T0349945

California

HUMBOLT

REDDING

CHICO

SACRAMENTO

STOCKTON

SAN FRANCISCO

OAKLAND

SANTA CRUZ

SAN JOSE

MONTEREY

FRESNO

BAKERSFIELD

SANTA BARBARA

LOS ANGELES

RIVERSIDE

PALM SPRINGS

SAN DIEGO

California

An American History

JOHN MACK FARAGHER

Yale UNIVERSITY PRESS

New Haven and London

Published with assistance from the income of the
Frederick John Kingsbury Memorial Fund.

Yale University Press books may be purchased in quantity for
educational, business, or promotional use. For information,
please e-mail sales.press@yale.edu (U.S. office) or
sales@yaleup.co.uk (U.K. office).

Designed by Mary Valencia
Set in type by Integrated Publishing Solutions
Printed in the United States of America.

Library of Congress Control Number: 2021946320
ISBN 978-0-300-22579-2 (hardcover : alk. paper)

A catalogue record for this book is available from the British Library.

This paper meets the requirements of ANSI/NISO Z39.48-1992
(Permanence of Paper).

10 9 8 7 6 5 4 3 2 1

Dedicated to the memory of my grandmother,
Maude McFarlin Delaley

Contents

1. A State of Diversity 1

2. Little Countries 10

3. Big White Birds 21

4. China Ships 30

5. Extending the Spanish Domain 39

6. The Wanderer 48

7. What Happened to My Chickens? 60

8. Undersea People 70

9. The Liberal Cause 78

10. Members of a Single Family 89

11. We Are Free 101

12. Viva California Libre 112

13. Wicked Foreigners 121

14. Yankee Doodle in Monterey 130

15. Overland to California 138

16. We Must Be Conquerors 148

17. The Horrors of War 159

18. Gold from the American River 169

19. A White Republic 178

20. Popular Justice 191

21. My Little Sister's Heart in My Hands 201

22. I'll Never Be Carried into Slavery 213

23. Bohemian Days 224

24. The Terrible Seventies 238

25. The Cow Counties 250

26. A Cosmopolitan City 263

27. The Remedy Is More Democracy 276

28. Bounty of the Mountains 289

29. Invisible Walls of Steel 300

30. Human Rights and Home Rule 310

31. The Man with the Hoe 320

32. End Poverty in California 332

33. Unite to Win 344

34. Make No Small Plan for California 357

35. Rebels and Forerunners 369

36. A Cyclone in a Wind Tunnel 381

37. A Complicated Ecosystem 393

38. The Impossible Dream 406

39. E Pluribus Unum 417

40. The First Step 430

Acknowledgments 445

Index 447

HEADING TO CALIFORNIA

1

A State of Diversity

The history of California has a lot to do with the lay of the land. Surrounded by deserts, mountains, and the Pacific Ocean, it is isolated from the rest of the continent. Driving into the state, you cross some pretty rugged country. In the state's far north, Interstate 5 crosses the Oregon-California border at Siskiyou Summit (4,310 feet), the steepest grade in the entire interstate highway system and the site of many trucking accidents during the winter.

West from Nevada, Interstate 80 follows the route of the old California Trail, ascending the mighty Sierra Nevada mountain range to the summit at Donner Pass (elevation 7,239 feet), named for a group of covered-wagon pioneers trapped there by an early winter storm in late 1846. Snowed in for months, the party lost thirty-four people to starvation or hypothermia, and survivors were forced to resort to cannibalism.

Routes into the southern part of the state are equally

challenging. Motorists traveling from Las Vegas to Los Angeles on Interstate 15 pass through the nation's hottest and most arid region. Back in the day, that trek was truly dangerous. In 1849 a group of pioneers lost their way searching for a shortcut, and many died of hunger and thirst in a desolate area forever after known as Death Valley, the lowest spot in North America at 282 feet below sea level. On the western horizon, the victims could see snowcapped Mt. Whitney in the Sierra Nevada, at 14,505 feet the highest point in the forty-eight contiguous states.

Or consider Interstate 8, which spans the Colorado River at Yuma, Arizona, before heading west to San Diego. For the Spanish, the Yuma crossing offered the only practical overland route for settlers coming from Mexico. When the Quechan (quit-SAN) people, who live along the river bottom, rose up against the Spanish and closed the crossing in 1781, they decisively shaped the course of California's history.

★

Geologists explain California's terrestrial isolation with the theory of *plate tectonics*. The earth's outer crust consists of massive continental and oceanic plates, floating on a sea of molten rock. When those plates collide, massive geological upheaval follows. California emerged from the violent impact of the North American and Pacific plates. Some four hundred million years ago, the ocean floor began to slide under the western edge of the continent, a process geologists call *subduction*. That forced molten and solid rock to the surface, creating California's many mountain ranges, including the 400-mile-long Sierra Nevada.

Twenty-five million years ago, for reasons yet unknown, the motion of this collision shifted from head-on to sideways. The San Andreas Fault, a visible scar on the land that extends the entire length of the state, marks that shift. Earthquakes, like the one that destroyed the city of San Francisco in 1906, remind Californians that the continental pileup continues.

The powerful action of water reshaped that landscape. Moist ocean air blowing in from the Pacific ascends to great heights as it passes over the mountains. As the air rises, it cools; water vapor condenses and falls as rain. Along California's northwest coast, where the mountains drop directly into the sea, the rainfall can exceed 120 inches per year. The mountains suck up nearly all the moisture, casting an enormous "rain shadow" over land to the east, creating vast deserts that can go for years without any measurable precipitation.

During the last ice age—a period lasting a hundred thousand years that ended about ten thousand years ago—enormous quantities of water in the mountain highlands froze, forming huge glaciers. Glacial movement carved out sheer canyons and dramatic valleys, like those at Yosemite National Park. Snowmelt from the Sierra Nevada created two powerful rivers, the Sacramento and the San Joaquin, that join in the Delta region and flow into San Francisco Bay. The sediment deposited by those rivers formed the floor of California's great Central Valley. In southern California, debris washing down mountain slopes produced the lowland of the Los Angeles Basin.

Scientists classify the climate of the southern coast—mild winters, long dry summers, and year-round sunny days—as "Mediterranean." That's what many people imagine when they think of California: white sandy beaches with bathers and surfers, the Hollywood sign and Disneyland, balmy breezes and plenty of sunshine. It's an image perpetuated by popular culture. Think of the annual New Year's Day broadcast of the Rose Bowl game from Pasadena, a city in southern California. From a hovering blimp, the television camera zooms in on the stadium, crowded with ninety thousand fans dressed in shirt-sleeves rather than winter coats. The camera pans to take in the vista of sun-drenched valleys and snowcapped mountains. For millions of viewers in more frigid parts of the country, such images have provoked a lot of "California dreaming."

Such scenes, however, represent only a fraction of California. The state includes more variation in climate than any other. Besides the mild southern coastal region, its climatic zones include alpine mountain highlands, semiarid valleys and grasslands, as well as parched deserts. Geological complexity produced climatic diversity, a patchwork of local ecologies. The California Department of Fish and Wildlife lists 178 major habitats in the state, populated by over five thousand plant species and at least a thousand animal species, many of them living nowhere else.

★

California's abundance began attracting human migrants some thirteen thousand years ago. The first people to arrive established themselves along the coast. Soon others created communities along the free-flowing northern rivers, with their abundant runs of spawning salmon and steelhead trout. Later waves of migrants settled the interior grasslands and foothills. Human residents have lived and thrived in every California habitat for thousands of years.

Natural abundance supplied the means for the growth of the largest indigenous population of any region now part of the United States. Native Californians lived in hundreds of small communities of astounding cultural variety. They spoke at least seventy-eight distinct languages, more than all the languages of Europe combined and more than any comparably sized region on the globe. The federal government recognizes 109 California bands and tribes as direct descendants of those original inhabitants. No other state comes close to this number.

California Landforms

Human diversity is the foundation of California's history. In the late eighteenth century, Spanish colonizers occupied the central and southern coastal zones, about a third of the state. Catholic missionaries and military officials hailed from Europe, but most colonists came from more varied backgrounds. The twenty-two adult men and women who founded the *pueblo* (town) of Los Angeles included two Spaniards, two men of African descent, nine Mexican "Indians," and nine individuals of mixed Spanish, African, and Native ancestry.

In the early nineteenth century, Russian fur traders established an outpost on the Pacific coast north of San Francisco, bringing with them native Alaskans who hunted for sea otters. Thirty years later an enterprising grifter from Switzerland named Johann August Sutter founded another large trading post at a site that later would become the state capital of Sacramento. Hawaiian laborers helped construct his outpost.

A new era opened in 1846 with the invasion and conquest of California by armed forces of the United States. Two years later, men constructing a mill dam discovered gold in the foothills of the Sierra Nevada. That sparked the world-famous California gold rush, drawing men and women from every state in the union, Black and White, free and slave, as well as Native Americans from many eastern tribes; thousands more came from Mexico and other countries in Latin America, the Pacific Islands and Australia, Europe and China. Gold rush San Francisco was one of the most multicultural places on the planet. The transcontinental railroad, completed by Irish and Chinese workers in 1869, brought tens of thousands as well, not only Americans but also immigrants from England, Ireland, Germany, France, and Italy. Pacific steamship lines carried large numbers of Chinese, Japanese, Filipinos, and Pacific Islanders to California ports.

In the twentieth century, the migration grew stronger as people arrived to work in the state's fields and factories. As a popular song of the 1920s put it, "California, Here I Come." Then, during the Great Depression of the 1930s, a flood of displaced farmers came by automobile, a trek chronicled in John Steinbeck's classic novel *The Grapes of Wrath* (1939). During and after World War II, the migrant tide became a tsunami, as hopeful Americans—rich and poor, rural and urban, Black and White—relocated to the golden shores. In 1962 the federal government announced that California had become the most populous state in the nation.

Although the migration of Americans from other states slowed in the last two decades of the twentieth century, powerful immigrant streams from Latin America and Asia continued to bring millions of new residents. By 2020, California's nearly forty million people made up the most diverse population of any state in the Union. California became "majority minority," meaning that a majority of the state's residents, 63 percent of the total population, were "minorities" or "people of color."

The history of California's human diversity includes stories of coming together and stories of coming apart. The mix of cultures led to invention and improvisation. California is the wealthiest state in the nation, first among its peers in both agricultural and industrial production, a world leader in high technology, and the center of the global entertainment industry. But ethnic difference has also led to conflict, turmoil, and violence. In a process repeated many times, newcomers overwhelmed natives. Soon the newcomers began to think of themselves as natives, fearful that the next wave of newcomers would overwhelm *them*.

★

Understanding the histories of the diverse places and peoples of California requires an imaginative leap back in time. That's something many people find difficult to do. Historical thinking does not come naturally. We focus intently on the present and the future, making it hard to imagine a past that extends back hundreds of years. To make sense of a period of time far longer than a human lifespan, we need to see the past in sequence. Understanding the order in which events take place is the key to unlocking the cause and effect of history.

Thinking historically also requires "historical empathy," the attempt to understand the thoughts, feelings, and actions of those who lived before us. They were like us in many ways: they lived and loved, worked and played, fought and died. Yet they were also very different from us. They laughed at jokes that today mystify us, they cherished values we find difficult to understand, they worshiped in ways that may seem strange and exotic. The British historian G. M. Trevelyan expressed this beautifully:

> The poetry of history lies in the quasi-miraculous fact that once, on this earth, once, on this familiar spot of ground, walked other men and women, as actual as we are today, thinking their own thoughts, swayed by their own passions, but now all gone, one generation vanishing after another, gone as utterly as we ourselves shall shortly be gone, like ghosts at cock-crow.

Here's a little thought experiment to kickstart your historical thinking. As a way of measuring historical distance and ordering it in sequence, imagine the past as a chain stretching back through time, generation preceding generation. Many of us have been fortunate enough to know at least one of our grandparents. They can tell us about people and events that took place fifty, sixty, seventy years ago, long before we were born. A grandmother might even tell stories she heard from her own grandmother, which would take us back four generations, more than a century. Yet many of those stories will have the ring of immediacy, echoing the experience, thoughts, and feelings of people who have long since passed away. Try imagining the world of your grandmother's childhood, then the world of *her* grandmother's childhood. Then compound that leap to your grandmother's grandmother's grandmother's grandmother. That takes us back some ten generations, to where this history of California begins.

INSIDE THE ROUNDHOUSE

2

Little Countries

Winter evenings in Native California villages were a time for storytelling. Imagine a community of Konkows (con-COWs), one of three closely related branches of the Maidu (my-DOO) people, who lived in permanent villages near today's city of Chico. Mothers and children of the village gather at the *kum,* a large conical earth lodge or roundhouse, the community's ceremonial and spiritual center. Crouching low, they enter through a small front door, descend a ramp to the subterranean earthen floor, and seat themselves on the cool ground, around a fire in the room's center.

The children fall silent, watching the patterns of light and shadow cast by the flickering flames. Suddenly they hear a shrill tone, and looking up in the direction of the sound they see a dark figure emerging, as if by magic, through the smoke hole in the ceiling. It is Storyteller. He blows on a bird bone whistle as he crawls down a ladder. A thrill courses through the small crowd of children as Storyteller begins his tale.

"Earthmaker, floating above primordial waters, sang this world into existence," he sings—for origin stories were always sung, and presented only on special nights like this one. "Earthmaker was pleased," Storyteller continues. "He went in the direction of the sunset, traveling across the rim of the world, counting all the countries. Then, returning to the spot where he had started, he began to create human beings. He made the first two, a man and a woman, then another two, then another." Storyteller details the differences among the people Earthmaker made, the size of their bodies, the colors of their skin, the distinctive sounds they make.

"Then Earthmaker spoke directly to them," Storyteller continues, his voice rising, his words punctuated by rhythmic whistling as the story reaches a crescendo. " 'You shall live here,' Earthmaker said to one couple. 'You shall live there,' he said to another. He pointed out the countries where the different people were to live. 'These places shall provide you with food of all kinds,' he said, 'and being clever, you will prosper. Your numbers shall multiply, you shall become a people.' "

Storyteller lowers his voice and his singing grows softer. "And Earthmaker told them," he says, "that your people shall have a name of their own, just as your country and every place within it shall have names of their own. And those names you shall teach your children as they accompany you to the meadows, oak groves, and streams. And I say to you, always shall you remain in the country where you were born. Content you shall be, living in a country that is little, not big. And never shall you drive another people from the country that they call their own."

When Storyteller finishes, the mothers and children begin dancing. Dancing, like storytelling, brought people together, strengthening the bonds of community. Afterward, the children offer Storyteller little gifts prepared by their mothers—a few cakes of acorn bread, or some smoked eel wrapped in wild grape leaves.

The children had listened to such stories and danced together in the *kum* many times before and would do so many times again. The Konkows celebrated in this way for generations, bequeathing their origin story to the young. Early in the twentieth century, a Maidu Storyteller named Hánc'ibyjim (aka Tom Young) repeated this version for a visiting anthropologist, a specialist in the study of human cultures who spoke the Maidu language. Then, using a system of phonetic writing, the anthropologist transcribed the story and produced an English translation, making it available to all of us.

★

Virtually all the native peoples of California told similar stories, tales assuring them that since the beginning of time they had lived in precisely the places Earthmaker intended. The homeland of the Maidus, some ten thousand people, lay in the foothills and mountains of the Sierra Nevada range, east of the river we know as the Sacramento. They were not a centralized tribe but a group of three distinct peoples speaking closely related dialects, residing in twenty or thirty villages. Most native Californians lived in much the same way, in hundreds of self-governing communities.

These "little countries" were remarkably compact, tucked into a valley, clinging to the banks of a creek, or perched on a bay. Parents taught their children to cherish the land of their birth, and most remained for the whole of their lives, although many groups practiced the custom of marrying outside the immediate community, which helped establish kinship connections between neighboring bands. That was the experience of Wiinu, a Mono Lake Paiute (PIE-oot) woman who lived near Yosemite Valley in the southern Sierra Nevada. In 1918, when she was ninety-five years old, she told an anthropologist that except for one terrible winter when soldiers of the United States forced her people onto a distant reservation, she had spent her entire life no farther than six miles from her birthplace.

Native Californians' strong preference for their own locale, a perspective known as "localism," developed over hundreds of generations and spanned thousands of years. Like every region of the world, California was settled by human beings who originated in Africa and spread to all the continents of the globe save Antarctica. The first men and women to arrive in California included hunting peoples in pursuit of large mammals like mammoths and mastodons, and aquatic coastal peoples who mostly relied on sea food. In an effort to diversify their quest, small family bands moved from place to place, exploiting every opportunity to hunt, fish, and gather. For the first Californians, localism was not an option.

Those first migrants were followed by others, speaking different languages and practicing different traditions. Over several millennia, wave after wave of newcomers washed across the barriers of desert, mountain, and ocean, flooding into California. A complicated history of pushing and shoving produced an intricate patchwork of language and culture. Bands competed for possession of the most valuable places—fishing sites along the shores and estuaries, hunting grounds in the grasslands, gathering places in the foothills. Warfare ran rampant. Mute testimony comes in the form of ancient human remains with skulls crushed by blunt objects and bones embedded with spear points. The fighting and dying among his people must have caused Earthmaker to weep.

★

Then, some two thousand years ago, things took a more peaceful turn. Another wave of migrants introduced a new technology to California: the bow and arrow. In the hands of an expert, this is a weapon of remarkable accuracy and power. During the gold rush, American miners on the Feather River watched as Maidu children with bows and arrows repeatedly shot a small coin off a distant stick. In another demonstration, a Maidu hunter dispatched an arrow that flew thirty feet and hit a target on a tree, penetrating to the depth of a foot. When first introduced, bows and arrows must have accelerated the violence between groups. But applied to hunting, it had a more positive impact. A man with a bow and a quiver of arrows could take down swift prey like deer or antelope as well as small quarry like rabbits and squirrels, supplying his extended family with more game than two or three men armed with spears.

Increased productivity allowed people to settle in permanent locations for the first time. And that, in turn, motivated them to develop more intensive methods for harvesting, processing, and storing the plant and animal foods of their locale. A single family, working several days in a grove of oaks, the most common native tree in California, could gather acorns enough to last a whole year. But the harvest had to be safely stored until it was processed to remove the bitter tannins, then ground into meal. Acorn meal was used to thicken soups and stews, make steaming bowls of porridge, and bake into flatbread.

Or consider the salmon coursing up the rivers of the northern region in enormous numbers to spawn. People hauled them in by the hundreds, then dried the flesh into a delicious jerky that kept for months without spoiling. Similar harvesting and storing techniques were applied to pine nuts (*piñons*), grass seeds, and edible roots of all kinds. Native women developed the complementary skill of basketmaking, using grasses and shoots to produce a diversity of shapes and sizes for hundreds of uses, including gathering, carrying, storing, and even cooking. California baskets, their intricate designs unique to the communities in which they were produced, are impressive artistic accomplishments.

Permanent village settlements within easy reach of important resource sites—oak groves, fishing spots, hunting grounds, grasslands—laid a foundation for localism, and the violent competition among groups gradually subsided. That said, Native California communities were certainly not conflict-free. People who live in small communities often get on each other's nerves. Personal fighting was common enough, and disputes between individuals, families, and even villages sometimes led to violence. Native California communities responded forcefully to outsiders who attempted to poach their resources.

But there also developed more of a "live and let live" attitude toward others, and village headmen did what they could to avoid violence with neighboring communities. If war broke out, as it sometimes did, it was usually limited to short skirmishes, and often ended with the first shedding of blood. There were exceptions, most notably the Quechan people of the Colorado River, who glorified war and were frequently in conflict with their neighbors, perhaps because they were river-bottom farmers with a different concept of land tenure. But most Native Californians practiced peaceful toleration.

This was a remarkable development—all the more so since California's intensive foraging economy encouraged population growth. On the eve of European invasion, California was the most densely populated region of the continent, north of Mexico. Historical demographers, who study past human populations, estimate that at least three hundred thousand Californians lived in hundreds of little countries.

★

The first White Americans to visit California in the nineteenth century were struck by its abundance. "No country in the

world was as well supplied by Nature with food for man,"
wrote Titus Fey Cronise in 1868. "Its hills, valleys and plains
filled with elk, deer, hares, rabbits, quail, and other animals fit
for food; its rivers and lakes swarming with salmon, trout, and
other fish, their beds and banks covered with mussels, clams,
and other edible mollusks; the rocks on its sea shores crowded
with seal and otter; and its forests full of trees and plants, bearing acorns, nuts, seeds and berries." Americans praised California, but they dismissed Native Californians as savages who
took advantage of nature's abundance simply by foraging whatever was edible. White Americans called them "Diggers." The
fact that the term rhymes with the racial slur for Black people
was entirely intentional.

But California Indians were not mere food *collectors;* they
were food *producers.* Their proactive management of plant and
animal populations literally created California's celebrated abundance. The state's most classic landscapes—the oak meadows
of Yosemite Valley, for example—were shaped by the labor of
generations of Natives. Ecologist M. Kat Anderson calls this
"tending the wild." Native women, she argues, were accomplished botanists, testing, selecting, and nurturing the plant
world. Native men were field zoologists, applying their intimate knowledge of animal behavior to hunting and fishing.

California Natives practiced an array of techniques that
included pruning, sowing, irrigating, and tilling. The Maidu
cut back elderberry bushes to increase their yield. The Pomo
(PO-mo) of the northern coast clipped the branches of red-
bud in the early spring to ensure the production of shoots suitable for basket making. The Cahuilla (kuh-WE-uh) of the Coachella Valley in arid southern California planted fan palm seeds
at their oases. The Paiute (PIE-oot) diverted water from the
Owens River on the eastern slope of the Sierra Nevada to irrigate stands of edible wild hyacinth. Using fire-hardened dig-

ging sticks, Native women turned over the soil as they foraged for edible roots and tubers. American pioneers may have sneered at "Diggers," but to a considerable extent the digging was responsible for the gardenlike quality of the California landscape they so admired.

Deliberate burning was the most significant, effective, and widely employed eco-management tool. Burning the underbrush removed combustible material and recycled nutrients. Burning increased the density of desired plants, enhanced the feed for wildlife, and kept insect populations under control. Native testimony makes it clear that they knew exactly what they were doing. "All open prairies were for gathering grass seeds," Lucy Thompson, a Yurok (yur-AWK) from the northwest coast, told an anthropologist. "The Douglas fir has always encroached on the open prairies. Therefore we have continuously burned to keep it from covering all the open lands."

Another Yurok, a man known as Klamath River Jack, defended controlled burning in a letter he sent to the United States Forest Service, which interpreted its mission as fighting all forest fires. "Fire burn up old acorn that fall on ground," he wrote. "Old acorn on ground have lots worm; no burn old bark, old leaves, bugs and worms come more every year. Indian burn every year, so keep all ground clean. Not much on ground to make hot fire, so never hurt big trees." Rosalie Bethel, a Mono from the southern Sierra Nevada, described the effect burning had on the mountain meadows of her country. "You would see all the beautiful wildflowers that grew after a fire," she said. "It gives nourishment to the plants and they grow. I remember as a child, it was the most beautiful sight you could see. Flowers would just cover the hillsides."

Never take it all: that was the fundamental principle of Native foraging. "We gathered Indian potatoes in May or June," remembered Virgil Bishop, another Mono. "We'd go back to the same area and gather them. My mother and grandmother would only take the best and the biggest. They never cleaned everything out. They would always leave some behind." In the words of Sam Young, a Wintu (win-TOO) from the far north of the state: "We Indians like to leave something for the ones who come after."

Lucy Smith, a Pomo elder from Sonoma County, considered the foraging ethic part of the Native Californian philosophy of "live and let live." She recalled her mother's teaching: "It's just like taking care of your younger brother or sister. When that baby gets to be a man or woman they're going to help you out. I thought mother was talking about us Indians and how we are supposed to get along. I found out later that she wasn't just taking about Indians, but the plants, animals, birds—everything on this earth. They are our relatives and we better know how to act around them or they'll get after us."

★

Native California was no Eden. Droughts, floods, or other natural disasters decreased the food supply and sometimes led to malnutrition, even starvation. Before the invasion of Europeans, Native people did not experience epidemics of contagious diseases, like smallpox, malaria, or bubonic plague, such as beleaguered the Old World. But like all human beings that lived before the development of modern medical science, they had to endure bacterial, viral, and parasitic infections, including tuberculosis, meningitis, and pneumonia, diseases that took their heaviest toll among the young. Child mortality was frightfully high among Native Californians. Newborns had only a three-in-five chance of surviving to adulthood.

Many of the stories told by Natives addressed such existential concerns. A principal character in those stories is Coyote. Native Californians spun tales about many spirit animals, but Old Man Coyote was the most popular. He is what historian

Dan Flores calls an avatar, a divine representation of the human condition. Very smart, and frequently helpful or compassionate, Coyote could also be vulgar, vain, and deceitful, a blunderer of the first order, often the victim of his own schemes. Coyote stories are about the foibles of human nature.

A story told by the Achumawi (ah-choo-MA-wee) people of the northeastern part of the state explains Coyote's origin. After Earthmaker fashioned the world, they say, he was proud but very lonely. He longed for someone with whom he could enjoy a real conversation. So he created Coyote, a spirit with a mind of his own. Coyote's independence, however, proved too much of a good thing. He arrogantly believed he knew best. As Earthmaker labored to give the world form and substance, Coyote stood by as his constant critic. Finally, exhausted by the persistent second-guessing, Earthmaker directed the other spirit animals to destroy Coyote. But despite everything they threw at him, he managed to survive. So Earthmaker gave up. "You have conquered me," he conceded, and he granted Coyote the gift of eternal life. From then on, Earthmaker seriously considered all of Coyote's suggestions about the way the world ought to work.

According to the Yana (YA-na) people, northern neighbors of the Maidus, Earthmaker wanted everything to be easy and comfortable for his human creatures. He told women to set their baskets outside their lodge doors at night, and in the morning they found them filled with meals, ready to eat. "That is no way to do," complained Coyote. "People should work for a living." Earthmaker listened, and thereafter, it was so. Earthmaker wanted women to bear children without pain. "No, that's not right," said Coyote. "Women must have a hard time; they must suffer in order to give life." And thereafter, it was so. Earthmaker wanted people to live forever, but Coyote objected. "Eternal life is dull," he said. "If people know they are going to die, they will take life more seriously. What's more, if people live forever, they will overrun the earth. People must die, and their families should mourn for them. Let them blacken their eyes and paint their faces with white clay. Let them make a great ceremony for the dead. Let them dance away their sadness."

But Old Man Coyote's ideas often backfired. Once, as he was going along, he saw the leaves of the cottonwood trees floating gently to the ground. He watched for the longest time, fascinated by the beautiful patterns the leaves made as they drifted with the breeze. "How do you do that?" he asked the leaves. "There's nothing to it," they answered; "you just fall off." Like humans, Coyote had aspirations. How wonderful it would be to fly, he thought. So he climbed the cottonwood and launched himself from a limb. But he didn't go all pretty like the leaves; he went bonk and nearly killed himself. But Coyote couldn't die. He kept going along, right into the next story.

The stories sometimes took a serious turn. Following Coyote's advice, Earthmaker introduced death into the world. But the first to die was Coyote's own beloved son. Coyote blackened his eyes, painted his face with white clay, and danced through the night. He mourned for his son, but he felt no better. So he went to Earthmaker. "I've changed my mind," he said. "I don't want people to die after all. Bring my son back to life." But Earthmaker shook his head. "It's too late," he said sadly, "it's too late." Earthmaker dug a grave for Coyote's son and covered his body with earth. "From now on, this is the way you must do," he said. And thus was the law of life and death established over all things.

Old Man Coyote, writes California poet Gary Snyder, is the original American antihero, never rising above the ordinary, always dealing with "the world as it is."

KUMEYAAY + THE SPANISH SHIPS

3

Big White Birds

ative Californians first encountered Europeans in
the mid-sixteenth century. The initial meetings were
fleeting, but foretold of troubles ahead. The Spanish
came to California to conquer, to seize Native homelands and
possessions, to force Native inhabitants into doing things
they would never have done on their own. Conquest is always
violent.

On the morning of September 28, 1542—the date provided by the Spanish record—a group of Kumeyaay (KU-me-
eye) families, digging for clams along the shore of their bay,
spied two large white shapes on the horizon. They were Spanish vessels, but to people who had never laid eyes on a sailing
ship they resembled huge sea birds. Watching as the shapes
approached and grew larger, they made out what appeared to
be black-bearded men dashing about on the birds' backs. Then,
the shock of recognition: These must be the invaders our desert cousins warned us about!

Historians estimate that approximately ten thousand Kumeyaays inhabited some thirty village communities along the coast of a region bisected today by the U.S.-Mexico border. Archeological evidence indicates that human occupation of the area goes back at least 12,000 years. The Kumeyaays fished in dugout canoes, harvested shellfish and clams, gathered acorns and seeds in the valleys and foothills, hunted for deer and small animals in the mountains. Their desert cousins, the Quechan people, grew corn, beans, and pumpkins on the floodplain of the river they called "Red Water," or *Colorado* in Spanish, 150 miles to the east. The two groups spoke related languages about as similar as Italian and Spanish. They met often to trade and swap information.

Some weeks before, Quechan traders had told the Kumeyaays about black-bearded strangers, mounted on strange and terrifying animals, who appeared at their villages. The strangers departed without incident, the Quechan said, but later they learned of burned villages and slaughtered residents in the interior. This was no tall tale. Conquistador Francisco Vásquez de Coronado, commanding an expedition of nearly two thousand men, had come north from New Spain in search of an empire called Cibola, somewhere in the unmapped territory of today's Arizona and New Mexico. But Cibola was pure fantasy, and Coronado found only small Native villages, on which he took out his frustration.

★

In 1542, the Spaniards had been in the Western Hemisphere for half a century. Columbus made landfall in the Bahamas in 1492, and the following year the Spanish monarchs dispatched the first colonizing expedition to the Caribbean. Conquistadors wreaked havoc on Native communities. During the first decade of colonization, the ravages of war, famine, and pestilence reduced the population of the Caribbean from millions to mere thousands. Native homelands became the estates of Spanish masters who imported enslaved African workers.

The Spaniards brought their own institutions and traditions. Europe was what historians call a "feudal" society, in which a small, privileged class of lords controlled virtually all the productive land. Law and custom required that the bulk of the population, the peasants residing in the countryside, labor on the land for the lords. In the Spanish Caribbean, this hierarchical social order transmuted into a plantation system, with enslaved Africans producing sugar and other tropical crops for a colonial elite whose privilege was protected by the royally appointed governor and his soldiers.

The Spaniards considered themselves the strong right arm of the Catholic Church, a hierarchical institution headed by the Pope in Rome. The ways in which religion echoes social relations are fascinating. Native Californians, living in their own little countries, without any authority ruling over them, believed in a multitude of spirit-beings. Spanish Christians, coming from a world where power was centralized, professed faith in a single all-powerful deity. The Christian God promised that all who were baptized would have "life everlasting" in the next world. Christians had the duty to spread that message. "Go ye into the whole world and preach the gospel to every creature," said Jesus, the Christ or messiah. This directive nourished a communal ideal, the fellowship of all humanity, embodied in the Golden Rule: "Do unto others as you would have them do unto you."

But this promise came with a stipulation: no tolerance for other religions. For Europeans, the world was divided into Christians and others. Religion, not race, was the difference of most importance. Spanish colonizers, the Pope decreed, had "full and free permission to invade, search out, capture, and subjugate pagans and any other unbelievers and enemies of

Christ wherever they may be," seizing "their kingdoms, duchies, countries, principalities, and other property." Conquest and conversion were thus both key parts of the colonial program. Native men and women who survived the initial onslaught would become what one Spaniard called "useful vassals for our religion and state."

★

In 1519 the Spaniards invaded Mexico and attacked the powerful Aztec (AZ-tek) empire, populated by several million people. The conquistadors plundered and looted, then established political control and put Natives to work as field hands, stock herders, and miners of precious metals. Galleons returned to Spain loaded with the looted treasure of the Aztecs. The Spaniards then extended their conquest to the Maya (MY-ah) civilization of Central America and the Inca (INK-ah) empire of Peru. The never-ending search for plunder was the Spanish viceroy's motive for dispatching Coronado across the Southwest in search of mythic Cibola. He also authorized an exploration of the Pacific coast of North America, a region the Spaniards called "California," a name borrowed from a popular story about a mythical land of great abundance.

Juan Rodriguez Cabrillo, a veteran of the conquest of Mexico, commanded the oceangoing expedition. During the siege of the Aztec capital (today's Mexico City), located on an island in the midst of a great lake, Cabrillo was assigned the task of preparing a fleet of vessels. Without tar to caulk them, he had his men prepare a mixture of pine resin and human fat, rendered from the bodies of dead Aztecs. Cabrillo's ships played an important role in winning the battle. Rewarded with a royal grant that entitled him to the labor of several hundred Natives, he dispatched armed gangs to round up workers. "He broke up homes," wrote an observer, "taking the women and girls and giving them to the soldiers and sailors in order to keep them satisfied." Cabrillo put his laborers to work mining gold, and they made him a fortune.

The Spanish had already charted the coast of lower or Baja California as far north as today's city of Ensenada. Cabrillo's assignment was to continue north to Alta California, searching out any and all "civilized peoples," which the Spaniards defined as societies with cities, rulers, and treasure. Ultimately, the Spanish aimed at conquest and colonization, but Cabrillo's assignment was to avoid violence if possible, gather intelligence, and determine if anything along the Alta California coast would be worth such an effort. He departed Mexico in late June and spent three months fighting headwinds and strong opposing currents before finally reaching the bay the Spaniards would call San Diego.

★

As the ships came nearer to shore, frightened Kumeyaay women and children ran for the safety of their village while the men took up a defensive position on the beach. Cabrillo ordered half a dozen armored soldiers into a small launch, and they rowed ashore. As the Spaniards disembarked, three Kumeyaay leaders stepped forward. Communicating as best they could using signs, they cautiously welcomed the strangers, who reciprocated with similarly peaceful gestures. Cabrillo offered some small gifts, which the Kumeyaay men accepted.

According to the Spanish account, "the Indians gave signs of great fear." Use of the term *Indian* for the Native inhabitants of the Western Hemisphere came from Columbus, who believed he had reached "the Indies," today's Indonesia. The name stuck and it is with us still, continuing to convey an impression of "otherness," a sense that these people are not like us. Rather than echo the colonial conquerors, it is better to call indigenous peoples by some version of the names they used for themselves, or use a more neutral term like *Native*.

The Kumeyaays did not hesitate to say why they were afraid. In the words of the Spanish account: "By signs, they said that in the interior men like us were traveling about, killing many native Indians." That came as no surprise to Cabrillo, who was well aware of Coronado's expedition. But Native knowledge of what was taking place in the interior concerned him, for it put the Kumeyaays on their guard and made his mission more difficult. After some additional formalities, the Spaniards returned to their vessels.

Cabrillo's ships were low on provisions, so later that day he dispatched a small party to shore. While one group went in search of water, another began casting their fishing nets into the surf. The Kumeyaays were outraged. Taking resources without their permission was not allowed. They responded just as they would to any similar theft, rushing to the attack. Arrows rained down on the Spaniards and three fell wounded. Their comrades dragged them to the launch and hurriedly returned to the ships. Cabrillo fumed, but following instructions, he did not retaliate.

The next morning several Kumeyaay leaders paddled out to the galleon in a dugout canoe and requested a parley. Cabrillo invited them aboard and offered gifts, including strings of Venetian glass beads. From long experience, the Spaniards knew how entrancing those sparkling objects appeared to people accustomed to adornments made only of feather, fur, and bone. Like other Californians, the Kumeyaays loved dressing up. The leaders must have asked themselves, How can we get more of these pretty things while keeping these dangerous strangers at a distance?

Like his hosts, Cabrillo was also taking stock. "These people are well disposed," notes the Spanish account, but "go about covered with the skins of animals." The Kumeyaays appeared to have no cities, no lords or king, no treasure. They made an unlikely target for conquest. Cabrillo pressed the leaders for information about their northern neighbors. Up the coast, they indicated, lived a people far more wealthy and powerful. The Kumeyaays were employing a tactic used by Native inhabitants the world over when confronted by curious colonizers: "What you're looking for you'll find over the horizon, so please leave now." Cabrillo decided to sail on.

★

A few days later, residents of the island of Pimu, some ninety miles northwest of San Diego, saw the approach of the Spanish ships. Named Santa Catalina by the Spaniards, the island is one of the eight Channel Islands lying off the coast of southern California. These islanders, who called themselves Pimuvit (PEA-moo-vit), were part of a group of perhaps fifteen thousand people speaking a common language and residing on the islands and the mainland, a region encompassed today by Los Angeles and Orange counties. They had no common name for themselves, but their descendants call themselves Tongva (TONG-vay). The islanders, excellent seafarers and fishermen, used large plank canoes to travel back and forth to the mainland.

As Cabrillo's vessels entered the cove near their village, the women and children fled and the men displayed their weapons. "A great number of Indians emerged from the bushes and grass," reads the Spanish account, "shouting, dancing, and making signs." The Spaniards indicated their peaceful intentions, and after a good deal of hesitation a number of Native men paddled out to the ship.

They accepted Cabrillo's gift of glass beads, which dazzled them. Using signs, an elderly leader told the same story of violent, bearded invaders that the Spaniards had heard from the Kumeyaays. That raised Cabrillo's interest, but mostly he was intent on assessing his hosts as potential targets of colonization. Once again, he found them wanting. Were there any great villages in the vicinity, he asked. Pointing toward the mainland, the Pimuvit indicated he would find them "over there." Cabrillo raised anchor and headed across the channel.

The next morning, as the Spaniards approached the mainland, they saw the smoke of many fires surrounding a shallow bay and estuary. Cabrillo called it the Bay of Smokes, but a later Spanish explorer named it San Pedro. Clustered along this shore was the densest concentration of villages in the region. Cabrillo, however, remained unimpressed. A large plank canoe filled with Natives paddled up to his vessel, but the frightened men refused to come aboard the ship. In response to Cabrillo's questions, they indicated that he would find even larger and wealthier villages farther north. The Spaniards sailed on.

They spent the next two weeks exploring the coastline from Malibu Canyon to Point Conception. This was the homeland of the Chumash (CHEW-mash), some ten thousand people who lived along the coast and in the immediate interior. Fishermen in a large canoe paddled up to Cabrillo's galleon but would not come aboard. He offered gifts, and the fishermen handed over a large catch of sardines, which the Spaniards found "fresh and very good." The Chumash villages did indeed appear larger than any the Spaniards had yet encountered. "We saw on the land a pueblo of Indians close to the sea, the houses being large like those of New Spain." That was a hopeful sign. Perhaps the Chumash would be worthy of conquest.

★

Cabrillo spent the next month sailing north along the central coast. He missed the entrance to San Francisco Bay, which is difficult to locate from the ocean side, but he discovered a good harbor, probably Monterey Bay, which he named "Bay of Pines." During this portion of the exploration, the Spaniards encountered few people, but Native Californians surely saw them. Many years later Essie Parrish, a Pomo from Sonoma County, related a story of such a sighting. "In the old days," she said, "before the white people came up here, there was a boat sailing on the ocean from the south. Because they had never seen a boat, the people said: 'This big bird floating on the ocean is from somewhere, probably from up high. Let us plan a feast. Let us have a dance.' When they had done so, they watched the ship sail way up north and disappear."

In November 1542, with the approach of stormy weather, Cabrillo returned to one of the Channel Islands off the southern California coast, planning to winter there before resuming explorations in the spring. These islanders, who may have been Chumash, were outraged when the bearded strangers established a base camp onshore and began fishing in their waters. According to the Spanish account, "the Indians never stopped fighting us." Near the end of December, during the Christmas season, the islanders attacked a party of Cabrillo's men who were engaged in filling water casks at a spring. Cabrillo led a small group of soldiers into a launch and hurried to the men's rescue. But as he disembarked on the rocky shore, he fell and shattered his shinbone. The wound became infected, and after several days of agony Cabrillo died.

His men raised anchor and departed. They had located no great kingdom ripe for invasion and conquest. Cabrillo's charts, the ship's log, and other documents were filed away and mostly forgotten. For some time, coastal Californians continued to watch for the return of the ships, but gradually memories of the encounter faded away. They would enjoy many feasts and join in many dances before they once again encountered the black-bearded strangers.

THE FIRST MILITARY ENGAGEMENT

4

China Ships

The flow of treasure from Spain's American empire—
the spoils of plunder and exploitation—provided the
monarchy with an annual bonanza. But it was never
enough. Military campaigns in Europe drained the royal treasury, and in 1557 Spain's King Philip II went bankrupt. To
increase revenue, he pressed for more colonies. Topping his
wish list was an outpost in the East Indies with access to the
lucrative Asian spice trade. Since the Portuguese controlled
the sea route around Africa, the Spaniards continued the work-
around pioneered by Columbus, sailing west to get east. In
1565 a large military flotilla departed from the Pacific coast of
New Spain, sailed across the ocean, and established a foothold
in an archipelago the Spaniards called the Philippines, in honor
of King Philip.

The westbound voyage from Acapulco, aided by prevailing trade winds, was relatively easy. Not so the return. Spanish
pilots made numerous attempts at the eastward crossing, but

failed each time. They suspected that the currents of the North Pacific, like those of the North Atlantic, rotated clockwise in a great spiral. That understanding had ultimately enabled them to master navigation of the Atlantic. But the enormous distances of the Pacific presented a more daunting challenge. Finally, a single Spanish sailing vessel pulled it off. Departing during the summer monsoon season, the vessel rode furious winds more than a thousand nautical miles northeast into the latitude of Japan. There they caught the eastward-flowing North Pacific Current, which carried them to within several hundred miles of the North American coast and the southbound California Current, which took them back to Mexico.

A few years later the Spaniards extended their Philippine conquest to the port of Manila on the island of Luzon, long an important trading center, where merchants from China exchanged silks, porcelains, and tea for local spices and exotic woods. Manila boasted a tradition of accomplished shipbuilding, and Native residents, called Filipinos by the Spaniards, were soon constructing galleons to carry trade goods to Acapulco. With a virtually inexhaustible supply of silver from their mines in Mexico and Peru, the Spaniards were able to purchase the Asian commodities they so desired. The first of the huge Manila galleons, loaded with treasure, reached Mexico in 1573, beginning a lucrative commerce that would continue for two and a half centuries. Popularly known as the "China ships" (*naos de China*), the galleons were manned almost entirely by Filipino sailors.

★

"The voyage from the Philippine Islands to America," wrote one passenger, "may be called the longest and most dreadful of any in the world." The trip took from six to nine months and provisions often ran short. In truth, high-profit cargo often crowded out essential foodstuffs, forcing sailors to survive on nothing but rice cakes and salt pork. That resulted in scurvy, a form of malnutrition caused by a dietary deficiency of vitamin C. Symptoms begin with fatigue, bleeding gums, and ugly bruises, followed by fever, convulsion, and death. Many sailors perished before reaching Acapulco. One galleon was found drifting off the Mexican coast, its entire crew and all the passengers dead.

This is where California enters the story. Spanish officials proposed establishing a provisioning station for the galleons in Alta California. Such a base could also provide additional security, because the hulking China ships were tempting prizes for pirates and privateers. In 1578 Francis Drake, commissioned by Queen Elizabeth I of England "to annoy the king of Spain," successfully navigated the treacherous Strait of Magellan and became the first privateer to venture into Pacific waters. For several months Drake and his crew attacked and looted Spanish ports and vessels along the Pacific coast of South America. His most impressive prize was a China ship carrying chests filled with pearls and precious stones, eighty pounds of gold ingots, and twenty-six tons of silver, a haul worth upward of $40 million in today's money.

With the booty literally bursting the seams of his vessel, Drake anchored at a bay somewhere along the coast of what one of his officers called "the Californias." They remained there for a month, repairing and provisioning the vessel. Before departing, Drake planted a cross and claimed the region, which he christened "Nova Albion" (New Britain), for his queen. When he returned to England, completing a remarkable circumnavigation of the globe, Queen Elizabeth declared all information concerning the voyage a state secret. The precise location of Drake's California landing remains a mystery to this day.

★

In 1585, the viceroy of New Spain authorized an expedition to locate a California refuge for the China ships. He unwisely elected to do so on the cheap, arranging for a makeshift exploration by one of the returning Manila galleons. The assignment fell to Pedro de Unamuno, master of the *Nuestra Señora de Buena Esperanza,* which departed the East Indies in the summer of 1587 and made landfall at a small bay on the central California coast in October.

As with Drake, the precise location is uncertain, but it may have been Morro Bay in today's San Luis Obispo County. From the deck of his vessel, Unamuno saw large pine trees suitable for ship masts as well as abundant aquatic life. "A ship in need could supply itself here," he noted. Accompanied by a company of soldiers from New Spain, he went ashore. Following a clearly marked trail through wooded country, a dozen Filipino scouts in the lead, they came upon a group of Native women gathering wild herbs. They were probably Chumash. Grabbing their children, the women fled into the woods. Unamuno raised a cross and made a formal claim to the site before returning to his ship.

Determined to explore the countryside more fully, the following morning Unamuno led a company of soldiers and scouts ashore. Imagine the scene as his men assembled on the beach. The Mexican soldiers, their steel helmets gleaming in the sun, dressed in heavy chain mail over quilted shirts hanging to their knees. The Filipino scouts, bare-chested and barefoot, wearing handloomed loincloths called bahags. All were heavily armed, the soldiers shouldering muskets, the scouts carrying lances and painted leather shields. Unamuno led them ten or twelve miles upriver, the farthest inland exploration of Alta California the Spanish had attempted. They encountered no Native inhabitants but saw many signs of them, including an abandoned camp where the party put up for the night.

Meanwhile, back at the bay, the Filipino crew spent the day refilling water casks, gathering firewood, and doing laundry on the bank of a free-flowing stream. Late in the afternoon a group of Chumash men, armed with bows and arrows, suddenly emerged from the woods at the edge of the beach. Assertive and aggressive, they attempted to seize the drying laundry, which probably included the Filipinos' colorful bahags. Native Californians, whose only cloth came from pounded tree bark and feathers, were fascinated by the closely woven, cotton fabric. The Filipinos tried to defend their possessions. Several soldiers fired their muskets, and the Chumash retreated. But regrouping, they charged the Filipinos, shooting arrows and throwing stones. All hands beat a hasty retreat.

The following day, as the returning exploring party came within sight of the galleon, Chumash fighters swept down on their rear. Two men died from lance thrusts and four more suffered serious wounds. Unamuno maneuvered his men into a defensive position. A number of Chumash were killed by musket fire. This military engagement, the first between Natives and colonizers on the California mainland, claimed the lives of an unknown number of Chumash, a Mexican soldier, and a Filipino scout.

Unamuno decided to sail on and explore farther south. But the weather turned foul, a thick fog enveloping the coastline, and that was the last he saw of Alta California. Days later, as the ship approached Acapulco, it was met by a Spanish vessel dispatched to warn them that privateers were in the vicinity. Only days before, English captain Thomas Cavendish had captured and looted another Manila-bound galleon.

★

King Philip ordered a continuation of California exploration, "for the security of the ships that come and go." Once again the assignment went to the master of a returning galleon, Sebastian Rodriguez Cermeño, a veteran of the Manila trade and formerly the chief pilot on the China ship captured by Cavendish. Cermeño's galleon, the *San Agustín*, left Manila in July 1595 and reached the northern California coast five months later. Sailing south, Cermeño came to a projecting point of land and a large bay "shaped like a horseshoe." With a contingent of soldiers and seamen, he went ashore, made contact with the inhabitants of a nearby village, and raised a temporary encampment on the beach.

Although historians aren't sure where Francis Drake anchored, they are certain that Cermeño landed at what today is called Drakes Bay. That's because the Spaniards left plenty of evidence behind. Within days of their arrival a powerful storm blew up. The *San Agustín* dragged anchor, beached, and was torn apart by pounding surf. The ship was a total loss, and ten or fifteen Filipino seamen died in an attempt to save its cargo. Archeologists have recovered hundreds of shards of Chinese porcelains destroyed in that wreck.

The villagers—Coastal Miwok (MEE-wok) people, whose homeland included this bay—salvaged what they could from the shipwreck. The crew had been constructing a smaller ship that Cermeño planned to use for a closer exploration of the coast, and that half-completed vessel now offered the only means of returning to Mexico. Cermeño demanded the return of the *San Agustín*'s masts, planks, and sails in order to outfit his rescue ship, but the Miwoks refused.

An ugly confrontation ensued as Cermeño's men attacked the village, chased the Miwoks off, and took what they wanted, including the villagers' cache of acorns, even though the intruders were ignorant of the method used to remove the tannin. "Our sustenance was nothing except bitter acorns," wrote Cermeño. "But if it had not been for these, all the people would have suffered and died." The loss of the *San Agustín* was a financial disaster of the first order, and the viceroy ruled that all further exploration of the Alta California coast would be conducted by vessels from Mexico, not China ships returning from Manila loaded with treasure.

★

The new viceroy, Gaspar de Zúñiga, count of Monterrey, commissioned Sebastián Vizcaíno, another veteran of the Manila trade, to conduct the next expedition. Like Cermeño, Vizcaíno had been an officer on the galleon captured by Cavendish, and he had a clear sense of the risks involved. "There is great gain to be gotten," he wrote, "but only if a man can return in safety." He was determined to find a refuge for the China ships along the Alta California coast.

Commanding a fleet of three vessels, in the late months of 1602 Vizcaíno made stops at San Diego Bay and Catalina Island (giving both places their modern names). He found Natives eager to trade. The Kumeyaays of San Diego offered animal pelts in exchange for colored beads. The Pimuvit of Catalina welcomed the Spaniards ashore, and a woman showed Vizcaíno several fragments of silk fabric she had obtained in trade from a bearded man in a disabled vessel. The Natives seemed familiar with the galleons that periodically anchored along the coast to take on provisions. "They are a people given to trade and traffic and are fond of barter," Vizcaíno noted.

While Vizcaíno was impressed with the cooperative Natives, the southern California coast left him cold. San Diego Bay, though first-rate, was too near Mexico to be of real service as a provisioning base. San Pedro, Cabrillo's "Bay of Smokes," was exposed to bad weather, and there were no good harbors on Catalina Island or along the Chumash coast. Sailing farther north, however, he came upon a large bay that delighted him. It was "all that could be desired as a waystation for the galleons," he wrote, "for besides being sheltered from all the winds, it has many pines for masts and yards, and live oaks and white oaks, and [fresh] water in great quantity, all near the shore." This was no doubt Cabrillo's "Bay of Pines," a discovery long since forgotten. Vizcaíno christened it Monterey, in honor of the viceroy.

"The land is thickly populated with numberless Indians," Vizcaíno reported, "of whom a great many came several times to our camp." The Ohlone (oh-LOW-nee) people, who resided along the coast from Big Sur to San Francisco Bay, seemed unsurprised by the ship and its crew and eager to receive cloth and beads. The inhabitants were "peaceable and docile," wrote Vizcaíno, "and can be brought readily within the fold of the holy gospel and into subjection to the crown of Your Majesty."

Returning to Mexico, Vizcaíno submitted a proposal for establishing a colony at Monterey Bay. But a new viceroy quashed the project, arguing that there were too many inherent dangers. Native Californians could be friendly, but experience showed that relations with them easily turned sour, and an outpost in Alta California was too far from Mexico to be defended or reinforced. What they needed, argued the viceroy, was a port on an island in the north Pacific. Indeed, in the 1660s the Spaniards established just such a port as a refuge for the China ships, on the Pacific island of Guam. Many years would pass before they returned to Alta California.

Yet the idea of a California refuge for the China ships remained under consideration. As late as the mid-eighteenth century, a former colonial governor of Manila proposed an outpost at Monterey Bay. "From the Philippines," he wrote, "three hundred men of all trades can be conveyed on a frigate . . . with all the nails, locks, tools, and everything necessary to found a town at once." Add soldiers and missionaries from

Mexico, and "a great spiritual and temporal conquest can be effected." The idea was feasible: California might have been colonized by Filipinos. But that plan would be rejected for a very different one.

TURN BACK

5

Extending the Spanish Domain

On the morning of April 11, 1769, the *San Antonio,* a 193-ton Spanish supply ship, entered San Diego Bay. From the deck, Captain Juan Pérez, a veteran pilot of China ships, saw a group of Kumeyaays watching from the shore. It had been decades since a European sailing ship had entered their bay, and the community had no memory of previous encounters. It's a huge whale, some of the Kumeyaays said, a huge whale with white wings. But as the ship drew closer they could see it was a vessel, larger than any they could have imagined. Over the next several years, California Natives living along the coast from San Diego to San Francisco would become very familiar with the sight of these ships.

One hundred and sixty-seven years after Sebastián Vizcaíno's exploration of the coast, the Spaniards had finally decided to colonize Alta California. Loaded with tools, farm equipment, and other heavy gear, the *San Antonio* had left the port of La Paz in Baja California two months before, manned by a crew of thirty-two. To avoid beating against the southward-flowing coastal current, Captain Pérez took his vessel out to sea, catching breezes that carried it to a latitude north of his intended destination. Then he turned toward shore and rode the current south to the gateway of the Kumeyaay homeland.

By then half his crew showed signs of scurvy. Captain Pérez himself was so weak he could barely stand. He and his men badly needed assistance. A sister ship, the *San Carlos,* carrying a company of twenty-five Spanish soldiers, had departed more than a month before him, and Pérez hoped to find the vessel already in the harbor at San Diego. But it was not there. Without the protection of the soldiers, Pérez decided against confronting the Kumeyaays, who lined the shore shouting and waving weapons. The captain ordered all hands to remain on board while they awaited the arrival of their comrades.

It took another eighteen days before the missing ship appeared at the entrance to the bay. By then two of Pérez's crew had died and only seven men remained fit for service. Using a small handheld spyglass, Pérez surveyed the *San Carlos.* Seeing no one on deck, he sent his pilot and a few able-bodied men over in a launch. They found virtually all hands, including Captain Vicente Vila of the Spanish Royal Navy, incapacitated. It had been a disastrous voyage. Heavy seas had tossed them so badly that the water casks in the hold shattered, forcing them to keep close to shore to take on water. That meant fighting the coastal current. It had taken them 110 days to reach San Diego, by which time everyone was stricken, both with scurvy and with some other disorder, possibly a form of dysentery contracted from contaminated water. Several men had died. Of the more than one hundred soldiers and sailors aboard the two ships, only sixteen were fit for service.

On May 1, lieutenants Pedro Fages and Miguel Costansó,

accompanied by a few armed men, went ashore. They hailed a group of Kumeyaay men, but the Natives kept their distance. When Fages sent an unarmed soldier forward with presents, several Natives warily approached. Using signs, the Spaniards communicated their need for water, and the Kumeyaays directed them to a river two or three miles away. Nearby was the village of Kosa'aay, where the hungry men bartered for fish and game.

The following day the Spaniards began the construction of an encampment on the beach. Using sails from the ships, they rigged up two hospital tents and ferried the sick to shore. "The cold made itself felt with rigor at night in the tents and the sun likewise by day," wrote Lieutenant Costansó, "which made the sick suffer cruelly, two or three of them dying every day." The Spaniards buried their dead on a sandy spit of land they called *Punta de los Muertos,* Dead Man's Point. Today it is the site of a lovely waterfront park.

The Kumeyaays struck the Spaniards as arrogant and contemptuous. "They are of haughty temper," Costansó noted, and "make great boast of their powers." Fearful of their hosts, the intruders kept to their encampment. The Kumeyaays were "evil-looking, suspicious, treacherous, and have scant friendship for the Spanish," wrote Lieutenant Fages. "We have taken shelter behind a breastwork garrisoned by two small cannon in case of attack by day, and at night I keep two sentinels on guard, changing them very two hours."

In their account of the encounter, the Kumeyaays recalled several ominous signs that accompanied the landing of the Spaniards, including a solar eclipse and a powerful earthquake, both events confirmed by the Spanish accounts. Those signs convinced the Kumeyaays, wrote Father Junípero Serra, "that some great event was about to take place, as indeed it was."

★

Why had the Spaniards waited so long before undertaking the colonization of Alta California? In the mid-sixteenth century, when enthusiasm for conquest was at its peak, they were discouraged by the absence of a great civilization to plunder. At the turn of the seventeenth century, flush times for the China ships, they were put off by Native resistance and the daunting task of supplying a distant outpost. The century and a half since had proved to be an era of diminished expectations. Disastrous epidemics in Mexico decimated the Native population, and a shrinking workforce triggered a downward economic spiral, cutting deeply into the flow of treasure to Spain.

Eroding colonial profits accompanied a decline in Spain's military power. It commenced with the defeat of its naval armada by the English in 1588 and continued with losses and defeats in the endless European wars of the seventeenth and eighteenth centuries. During the most recent conflict—the Seven Years' War from 1756 to 1783, pitting France and Spain against Great Britain and the German states—British naval forces seized and occupied Havana on the island of Cuba and Manila in the Philippines, Spain's two most valuable colonial ports. Both were returned to Spain following the war, but the temporary loss was a profound shock to the Spanish monarchy, which became preoccupied with the expansion of rival empires.

Russian fur traders had planted outposts in the Aleutian Islands of the north Pacific, while their British counterparts had extended their reach all the way across the North American continent. Spanish authorities worried about the vulnerability of New Spain and its silver mines. "It cannot be denied," an influential report concluded, "that if any foreign power should find means of building fortifications in California and maintain superiority there, the empire of Mexico would be in the utmost danger."

In 1765, Charles III, the Spanish monarch, appointed José de Gálvez, a trusted royal advisor, to oversee the reform of New Spain's administration, focusing particular attention on the northern borderlands. To secure the frontiers, the Spanish relied on Christian missions and military outposts called *presidios*. Missionaries, supported by soldiers, were tasked with enticing Native peoples to their missions, converting them to Catholicism, and teaching them to farm. The goal was to transform them into a well-trained, reliable, subject labor force. Gálvez proposed extending that system to Alta California, creating a buffer against the possible expansion of competing colonial powers.

The northern missions, from Tejas (Texas) to Baja California, were staffed and managed by the Jesuits, a highly disciplined religious order committed to spreading Catholicism across the globe. So successful were they that the Spanish crown feared they might challenge the sovereign power of the monarchy, so in 1767 Charles ordered the Jesuits expelled from Spain and all its colonial possessions. Administration of the frontier missions was handed over to the more compliant Franciscan order, and Gálvez appointed Father Junípero Serra, a veteran Franciscan missionary, as "father-president" of the Baja missions. Serra forged a close working relationship with the local military governor, Captain Gaspar de Portolá.

Consulting with Serra and Portolá, Gálvez drew up a plan for the colonization of Alta California. It began with the establishment of missions and presidios at San Diego and Monterey, followed by the construction of additional missions in all the Native population centers in between. Because of the great distance and the difficulty of resupply, the colony was designed to be self-supporting, with Native Californians themselves providing the labor. The enterprise would begin with the supply vessels sent to San Diego, which would link up with overland parties driving livestock north from Baja. A contingent would then push on to Monterey. "The object," Gálvez wrote, "is to establish the Catholic faith, to extend the Spanish domain, and to check the ambitious schemes of foreign nations."

★

On May 3, 1769, as the sailors and soldiers at San Diego set up their forlorn encampment, the first of the overland parties entered the southern portion of Kumeyaay territory. The lumbering caravan of approximately fifty men, led by Captain Fernando de Rivera, included two Franciscan missionaries and twenty-five mounted Mexican *soldados de cuera* or leatherjackets, named for the padded leather vests they wore as protection from Native arrows. They were accompanied by fifteen or twenty Cochimí (ko-chi-MEE) converts from the Baja missions, in charge of more than a hundred pack mules and several hundred head of cattle.

The livestock kicked up a huge cloud of dust, visible for miles, alerting the residents of a Kumeyaay village near today's port of Ensenada, Mexico. "As soon as they saw us," wrote Franciscan missionary Juan Crespí, "they ran off to the hills and commenced a lot of shouting, seeming by their gesturing to be telling us to turn back." That was something the Spaniards would not consider. Soldiers and missionaries alike believed they were endowed by God, Church, and King with the right to assert sovereignty over the lands of pagans. They considered themselves cultural superiors, *gente de razón*—people of reason—while the Kumeyaays were just "Indians."

Not long after, the expedition was confronted by a party of Kumeyaay fighters, who arrayed themselves along a ridge overlooking the trail. They "shouted at us a great deal in a loud chorus," wrote Father Crespí, "all naked, heavily armed, and with large quivers on their backs and bows and arrows in their hands." Captain Rivera tried to convey his peaceful intentions, but the fighters refused to parlay. They shadowed the caravan for several days, at one point shooting several arrows that struck the ground near Captain Rivera. He ordered his men to fire a musket volley over the fighters' heads, which sent them running for cover.

The Kumeyaay fighters, who may have received word of the ships anchored at San Diego, were doing what they could to repulse the Spaniards. But, like other Native Californians, the Kumeyaays had no central leadership. Villages and individuals were free to do as they pleased. Small groups of Kumeyaay women and children began visiting the Spanish encampment in the evenings, begging for beads and cloth. Soon a throng of Kumeyaay men, women, and children were following the party, clamoring for presents. The Cochimís of northern Baja spoke a related language, so they were able to communicate with the Kumeyaays, translating what they learned into Spanish.

The overland party finally arrived at San Diego. "To our sorrow," wrote Father Crespí, "we found the camp turned into a hospital, with nearly all the soldiers and sailors perishing from scurvy." The burying ground became more crowded with each passing day. By the time the second overland caravan arrived—sixty or seventy men commanded by Governor Portolá and including Father-President Serra—thirty-one graves marked Dead Man's Point. Many men remained sick and suffering. A cautious leader might have aborted the project, but Portolá prided himself on his daring. He dispatched a few able-bodied sailors back to Mexico in the *San Antonio* for resupply. "I shall stop at no hindrance, obstacle, or risk," he wrote to Gálvez. "My resolve has been either to die or to fulfill my mission." He was determined to push on to Monterey.

★

A week later Portolá set out with a party of seventy-four men, including three dozen mounted leatherjackets, fifteen Christian Cochimís from the Baja missions, and ten Mexicans driving a pack train of two hundred mules. Three missionaries stayed behind at San Diego, protected by eight leatherjackets. Twenty or thirty ailing men remained confined to their beds. Eight Cochimís gathered roots and seeds, shellfish, and small game to augment the food supply. They also cleared a garden patch and planted beans and corn. The Cochimís would continue to supply the labor until a sufficient number of Native Californians had been converted. On July 16, Father Serra ordered a large wooden cross erected on a low hill and dedicated the site with a mass. Mission San Diego had been founded.

But the Kumeyaays wanted nothing to do with it. They were repelled by the sour smell of the Spaniards, who believed bathing threatened their health. The Kumeyaays, who loved swimming in the Pacific surf, "thought we were like animals," observed Franciscan missionary Luis Jayme. With all the sickness and dying among the Spaniards, wrote Jayme, the Natives concluded "it was bad to become a Christian, for they would die immediately." In the face of Spanish weakness, the Kumeyaays paraded their strength, even poking fun at the armed leatherjackets by aiming imaginary muskets and mimicking the sound of gunfire, then laughing uproariously.

Yet they remained eager for Spanish things. As soon as Portolá and the majority of the soldiers left for the north, Natives began pilfering tools, pottery, and furnishings from the encampment. Metal, glass, and ceramics impressed them as objects with great spiritual power. They were especially attracted to woven fabric, particularly the large canvas ship sails that sheltered the sick, which a group of Kumeyaays attempted to steal one night. The leatherjackets chased them off, but over the next several days Kumeyaay men prowled the outskirts of the encampment, leaving only after being warned off by armed guards. The Spaniards lived in constant fear of a surprise attack.

It came on the morning of August 15, just after Serra finished celebrating mass. Four of the eight soldiers were on board the *San Carlos,* two were guarding the horses, and two were sleeping. Twenty or thirty Natives stormed the compound and began pulling down the sails and ripping sheets off the sick. The guards, joined by the expedition's carpenter and blacksmith, came running. They fired their muskets, and the Kumeyaays responded with a volley of arrows. "Long live the faith of Jesus Christ," roared the blacksmith, "and may these dogs, its enemies, die!" Hit by an arrow, he went down, but it proved a minor wound. A missionary and a Christian Cochimí were also wounded. Father Serra took refuge in a hut. Suddenly his Cochimí servant boy staggered in, an arrow protruding from his neck. Serra administered the last rites as the boy bled to death, the first member of the expedition to die by violence.

The leatherjackets chased off the attackers and claimed to have killed at least three. The residents of Kosa'aay abandoned their village, and for many days the Spaniards saw no Natives at all, although they could hear the distant cries of mourning women. The soldiers hastily constructed a stockade around their encampment, and everyone hunkered down, praying that relief would soon arrive from New Spain. The Kumeyaays, Lieutenant Costansó wrote, were "influenced solely by their greed and their desire to rob." Surely that was an objective, but a minor one. Strangers had invaded their country, set up an encampment, and showed no sign of leaving. "They did not know why the Spaniards had come," wrote Father Jayme, "unless we intended to take their lands away from them." How else could patriots respond?

TARABAL LEADS ANZA'S EXPEDITION

6

The Wanderer

Governor Gaspar de Portolá and his men returned from their expedition along the California coast in late January 1770 after pushing as far north as San Francisco Bay. "It is a very large harbor," reported Father Juan Crespí. "Not only the navy of our Most Catholic Majesty but those of all Europe could take shelter in it." Portolá, however, did not recognize the significance of the discovery. He had failed to locate Monterey Bay, which left him in a funk. He did have one piece of good news. All hands had survived the arduous journey, despite an attack of scurvy, which cleared up once the leatherjackets began emulating the Christian Cochimís, consuming grass shoots, seeds, and berries they foraged along the trail. Finally on the return march, after finishing off the last of their food stores, the men slaughtered and ate their pack animals. They arrived back at San Diego, as Portolá put it, "smelling frightfully of mules."

The thousand-mile expedition would have been impossible without the contribution of the Christian Cochimís, who blazed the trail. They also acted as go-betweens with the many Natives encountered along the way, most of whom were friendly and eager for presents. The languages spoken north of San Diego, however, were as alien to the Cochimís as to the Spaniards, and miscommunication characterized the encounters with Native communities. At one village a headman greeted the Spaniards. "He told us by signs, which we understood very well, that we must come to live with them," wrote Father Crespí, "telling us that all the land we saw was theirs and that they would divide it with us." That sounds like wishful thinking.

According to Lieutenant Miguel Costansó, the crude sign language employed by Spaniards and Natives amounted to a "pantomime from which, truly, one could understand little." A Christian Native named Pablo Tac later offered an indigenous account of the first appearance of the Spaniards. "What is it that you seek here?" the headman demanded of the strangers. "Get out of our country!" But unable to understand what he said, the Spaniards merely nodded. According to Tac, the men and women of his village "never wanted another people to live with them." That sounds more plausible.

The situation at San Diego remained perilous. Missionaries and leatherjackets alike hunkered down, surrounded by angry Kumeyaays. What's more, during Portolá's absence the infectious disease plaguing the encampment claimed another nineteen lives. The expedition had lost a total of at least fifty men. Unless the *San Antonio* soon returned from Mexico, Portolá concluded, he would have to abandon the enterprise. He dispatched a small force of mounted leatherjackets back to Baja for supplies, but Kumeyaay fighters harassed them along the trail, slowing their progress. Finally, after six weeks of anxious waiting, Portolá ordered the *San Carlos,* still anchored in San Diego Bay, loaded for evacuation to Mexico. Father-President

Junípero Serra angrily declared his determination to remain, come what may. But conflict was averted when the *San Antonio* arrived in mid-March with reinforcements and several tons of supplies. The Spanish colonization of California would continue.

★

Father Serra believed correctly that Portolá had actually reached Monterey Bay but simply failed to recognize it. Eager to try again, Portolá set out in April with twenty mounted leatherjackets, a string of pack mules, and a herd of cattle driven by Christian Cochimís. This time he found what he was looking for. Serra and a small party followed in the *San Antonio,* and in early June the two groups rendezvoused at the bay. On the slope of a gentle hill, Serra conducted a founding ceremony for the mission he named San Carlos Borromeo. The Cochimí workers immediately began clearing land, grubbing stumps, digging ditches, and planting crops. They herded the livestock onto the rolling hillsides to graze. The Cochimís were essential, wrote Serra, as "laborers, vaqueros, and mule drivers."

Monterey was homeland for the Ohlone people, perhaps as many as ten thousand living in several dozen village communities scattered along the coast. Unlike the Kumeyaays, the Ohlones did not offer resistance. Eager for glass beads and fabric, a number of them went to work for the missionaries, and within months they were joined by dozens more. Father Serra convinced himself that the power of his gospel message *pulled* them to the mission. It is more likely, however, that forces beyond their control *pushed* them there.

The grazing cattle and foraging hogs of the Spaniards produced a significant and sudden change in the local ecology, lowering the productivity of Native gathering and hunting and generating conflict between neighboring villages. Historian

Steven Hackel calls this "the awful, if accidental, genius of Spanish colonization": creating a subsistence crisis while simultaneously offering the remedy of mission agriculture and stock raising. As the animals reproduced and multiplied, the negative consequences compounded and the number of Ohlones seeking to join the Spaniards increased. The same process would play out at each of the missions the Franciscans founded.

A second disastrous consequence of colonization soon became apparent. Native men, women, and children began to fall sick and die from the common maladies spread by the Spaniards—bronchial infections, digestive ailments, and sexually transmitted diseases—to which the Ohlones had no acquired immunity. The missionaries professed themselves powerless to prevent the scourge. They had no understanding of the way those illnesses were transmitted, of course. It would be another two hundred years before the germ theory of disease was widely accepted. But the missionaries knew full well that sustained contact with Spaniards meant sickness and death for Natives. That's what had happened at the missions in Baja, and the Franciscans watched as it happened again in Alta California. Nevertheless, they pushed ahead, extending their missions into new territory.

Although Mission San Diego came first, San Carlos Borromeo, which fully embodied the ideals and policies of Father Serra, became the model for the nineteen missions that followed. Serra, an indomitable man in his late fifties, had no doubts about his work. The bright light of his Christian faith blinded him to all other forms of religious experience. He professed to love Native Californians yet despised their culture. "They are our children," Serra wrote, and "we look upon them as a father." Children need assistance, guidance, discipline, sometimes punishment. Transforming them into Christian believers and royal subjects would require much work—quite literally. Serra believed that regimented physical labor would teach the self-control that Natives lacked. Enforcing discipline required that the mission be organized much like a monastery, what social psychologists call a "total institution," one that controls virtually every aspect of daily life.

Conversion was voluntary, but once Natives accepted baptism they forfeited their freedom. "To become Christians," wrote missionary Pedro Font, Natives "must settle permanently in the mission and give up living in the wild." Reacting with horror to confinement, many wanted to leave. But that was not allowed. "Should they run away," warned Father Font, "they will be found, caught, and punished."

The Franciscans had few reservations about inflicting physical pain. Serra believed that "spiritual fathers should punish their sons, the Indians, with blows." On one occasion he ordered four misbehaving converts punished with "two or three whippings on different days," which would "serve as an example and a spiritual benefit to all." He believed in the positive value of physical pain, and willingly subjected himself to it as well. He walked barefoot on the roughest trails, wore a hair shirt beneath his habit, and flogged himself bloody each evening before going to bed. Introduced to such practices, Native converts had second thoughts about what they'd signed up for. Was this what was required of a Christian? Many fled the mission.

Father Serra relied on the leatherjackets to bring them back. Frequently the soldiers flaunted their power and abused Native women. Serra returned to this problem time and again in his correspondence. "The soldiers, without any restraint or shame," he reported to the viceroy, "behave like brutes toward the Indian women." Assaults and rapes took place regularly. "It is as though a plague of immorality has broken out." In truth, the sexual abuse of Native women by Spanish colonizers had been happening since the day Columbus first landed in the Caribbean. Spanish officers found such behavior impossible to curb, fearing that if they punished offending soldiers, they would encourage Native resistance. Serra complained, but little changed. As much as the Franciscans were appalled by the conduct of the leatherjackets, the missions would have been impossible without their protection.

★

Father Serra had ambitious plans for "a ladder of missions" stretching from San Diego to San Francisco, and before he died in 1784 he founded nine of them. One of the first was Mission San Gabriel in southern California, established in 1771 near several Tongva villages in what is today the city of Montebello. Things quickly turned sour. The leatherjackets raped a Native woman, then killed and decapitated her outraged husband, mounting his head on a pike at the entrance to the mission.

The violence shocked the missionaries, but their fear of Native retaliation exceeded their disgust. The abuse by leatherjackets continued. "Six or more soldiers would set out together on horseback every morning," Serra reported, "and clever as they are at lassoing cows and mules, would catch an Indian woman with their lassos to become prey for their unbridled lust. At times some Indian men would try to defend their wives, only to be shot down with bullets."

It is hardly surprising, then, that the missionaries at San Gabriel enjoyed little success in converting local inhabitants. Two years passed, "not only without making any serious progress," Serra wrote, but "each day turning away the hearts of the gentiles, pushing them further away." According to Pedro Fages, who succeeded Portolá as governor of Alta California, Native men believed "that we are exiles from our own lands who have come here in quest of their women." One convert told Serra that some Natives wondered if the Spaniards were "the sons of the mules on which they rode," perhaps because they smelled so much like their animals. To change those perceptions, Serra requested his missionary colleagues in Baja to send a group of Christian Cochimí families north, so the Natives might see "that there are marriages also among Christians." The missionaries needed the Cochimís not only as workers, but as living examples.

Six Cochimí families arrived at Mission San Gabriel in the spring of 1773. The Spaniards were fastidious record keepers, yet they consistently failed to note the names of the Natives who assisted them. Thanks to some historical sleuthing, however, we know the Christian names of one of those couples: Sebastián Tarabal, an energetic man in his late twenties, his wife María Dolores Kinajan, and their infant daughter. Tarabal was one of the Cochimís assigned to the 1769 expedition, trekking overland to San Diego with Portolá, then to Monterey, before rejoining his family in Baja. A married Christian couple with a child, Tarabal and his family were a shining example of what the Franciscans hoped to accomplish.

★

In those early years, Mission San Gabriel was a primitive compound with a rude chapel constructed of willow poles and several dozen adjacent brush dwellings for missionaries, leatherjackets, and the small number of Natives who accepted baptism. The Tongva language was unintelligible to the Comichís, who lived in separate quarters. As experienced farmers, they supervised the labor of Tongva converts, which generated a good deal of mutual resentment. The Cochimís grew discontented and homesick. In the fall of 1773, only a few months after they arrived, Sebastián Tarabal, his wife, and a Cochimí kinsman went missing. The report of their absence made no mention of the daughter, who may have perished in one of the mission's frequent epidemics, provoking her parents to flee.

Fearing capture by leatherjackets, they avoided the trail to San Diego and instead headed southeast toward the Colorado River, homeland of the Quechans, with whom they shared a language. The route was treacherous, crossing desolate mountains and scorching deserts. But after his extensive travels with Portolá, Tarabal must have felt confident in his ability as a guide. He successfully led them from one waterhole to the next. Approaching the Colorado, however, in a trackless area known as the Algondones Dunes, he lost his way. His wife and kinsman died of dehydration, but Tarabal himself made it to the river, where some Quechans found him and nursed him back to health.

The Quechan homeland centered on the confluence of the Colorado and Gila rivers, where sandbars and shoals formed a passable ford. The strategic importance of this crossing was well understood by Spanish officials, for it offered the possibility of an overland route to Alta California. The ocean passage was unreliable, and the trail north from Baja linked two underdeveloped regions. The Spaniards needed an overland route connecting the province of Sonora with Alta California, enabling them to populate their new colony with Mexican settlers.

Franciscan missionaries made friendly contact with a leader of the Quechans, a man the Spanish knew as Salvador Palma. Chief Palma expressed interest in an alliance, perhaps in the hope it would assist in consolidating his authority. So in 1773, on orders from the viceroy of New Spain, Captain Juan Bautista de Anza, commander of the presidio of Tubac, near today's city of Tucson, assembled a large party of mounted leatherjackets and muleteers. As the expedition prepared to depart, Chief Palma and his entourage arrived with Tarabal, the fugitive Christian Cochimí, in tow.

Listening to Tarabal's story, Anza immediately recognized

his value. Having just blazed a trail across the desert and mountains, he had the ability to lead Anza's expedition to Alta California. Rather than treat Tarabal as a fugitive, Anza made him his personal servant, muleteer, and guide. "We were assured by the Indian Sebastián that he would lead us to the watering places," a member of the expedition jotted in his journal. And that is precisely what Tarabal did, successfully leading them on a northwesterly course across the desert. Anza took the expedition "wherever the Indian Sebastián wanted to take them," Father-President Serra reported.

After two months of exhausting travel, they arrived at Mission San Gabriel, then pushed on to Monterey. Tarabal certainly earned the name Anza gave him: *El Peregrino,* the Wanderer. The next year Anza and Tarabal repeated the trip, this time escorting a party of more than two hundred Sonoran colonists, including women and children. They became the first Spanish-speaking settlers of San Francisco Bay. With Tarabal's assistance, Juan Bautista de Anza appeared to have cleared the way for the full colonization of Alta California.

★

But serious obstacles remained. When Anza arrived at San Gabriel he learned that a second uprising of the Kumeyaays had taken place at San Diego, this one considerably more serious than the attack of 1769. Sometime after midnight on November 5, 1775, several hundred Kumeyaays from at least fifteen villages overran, pillaged, and burned the mission, killing three Spaniards, including Father Luis Jayme. The reason for the violence was depressingly familiar. "A feeling of resentment spread among the Indians," the official Franciscan account concluded. "They saw how the pack animals and the cattle were constantly eating the grass from which they had hitherto supported themselves." As a Kumeyaay leader put it, they wanted to destroy the mission "in order to live as they had before."

And once again, the spark that ignited the rebellion was the sexual abuse of Native women. In one incident, three soldiers raped a group of young girls, leaving one of them dead. "The soldiers are committing a thousand evils, particularly of a sexual nature," Father Jayme wrote shortly before his violent death. "Very many of them deserve to be hanged."

Christian Kumeyaays took an active part in the uprising. In the midst of the attack, Father Jayme appealed to them to remember their faith, but they seized him, stripped him naked, shot him full of arrows, and beat his face to an unrecognizable pulp. The uprising marked an end to Father Serra's optimism, but he still attempted to find the divine plan in the disaster. "Thanks be to God," he wrote. "Now that the terrain has been watered by blood, the conversions of the San Diego Indians will take place." But he was wrong about that. Mission San Diego failed to attract large numbers of converts. Most Kumeyaays remained intractable opponents of the Spaniards.

Fearing a general uprising in Alta California, the viceroy dispatched more soldiers and plans were made to strengthen Spanish control of the Quechan crossing. Captain Anza saw the situation clearly. "If the peoples who dwell along this great river [the Colorado] are attached to us, we will effect its passage without excessive labor," he wrote. "If they are not, it will be almost impossible to do so." Chief Palma accepted an invitation to Mexico City, where the viceroy entertained him lavishly, and he went home eager to exploit the new alliance. Franciscans established two missions among the Quechans, and colonists from Sonora settled nearby.

It took only two or three years for the relationship between the Quechans and the Spanish to deteriorate. Soldiers abused Native women, and settlers allowed their livestock to graze Native fields. "Much damage was done," a Franciscan reported, "by this multitude of animals in the maize-fields and sown lands of the Indians."

Fed up, in 1781 the Quechans rose in revolt, led by Chief Palma himself. Aiming to eliminate the Spaniards from their world, they burned and destroyed both missions and the settlement, killing 105 leatherjackets, missionaries, and settlers and taking 76 men, women, and children captive. The Spanish sent a military force that succeeded in redeeming most of the captives, but the Quechans repelled their attack and continued fighting back against subsequent military expeditions for the next two years. It was the most significant defeat of the Spaniards by a Native people in the history of colonial California. By closing the river crossing, the Quechans effectively prevented Alta California from becoming a settlement colony. They remained independent and indomitable until finally subdued by the U.S. Army in the 1850s.

The Franciscan Francisco Garcés was among those murdered during the Quechan uprising. Even before his death, Father Garcés had become legendary for his missionary travels in the Southwest, usually accompanied by Sebastián Tarabal. The two men first met on Anza's expeditions. Afterward, Garcés arranged for Tarabal to be his permanent guide. They traveled thousands of trackless miles together, bringing the gospel message to dozens of villages. Enthralled Natives listened intently as Garcés and Tarabal sang the "Alabado," the Catholic hymn of praise, in unison.

Historian Robert Kittle believes the two men became friends. "Sitting together for hours around the campfire under starlit desert skies," he writes, they "developed an attachment that was rare between any Spaniard and Indian." Once, unavoidably separated for several days, Garcés found himself "haunted" by the thought that Tarabal had come to harm. "All I wanted," he wrote in his journal, "was relief from my fears."

They were staying at a Mojave (mo-HAV-ay) village on the Colorado River when Garcés announced his intention to visit the remote Hopi (HO-pea) pueblos in the vicinity of the Grand Canyon. The Mojaves warned him that the Hopis were dangerous, and fearing harm, Tarabal refused to go. Garcés went alone and was gone far longer than he had planned. When he finally returned, he found that Tarabal had left, headed for parts unknown. Garcés never saw him again, and Tarabal disappears from the Spanish historical record. The missionary mourned his absence, despite the Mojaves telling him he shouldn't care, that Tarabal had revealed his "bad heart" by abandoning his master. More likely, Sebastián Tarabal simply slipped off into the wilderness again, inveterate wanderer that he was.

FATHER BOSCANA + THE DANCERS

7

What Happened to My Chickens?

The Kumeyaays stubbornly resisted the missionaries. "A wounded spirit animated their memory eternally," said Pablo Tac, a Luiseño and northern neighbor of the Kumeyaays. With memories of invasion and rape, the Kumeyaays tried to keep their distance, but the ruination caused by grazing cattle and sheep forced many of them to resort to the mission for their subsistence. Conversion and forced labor followed, although most converts continued to reside in their natal villages. By 1799, thirty years after the founding, the Franciscans had recorded the baptism of 2,343 Kumeyaays at Mission San Diego, half of them children under the age of ten. They also recorded the death of 1,045 converts, a mortality rate double what it had been before the invasion. Most were victims of infectious diseases that spread from missionaries and leatherjackets to mission converts and villagers.

The Kumeyaays, said one of the missionaries, were "exceedingly desirous of preserving the customs of their elders."

In stories and songs passed down through the generations, they rehearsed their fear and hatred of the missionaries. One such tale was repeated by an elderly Kumeyaay woman named Alejandrina Murillo Melendres in the mid-twentieth century:

> Coyote was going along and came to the house of an old woman with a hen and a rooster. The hen had seven chicks. Coyote wanted to eat them, but he couldn't carry them all at once. "Give me a chick," he said to the hen. "I'll take and baptize it." "All right," said the hen. Coyote carried off the chick and ate it. The next day he came back. "I'm taking another one to baptize; the first one is sad, all by himself," he said. "All right," said the hen. Coyote carried off the chick and ate it. He did this with all the chicks. He ate every one. Then he went again to the hen. "Come and see your children, all baptized, very big and beautiful," he said. "All right," said the hen. Coyote carried off the hen and ate her. Then he went to the rooster. "Your wife cries for you to come," he said. "All right," said the rooster. Coyote carried off the rooster and ate him. Then the old woman came. "What happened to my chickens? Who robbed me?" She went to look. In a cave, under a stone, she found a lot of feathers. She got furious, but what could she do? The chickens were all gone.

This dark-humored tale was an analog of real events. Coyote mimics the missionaries, adopting their practice of taking first the young, then the mother, followed by the husband. All are lost, just as Kumeyaay converts were lost to unknown maladies and an alien religion. That made the Kumeyaays furious, but what could they do? This Coyote tale spoke not only to the Kumeyaay experience, but to the experience of all mission converts among Native Californians.

★

Junípero Serra died at his post in 1784, but other Franciscans continued his work. By 1805, with military support, nineteen missions operated along coastal California from San Diego to San Francisco, each strategically sited near concentrations of Native inhabitants: five in southern California, including large establishments among the Tongvas at San Luis Rey and San Gabriel; five along the Chumash coast, the largest at Santa Barbara; two for the Salinan (SAL-in-an) people of the Salinas Valley; and seven among the Ohlones, including Santa Clara, San José, and San Francisco.

For Native Californians it was, in the words of historian Randall Milliken, "a time of little choice." At first most Natives tried to avoid the missionaries, but soon their world began to change for the worse. A newly established mission typically experienced two or three years of slow growth, then a sudden burst of conversions as the Native foraging economy collapsed under the onslaught of grazing livestock. "Experience has taught that the foremost sermon with which these unfortunate savages can be reduced to our Holy Faith is food and clothing," one missionary wrote. "Faith enters through the mouth."

With Natives supplying the labor, the missions gradually went from brush structures to modest buildings of adobe and stone. In the pattern of Mission San Carlos Borromeo, Native converts resided in an adjacent mission village, but young, unmarried women and men were housed in single-sex dormitories. There were quarters for the missionaries, a barracks for the leatherjackets, workshops and barns, and a sanctuary or chapel. The ubiquitous bells rang out the day's schedule, announcing the time to rise, worship, eat, work, and sleep. Men and women alike worked in fields and workshops, producing virtually all the grain, meat, soap, candles, shoes, furniture, and other basics required for the colonization of Alta California. A small number of converts became mounted vaqueros, responsible for the livestock, but the Franciscans prohibited most from getting near the horses, fearing that if they learned to ride they would become rebellious.

The mission offered Natives an alternative to starvation but provided no refuge from disease. Dysentery, diphtheria, tuberculosis, measles, syphilis, and other debilitating and deadly infections spread rapidly among the Natives. Soon after joining the mission, wrote one leader, the converts "become extremely feeble, lose weight, get sick, and die." Missionaries comforted themselves in the belief that the souls of the dead had been saved.

Historical demographers calculate that during the mission period convert deaths outnumbered births by better than two to one. Such a pattern leads to annihilation. The coastal population among which Franciscans established their missions fell from an estimated sixty thousand in 1770 to less than twenty thousand by 1830. To keep the missions functioning, Franciscans kept expanding their recruitment to outlying areas, ensnaring ever more Native people in the mission trap.

★

The Franciscans rarely recorded the thoughts and voices of their converts. But after the collapse of the mission system in the 1830s (more on that below), a number of survivors recounted some of their experiences and they were recorded for posterity. Their perspective was uniformly negative. "We were treated unjustly," declared Fernando Librado, who lived most of his life at Mission San Buenaventura, in today's city of Ventura. "All of our possessions, game, land, and foodstuffs were taken away." According to Lorenzo Asisara, raised at Mission

Santa Cruz, the missionaries were relentlessly cruel. "They treated us very badly. They made us work like slaves." Julio César of Mission San Luis Rey agreed. "The way the Indians were treated was not good at all," he said. "They only gave us food, a loincloth, and a blanket which they replaced each year. They did, however, give us plenty of whippings for any wrong-doing, however slight."

Franciscan leaders not only condoned corporal punishment, they believed in it. California Natives were "a people of vicious and ferocious customs," declared Father-President Fermin Lasuén, Junípero Serra's successor. "It is a duty imposed on us to correct and punish men of this kind." The punishments were mild, he asserted, with an upper limit of twenty-five lashes. That's twenty-five lashes on the bare back, applied with a hemp or rawhide whip with several knotted braids. According to Lorenzo Asisara, the converts at Santa Cruz were "very severely treated by the padres, often punished by fifty lashes on the bare back. Any disobedience or infraction brought down the lash without mercy on the women the same as the men. We were always trembling with fear of the lash." "Padre, take back thy Christianity," a convert at Mission San José told the missionary after receiving punishment. "I want none of it. I will return to my country."

In 1797, a company of leatherjackets captured a large group of fugitives from Mission San Francisco. A Spanish officer interviewed the fugitives and recorded their reasons for running away. A convert named Tiburcio fled after the missionary "ordered him whipped because he was crying" following the death of his wife and daughter. Magín left because "they had put him in the stocks when he was sick." Ostanso, because his wife, child, and two brothers had died. Román, because of the many whippings he suffered. Claudio, because he was "clubbed every time he turned around." José Manuel, because he was hit with a heavy cane, "rendering one hand useless." Homobon, because his brother died, "and when he cried for him at the mission they whipped him." Liborato, because his mother, two brothers, and three nephews had died. Timoteo, because they whipped him when he was sick and unable to work. As for Próspero, the padre "ordered him stretched out and beaten" after he was caught hunting ducks to feed his family. This sampling of testimonials paints a chilling portrait of mission life.

★

When French naval officer Jean-François de Galaup, comte de Lapérouse, paid a visit to Mission San Carlos in 1786, he wrote that it "brought to our recollection a plantation at Santo Domingo or any other West Indian island." He was not the only observer who made such a comparison. The converts, wrote an American fur trapper at Mission San Gabriel forty years later, "are complete slaves in every sense of the word." Some modern historians have compared the missions to concentration camps.

But such characterizations obscure the truth. The missions were Native communities under European domination. Converts preserved as much of their traditional culture as they were able. Few missionaries bothered to learn the Native language, which provided the converts with a degree of privacy and autonomy. Parents continued to teach their children stories and songs, communicating traditional ideas and values. Converts were also allowed to pick their own leaders, known as alcaldes, and often they chose the same individuals who had previously served as village headmen.

They also continued many of their traditional cultural practices, incorporating music and dance into Christian ritual. "So great is the affection which they have for their dances," reported Father Gerónimo Boscana, a missionary at Mission San Juan Capistrano, "they will spend days, nights, and whole weeks dancing." According to Pablo Tac, his Luiseño people at Mission San Luis Rey danced for joy and for sorrow, for the newborn and for the dead.

Tac was a committed Christian who rejected the old spiritual beliefs. He was also a brilliant student, and the Franciscans sent him to Rome to study for the priesthood, where he died at a very young age. But Tac left a fascinating essay on the conversion of his people, in which he described Luiseño dancers adorning themselves in feathers, "like the ancients." But "now that we are Christians," he added, "we dance only for ceremony." Father Boscana doubted that. Dancing, he worried, perpetuated traditional beliefs. Story, song, and dance linked the converts to their old life. Despite every effort to "make them forget the ancient beliefs of paganism," another Franciscan wrote, the converts continued "to carry on certain pagan practices."

The bonds of community could produce sparks of resistance. In 1776, after a devastating flood that destroyed the primitive structures at Mission San Gabriel, the Franciscans relocated to higher ground several miles away in what is today the city of San Gabriel, where the mission church remains intact. The area included a dozen or more densely populated Tongva villages, and the mission introduced all the familiar troublesome effects. Finally, after nearly a decade of disruption, the residents of several villages decided to act.

The principal instigator was the alcalde of the mission, a Tongva whose Christian name was Nicolás José. One of the first to be baptized at San Gabriel, he was an active participant in Catholic rituals. But he also returned frequently to his natal village to join in dances and ceremonies. He kept both worlds in balance, it seems, until an epidemic claimed the lives of a third of his community, including his wife and children. Turning against the mission, he approached the sister of his village headman, a young woman named Toypurina with a reputation as a powerful shaman who could communicate with the spirit world. Toypurina recruited other local leaders and they made a plan to invade the mission compound at night and murder the Franciscans and leatherjackets as they slept.

But the plot was discovered; the leaders were arrested and subjected to intense interrogation. Toypurina acknowledged her guilt. "I am angry with the padres and all of those of the mission," she declared, "for living here on my native soil and for trespassing upon the land of my ancestors and despoiling our homeland." Seventeen men were punished with public lashings, so all the Tongvas could see the consequences of attempted rebellion. Nicolás José and Toypurina were both sent north, he to perform six years of hard labor at the presidio of San Francisco, she exiled to Mission San Carlos.

★

Virtually every mission experienced violent confrontations. One of the best documented is the murder of a Franciscan missionary by Ohlone converts at Mission Santa Cruz. Father Andrés Quintana arrived at the mission in 1804 and soon developed a reputation for punishing converts for the slightest offense, applying the lash with enthusiasm. The breaking point came in 1812 after he flogged two young men with a whip enhanced with iron wires, nearly killing them. Outraged converts, both women and men, met secretly to decide how to react. Years later one of the conspirators told the story to his son, who repeated it to a historian, who committed it to print.

The case against Father Quintana was made by Lino, his personal servant, who had suffered the missionary's wrath many times. "We are not animals," he said. "God does not command this kind of punishment." But what could they do? "We cannot just run him off." That's what they would have done in the old days—simply exiled this evil person from their community. Now, they agreed, murder was their only option. "Let us kill the padre without anyone being aware, except those of us here," said Lino's father, a former headman named Ules. A woman named Yaquenonsat, a respected shaman like Toypurina, proposed a plan which the group adopted.

That night she went to Father Quintana to report that her elderly husband had fallen seriously ill and wished to confess. Quintana was about to sit down to supper and was reluctant to let his meal get cold, but Yaquenonsat pleaded and he agreed to accompany her. She led the missionary through the orchard, where her co-conspirators were supposed to seize him. But their nerve failed and they allowed him to pass. Quintana examined the old man, told his wife not to worry, and went back to his supper. Yaquenonsat returned to the orchard, where she angrily confronted the men. "If you don't do what you've promised," she threatened, "I will inform on you all." All right, they said, let's try again. So Yaquenonsat went back to Quintana, informing him that her husband had taken a turn for the worse and needed to confess. Quintana was eating, but Yaquenonsat begged, and he relented. This time, as they passed through the orchard, the men seized him.

Quintana immediately knew what was up. "Oh my sons, what have I done to you for which you would kill me?" he cried. "Because you have made a whip of iron," they told him. He only used the whip on "bad people," Quintana responded. "Well, you're in the hands of the bad people now," said one of the men. The missionary dropped to his knees and begged for his life, promising that if they spared him he would leave that very night and never speak of what they had done. You're leaving tonight for sure, they told him, but "you're going to heaven." They smothered Quintana with his own cape, carried the body to his room, and arranged it in bed. Before leaving, a man named Donato, a frequent victim of Quintana's, took out

his knife and cut off the missionary's testicles. "These balls belong in the outdoor privy," he said.

When Quintana's body was discovered the following
morning, it was assumed he had died in his sleep. A superficial
examination failed to notice the mutilation. Most mission Natives knew the truth, but they kept the secret. A year or two
later, a soldier who understood the native tongue overheard
two women chatting about the murder, leading the Franciscans to launch an official investigation that broke the code of
silence. Nine men were convicted and sentenced to receive
two hundred lashes apiece and long terms of forced labor. All
but two of them died before completing their sentences. The
Spanish considered the murder an act of rebellion. To the
Ohlones, it was an act of communal justice.

FORT ROSS

8

Undersea People

The Coast Miwok people living along the north shore of San Francisco Bay marveled at first sight of the strangers in their double-hatched kayaks, plunging through the heavy surf and gliding across the water, their faces masked by the colorful bentwood visors protecting their eyes from sea glare, their torsos covered in waterproof parkas made from strips of translucent sea lion gut. The Miwoks might easily have mistaken them for a pod of sea monsters.

The Aleuts (AL-e-oots), experienced sea otter hunters from the Aleutian Islands, first appeared in California in early 1809, brought by the Russian America Company. From a base camp at Bodega Bay, fifty miles north of San Francisco, the Aleuts scoured the coast, taking hundreds of otters for their valuable pelts. Then they entered the great bay itself, shouldering their kayaks and tramping several miles across the Marin peninsula to avoid being spotted by leatherjackets at the San Francisco presidio, overlooking the entrance to the bay that would be christened the Golden Gate. Several weeks later a company of leatherjackets out on patrol stumbled across a temporary camp of several dozen Aleuts on a beach south of the mission. The soldiers fired their muskets and four hunters were killed. But most of them escaped and continued their expedition for several weeks before returning to Bodega Bay in late April with more than two thousand pelts. Spanish fears of Russian expansion into California had finally become fact.

Since the early eighteenth century Russian fur traders, known as *promyshlenniki,* had been in eager pursuit of the North Pacific sea otter, whose coastal habitat ranged from the Kuril Islands north of Japan, across the Aleutian chain to Alaska, and down the North American coast as far south as Baja California. Unlike other marine mammals, sea otters have no blubber to protect them from cold Pacific waters, relying instead on dense fur, the thickest of all mammals. Their tanned pelts, remarkably heavy and lustrous, were prized by the Chinese, who paid extraordinary prices for them. To supply the demand, Russian traders relied on the aquatic prowess of the Aleuts, whom they ruthlessly exploited. They attacked Aleut coastal villages, taking women and children hostage and forcing the men into service. What violence and atrocity did not accomplish, disease did, and by the end of the century the Native population of the Aleutians had fallen by 80 percent.

By that time, fur traders from other nations had entered the trade. British and American merchant traders plied the waters south of the Russian sphere of operations, the coast of today's British Columbia and Washington state, bartering with Native hunters for sea otter pelts, which they transported to China, exchanging their haul for silk, porcelain, and tea. That trans-Pacific voyage usually included a stopover for provisions in Hawai'i, known then as the Sandwich Islands, named in honor of a British earl. The Hawaiian Islands were densely populated by several hundred thousand people of Polynesian descent calling themselves Kānaka Maoli (KA-nak-ah MY-oh-lee). The Kānakas were a seafaring people, and soon their young men were joining the crews of visiting ships.

In 1799, in the face of mounting competition, the Russian state chartered a royal monopoly known as the Russian America Company, granting it exclusive rights to the sea otter trade. Overhunting had decimated the otter population of the Aleutians, so the Company extended its operations south, directly challenging the British and American trade with coastal Natives. The Russians established their American headquarters at Sitka in southeastern Alaska, in the homeland of the maritime Tlingit (KLINK-kit) people. The Tlingits, who acquired firearms by trading with the Americans, proved fierce opponents. Twice they attacked and destroyed the Russian offices and warehouses at Sitka, and their resistance forced the Company to adopt a more measured approach to Native people. Aleut hunters became contract employees, still bound to service, but by indebtedness to the Company rather than threats of violence to their families.

★

Despite the Spanish assault on the Aleut boatmen in 1809, the lucrative hunting expedition to San Francisco Bay persuaded the Russians to establish a permanent outpost along the northern California coast. Ivan Kuskov, the administrator in charge, chose a location fifteen miles north of Bodega Bay, on a bluff more than a hundred feet above the Pacific, providing an excellent view of the coastline. The site, with ready access to fresh water and abundant timber, was known to local Pomo residents as *Métini*.

A young girl named Lukaria witnessed the arrival of Kuskov and his party during the winter of 1811–12, later recounting what she had seen. "We detected something white sailing on the water," she said. "We didn't know what it was, we hadn't seen anything like that before." Looking down on the ship from the bluff, they could see men emerging from below deck. To the Pomos it appeared as if they were arising from the bottom of the sea, so they called them the "Undersea People."

Kuskov distributed gifts and parlayed with local leaders, indicating through sign and gesture his desire to plant a settlement. A shrewd and courteous negotiator who had previously arranged a peace treaty with the Tlingits, Kuskov attempted to charm the Pomos and their Coast Miwok neighbors. "These lands are ours," declared a Pomo headman. No problem, Kuskov replied, he only wished for land enough to build an outpost. Native leaders hesitated, yet they also sensed an opportunity, given voice by one of the Miwoks. The leatherjackets from San Francisco, he told Kuskov, often invaded their country in search of fugitives from the missions and sometimes kidnapped his people. The Russians would be welcome if they agreed to help "defend the inhabitants from Spanish oppression." The Natives "do not recognize Spanish authority at all," one Russian reported, "and always kill them when they meet north of San Francisco Bay, which they consider the ultimate Spanish border."

The Native perspective came as good news to Kuskov. The informal agreement struck by the two sides that winter—the Pomos and Coast Miwoks agreeing to allow the Russians to plant an outpost in exchange for guarantees of protection against the Spaniards—was formalized by an official treaty in 1817. Known as the Métini Protocol, it is the only written agreement between a colonial power and Native Californians before the twentieth century.

The Russians constructed an impressive redwood stockade with blockhouses and cannon at the corners. It enclosed a three-acre compound complete with offices and residences, a large warehouse, a blacksmith shop, and other workspaces for Russian craftsmen. This was far more elaborate than anything the Spaniards had constructed in California. The Russians named their base *Kolonia Ross,* Ross being an old name for Russia. Fort Ross, as it is known in English, is now a state historic park.

Learning of the Russian landing, a few weeks later a Spanish officer leading a small party of leatherjackets came to investigate. Meeting with Kuskov, he insisted that Spanish California extended "as far as the North Pacific." If the Russians did not immediately vacate the premises, the Spaniard insisted, they would be expelled by "force of arms." That was an empty threat and Kuskov knew it. There were fewer than four hundred Spanish soldiers in all of California, scarcely enough to patrol the missions and garrison the presidios at San Diego, Santa Barbara, San Francisco, and Monterey, the capital. What's more, the Spanish monarch had been deposed by the French army of Napoleon Bonaparte, and Mexico and other Spanish colonies of the Western Hemisphere had erupted in revolt. Supply ships from the south no longer arrived in California, and the leatherjackets had not been paid in years. In the words of one Russian who visited Alta California, the soldiers were "destitute of almost every article of clothing."

So rather than fighting, local Spanish authorities and the Russians reached an informal accord. Ignoring the royal ban on foreign trade, the Spanish governor offered to sell the Russians large quantities of grain, wine, livestock, and other agricultural goods in exchange for badly needed manufactured goods. Spanish California was thrown a lifeline by Fort Ross.

★

The Franciscans sought to transform Natives into Christian subjects of the Spanish crown, but the Russians only cared about commerce. While they certainly exploited their Native workers, they made no attempt to proselytize them. The interior of the stockade at Fort Ross—where administrators, military officers, and sea captains had their quarters—was a "little Russia." Outside those walls, diversity prevailed. A group of Pomos and Coast Miwoks who worked at the post resided in a cluster of brush structures on the landward side of the stockade, nestled against the foothills away from the wind and fog. Aleut hunters, by contrast, sited their own dwellings on the edge of the bluff, overlooking their beloved Pacific. Ordinary Russian workers lived in a third cluster of log houses constructed of local redwood. Mixed in among these groups were other Pacific peoples, including Filipino and Kānaka seamen.

Russian workers and Aleut hunters were soon marrying local women and raising mixed families. From the Native perspective, those sexual unions helped cement their connection with the Russians, whose support protected them from the Spaniards. By 1820, just a few years after its founding, the resident population of approximately three hundred souls at Fort Ross included fifty-six mixed marriages and fifty-four young mixed children. One Aleut hunter proudly introduced his Pomo wife to a Russian visitor. Not only had she learned his language, he boasted, but she had also become adept at repairing his parka. Pomo and Miwok women learned to prepare seal steaks, certainly not part of their traditional diet, and Aleut men learned to tolerate acorn mush, although few claimed to like it.

Despite a great deal of mingling, for the most part the cultures remained distinct. The marriages were unions of convenience, accepted as such by both parties. When Russian workers or Aleut hunters completed their contractual service and returned home, they usually left their Native wives and children behind. Open-minded colonial customs were unacceptable back home, and most women would not consider leaving their kinfolk. On an inspection tour of the grounds, a Russian encountered "a rather comely young woman preparing food." He spoke to her and was surprised when she replied in good Russian. "She invited me to eat her acorn porridge and complained about the rain. When I inquired, I found that she had lived for some time in the Ross settlement with a *promyshlennik,* and then returned to her people."

★

At the missions, Franciscans drove converts to work harder in order to supply the basic needs of the leatherjackets. "The lot of these so-called Christian Indians," wrote a Russian visitor to San Francisco, "merits all kinds of pity. Even the situation of Negro slaves cannot be worse." With the population of converts falling because of disease, the Franciscans decided to extend their reach, founding two new missions on the north side of San Francisco Bay—San Rafael in 1817 and San Francisco Solano, in present-day Sonoma, in 1823.

In response, a flood of Natives sought refuge at Fort Ross. One Russian saw crowds of them outside the stockade in 1818. Administrator Kuskov "persuaded them to settle in the forests and mountain gorges and then to attack the Spanish unexpectedly," he wrote. "The savages followed his advice [and] once the Spanish became aware of this, they gave up their pursuit." A local Miwok leader told a visiting Russian naval officer he was "very glad" the Russians were there, because they offered protection from the Spanish, "who catch them with lassos, like wild beasts, put them in irons, and force them to work."

As the sea otter population declined from overhunting, farming took on more importance at Fort Ross. The Company grew wheat and other grains, potatoes, and root crops, which supplied operations in the north. At first, Pomo men and women worked the fields willingly for food and clothing, but as the Russian managers pushed them to produce more, they began

running away. By the late 1820s the Company was using violence to force them to labor. When Admiral Ferdinand von
Wrangel, governor of Russian America, visited Fort Ross in
1834, he was shocked to see the way Company managers recruited their workforce. They attack Native villagers "by surprise," he wrote, then "tie their hands, and drive them to the
settlement like cattle to work. Such a party of 75 men, wives,
and children was brought to the settlement during my presence." Natives, who at first welcomed the Undersea People as
allies against the Franciscans, now fled from them as well.

BOUCHARD'S MEN ATTACK MONTEREY

9

The Liberal Cause

Early on a November morning in 1818, a watchman at
the Monterey presidio sighted two black warships on
the horizon, both bristling with cannon. The soldiers
had been anxiously watching for them since receiving a report that a privateer, sailing under the flag of the newly independent nation of Argentina, had outfitted two vessels in the
Sandwich Islands, preparing for an assault on the Spanish colony of California.

The warships were commanded by Hipólito Bouchard, a
native of France who had served in the French navy. A strong
supporter of the French Revolution, Bouchard grew increasingly distressed at the conservative turn in French politics, and
in 1809 he left the country of his birth for Argentina, where he
joined the fight for independence from Spain. He participated
as an officer in both naval and land operations and won a reputation as a courageous leader with a mercurial temper. In 1817,
Bouchard obtained "letters of marque" from the Argentine

government authorizing him to attack and plunder Spanish ships and possessions wherever he found them. Lacking the resources to organize a navy, Argentina followed the example of the United States, which during its own struggle for independence relied on a fleet of privateers.

Pablo Vicente de Solá, colonial governor of California, was committed to the continuation of Spanish rule. But a struggle for independence had erupted in New Spain, seriously disrupting support for the distant California colony. Not a single supply ship had arrived from Mexico since 1810, and as a result the armory at the Monterey presidio contained little ammunition and even less gunpowder. The leatherjackets had not been paid in years and morale was abysmal. Governor Solá ordered the evacuation of military dependents and civilians, and directed that all government records be removed to the interior. Desperate for assistance, he authorized Franciscan missionaries to arm Native Christians to augment his pitiful defenses. "I am keeping everyone on the lookout, to prevent the pillage of the missions," he notified the viceroy in Mexico City.

Privateers financed their operations through pillage and plunder. But Commander Bouchard was something more than a mere pirate. A passionate believer in republicanism, he sought to spread the gospel of revolution and fan the flames of popular insurrection. He conceived of his mission as a campaign for what one of his men called "the liberal cause," seeking to make peripheral Spanish colonies like California into "rallying points for expeditions destined to help the patriots overthrow the King of Spain," who had been restored to the throne in 1813.

Bouchard circumnavigated the globe in his quest for plunder and principle. He departed Buenos Aires in July 1817 aboard the heavily armed frigate *Argentina* with an audacious plan to attack Manila, Spain's most lucrative port, halfway around the world. Sailing across the Atlantic and rounding the Cape of Good Hope, the southernmost point of the African continent, he anchored at the island of Madagascar to take on supplies. There he encountered several slave ships about to depart with cargos of African captives. Declaring his hatred of what he termed the "vile commerce" of slave trading, Bouchard impounded the ships and freed the Africans, several of whom joined his crew.

He reached Manila in early 1818 and blockaded the port. "I cruised for three months in front of them," he later wrote, "without a single ship daring to leave." He sank sixteen vessels attempting to resupply the city. Food grew scarce and prices rose, but the inhabitants of Manila did not rise in insurrection, which puzzled and infuriated Bouchard. Finally, with many of his men incapacitated by scurvy, he set sail for the Sandwich Islands, the mid-Pacific rendezvous for ships and sailors of many nations.

On the island of Hawai'i, Bouchard met an English pilot named Peter Corney, a veteran of the sea otter trade, who told him of the vulnerable state of Spanish California and filled his head with exaggerated claims of "wealthy missions." Bouchard obtained a second vessel, the *Santa Rosa,* and appointed Corney as its captain. Together, the two men recruited a diverse crew of some four hundred men, including eighty Kānakas or "Sandwich Islanders," and sailed east. Their first stop in California was Fort Ross, where they took on provisions and, according to some sources, purchased gunpowder. Then it was on to Monterey.

★

On November 23, 1818, Bouchard dispatched a messenger ashore with an ultimatum for Governor Solá: "Surrender your city or it will be reduced to cinders." Solá responded with scorn. The inhabitants of California "were faithful servants of the king," he declared, and "would shed the last drop of blood in his service." Like the governor, the Franciscans and the small population of colonists supported the Spanish empire. In Monterey, as in Manila, there would be no republican uprising.

It would be destruction then. Solá blasted the privateer with what powder and shot he had, inflicting serious damage to one of the vessels. But braving the fire, Bouchard led two hundred men ashore in a cold rain and stormed the battery of cannon. "We halted at the foot of the hill where it stood," Corney wrote, "then beat a charge and rushed up, the Sandwich Islanders in front with pikes. The Spaniards mounted their horses and fled. A Sandwich Islander was the first to haul down their colors."

Governor Solá and his leatherjackets fled to the interior, leaving the capital of the California colony to the attackers. Bouchard raised the flag of independent Argentina over the presidio and ordered Monterey torched. "All the sailors were employed in searching the houses for money, breaking and ruining everything," said Corney. "The Sandwich Islanders, quite naked when they landed, were soon dressed in the Spanish fashion." By the time Solá returned, his force augmented by several hundred armed Native Christians, Bouchard and his men had sailed off.

A few days later the two warships anchored two hundred miles south at a cove on the Chumash coast, the landing place for Rancho Nuestra Señora del Refugio, owned by José Francisco Ortega, late comandante of the Santa Barbara presidio. Ortega and his extended family were fervent royalists and wealthy smugglers, which made them perfect targets for Bouchard. The residents of the rancho fled into the coastal hills, allowing Bouchard's men to plunder the place at will, seizing trunks of Chinese silks, boxes of fancy lace handkerchiefs, and piles of silver and gold jewelry. They left the place a smoking ruin.

Reaching Santa Barbara, Bouchard observed a large force of leatherjackets and converts assembling to defend the town and chose to pass it by. He anchored at one of the Channel Islands, where he spent several days repairing the damaged ship, then sailed on to the landing for Mission San Juan Capistrano, sixty miles north of San Diego. Bouchard sent the Franciscans a request for provisions, promising to depart without incident if they cooperated. But the missionaries responded with what he considered an insulting refusal, so Bouchard ordered the mission and the adjacent village sacked and burned. "We found the town well stocked with everything but money," Corney laughed. Aside from the contraband taken from the Ortega rancho, Bouchard got very little of value in California. Before departing the mission, however, his men liberated several barrels of wine, got magnificently drunk, and had to be whipped back to the ships; only then did Bouchard sail off, leaving California behind.

★

With that, California returned to its isolation from the revolutionary events sweeping the hemisphere. Bouchard had assumed that California would resemble Argentina, where homegrown elites believed their interests were best served by political and economic independence from Spain. But in California, where missionaries controlled virtually all the good land along the coast, there was no elite landowning class. The small number of colonists stood solidly with the establishment of military officers and missionaries, united in a common goal—the exploitation of the Native workforce.

Despite the shocking reduction of the indigenous population along the southern and central coasts, Native Californians continued to greatly outnumber colonists. In the places where neither missionaries nor their diseases had yet penetrated—in the Delta and the Central Valley, along the rocky northern shore, in the deserts and mountain highlands—another quarter million Native people continued living the old life. The small force of leatherjackets was responsible for keeping Native Christians at their labors while defending the frontier against the unconverted. Without the soldiers there would be no missions, without the missions no colony. The idea of overthrowing the very force that protected them surely struck the colonial residents of California as absurd.

Most California colonists were the offspring of the several hundred soldiers dispatched to the territory over a half century of Spanish rule. Although the small corps of commissioned officers were Spaniards, the corporals, sergeants, and ordinary soldiers were men of mixed ancestry, what Spaniards termed *castas,* whether *mestizos* (Native and Spanish), *mulatos* (African and Spanish), or *pardos* (various combinations of all three). Elsewhere in Latin America, Spaniards scorned castas as social inferiors, but in frontier California cultural unity prevailed. "Only two *castas* are known here," wrote a missionary, "the *gente de razón* and the Indians." Despite their mixed ancestry, all the colonists were considered "people of reason," a term that had less to do with intelligence than with common cultural heritage. Natives, by contrast, were dismissed as uncivilized, *gente sin razón,* people without reason, or at least without a culture that colonists were obliged to respect.

Had Spain succeeded in populating California with large numbers of settlers from Mexico, colonial society surely would have developed very differently. In 1777, Juan Bautista de Anza had escorted nearly 250 Sonorans across the desert and mountains, and several smaller migrations at about the same time brought in several hundred more. Those settlers were granted small plots of land to farm at three pueblos or towns—San José on the southern shore of San Francisco Bay, Branciforte (later renamed Santa Cruz) at the northern end of Monterey Bay, and Los Angeles in southern California. Had the migration from Sonora continued, those pueblos might have become the seedbed for a different kind of colony, perhaps more like Argentina. But when the Quechan people blocked the crossing of the Colorado River in 1781, they ended that possibility. California became known as "the Siberia of Mexico," a far frontier, a place of exile. Had the migrations continued, had towns multiplied and grown, had commerce expanded, who knows? But that was not to be.

★

California colonists showed little interest in Commander Bouchard's militant version of the liberal cause. Yet many of them had already embraced *economic* liberalism. The Spanish empire tightly regulated markets and prohibited trade with outsiders. Officials in New Spain, however, were powerless to prevent foreign interlopers from trading with Californians. Russians with their Aleut hunters were joined by British and Yankee traders, eager to exchange manufactured goods for valuable sea otter pelts. This illicit trade thrived at isolated locations along the coast, like the Ortegas' Rancho Refugio. When the independence struggle cut off official trading connections with Mexico, smuggling became the mainstay of the California economy.

Local authorities were mostly tolerant. "Necessity makes licit what is illicit by law," declared José Dario Argüello, Governor Solá's predecessor. Foreign traders were allowed to go about their business, although officials kept up the pretense of Spanish regulation by selectively detaining a few. One detained American trader admitted doing business with the governor himself. "The guilt for this is upon myself," he said, "if it is guilt to give something to eat to the hungry and to clothe the naked soldiers of the King of Spain." Government officers, missionaries, and ordinary colonists grew accustomed to free trade, one of the founding principles of the liberal cause.

In early 1822, three years after Bouchard's raid, Governor Solá received an official dispatch announcing that after a dozen years of violent conflict, Mexico had secured its independence from Spain. The new authorities in Mexico City expressed concern about the royalist sentiments of both the governor and the missionaries, but they had no need to worry. Although the Franciscans deplored the turn of events, they kept quiet, and Solá switched sides with remarkable ease. On April 11 he took the oath of allegiance to independent Mexico before an assembly of soldiers and colonists in Monterey, followed by a celebration featuring fireworks and cries of "*Viva la Independencia!*" The revelers included Native Christians from nearby Mission San Carlos. "Now anybody may dance when he wants to," one of them exclaimed.

A council of military officers chose Solá as California's first representative to the new national congress in Mexico City, and named Luis Antonio Argüello, the California-born son of Solá's predecessor, as his interim replacement until a new governor arrived. Colonists accepted these changes with little complaint. Far more important to them was the announcement that California's ports were now open to international traders.

The sea otter population, however, was seriously depleted, and Californians needed another primary product to exchange. They found it in the herds of cattle grazing on mission lands. For years the missionaries had been exporting tallow— rendered beef fat—for the manufacture of candles to illuminate the mines of Mexico and Peru. But during the heyday of smuggling in the 1810s they also found a market for their cattle hides. In New England, the production of boots and shoes was being industrialized, creating a strong demand for leather, and by the 1820s the hide trade had become the principal driver of the California economy, with dozens of British and American trading vessels carrying off large cargos. The missions became profit centers.

★

From 1822 to 1848 more than a million cattle hides were exported from California. Richard Henry Dana, a Yankee serving on a merchant vessel, described the process of loading them at Santa Barbara, where there was no wharf or pier. "We rake them upon our heads, one at a time, or two, if they are small, and wade out with them and throw them into the boat," he wrote. "I have often been laughed at myself, and joined in laughing at others, pitching themselves down in the sand, trying to swing a large hide upon their heads, nearly blown over in a little gust of wind."

The cattle were tended, slaughtered, and skinned by Native workers. Many mission converts became vaqueros or cowboys, mastering the equestrian skills of riding and roping. But the expansion of trade meant they had to work all the harder. The converts, one Franciscan reported, "bitterly complained that nothing was paid to them for their toil and labor." Fugitivism, always a problem, became more acute. Many runaways escaped into the interior on the backs of mission horses. "A considerable number have withdrawn from the mild rule of the friars," said Father-President Mariano Payeras, "and have become one body with the savages with whom they carry out whatever evil their heart and malevolent soul dictate."

By the 1820s the plains of the Central Valley teemed with herds of wild horses. Unconverted Natives learned to capture, train, and ride them. Native communities on the periphery of the coast turned aggressive, determined to defend against mission expansion. They conducted mounted raids on outlying mission stations, killing vaqueros and stealing livestock. California became a source of stolen horses and mules supplying a wide-flung trading system that included Mexican merchants from New Mexico, American fur trappers in the Rockies, and British traders on the Columbia River.

The missionaries intensified their policing. With leatherjackets impoverished and demoralized, Franciscans increasingly relied on Native militia companies—first officially authorized by Governor Solá during Bouchard's attack—deploying them to round up fugitives and defend mission herds against raiders. At Santa Barbara, the Franciscans organized a company of Chumash converts, including a contingent of mounted lancers. "It would cause me joy," the father-president of the missions wrote to Governor Solá, "if you could see the preparation and enthusiasm of these Indians." Native converts learned to take commands from their own leaders in the style of European warfare, acquiring in the process a new appreciation of their collective power.

It was only a matter of time before they employed their newfound military skills for their own purposes. On February 21, 1824, following the flogging of a convert at Mission Santa Inés, north of Santa Barbara, Christian Chumash rose up in what would become the largest revolt in the history of the coastal California missions. They attacked leatherjackets with bows and arrows, then burned buildings, before marching en masse to Mission La Purísima, some twenty miles away, where missionaries, soldiers, and their dependents holed up in a storehouse. The rebels allowed the Spaniards to evacuate unharmed, then took over the mission and erected defensive fortifications. They sent runners carrying the news to converts at all the missions in Chumash country.

The following day, converts at Mission Santa Barbara attacked the guard, wounding two men and chasing the leather jackets away. The presidio's comandante counterattacked with his entire force, but the rebels turned them back, firing muskets as well as arrows. When the leatherjackets withdrew to lick their wounds, Chumash men, women, and children took the opportunity to flee into the hills, beginning a long march of nearly a hundred miles over the coastal mountains to the Central Valley. There they established a large encampment near Tulare Lake, at the time the largest freshwater lake west of the Mississippi, near today's city of Bakersfield. When the leatherjackets retook the mission, they torched the Chumash village and slaughtered the sick and elderly stragglers left behind.

The rebels remained in control at Purísima for several weeks. Word of the uprising spread, and the missionaries feared outbreaks at other missions. But the leatherjackets mustered their forces and in March retook Purísima in a furious battle. A number of Chumash leaders were executed, while others were sentenced to long terms of hard labor. The missionaries negotiated the return of many converts, but most of the fugitives remained in the San Joaquin Valley. They established a refugee community in the foothills of the Sierra Nevada, where for years they lived independently. A group of American fur trappers found them there in the early 1830s, a self-contained community of seven or eight hundred residents, with large fields of corn, pumpkins, melons, and other crops, as well as horses which they rode and traded. That was their version of the liberal cause.

CALIFORNIOS AT HOME

10

Members of a Single Family

Pablo Vicente de Solá, the last Spanish governor of California, found the ignorance of the California colonists appalling. Virtually all of them were illiterate. Only a handful of soldiers could sign their names, and the officers were poorly educated. The Franciscan missionaries expressed profound skepticism about the value of popular education, fearing that reason threatened faith. But Governor Solá—a conservative, but also a believer in Enlightenment rationalism—considered education the key to unlocking California's development. "The country cannot progress if the young are not educated," he told a missionary. During his seven years as governor, Solá established schools at several pueblos and presidios, including classes for girls at Santa Barbara and Monterey. But the colonial budget made no provision for schools, and the ones Solá founded closed after he departed in 1822.

At the Monterey presidio, a former governor had established a small primary school for the sons of officers, with a curriculum that focused on the memorization and recitation of Catholic doctrine. The schoolmaster, a retired corporal, enforced strict discipline, punishing infractions with an iron-tipped lash. Offending students were stripped to their underclothes and stretched out on a bench, a handkerchief stuffed in their mouths to muffle their cries as they took the blows. The school, a former student recalled, was "a torture chamber designed to extinguish the light of reason."

Solá paid the school a visit soon after becoming governor. An imposing man in his late fifties, he had an infamous temper that kept subordinates on their toes. But in the company of children he loosened up, telling stories, passing out sweets, and insisting that students address him as "Uncle Pablo." He asked the schoolmaster how the boys were doing with their lessons. Making wonderful progress, the teacher reported. The brightest among them was able to sing an entire mass. Impressive, Solá allowed, but smart boys ought to learn something more than religious ritual. He told the schoolmaster to send the best students to his office the next day.

Three boys, ages seven to nine, appeared the following morning. Mariano Guadalupe Vallejo, Juan Bautista Alvarado, and José Antonio Castro immediately impressed Solá as quick-witted youngsters. From his bookshelf he pulled a copy of *Don Quixote* by Miguel de Cervantes. "Read this," he told them, "it is written in good Castilian." They did as they were instructed and returned a few days later, eager for more to read. Solá provided them with Mexican newspapers, volumes of Spanish law, and selections from his personal library. He would remain their personal tutor until he left the governorship in 1822. By then the boys were adolescents and Solá had become well acquainted with their strength of character. Shrewd Alvarado, passionate Castro, strategic Vallejo. Spurred by Solá's encouragement, they would rise steadily in prominence and position, becoming three of the most important leaders of their generation.

★

The boys grew up in the close-knit world of the colonial California military. From their soldier fathers they inherited social position, providing them the opportunity for education and access to the elite. But they also enjoyed the benefit of strong and protective families. Successful colonization required not only missions, presidios, and pueblos, but also families, without which there could be no real communities. And there could be no families without women.

Wives and mothers were central to the domestic economy —in charge of the garden and kitchen, producing food, clothing, candles, soap—assisted by Native servants. When their husbands left on military assignments, women assumed charge. One Mexican observer described the daughters of one soldier "looking after the livestock, cutting wood, loading country carts, and generally doing all kinds of work done by men." Pioneering could be gender-bending.

Nevertheless, colonial California families were patriarchal. Fathers and husbands ruled over women. That was clear in numerous ways. "The daughters had little liberty in choosing the men that they would marry," wrote Antonio Coronel, who relocated to California as a young man. And once married, women typically had many children—large family size being a leading indicator of women's subordination.

Consider young Mariano Guadalupe Vallejo, son of Sergeant Ignacio Vicente Vallejo and María Antonia Lugo, herself the daughter of another leatherjacket, Francisco Salvador Lugo. On the day of her birth in 1776, her parents consented to her betrothal to Vallejo, then in his twenties. In the early days, the Hispanic population of colonial California was overwhelmingly male, and this extraordinary arrangement suggests the intensity of the competition among men for brides. When the couple wed in 1790, Maria Antonia was fourteen, Sergeant Vallejo forty. Over the next quarter century she bore thirteen children.

When Vallejo was away on distant postings, as was often the case, Señora María Antonia became head of the household, managing the servants, supervising the courtship and engagement of her eight daughters, cultivating important relationships of kinship and friendship. Women also benefited from the Spanish legal tradition, in which family property was owned jointly by husband and wife. As José Fernandez, another Mexican, observed, "California women have a lot of control."

★

Señora María Antonia's eldest daughter, María Josepha, was fourteen when she married Sergeant José Francisco Alvarado, a second-generation leatherjacket. Their firstborn and only child was Juan Bautista Alvarado, the second of Solá's three students, making him the nephew of Mariano Guadalupe Vallejo, although he was only two years younger. "My mother was a spirited woman," Alvarado said years later, and he told a story that he'd heard from her, of a desperate ride she undertook not long after his birth. Learning that her husband was ill at Mission San Luis Obispo, one hundred and fifty miles south of Monterey, she bundled up the baby and started out on horseback, determined to reach her husband and nurse him back to health. But on the way she met the messenger bearing the bad tidings that Sergeant Alvarado had died. She turned around and rode home. Some years later María Josepha married another presidial officer and bore nine more children.

José Antonio Castro, the third student, was the son of Corporal José Tiburcio Castro, who came to California with Portolá in 1769. Corporal Castro married twelve-year-old María

Rufina Álvarez and they relocated to Monterey, where José Antonio was born. The Castro and Alvarado families were linked by several marriages, making José Antonio Castro and Juan Bautista Alvarado cousins. Alvarado would later marry another cousin, fifteen-year-old María Modesta Castro.

"When I was a child," one of the extended Vallejo clan later wrote, "there were fewer than fifty families in the region about the bay of San Francisco, and these were closely connected by ties of blood or intermarriage." The six or seven hundred colonial families of California created a dense web of kinship, reinforced by the custom of *compadrazgo* or god parentage, a widely practiced Hispanic tradition. Anthropologists call this "fictive kinship," but colonists considered it as real and enduring as parenthood itself. "They all treated one another as cousins," wrote another Mexican observer. "They considered themselves as members of a single family."

★

In 1824 independent Mexico adopted a constitution modeled after that of the United States of America. Because Alta California did not meet the population threshold for statehood, Mexico's founders declared it a territory, with an appointed rather than an elected governor. Male citizens over the age of eighteen, however, were eligible to vote for a delegate to the national congress and the seven members of the territorial legislature. Those were "indirect elections," in which voters cast ballots for "electors," leading men of property, who then chose the legislators. This system, in use throughout Mexico, insured that leadership positions remained among members of the elite.

That's not democracy as we understand it—although the U.S. presidential Electoral College originated in the same distrust of ordinary voters—but the new electoral system was considerably more representative than the arbitrary military rule it replaced. Moreover, town councils and mayors (alcaldes) were directly elected by male citizens, which resulted in considerably more social diversity among leaders at the local level.

The first appointed territorial governor, Lieutenant-Colonel José María Echeandía, arrived in California in 1825. Echeandía and his entourage of assistants and advisors were veterans of the Mexican independence struggle and passionate advocates of the liberal cause—equal rights, republican government, and a free market economy. When Echeandía realized that liberal principles were generally unknown in California, he encouraged young men to join study groups, reading classic liberal texts and discussing politics. It was from Governor Echeandía, Juan Bautista Alvarado later recalled, that he and his contemporaries first learned "the true principles of republicanism and liberty."

Alvarado, Vallejo, and Castro were avid readers—Governor Solá had seen to that. "The missionary fathers were adamantly opposed to the circulation of books among us that might inspire liberal ideas," Vallejo remembered. "They knew that books were the most fearsome emissaries of the goddess of liberty." During Echeandía's term as governor, Vallejo purchased a small library from a foreign merchant that included works by Enlightenment luminaries—Voltaire, Rousseau, and others—most of them on the Church's list of banned books. When Franciscan father-president Narciso Durán learned that Vallejo had shared the books with Alvarado and Castro, he excommunicated all three of them. On appeal, Durán agreed to grant absolution if they promised not to loan the books to others. Among conservatives, Vallejo became known as "the heretic."

★

These young men, like others of their generation, shared a deep concern about their future prospects. The traditional way to wealth and position was through the ownership of land, but the children of the original colonists, the first generation of

Spanish-speakers born in California, had almost no stake in real property. During the period of Spanish rule, governors issued a number of "grazing permits" to retired military officers. The Ortega family's Rancho Refugio was one such. But with those few exceptions, Franciscans held all the productive land along the coast, from San Diego to San Francisco Bay.

With independence, California's ports opened to foreign merchants and the hide and tallow trade boomed. Nearly all the profits went to the Franciscans. Yet they refused to swear an oath of allegiance to the new republic of Mexico. How could it be considered fair, asked Governor Echeandía, for disloyal missionaries to enjoy the loaf while loyal citizens got the crumbs? The colonists ought to have a stake in their own country. His argument struck the rising generation forcefully. Soon these young men, most born around the turn of the nineteenth century, began referring to themselves as *Californios,* a term that not only emphasized their identification with the land of their birth, but suggested their right to own and control it.

The way the Californios saw things, there were two ways to accomplish their goal. One was to open new areas for settlement, which would require waging aggressive war on unconverted Native communities beyond the mission frontier. In 1819, before the conclusion of the Mexican war for independence, the United States and Spain had negotiated a treaty establishing California's northern boundary at the forty-second parallel. The northern portion of the territory, with the exception of Fort Ross, remained Native country, and the Californios worried that unless they secured control it would be seized by another colonial power, perhaps the Russians, more likely Great Britain or the United States. The Californios therefore focused attention on the north, especially the fertile country immediately north of San Francisco Bay, where the coastal mountains are punctuated with grassy hillsides and broad valleys, perfect for cattle grazing—and not incidentally, a hotbed of Native opposition to further colonial expansion.

The second Californio strategy was to convert existing mission lands into private property, replacing religious with secular authority, a process known as *secularization*. In theory, the Franciscans held all mission assets in trust for Native Christians. The time had come, Echeandía insisted, for the Natives to collect their inheritance. Each family of Native Christians ought to receive a share of the mission estate sufficient for their needs—a plot of land, a few head of livestock, and farming tools. Once Natives received their due, there would be plenty of land remaining for Californios. Franciscan missionaries agreed that the mission estate rightfully belonged to Native Christians, but they insisted that they were incapable of managing it themselves. The argument was certainly self-interested: the Franciscans wanted to preserve the missions, along with the power over Natives that went with them. But they also feared that whatever the Californios said about rights, secularization would end in the ruination of Native Christians.

Rejecting the Franciscan argument, in 1826 Echeandía issued a proclamation inviting married Christian converts to apply for grants of land. The program was modest, and the missionaries did what they could to stifle it, yet it raised the hopes of many Native Christians. Conservatives were fearful. "Echeandía led the Indians to believe that they too were free men and citizens," recalled Angustias de la Guerra y Noriega, daughter of the comandante of the Santa Barbara presidio, where the Chumash had risen in revolt only a year before. "My father advised him to temper his enthusiasm and try to keep the Indians in check, because many of them were traitors. He said that on any given day the Indians could revolt and kill the white people, including Echeandía himself." Echeandía acknowledged that Native Christians were sometimes insubordinate, but blamed the fact that "they do not enjoy all the fruits of the labor which they perform." When he visited Mission San Luis Rey, the Christian Luiseños greeted him enthusiastically, hoisting him onto their shoulders and cheering.

★

Frustrated by the slow pace of secularization, in 1828 several hundred Native Christians, most of them Yokut (YO-kut) people of the Central Valley, abandoned Mission San José on the east side of lower San Francisco Bay and returned to their original homeland. The Yokuts were one of the largest Native groups in California, including some seventy thousand people. Over the previous decade, many had become accomplished horsemen. The San José fugitives were led by a Christian Yokut, a charismatic leader named Estanislao (eh-STANIS-lao), the former Native alcalde at the mission.

Estanislao and his followers established a refugee community on the banks of a tributary of the San Joaquin River, near today's city of Modesto. It attracted hundreds of fugitives from a variety of Native groups, including some of the Chumash who had fled to the Central Valley in the aftermath of their revolt four years before. From their refuge, Estanislao's people launched mounted raids on missions and ranchos of the Bay Area, attacking colonists and stealing horses. Estanislao and his followers had "declared themselves in rebellion," wrote Franciscan father-president Narciso Durán. They recruited Native Christians from other missions to join them in putting Native people back in control of California.

In early 1829, the San Francisco presidio launched a military expedition against the rebels. In the densely wooded country along the river, Estanislao's men constructed a log fortress, protected by trenches for defensive cover. The Californios besieged the fortress, but the Natives taunted them.

"Cowards, cowards," they cried, "come on and get us if you are real men." Stung by the insults, the leatherjackets launched an assault and were badly mauled. The soldiers, Estanislao declared, were nothing to fear, "because they are few in number, are very young, and do not shoot well."

By that time, Mariano Guadalupe Vallejo, who had chosen a military career, was a twenty-two-year-old lieutenant at the Monterey presidio. He had just returned from a successful expedition against mission fugitives in the San Joaquin Valley, killing several dozen Natives and recovering a herd of horses. Vallejo practiced a ruthless style of warfare, aimed not at retaking deserters but at destroying the communities that sheltered them. Governor Echeandía had serious qualms about the morality of such tactics. But unwilling to argue with success, he placed young Vallejo in command of a large force and dispatched him against Estanislao's community, ordering the "total defeat of the Christian rebels and the wild Indians aiding them." With more than a hundred leatherjackets, Native militia, and a company of field artillery, Vallejo commanded the largest military expedition yet mounted in California.

Reaching the fortress, Vallejo called on Estanislao to surrender, but the Native commander swore resistance to the death. Vallejo commenced an artillery barrage that drove the rebels from their entrenchments. As they attempted to cross the river, many were shot and killed. The water, read one account, was "swollen with corpses." The river became known as *Río Estanislao,* the Stanislaus. Remaining rebels retreated several miles upstream, but Vallejo chose not to pursue them, and Estanislao survived. He later returned to Mission San José, where the Franciscans, much to the Californios' disgust, welcomed him back into the Christian community. Vallejo nevertheless proclaimed his expedition a great victory, and was greeted as a conquering hero upon his return to Monterey. Soon thereafter he won election to the legislature.

Over the next several years, the Yokuts and other Native societies of the interior were shaken to their core by epidemics sweeping inland from the coast. Disease followed in the wake of contact. Malaria, measles, smallpox, and other maladies claimed thousands of lives, critically weakening the ability of the survivors to resist invasion. Mariano Guadalupe Vallejo made the most of this opportunity, continuing to wage war against the Native societies north and east of San Francisco Bay, killing hundreds of people and opening new grazing lands for himself and other Californios.

★

Vallejo's boyhood friends, Alvarado and Castro, went directly into political service. In 1827, at the age of nineteen, Alvarado accepted an appointment as secretary to the legislature, preparing its agenda, keeping the minutes, and attending to correspondence. Castro became secretary to the town council of Monterey. Both men were passionate advocates for their California homeland, and they frequently found themselves in conflict with officials from Mexico.

At a Monterey celebration of Mexican Independence Day in September 1830, a Mexican officer proposed a toast that concluded with a condescending aside concerning the "ignorant Californios." Alvarado responded with a toast of his own. "To those who appreciate the frank hospitality of the Californios," he began, then added: "I loathe every man who, forgetting his own education and good taste, might insult them, as just happened in this room." The crowd fell silent as the Mexican officer stepped up to Alvarado and tossed a drink in his face. Castro rushed to his friend's defense. "You son of a bitch," he shouted at the officer. "You Mexicans seized all the good land for yourselves and left nothing for my countrymen. Take this. . . ." He delivered a hard slap across the man's face, and the room exploded in pandemonium. Military authorities later arrested Castro and he paid a fine.

That same year, Governor Echeandía presented an expanded plan of secularization that the California legislature approved. It provided for the immediate conversion of the missions into pueblos and Native converts into citizens, with each Christian family granted a small portion of the mission estate. Not long thereafter, Echeandía received a dispatch from Mexico informing him that he had been replaced. Conservative supporters of the Church had overthrown the liberal regime in Mexico City, and a new president had appointed another governor for California. Expecting his successor to take a different position on secularization, Echeandía rushed to put his plan into effect. The stage was set for a confrontation that would become a defining moment for Californios and Natives alike.

THE LUISEÑOS REFUSE TO WORK

11

We Are Free

Colonel Manuel Victoria had served for several years as governor of Baja, and the new appointment extended his authority to Alta California. Victoria was both a hero of the Mexican war of independence and an avid supporter of the Church. He arrived in Monterey early in 1831, and after taking the oath of office immediately issued a decree suspending Echeandía's secularization program, which he denounced as "a scheme of plunder." The Franciscans were overjoyed. "God willed that Victoria should arrive," declared Father-President Narciso Durán.

The Californios were stunned. But shock turned to outrage when Victoria refused to convene the territorial legislature for its regular session. The delegates bombarded the governor with letters of protest, and Victoria responded with a manifesto escalating the conflict. The legislators flattered themselves as humanitarians and patriots, he declared, but their support of secularization was nothing but "personal interests disguised in the trappings of philanthropy." Since Californios had demonstrated they could not be trusted, he announced that he was suspending the legislature indefinitely. Moreover, if the political controversy did not subside, he threatened to abolish all elective offices and impose military rule. His assault on republican government galvanized the opposition. Still, the underlying issue remained secularization. Californios, wrote Father Durán, were consumed with "hatred for Victoria for having rescued the prey [the missions] which they deemed already within their clutches."

Instead of returning to Mexico, former governor Echeandía remained in California, trading cold and foggy Monterey for balmy San Diego. And behind the scenes, he continued to agitate for the liberal cause. With his encouragement, three Californios from the southern part of the territory emerged as Victoria's fiercest critics. José Antonio Carrillo, Pío de Jesús Pico, and Juan Bandini had all served in the legislature. Carrillo and Pico were the California-born sons of presidial officers. Bandini was a wealthy merchant from Peru, but he had been in the territory so long that everyone considered him an honorary Californio. Writing letters of protest and making a public case against the governor, the three rebels soon came to Victoria's attention. In mid-November he headed south from Monterey, determined to silence them.

Learning Victoria was on his way, the three men decided to act. On an evening in late 1831, accompanied by a dozen armed confederates, they seized control of the San Diego presidio and issued a manifesto vowing to restore republican government to California. Captain Pablo de la Portilla, comandante of the presidio, agreed to join the rebellion if former governor Echeandía would consent to be their leader. Without hesitation Echeandía signed on, and a day or two later a score of rebels and fifty mounted leatherjackets, with Echeandía in command, set out for Los Angeles, where they expected to confront Victoria.

★

In Los Angeles, the rebels learned that the governor, accompanied by a company of leatherjackets, had arrived at Mission San Fernando, twenty-five miles to the northeast. Reinforced with a large company of Angeleno volunteers, on the morning of December 5 Captain Portilla led a force of more than a hundred men, mounted and armed, to Cahuenga Pass, a narrow canyon through the foothills separating the Los Angeles basin from the San Fernando Valley. From the high ground, they could see the governor and fourteen leatherjackets approaching on horseback.

Victoria had not anticipated such a large force of opponents. Captain Romualdo Pacheco, in command of the leatherjackets, was greatly concerned and advised the governor to withdraw and secure reinforcements. Victoria was a brave soldier who had served valiantly during the Mexican war of independence. But he was also an impulsive hothead, and he treated Pacheco's suggestion as evidence of cowardice. "Officers in skirts," he replied scornfully, "should move to the rear." Pacheco jerked to attention. "I'm a man with balls," he said, "as you'll soon see." They continued to advance.

The governor led his men to within shouting distance of the rebels. Scanning their ranks, he recognized Captain Portilla, whom he had met upon his arrival in California. "Leave that pack of scoundrels and join me!" he shouted to Portilla, then motioned his men to advance. "Halt!" Portilla shouted back. The command struck Victoria like a thunderbolt. "I'm not a man to be halted!" he sputtered, then barked out an order for his men to open fire. Reluctant to draw down on their fellow leatherjackets, the men responded with a musket volley aimed well over the heads of their opponents. No one was hit, but the Angeleno volunteers with Portilla were unnerved. Wheeling their horses, most of them retreated in disorder.

Victoria flew into a rage. He was not accustomed to commanding "men in petticoats," he stormed. For Captain Pacheco, that insult was a match applied to his own short fuse. Drawing his sword, he spurred his horse forward, galloping toward the enemy. His charge was answered by one of the few Angelenos who had stood his ground, a ranchero named José María Ávila, an accomplished horseman and a noted daredevil. Men on both sides watched as the two champions raced toward each other like jousting knights. Ávila carried a lance, which he thrust at Pacheco, who adroitly swerved to avoid it. As the riders passed each other, Ávila pulled a pistol from his sash and fired wildly over his shoulder. By sheer chance, the ball found its mark, tearing into Pacheco's back and hurling him from the saddle. He was dead before he hit the ground. Ávila continued on, his lance extended, bearing down on Victoria himself. The governor suffered a grievous wound before the leatherjackets shot and killed Ávila.

The rebels fled, but Victoria's men made no attempt to pursue them. Instead they carried their fallen commander to Mission San Gabriel, where he received medical attention. Victoria survived the wound, but, humbled and humiliated, he summoned Echeandía to his bedside and formally surrendered the governorship. As soon as he was fit for travel, he returned to Mexico by sea.

★

It was a decisive moment: despite cowardice in the face of confrontation, the Californios had succeeded in deposing a sitting governor. Echeandía called the legislature into session in Los Angeles and the delegates issued a proclamation defending the rebellion. Victoria had "treated citizens with contempt," they wrote, "smothering the liberty of speaking and writing, guaranteed by the law." His every step, they asserted, had been "directed by the missionaries," who were determined to maintain "the condition of slavish oppression in which the converts are held under the detestable mission system."

So far so good. But self-confidence in the flush of victory overwhelmed the good sense of the legislators. They took the radical step of naming Pío de Jesús Pico, the most senior among them (he was all of thirty-one), as interim governor of California. They wanted to administer the oath of office in the church on the Los Angeles plaza, but the parish priest barred the door. So, in a minor act of daring that made his reputation, the legislature's secretary, Juan Bautista Alvarado, climbed through a skylight and retrieved the altar cloth and chalice for the ceremony. Then his uncle and contemporary, Lieutenant Mariano Guadalupe Vallejo—"the heretic"—administered the sacred oath to Pico at the door of the church. Echeandía warned them that they had gone a step too far, but the Californios wanted to govern themselves and saw this as a golden opportunity. After several days of sober reflection, however, they relented, calling on Echeandía to return as governor, notwithstanding Pico's loud objection.

A year of political chaos followed. The senior-ranking officer at Monterey came south with an armed company, determined to arrest the legislators for treason. Captain Portilla mobilized the San Diego presidio and Echeandía issued a call for Native Christians to join in resisting those who intended to keep them in bondage. By March, some five hundred armed Natives had mobilized, terrifying Californios up and down the territory, who were still quaking from Estanislao's rebellion only months before. But Echeandía's maneuver worked. The northerners turned back and the Native army dispersed.

Echeandía remained in the south, and the legislature adjourned for the remainder of the year, waiting to see how the authorities in Mexico City would react.

★

A new governor arrived in January 1833. Brigadier General José Secundino Figueroa, a distinguished veteran of the Mexican independence struggle, had spent several years as the commander of military forces on the northern frontier of Sonora. The appointment pleased Echeandía, who told Californios that he and Figueroa shared political views. Why would a conservative Mexican president chose a liberal? Perhaps, some historians speculate, to get him as far away from Mexico City as possible. Whatever the reason for his appointment, the Californios found Figueroa an accommodating leader, a man who consulted widely, listened carefully, and willingly accepted advice. In one of his first acts, he issued a general amnesty to all involved in the revolt against Victoria.

Figueroa came with instructions: he was to proceed with the colonization of the region north of San Francisco Bay. Soon after his arrival, he learned that Admiral Ferdinand von Wrangel, governor of Russian America, had recently paid a visit to Fort Ross. Concerned that this might signal an expansion of Russian operations, Figueroa asked Lieutenant Vallejo to investigate. Vallejo visited the colony and reported that it was weak and posed little danger. Figueroa then ordered the young lieutenant to establish a new presidio at Mission San Francisco Solano, in today's town of Sonoma, and use whatever force was required to subdue the Native inhabitants. Over the next few years, Vallejo and his leatherjackets secured hundreds of thousands of acres for colonization, the first time the military had been employed for the express purpose of dispossessing Native Californians. The territorial legislature—which by then included José Antonio Castro, representing Monterey—applauded these measures.

Governor Figueroa was also ordered to resolve the local conflict over secularization. After several months spent discussing the matter with both Franciscans and Californios, he announced a moderate plan that preserved the missions but provided small plots to a limited number of Native Christians, bitterly disappointing the Californios.

But before the plan could be put in operation, it was overtaken by events. There had been another convulsive political turn in Mexico City. General Antonio López de Santa Anna, celebrated as a national hero for turning back an attempted Spanish invasion in 1829, led a coup against the conservative government, then won the subsequent election for president. Bored by the work of governing, however, Santa Anna retired to his hacienda, leaving the nation in the hands of his vice president, Valentín Gómez Farías, a committed liberal. Farías pushed the Mexican Congress to pass an act mandating the immediate secularization of all California's missions, which it did in August 1833. When, several months later, Figueroa received the news, he suspended his own plan and asked the legislature for advice on the development of a new one that conformed to the new law.

★

The Californios did everything they could to convert Governor Figueroa to their cause. In late 1833, he was asked to arbitrate a dispute among the heirs of Manuel Nieto, a former sergeant in the Spanish army who in 1784 had been granted "grazing rights" to a huge parcel of land southeast of the pueblo of Los Angeles. Figueroa approved the partition of the land into five large ranchos, and deeded them permanently to Nieto's heirs. He then purchased one of them—Rancho Los Alamitos, in today's city of Long Beach—for himself, paying practically noth-ing for it. The transaction looks a lot like a bribe. "By taking over a vast ranch," writes historian C. Alan Hutchinson, "Gov-ernor Figueroa was acquiring the same vested interests as the Californians, and would perhaps be less likely to oppose their desire for more land." Three weeks later, Figueroa approved the legislature's new plan for secularization.

Denouncing the missions as "entrenchments of monas-tic despotism," Figueroa ordered the Franciscans to relinquish control. He appointed civil administrators to oversee the con-version, supervising the distribution of land and livestock. But just as the program was getting underway, he and the Califor-nios were confronted with another crisis. Vice President Farías had come up with a plan of his own, authorizing a company of Mexican colonists to take charge of converting the mission estates into private property. Governor Figueroa was to be re-placed by a liberal Mexican politician.

A group of some two hundred colonists arrived in late 1834. They included craftsmen, artisans, and most importantly school teachers, which the Californios had been requesting for many years. But rather than welcoming them, the Californios reacted with outrage. They wanted control of the distribution of mission lands themselves, and saw the Mexican colonists as usurpers. Fortunately for them, Mexican politics took yet another lurch, this time to the right. Conservatives opposed to the policies of Vice President Farías convinced President Santa Anna to reassume power. He did, sweeping away many programs, including Farías's plan for California. When Gover-nor Figueroa received the news, he happily sent the leaders of the new colony packing, earning him the eternal gratitude of Californios.

★

Realizing the need to act swiftly before Mexican policy shifted once again, Figueroa and the Californios pushed ahead with secularization. For Native Christians, however, the plan contained a poison pill. To be eligible for grants, they had to agree to remain at their respective missions for an unspecified period of transition, during which the administrator in charge had the authority to compel them to labor as farm workers or vaqueros. If secularization meant replacing missionaries with administrators, most Natives wanted nothing to do with it. One historical study suggests that nearly two-thirds of mission converts had returned to their home communities by the early 1840s.

The Luiseños of Mission San Luis Rey "absolutely refused to obey orders," reported Captain Pablo de la Portilla, rewarded for his support of the revolt against Victoria with an appointment as civil administrator of that large and productive mission. "They said they had at length become a free nation," he continued, "and to prove it they left their houses and wandered off, abandoning the mission." Portilla tried to persuade them to return. "But all in vain," he reported. "They would listen to no reason. They all with one voice cried out: 'We are free. It is not our pleasure to obey. We do not choose to work!'"

Appointment as a civil administrator was a lucrative political plum. Many leading Californios—including Vallejo, Alvarado, and Castro—held such positions during secularization. They drew salaries, not only for themselves but for their extended families as well. But they profited only if Native Christians continued providing the labor. Some did remain, perhaps because it was the only life they knew. Administrators often abused them, and appropriated the assets of the missions for themselves, their families, and their friends. "Those in power rob us," a group of Luiseños complained. "To stand by and watch these men take over the missions which we have built, the herds we have tended, and to be exposed incessantly, together with our families, to the worst possible treatment, even death itself, is a tragedy!" A few Native Christians gained ownership of small plots, but the vast majority ended up landless and impoverished, just as the Franciscans had predicted.

★

Governor Echeandía made only a handful of land grants during his seven years as governor. Governor Figueroa, however, over the course of his three-year term and in close consultation with the legislature, issued a total of sixty-six grants. The largest was Rancho Petaluma, ten square leagues (approximately 67,000 acres, or nearly a hundred square miles) of fertile, well-watered land, essentially the entire estate of former Mission San Francisco Solano. It went to Mariano Guadalupe Vallejo, a measure of the high regard the Californios had for the man most responsible for extending the area of settlement in the north. Henceforth, Vallejo would be known as Don Mariano, the honorific title of an elite landowner. Juan Bautista Alvarado was awarded Rancho El Sur (along the beautiful Big Sur coast), and José Antonio Castro received Rancho Sausal in the lower Salinas Valley, encompassing today's city of Salinas. Both those grants were carved from the estate of Mission San Carlos, founded by Junípero Serra.

By 1836 all the missions were under the control of civil administrators. The Franciscans departed and returned to Europe. The missions were closed. Yet Natives continued to supply the labor that powered the colonial economy. The new ranchero class would rely on them, as had the missionaries. California's missions laid the foundation for what came after. But at what cost? Conquest, disease, forced labor, and demoralization cost the lives of tens of thousands of men, women, and children.

Most Native Christians left the former missions in disgust. They returned to their old haunts, or joined unconverted Native communities on the periphery of colonial settlement. A large number relocated to the outskirts of Los Angeles and San José, taking work as domestic servants or unskilled laborers. In 1830 the mission population was estimated at about twenty thousand. Ten years later no more than a thousand Christian Natives continued to reside in the crumbling compounds. The mission era of California history was over. The rancho era had already begun.

A VIEW OF MONTEREY

12

Viva California Libre

Governor José Figueroa died in September 1835 following a short illness. He was only forty-three years old, and his death came as a shock to the Californios. They wanted to govern themselves, but Figueroa had won their admiration and respect by supporting their goals. Indeed, by purchasing a rancho he became something of a native in the eyes of the Californios. The legislators passed a resolution praising the late governor as "the Father of California."

Mariano Chico, Figueroa's successor, arrived in the spring of 1836. He was the appointee of Mexican president Antonio López de Santa Anna, who the previous year had scrapped the federal constitution, dissolved the national congress, and established a centralist dictatorship backed by Mexico's military. Chico echoed Santa Anna in his contempt for republican government and his opposition to secularization. He also promised to avenge his old friend, deposed governor Manuel Victoria. It was déjà vu for the Californios.

In his inaugural address, Chico offered his vision of California as "a model of subordination and obedience to supreme authority." That was not the way Californios saw things. As Pablo de la Guerra y Noriega, son of a former comandante of the Santa Barbara presidio, put it, "Chico promises us honor, glory, and grandeur if we meekly follow his politics, which amounts to telling us to renounce our rights as free men and simply accept his centralist plan." That was something few Californio leaders were willing do.

In opposing Santa Anna's centralism, Californios weren't alone. Several Mexican states protested the loss of political autonomy, including Tejas, where settlers from the southern United States outnumbered Tejanos. Those troubles were headline news before Chico departed Mexico, and he came to California with a deep suspicion of *extranjeros* (foreigners), especially Americans. Monterey, he thought, had far too many of them. With the expansion of the hide and tallow trade over the previous fifteen years, an émigré community of perhaps a hundred men (and a handful of women) had sprouted in the capital. The extranjeros included respectable merchants, commission agents, accountants, and clerks from Great Britain and the United States. But there were also ship-jumping sailors from a number of nations and rough-hewn fur trappers from the United States who came to California to exploit the beaver population of the interior rivers.

California was relatively open to international migrants, who were merely asked to register their arrival with the authorities. Most assimilated readily to local customs, converting to Catholicism, marrying daughters of the country, and becoming naturalized Mexican citizens. But Governor Chico distrusted all of them. He was "violently incensed at the foreign residents," noted an American merchant, threatening jail and worse for any who dared meddle in local politics. But in the election for the legislature, held a few weeks after Chico's arrival, the citizens of Monterey defied the governor by choosing David Spence, a Scots merchant and a naturalized Mexican citizen, to represent them. That only intensified Chico's ire. Juan Bautista Alvarado, elected to the legislature the year before, warned him that if he succeeded in chasing the extranjeros away, they would take their trade and capital with them, to the detriment of California. The governor responded that he couldn't care less.

Chico persisted in making enemies. He ordered the homes of foreigners and citizens alike searched without warrant. He picked a fight with the Monterey town council and threw the alcalde in jail. Traveling to southern California, he managed to alienate the citizens of Santa Barbara and Los Angeles. Alvarado and Castro, colleagues in the legislature, drafted articles of impeachment and conspired with other Californios to drive Chico from office. Catching wind of the opposition, and fearing a replay of Victoria's humiliation, the governor made a precipitous decision to return to Mexico. He would be back, he vowed, accompanied by a strong military force that would compel the Californios to submit. As he boarded the vessel taking him south he offered a departing threat. Punning on his own name (*chico* means "little" in Spanish), he exclaimed: "I leave Chico. I shall return Grande." But it proved an empty boast. He never set foot in California again.

★

Chico named Lieutenant Colonel Nicolás Gutiérrez, the highest-ranking military officer in the territory, as interim governor. Gutiérrez was in southern California at the time, and several weeks elapsed before he returned to Monterey. That gave Californios time to organize. After their success at deposing two Mexican governors, Victoria and Chico, they felt supremely self-confident. Why should they submit to another? The governorship, they believed, ought to be held by a native son. When he arrived, Gutiérrez was confronted with strong opposition from the legislature. Rather than conciliate, as Figueroa had done, he turned surly and arbitrary. Alvarado, the legislator with the most seniority, attempted to negotiate, but Gutiérrez dismissed him. He had "no need of legislators of pen and voice," he said, as long he had "plenty of legislators of sword and gun." Taking this as a direct threat, the legislators fled to the interior.

At a public meeting held in the chapel of former mission San Juan Bautista, the legislators passed a resolution condemning Gutiérrez. If the acting governor did not vacate his office voluntarily, they declared, the people of California would rise up and depose him. According to Alvarado, his fellow Californios greeted the resolution with enthusiasm. The pueblo of San José sent an armed brigade. David Spence promised the material support of the Monterey émigré community. Isaac Graham, an American trapper from Tennessee who operated a distillery and grog shop, organized an armed company of fur trappers known as *los rifleros americanos.*

Alvarado asked his uncle Don Mariano to lead this motley force, but he declined, saying that as a Mexican military officer he ought not take up arms against the government. Alvarado instead gave the command to his friend José Castro. But fearing a loss of support if Don Mariano's refusal became public, he assured his followers that his uncle would soon arrive with a company of leatherjackets. Then he dispatched a messenger to Gutiérrez with an ultimatum: step down or face the consequences.

When Gutiérrez did not comply, Alvarado and Castro marched back to Monterey with a force of a hundred rebels. Arriving on November 3, 1836, they found Gutiérrez, his officers, and fifty leatherjackets barricaded in the presidio. That turned out to be a foolish move, since the rebels immediately seized the coastal battery on the heights, which provided them with a commanding position. "We sent a flag of truce with a demand that Gutiérrez should surrender," Alvarado wrote to Don Mariano the following day. "The reply being delayed, we fired a cannon shot and the ball was so well directed that we put it into the comandante's house." Gutiérrez and his leather-jackets scattered in fear. Isaac Graham, leading los rifleros americanos, urged Alvarado to storm the presidio, but he refused. In truth, firing on his own countrymen had unnerved him. He decided to wait, which was a wise decision, for within the hour Gutiérrez surrendered. He and his officers were loaded onto a waiting vessel and dispatched to Mexico.

Alvarado later recalled that Isaac Graham then urged him to declare California's independence, opening the way for annexation by the United States. Graham had come prepared, with a handmade lone star flag to raise over the capital. American settlers had flown a lone star flag in Baton Rouge when they declared the district of West Florida independent of Spain in 1810 and invited incorporation by the United States. Americans in Tejas fought for independence under a similar lone star banner. Graham's suggestion horrified Alvarado. The rebels were fighting for home rule not independence, and they certainly wanted nothing to do with American annexation. In the name of the legislature, Alvarado issued a proclamation. "California is free," he declared, "and will sever its relations with Mexico until she ceases to be oppressed by the present dominant centralist faction." He appealed for unity. "Californios, let us be united and we shall be invincible."

★

Unity was difficult to come by, however. The residents of southern California feared the northerners would claim the lion's share of offices and benefits, the most important of which were the duties on imports, collected at the Monterey custom house.

Their suspicions were confirmed when the legislature named Alvarado interim governor and promoted Don Mariano to the rank of general and territorial comandante, a position he happily accepted, despite his earlier reluctance to join the revolution. But prominent Californios from the south—including Pío Pico, Juan Bandini, and José Antonio Carrillo, the men who had led the rebellion against Victoria—condemned the uprising. Alvarado, Castro, and Vallejo were compelled to go south with an armed force to persuade the southerners, one way or another.

They encountered some initial violent resistance, but that soon dissipated. Negotiations, however, wore on for months before the southerners finally acquiesced to Alvarado's governorship. The agreement had relatively little to do with policy and a great deal to do with the family connections among the Californio elites. In one telling incident, Don Mariano ordered the arrest of José de la Guerra y Noriega, former comandante of the Santa Barbara presidio and the most prominent man in southern California. Despite many appeals for his release, Don Mariano refused.

Finally he was approached by Guerra y Noriega's wife, María Antonia Carrillo, his first cousin. "Guadalupe," she said to him, using the familiar name by which he was known within the family, "you have treated my husband harshly. Revoke the order of arrest." Don Mariano explained that his actions were official, not personal. Among relatives, Doña María reminded him, everything was personal. She begged him to "reestablish harmony." Don Mariano released the prisoner. "In Alta California," he wrote years later, "we are all related to one another, and if one has the strength to resist the entreaties of the men, he must inevitably succumb to the tears and sighs of the women."

But how would Mexico respond? It was feared that former governor Chico would arrive at Monterey with a warship, like the privateer Bouchard had, and crush the new regime. But Mexico was preoccupied with the province of Tejas, where rebels had defeated a Mexican army led by President Santa Anna, captured Santa Anna himself, and forced him to agree to the independence of the province, which was renamed the Republic of Texas. So instead of an armed force, the central government sent a commissioner to negotiate, and in the summer of 1837 he and Alvarado agreed to a compromise. The rebels would accept the legitimacy of the regime in Mexico City, and in turn the centralists would elevate California from a territory to a department, giving the Californios the right to choose their own governor. Some time later they confirmed Alvarado as governor and Don Mariano as general and comandante of the Mexican military in California.

★

The rebels claimed to speak for all California's inhabitants. But what about the Natives? Native Christian converts outnumbered Californios by at least three to one, and outside the coastal district, tens of thousands of unconverted Natives continued to live in homelands under their own control. What did Natives think of the revolution of 1836? The documentary evidence bearing on this question is scanty, but there is at least one suggestive story. One day, during the months of negotiation in southern California, Alvarado and Castro were traveling together outside Santa Barbara when they encountered an elderly Chumash convert named Cristóbal Manojo, a man known for his sharp wit and ironic sense of humor. "Viva California libre!" he shouted when he recognized the two rebel leaders. "Viva!" they replied. Then Manojo exclaimed, "Take what you can get!" Puzzled, the Californios asked him what he meant. "Well," Manojo said with a smile, "you steal everything anyway." And with that he went on his way like Old Man

Coyote, chuckling to himself. Alvarado and Castro were left scratching their heads.

"Take what you can get!" That could have been the motto for the new Californio regime. During his time as governor, Alvarado made 180 more grants of former mission land. Indeed, more than three-quarters of all the land grants in Alta California were issued during the ten years that followed the uprising of 1836. The vast majority of those, made by the governor in consultation with the legislature, went to prominent individuals representing less than a quarter of all Californio families.

Some grants were small, others were huge. Half of all the granted land went to a small group with familiar names: Alvarado, Bandini, Carrillo, Castro, Guerra y Noriega, Ortega, Pico, Vallejo, and a few others. By the mid-1840s, a group of some three dozen Californio families controlled nearly 4.5 million acres (7,000 square miles) of grazing land. At huge Rancho Petaluma, Don Mariano employed several hundred vaqueros, field hands, and domestics, many of them the very Native men and women who had once called the place a homeland. Don Mariano and men like him made up a ruling rancho elite that dominated the social, economic, and political life of California. They turned the missions into their own private estates.

A considerably larger group of smaller landowners, families with little political clout, labored for themselves, perhaps with the assistance of a Native servant or two. But three out of four Californio families received no land at all. They worked as skilled vaqueros or majordomos on ranchos, or as artisans and laborers in the pueblos. The bulk of California's labor continued to be supplied by former mission Natives, bound to the new ranchos by force, by indebtedness, or simply by habit.

Other former mission Natives clustered in shanty towns on the edge of the pueblos.

About a quarter of the land grants went to foreigners who had become naturalized Mexican citizens. David Spence of Monterey, for example, was awarded a large spread in the Salinas Valley. But most of the extranjero grants were for land in the frontier region, north of San Francisco Bay or in the lower Sacramento Valley. In the decade to come, these men, many of them Americans, would play an increasingly important role in California's story.

SUTTER'S FORT

13

Wicked Foreigners

In August 1839 three small transport vessels left the village of Yerba Buena on San Francisco Bay and sailed north, passing through San Pablo and Suisun bays and entering the maze of waterways known as the Delta, the largest estuary in western North America, where the Sacramento and San Joaquin rivers converge. Johann August Sutter, a merchant trader from Switzerland, had secured Governor Alvarado's permission to establish a trading post and settlement on the Sacramento River. Sailing upstream some forty miles, his small flotilla came to a fork where the *Río Americanos* (named for American beaver trappers) tumbled down from the Sierra to meet the Sacramento. "Suddenly," Sutter later recalled, "I saw in an open space two hundred warriors painted yellow, black, and red, armed and keen for fight." They were Miwoks, defending their homeland.

Colonizers on deck, Natives on shore. There had been many such encounters before. But after three generations, the

Miwoks knew the protocol. They staged a ferocious welcome, but were far more interested in trading than fighting. Many were former residents of Mission San José. With secularization they had returned to their homeland, but not to their old way of life. They still gathered acorns in the oak groves and hauled salmon from the river, but they also tended livestock, rode horses, and found a variety of ways to profit from their position on the margins of Mexican California. They hunted and trapped, selling their pelts to itinerant fur traders. They raided ranchos and rustled horses, exchanging them with renegade stock dealers. When Sutter's vessels approached, they envisioned new opportunities.

Sutter had aims of his own. A garrulous charmer with notable powers of persuasion, he was, in the words of Albert Hurtado, his foremost biographer, "a confidence man." Fleeing Europe to avoid debtor's prison, Sutter swindled his way from New York to Missouri, hounded by creditors and shadowed by county sheriffs. For several years he conducted business in Santa Fe, New Mexico, where cross-border trade boomed between the United States and Mexico. He first learned about California when he purchased and resold a herd of horses rustled there, netting a fine profit. California was the place for him, he thought, a country with plenty of opportunity and no sheriffs to get in his way.

Sutter joined a fur trade caravan headed for the Rockies, where he peddled rotgut whiskey to mountain men at the annual fur trade rendezvous. He traveled to the Oregon Country with a party of missionaries and bamboozled Hudson's Bay Company officials at Fort Vancouver. He caught a merchant ship to Hawai'i, where he learned the contours of the trans-Pacific trade, arranged for transport to California, and hired a dozen Kānaka workers. En route he paid a visit to Fort Ross, an operation that greatly impressed him. In Monterey he captivated Governor Alvarado with a plan for a large, self-sufficient trading establishment in the Central Valley. With Alvarado's endorsement, Sutter obtained supplies and outfitted his vessels on credit from Monterey merchants.

Governor Alvarado too had his motives. Sutter's establishment would be the first permanent outpost in the Central Valley, a region that offered enormous opportunity for the expansion of settlement. That would require breaking the power of the Miwoks, the Yokuts, the Maidu, and others like them, a project that Sutter promised to support. Given his record as a dealer in stolen California horses, however, his promise wasn't worth very much.

Alvarado also expected that Sutter's presence in the interior would counter the growing power of Don Mariano, who controlled the fertile Sonoma and Napa valleys. Relatives, boyhood companions, and close associates for thirty years, the two men had recently become estranged. The cavalier way Alvarado leveraged his name and reputation during the 1836 uprising wounded Don Mariano's pride. Moreover, Alvarado took the position that in a republic the military should be under civilian control, which made Don Mariano his subordinate, an intolerable situation for a man who ruled his rancho like a feudal baron. Don Mariano railed about the "clique at the capital," while Alvarado complained that his uncle had become "the autocrat of Sonoma."

★

Sutter's frightened men pulled their firearms, but their boss ordered them to hold their fire. He had to proceed with care. While the crew covered him with their muskets, he disembarked and conversed in broken Spanish with Miwok leaders, promising presents if they would hear him out. He had the men unload bolts of fabric and bags of beads, but before distributing the goods he made his pitch for permission to build an outpost. He promised good prices for Miwok pelts and horses. He promised to pay them for their labor. Then, so there would be no misunderstanding about who was boss, he ordered his men to unload a small field cannon, which they fired off several times.

The Miwoks went to work for Sutter. They brought him beaver pelts by the score, which he sent downriver to exchange for livestock and trade goods. They dug irrigation ditches and broke new ground for planting. They herded his horses and cattle. In exchange they received goods at his store, including plenty of cheap brandy. Most soon ran up debts they would never pay off. That was Sutter's preferred method of control, although he did not hesitate to use violence when he thought it necessary. If they failed to perform at the desired pace, one of the Miwoks told a visitor, Sutter's foreman "whipped them with a big whip made of cowhide." When a dissatisfied group of Miwok vaqueros stole some cattle, Sutter personally led a night raid on their camp that killed as many as thirty men.

Sutter's Kānaka employees built the first structures, Polynesian grass shacks, where the city of Sacramento would later rise. The Miwoks, using skills learned at the mission, constructed adobe buildings to house his warehouse and store. The outpost soon became a prominent stopping point for traders and trappers, some of whom Sutter hired. By the spring of 1840 several dozen American and British men were working for him in a variety of capacities. Many took up residence with Native women in a cluster of huts constructed in both Miwok and Kānaka style. Eventually this diverse frontier compound was enclosed with eighteen-foot adobe walls. It drew mountain men, trappers, and other Americans from the East. Sutter called his establishment *Nueva Helvetia* or New Switzerland, but throughout the American West everyone knew it as Sutter's Fort.

★

By 1840 approximately five hundred men from the United States, Great Britain, and elsewhere were living amid five or six thousand Californios in Alta California. Most were reputable citizens, but some were troublemakers, and Californio authorities were increasingly concerned. Alvarado grew highly suspicious of the dozens of Americans residing at Sutter's Fort— "a throng of depraved creatures," he called them—and worried that he had made a serious mistake encouraging Sutter. But Alvarado's immediate attention focused on Isaac Graham and his rifleros, the American fighters who had taken part in the 1836 revolution. From the moment Alvarado rejected Graham's lone star flag, the rifleros loudly proclaimed their discontent. In the grogshops of Monterey they raised their cups to the newly independent Republic of Texas, toasting "California Next!"

Push came to shove in March 1840 when a Catholic priest informed Alvarado that a dying American had confessed to a scheme supposedly concocted by Graham: the rifleros would seize Monterey by force and declare California independent. The evidence was hearsay, but for Alvarado sufficient. He presented the legislature with a plan to immediately deport all foreigners without valid papers, an honorable profession, or a wife from a respectable Californio family. They quickly approved it and José Antonio Castro, comandante of the Monterey presidio, seized Graham and several American associates in a violent raid.

Over the next few weeks local authorities throughout California arrested and jailed several dozen Americans and Englishmen, and at the end of the month Castro escorted them by sailing vessel to Mexico, where they were to be tried for attempted insurrection. "The country has been saved from imminent danger," declared Alvarado. Californios had no more to fear from *los malditos extranjeros,* "the wicked foreigners." How wrong he was.

Several weeks later a large American warship sailed into Monterey Bay. Word of the arrests had spread quickly through the Pacific trading network, and Captain French Forrest, in command of the USS *Saint Louis,* armed with twenty guns and a full complement of 125 men, had come to investigate. Forrest sent a messenger ashore with a note demanding that Governor Alvarado provide an explanation for the outrageous expulsion of American citizens. Everything had been done in accordance with the law, Alvarado replied—and then, before Captain Forrest could respond, he and fellow government officials left the capital for the interior. Forrest took his gunboat diplomacy no further and sailed away, but the Californios were thoroughly spooked.

Their apprehension intensified when Castro returned from Mexico with a disheartening story. The Mexican state, deeply in debt to London creditors, had acquiesced to British demands and released all the prisoners, Americans as well as Brits. Castro himself had been jailed for illegally arresting them. Graham and a number of his men soon returned to Monterey, determined to avenge their mistreatment. If nothing else, the fiasco vividly demonstrated just how little support the Californios could expect from Mexico City.

★

The return of Isaac Graham and his rifleros was followed by the arrival of the first large parties of overland emigrants. In early November 1841 a group of fifty or sixty men, women, and children, led by William Workman and John Rowland, arrived at Mission San Gabriel after a 1,200-mile trek from Santa Fe. They were the first settlers to make the desert crossing to California since Anza's expedition. Workman and Rowland had moved from Missouri to Santa Fe two decades before, prospered in business, married New Mexican women, and become naturalized Mexican citizens. With the revolt of Americans in

Texas, however, and the increasing hostility of their neighbors, they made the decision to relocate to California with their extended families. Local authorities welcomed them with open arms.

A few days earlier, four hundred miles to the north, a group of thirty-two American men, one accompanied by his wife and infant child, stumbled into the Central Valley after a nightmarish overland journey. Led by John Bidwell and John Bartleson, they were the first Americans to attempt a wagon crossing from Missouri to California. Unlike the Workman-Rowland Party, these men had no prior experience in Mexico. Arrested by patrolling leatherjackets, they were escorted to Sonoma, where Don Mariano interviewed them and issued temporary visas.

Don Mariano believed that the Bidwell-Bartleson Party signaled the commencement of a major migration to California from the United States. He was right. Over the previous twenty years, thanks to an exceptionally high birth rate and large-scale European immigration, the population of the United States had nearly doubled. Along the nation's western frontier, whence the Missouri migrants had come, the growth was even more explosive. It was only a matter of time, Don Mariano expected, before American pioneers began streaming into California. They had demonstrated a talent for developing new country, and he thought their coming might be a good thing. The problem was how to manage them. Neither he nor anyone else had any idea that within ten years several hundred thousand Americans would arrive in California. There would be no way to manage that.

★

The Missouri migrants found refuge at Sutter's Fort. Sutter was in the process of expanding his operations, and he needed more men. The Russian America Company, concluding that

Fort Ross was no longer a paying operation, had sold all their movable property to Sutter. They had first offered it to Don Mariano, who was eager to extend his domain. But being a cautious man, he decided to seek approval from Mexico City before acting. The Russians, anxious to liquidate and unwilling to wait, offered everything to Sutter on credit. The deal netted Sutter several hundred head of cattle and horses; a number of redwood buildings, which he dismantled and transported to his Sacramento site; all the equipment and tools necessary to run a dairy, a lumber mill, a tannery, a blacksmith's forge, and a cooperage for making casks and barrels; and a twenty-ton schooner. The haul also included a trove of military uniforms and a complete armory, which Sutter used to arm and outfit his Miwok militia. He had become a power unto himself.

Don Mariano was outraged. The Russian withdrawal gave him the opportunity to expand his operations all the way to the coast, but the transfer of livestock and equipment from Fort Ross to Sutter's Fort traversed his rancho, and his vaqueros clashed with Sutter's men a number of times. He protested to Sutter, but the squire of the Sacramento refused to be intimidated by the autocrat of Sonoma. "I am strong now," Sutter responded in a letter. "It is too late to drive me out of the country." If Don Mariano tried to rein him in, Sutter wrote, "I will make a declaration of independence and proclaim California a republic."

Don Mariano took the threat seriously. In early 1842, acting in his capacity as comandante of California, he dispatched a rider with an urgent message to his superiors in Mexico City, enclosing a copy of Sutter's threatening letter. California required immediate protection against foreign encroachment, he argued, and he urged the authorities to send no fewer than two hundred armed men. Since he and Alvarado disagreed over the relationship between civil and military authority, he also recommended the appointment of a new governor with military rank.

Equally concerned, Alvarado had already sent his own courier to Mexico City with a request for troops. "There are ambitious schemes affecting this department," he wrote, "endangering the integrity of Mexican territory." Everything in California was about to change.

COMMODORE JONES + THOMAS LARKIN

14

Yankee Doodle in Monterey

On October 19, 1842, two formidable warships of the United States Navy bore down on the central California coast. Together, the frigate USS *United States* and the sloop-of-war USS *Cyane* boasted a total of seventy-eight guns and upward of seven hundred officers, sailors, and Marines. Before lights out that evening, the commander of the Pacific Squadron, Commodore Thomas ap Catesby Jones (*ap* meaning "son of" in Welsh), addressed his men. "We are now approaching the shore of California," he announced, "the territory of Mexico, the enemy of our country, whose flag it is our duty to strike, and hoist in its place our own." They would arrive at the capital of Monterey on the morrow, and it was their duty to meet and overcome any resistance. "This may or may not be an easy task," said Jones. "We are prepared for the worst, while we hope for the best."

For several years, the United States had expressed interest in acquiring California, especially San Francisco Bay, considered vital to the growth of the nation's trading interests in the Pacific. In 1835 President Andrew Jackson offered to purchase the northern part of the territory, but, infuriated by Jackson's support of American rebels in Tejas, the Mexicans refused. President John Tyler renewed Jackson's offer in 1841, by which time Tejas had become the independent Republic of Texas and was petitioning for admission to the union of states. If the U.S. Congress agreed, Mexican diplomats warned, their nation would consider it an act of war. Many officials believed war with Mexico was inevitable, and before Jones departed Washington, the navy secretary informed him that if war broke out he was to seize Monterey and lay claim to California by right of conquest.

In early September 1842, while Jones was anchored with the Pacific Squadron at the Pacific port of Callao, Peru, the American chargé d'affaires delivered a letter from a U.S. consular official in Mexico warning that relations between the two nations were rapidly deteriorating. Given the time it had taken for the letter to arrive, Jones figured that "hostilities must have already commenced." He immediately set sail for Monterey.

Jones anchored his warships within firing distance of the Monterey presidio on the afternoon of October 19 and sent an officer ashore with an ultimatum: Governor Juan Bautista Alvarado had until the following morning to surrender California or suffer the destruction of his capital. "Señor Alvarado was in shock as he read the note," wrote a Californio who was present. "His face suddenly became pale and then immediately turned red, as if blood was about to burst from his eyes." Alvarado vividly remembered the attack by the privateer Bouchard when he was a boy, twenty-four years earlier. And only two years before, he and other officials had fled the capital during U.S. Navy captain French Forrest's "visit" to Monterey.

With fewer than thirty able-bodied soldiers and a few old

artillery pieces, resistance was out of the question, so Alvarado played the only card he had. He would not resist, he informed the American officer. But he had no authority to surrender California because he was no longer governor. His successor, Brigadier General José Manuel Micheltorena, had already arrived in the territory and was currently making his way north from San Diego.

★

In response to concerns of Don Mariano and Governor Alvarado about the rising number of American settlers, President Santa Anna relieved them both of duty and appointed Brigadier General Micheltorena to a unified command as both governor and comandante of California. The Californios knew nothing about it until Micheltorena's arrival at San Diego. Don Mariano claimed to be pleased, but Alvarado could not hide his bitter disappointment. His dismissal from the governorship, he believed, repudiated the compromise he had negotiated, keeping California within the Mexican federation.

Micheltorena came with a clear mission: to prevent California from following the same course as Texas. But the Mexican state was practically bankrupt, and President Santa Anna had not provided Micheltorena with the means his assignment required. He arrived in California with a battalion of three hundred men, but the majority of them were former convicts, recruited directly from their prison cells. They were untrained, undisciplined, and underequipped. An American merchant who saw them disembarking in San Diego was appalled. "They presented a state of wretchedness and misery unequaled," he reported. The soldiers became infamous in California for stealing food and clothing simply to survive.

After several weeks attempting to whip his men into shape, Micheltorena began a slow march north toward the capital. But shortly after he set out, messengers from Monterey arrived with the alarming news of the American invasion. "Would that I were a thunderbolt to fly and annihilate the invaders," Micheltorena stormed. But rather than flying northward, he turned his men toward Los Angeles. There he holed up, awaiting further reports.

★

On the morning of October 20, Commodore Jones sent 150 sailors and Marines ashore. As the Marine band played "Yankee Doodle," they marched to the presidio, lowered the Mexican flag, and raised the stars and stripes. Jones issued a proclamation in English and Spanish. California was now a possession of the United States, he declared. As long as the inhabitants remained in the peaceful pursuit of their occupations, he would guarantee the security of life and property "from the consequences of the unjust war into which Mexico has plunged you."

What war? No one in Monterey had any knowledge of such a war. Thomas O. Larkin, a Massachusetts merchant who had resided in Monterey for a decade, provided Jones with copies of several recent Mexican newspapers, none of which made any mention of war with the United States. Jones stewed for several hours before concluding that he had made a precipitous mistake.

He ordered the Mexican flag rehoisted and dispatched a perfunctory note to Governor Micheltorena in Los Angeles. Sometimes described as an apology, it was hardly that. "I have received new communications from Mexico," Jones wrote, "which induce me to believe that friendly relations have been reestablished between the two nations." In fact, relations were never broken and Jones had received no "new communications." The Mexican minister in Washington later demanded that Jones be reprimanded, but the navy secretary instead issued a statement praising his "ardent zeal."

The surrender and brief occupation of Monterey by Commodore Jones laid bare American intentions regarding California. It also suggested how easily a conquest might be accomplished. A French naturalist on an expedition along the California coast offered a concise judgment when he heard what had happened. "It is evident," he wrote, "that California will belong to whatever nation chooses to send there a man-of-war and 200 men."

★

Governor Micheltorena spent several months in Los Angeles before relocating to Monterey in late summer 1843. The Californios, who still aspired to run their own government, opposed him at virtually every turn. They resented the presence of Mexican authorities, and were outraged by his disorderly soldiers. Alvarado suggested that the governor execute a few as an example to the rest, but as Micheltorena wrote to his superiors in Mexico City, "it was hard to shoot a hungry, unpaid soldier for pilfering food."

The governor convened a meeting of leading Californios to advise him. Don Mariano suggested sending the battalion to the northern frontier, where it could live on his abundant beef and assist in hunting Native horse thieves. The Mexican officers protested. They had not come "to fight Indians for Californios." Growing frustrated, former governor Alvarado gave an incendiary speech. Their homeland was under assault, he said. Each year more Americans arrived from the East. Warships of the United States operated with impunity in California waters. Yet Mexico's response was to send an army incapable of defending the department. The meeting broke up in confusion. Micheltorena accused Alvarado of plotting against the government and ordered his arrest.

Alvarado was soon released—but he and José Antonio Castro were indeed up to their old tricks. In the summer of 1844 a group of prominent Californios secretly met with the

British consul in Monterey. They were preparing to drive Micheltorena from office and declare California's independence, they told him. Could they rely on Great Britain for protection? The consul supported that idea, but the British Foreign Office rejected it, fearful of alienating the Mexican government, which remained deeply in debt to British creditors. The Californios decided to go ahead with their plan anyway.

They began their revolt in November by seizing a cache of government munitions stored at the former mission of San Juan Bautista. Alvarado succeeded in rallying a few hundred men with his oratory, and Castro organized several dozen rancheros and vaqueros into a rough cavalry force. Governor Micheltorena, who did not trust his own troops, negotiated an agreement with the rebel leaders, agreeing to send the convict army back to Mexico. But at the same moment, he secretly made a deal with Johann August Sutter and Isaac Graham. In exchange for promises of large land grants, they promised a force of rifleros americanos and Sutter's Miwok militia to fight with Micheltorena against the Californios. For Sutter, this was simply business. For Graham, it was sweet revenge.

★

When Alvarado and Castro learned that Micheltorena had enlisted the support of Graham's wicked foreigners, just as they themselves had done eight years before, they professed outrage. "Sir, you have aroused the country," they exclaimed. "The sons of California will do us justice, and we will shed our blood rather than permit our country to endure this infamous oppression." Outnumbered by Micheltorena's newly augmented battalion, they fled south with their small force, the governor's several hundred men, including at least fifty Americans, in hot pursuit.

In Los Angeles, Alvarado made his case to the town council. Although Angelenos had their own bitter memories of the convict army, they mistrusted the northerners. Alvarado and Castro had to employ a combination of threat and inducement to get their way. Local leaders finally came around when Alvarado pledged that once they ousted Micheltorena, the succeeding governor would be a Californio from the south. The legislature convened and passed a resolution deposing Micheltorena and appointing Pío Pico as his successor. Pico then issued an order that all inhabitants, citizens and foreigners alike, present themselves for militia service. Some fifty American settlers living in southern California enrolled in the Californio army.

On February 20, 1845, several hundred fighters crossed Cahuenga Pass and confronted Micheltorena's force not far from where the Californios had succeeded in deposing Governor Victoria fourteen years before. The two sides commenced a lengthy artillery duel that continued through the day. The thunder of the guns frightened the residents of Los Angeles, watching from the hills, but did little damage. That evening, the Americans on both sides of the conflict found an opportunity to fraternize. This was not their fight, declared the southerners. But they had been promised land, replied the northerners. When Pío Pico learned of their concern, he pledged to honor their land claims when he became governor. Isaac Graham objected, but the Americans on both sides agreed to withdraw.

Without the rifleros, Governor Micheltorena raised the white flag. Following a brief negotiation, he marched his convict army to the port of San Pedro and was soon on board a vessel headed for Mexico. For a third time, the Californios had deposed a sitting governor. The rifleros trudged back to their homes in the north, and Isaac Graham bitterly retired to his farm, remaining a recluse until his death in 1863.

Pío Pico—who resided in a townhouse on the Los Angeles plaza, built with the fortune he accumulated while civil administrator of former Mission San Luis Rey—announced he would govern California from the south. The northerners wanted their fair share of offices, of course, and in a compromise the legislature appointed Castro military comandante and Alvarado chief customs inspector, positions based at Monterey. All these appointments were later approved by the Mexican government.

But over subsequent months regional and personal jealousies among the Californios continued to break out in persistent conflict. "The Californians are now free to govern themselves," wrote merchant Thomas O. Larkin, "which freedom they exercise by not governing at all." In 1846, leading Californios remained divided among themselves as the moment of their greatest peril approached.

NANCY KELSEY CROSSES THE SIERRAS

15

Overland to California

"A new era in the affairs of California is about to arise," Lansford W. Hastings wrote in a March 1846 letter to merchant Thomas O. Larkin in Monterey. "The eyes of the American people are now turned westward, and thousands are gazing with the most intense interest and anxiety upon the Pacific shores." Hastings, writing from Sutter's Fort, had put a bet down on that westward turn. The previous year he published *The Emigrants' Guide to Oregon and California,* and he was confident of the results. "The emigration of this year," he predicted, "will not consist of less than *twenty thousand* human souls." He and Johann August Sutter were ready for them.

Hastings cut a dashing figure. Fourteen-year-old John McBride met him on the trail to California, and many years later his memory of Hastings remained vivid. "He was a tall, fine-looking man with light brown hair and beard," McBride recalled, "dressed in a suit of elegant pattern made of buckskin, handsomely embroidered and trimmed at the collar and openings with plucked beaver fur, an ideal representative of the mountaineer."

Appearances can be deceiving. Hastings dressed the part, but he was no mountain man. Born to a middle-class Ohio family, he made his living as a lawyer, land speculator, and inveterate schemer. In 1842, at the age of twenty-three, he joined the first wagon train to make the overland journey all the way to Oregon, where he found legal work specializing in land claims. Unhappy with the climate, however, he joined a party of some two dozen Americans headed south to California.

Hastings fell in with Sutter, a man cut from similar cloth. Sutter eagerly wished to attract more Americans to his outpost, men to employ in his shops and families to settle as tenants on his enormous land grant in the Sacramento Valley. Given his experience with Oregon land claims, Hastings seemed the perfect partner. In exchange for a promise of land, the young man agreed to return to the States and do what he could to drum up enthusiasm. Before departing, he announced his intention to publish a book promoting overland emigration.

Hastings returned to Ohio and quickly churned out a manuscript. The book, which came off the press in the spring of 1845, portrayed California as a farmer's paradise. "In my opinion," Hastings wrote, "there is no country in the known world possessing a soil so fertile and productive, with such varied and inexhaustible resources, and a climate of such mildness, uniformity, and salubrity." West of the Sierras, snow, ice, and frost were unknown. Livestock could forage during the winter, needing neither shelter nor hay. Farms abounded in crops of every kind. In California, everything grew bigger and better.

This Eden was wasted on its current inhabitants. Hastings ridiculed Native Californians as miserable "Diggers," and scorned Californios as "scarcely above the barbarous tribes by whom they are surrounded." The political and military authorities were weak and corrupt, he assured his readers, and emigrants from the United States had nothing to fear from them. "The impromptu conquest of California by Commodore Jones," he wrote, "taught them the propriety of respecting the rights of foreigners." Americans in California were "resolved to throw off the Mexican yoke." Sooner rather than later, they would "play the Texas game," Hastings predicted, and form their own republic. "I strongly suspect," a newspaper editor commented, "that Captain Hastings aims at the highest executive office himself." Indeed, Hastings imagined becoming the Sam Houston of California.

Hastings toured the Mississippi Valley promoting his book and recruiting prospective emigrants before once again setting out for California with a mounted company late in the summer of 1845. They arrived at Sutter's Fort on Christmas Day, lucky to have avoided early winter storms in the Sierras. Hastings proudly displayed copies of his book and predicted a flood of emigrants the next year. He also announced that he had discovered, in the harsh desert region between the Rockies and the Sierras, a cutoff that made the trek "400 miles shorter." He planned to be back on the trail in the summer of 1846, directing emigrants to this "better and more direct route."

★

The remarkable overland migration of tens of thousands of Americans to the Pacific coast resulted from a convergence of circumstances. Intense land speculation during the 1830s led to a rapid sell-off of public land in the trans-Appalachian West. Then the Panic of 1837 plunged the nation into a sustained economic depression that continued for more than a decade. By the early 1840s, many rural Americans had resolved to better their circumstances by heading for the frontier. Most relocated to the first tier of trans-Mississippi states—western Louisiana and the Gulf coast of Texas, Arkansas and Missouri, Iowa and Minnesota. From 1840 to 1870, the population of those states grew from a few hundred thousand to more than four million. Over roughly the same period a total of 350,000 people took the overland trail to Oregon or California. Although overland migrants to the Pacific coast made up a minority of American frontier settlers, that still amounted to a lot of people.

The two thousand miles across plains, mountains, and deserts were counted off at the rate of twelve to fifteen miles a day, the speed of oxen and farm wagons. That added up to a journey of five or six months. Emigrants departed as soon as the spring grass was high enough for livestock to graze, praying they would make it over the Sierra Nevada range before the first winter storms. They followed trails laid down long before by hunters and trappers, following the Platte River trail to Fort Laramie, then heading west across the broad expanse of South Pass in the Rocky Mountains.

The approximate halfway point was Independence Rock, a large granite outcropping on the Sweetwater River in today's Wyoming, on which thousands of emigrants would inscribe their names, which remain legible today. Another ten days of hard travel brought them to the crossing of the Green River, where the trail bent northwest toward the Hudson's Bay Company outpost of Fort Hall, in what is now southeastern Idaho. A day or two beyond came the parting of the ways, the right fork leading to Oregon, the left to California. This was where the overland emigrants realized the heart-breaking truth. As one man put it, "The nearer California, the worse the road."

Before the California gold rush of 1849, which attracted single men by the tens of thousands, the migration to the Pacific was almost entirely a family affair. Wagon companies were made up of extended families, people linked by blood and marriage. Families from the same rural districts often traveled together. "How do the old woman and the girls like the idea of such a long journey?" one farmer asked a neighbor about to depart for the coast. "They feel mighty pert about it," came the reply, "and Suke says she shan't be easy till we start." Other women were not so enthusiastic. "Oh, let us not go," cried Mary Jones when her husband told her of his decision. But, she lamented, "it made no difference." A large number of women recorded their reluctance in the diaries and journals they kept along the way. The number of men kept at home by reluctant wives is unknowable, but was surely large.

Women were on the trail from the beginning. When Nancy Kelsey's husband Ben declared his intention of going to California with the Bidwell-Bartleson Party in 1841, she insisted on accompanying him. "I can better endure the hardships of the journey than the anxieties for an absent husband," she declared. She was the only woman in a company of several dozen men, a seventeen-year-old mother traveling with an infant daughter. "She bore the fatigues of the journey with heroism, patience, and kindness," recalled one of the men. "Her cheerful nature and kind heart brought many a ray of sunshine through the clouds that gathered round a company of so many weary travelers."

The company lost its way in the desert and had to abandon the wagons. Ascending to the crest of the Sierras on horseback, the men scattered to find the best descent to the Central Valley. "I was left with my babe alone," Mrs. Kelsey recalled. "And as I sat there on my horse and listened to the sighing and moaning of the winds through the pines, it seemed the loneliest spot in the world." After finding their way to Sutter's Fort, she told her husband what she had known for several weeks. She was pregnant.

★

From 1841 to 1845 approximately four hundred American emigrants traveled overland to California. The migration of 1846 was the largest yet, some fifteen hundred individuals—nowhere near the twenty thousand Hastings had predicted, but more than three times the total of the previous five years. And for that, Hastings was largely responsible. Nearly every wagon train included someone traveling with his guidebook in hand.

Many of the emigrants took note of a suggestion Hastings made in his discussion of the route beyond Independence Rock. "The most direct path," he wrote, "would be to leave the Oregon route about two hundred miles east from Fort Hall, thence bearing west-southwest to the Salt Lake." Hastings was simply speculating, drawing lines on a blank map. By the time he stationed himself on the trail to meet the emigrants of 1846, however, he claimed—falsely—to have firsthand knowledge.

In late June, the first wagon companies to arrive at Independence Rock found Hastings waiting with news of his shortcut. It turned southwest well before reaching the crossing of the Green River, continued to the trading post of mountain man Jim Bridger, took a canyon route through the last range of the Rockies, then skirted the southern shore of the Great Salt Lake and headed directly across the desert to link up with the established trail. Hastings claimed that the cutoff had "an abundant supply of wood, water, and grass," although acknowledging that there was a waterless section of some forty miles. He offered to act as guide for any and all who were interested. Most California-bound emigrants stuck with the old trail, but a number went with Hastings. Before departing, he left a notice for companies bringing up the rear. Form yourselves into large parties, he advised, and take the road to Bridger's. He would meet them there.

★

The heavily loaded wagons of James Frazier Reed and George and Jacob Donner were slow and cumbersome. By the time they reached Fort Laramie their party of thirty-three—including wives, children, teamsters, a handyman, and a cook—had fallen to the rear of the migration. They knew they had to pick up the pace if they were to make it over the mountains before the first snow. They consulted a copy of Hasting's *Guide* and wondered about the cutoff. Reed ran into an old friend, an experienced frontiersman, and asked him about it. "Take the regular wagon track and never leave it," the man advised. "It is barely possible to get through if you follow it, and it might be impossible if you don't."

Nevertheless, when Reed and the Donners found the notice Hastings had left at Independence Rock, they were enthusiastic about the time it could save them. With a number of families joining them, they formed a train of two dozen wagons and chose George Donner, a vigorous man in his early sixties, as their captain. The eighty-seven people of the Donner Party, as it would be known forever after, represented a cross-section of the American migration to California. They were people of German, Irish, English, French, and Mexican ancestry; Protestants, Catholics, Mormons, and at least one Jew.

One Oregon-bound emigrant watched as the party made the turn for Bridger's. The men were in fine spirits, he recalled. But Tamsen Donner, the captain's wife, was "gloomy, sad, and dispirited." Why, Mrs. Donner wrote in her journal, would her husband and the other men "confide in the statement of a man of whom they knew nothing, but who was probably some selfish adventurer." Hastings was precisely that. In fact, he had never actually traveled over the cutoff he promoted. At that very moment he was ahead of them, exploring it for the very first time.

When the Donner Party reached Bridger's Fort on July 31, Hastings had already gone ahead, leaving vague instructions. So they set out on their own. At the mouth of a canyon leading through the mountains they found another note. The way ahead was impassable, Hastings had written, and they would have to find another. There and then they should have turned back and joined the main trail, but that would mean a late crossing of the Sierra Nevada. Better, they decided, to forge ahead.

But ahead they found no trail at all. It took them eighteen days to travel thirty-six miles through the Wasatch mountain range before they reached the Great Salt Lake. Exhausted and demoralized, they now had a desert to cross. They found another note from Hastings: "2 days—2 nights—hard driving—cross desert—reach water," he had scribbled. They loaded up all the grass and water they could carry and set out, but it took several days before they finally reached the oasis. When the desperately thirsty livestock smelled water, they stampeded, and the emigrants lost several days more searching for lost animals.

By the time they rejoined the old trail it was late September. Hastings's shortcut had cost them more than a month. It took another four weeks to reach the flanks of the Sierra, looming before them like a colossal granite wall. With extraordinary effort they made the ascent, reaching the summit at what is now called Donner Lake, an elevation of 6,000 feet. Snow already covered the ground, but they took heart: Sutter's Fort was just a few days ahead.

On the night of October 30, however, a ferocious winter storm engulfed them. Louis Keseberg, sleeping with his family around a campfire, awoke covered with snow. He sat up and looked around. "The camp, the cattle, my companions, had all disappeared," he remembered. "I shouted at the top of my voice. Suddenly, here and there, all about me, heads popped up through the snow. The scene was not unlike what one might imagine at the resurrection, when people rise up out of the earth." But there would be no resurrection for the Donner Party. They were condemned to a frozen hell. A few men successfully made it to Sutter's and raised the alarm, but continuing storms prevented rescue. It was the worst winter in many years.

The stranded emigrants constructed rough shelters. It continued to snow until the drifts were fifteen to twenty feet deep, covering the treetops. Oxen wandered off and were lost; those that remained were slaughtered for meat. November turned to December. The meat ran out and people survived on boiled rawhide and bones. December turned to January. People began dying, the young and the elderly first. January turned to February. The living did what they had to do to survive, consuming the flesh of the dead. The first rescue party finally arrived that month, but it took two more months and four attempts before the last survivors were evacuated in April. Thirty-six people perished.

★

Hastings did not become the Sam Houston of California. He would fight with the Americans against the Californios, practice law, and serve as a delegate to the convention that wrote a constitution for American California. When asked about the Donner horror, as he was many times, he simply said he was sorry, that he had meant well. But as the story of the Donner Party became an indelible part of California's history, an undercurrent of hostility sabotaged Hastings's political career. Eventually he was reduced to accepting an appointment as the postmaster of an Arizona town, described by one observer as consisting of "a store and a boarding house, with a population of ten or fifteen persons." That number included Hastings, his wife, and their five children.

He still dreamed of glory. After the death of his wife in 1862, Hastings placed his children in foster care and relocated to Louisiana. He supported the Confederacy during the Civil War, and proposed raising a force of volunteers to seize California, but his convoluted plan went nowhere. After the war he promoted a scheme to settle a colony of former slave owners in Brazil, where slavery remained legal, and in 1867 he published *The Emigrants' Guide to Brazil.* Three years later, while accompanying a shipload of planters headed for this new paradise, he contracted yellow fever and died.

THE BEARS TAKE DON MARIANO PRISONER

16

We Must Be Conquerors

Western expansion dominated the U.S. presidential campaign of 1844, pitting Democrat James K. Polk of Tennessee against Whig Henry Clay of Kentucky. Incumbent president John Tyler had raised the issue of westward expansion in April of that year when he signed a treaty of annexation with the Republic of Texas and forwarded it to the Senate for ratification. Mexico immediately severed diplomatic relations and warned that if Texas became a state it would mean war. Violent conflict was averted when the treaty failed to win the required two-thirds Senate majority, but the annexation of Texas became the principal issue in the presidential campaign.

Both candidates were slave owners. But the Whig Party included many antislavery northerners, and since the Republic of Texas had enshrined slavery in its constitution, Clay opposed its admission to the Union. Polk and the Democrats, however, ran a full-throated campaign, advocating not only

Texas statehood but also the acquisition of the Oregon Country, claimed by both Great Britain and the United States. In the words of a Democratic Party propagandist, such expansion was "the fulfillment of our manifest destiny to overspread the continent." Polk won a narrow victory in an extremely close contest.

After the election but before the inauguration, lame-duck president Tyler, also a slave owner, made a final attempt to get Texas into the Union, this time by means of a joint resolution of Congress, requiring only simple majorities in the House and Senate. Polk endorsed Tyler's parliamentary maneuver, and the resolution passed shortly before he assumed office. Mexican officials fumed, but decided to wait and see what the new administration would do.

With Texas statehood apparently a settled question, President Polk turned to his other expansionist aims. His principal foreign policy goal, he told his cabinet, was the conquest of Mexican California and the extension of United States sovereignty to the Pacific coast. Though claiming to be willing to negotiate, he was determined to succeed by hook or by crook. He first took up the question of the Oregon Country, blustering about the nation's right to the entire region south of Russian America ("Fifty-four Forty or Fight!")—not only the future states of Oregon, Washington, and Idaho, but the future province of British Columbia as well. Fearful of a confrontation with the powerful Royal Navy, however, Polk reached an amicable resolution with the British, extending the international boundary across the disputed territory at the 49th parallel.

When it came to Mexico, which Polk did not fear in the least, he adopted a policy of overt intimidation. He first ordered an army of four thousand under the command of General Zachary Taylor into the new state of Texas, then sent an emissary named John Slidell to Mexico City to negotiate the purchase of California. Perhaps he could bully the Mexicans into a sale, or else bait them into firing the first shot in a war Polk was sure the United States would win. Either alternative was acceptable to him. The navy secretary sent instructions to Commodore John D. Sloat of the Pacific Squadron, which included a dozen warships, half the entire U.S. Navy: once he had "ascertained with certainty" that Mexico and the United States were at war, he was to sail to California and occupy its ports.

★

Polk had another trick up his sleeve. Sooner or later, he believed, American settlers in California would "play the Texas game," as Hastings suggested in his book. Perhaps Polk could push that along. In the spring of 1845 he met with Captain John Charles Frémont of the Army Corps of Topographical Engineers. Previously, Frémont had led two expeditions exploring the far West, and had published a best-selling account of his adventures that made his reputation as the nation's "Pathfinder." He was about to embark on another trip, exploring and mapping the eastern flank of the Rockies. But Polk gave him secret orders to head directly to California. The president provided "no distinct course or definite instruction," Frémont recalled years later, but "the *probabilities* were made known to me as well as what to do when they became *facts*. . . . I was given discretion to act."

Following a swift march across the continent, Frémont and his company of sixty heavily armed men arrived in California in December 1845. He visited Monterey and paid his respects to Comandante Castro and former governor Alvarado. Both men were unnerved by the arrival of an American army officer in command of an armed company. But merchant Thomas O. Larkin, whom President Tyler had appointed American consul to California, vouched for the young officer. Larkin enjoyed good relations with the Californio leaders, so, taking

Larkin's word for it, Castro gave Frémont permission to graze his horses in the Central Valley, a considerable distance from the capital, before moving on. But for the next two months Frémont and his men loitered in the countryside outside Monterey. He was stalling for time, waiting for probabilities to become facts.

Fed up, Castro ordered the Americans out of California. Frémont, whose impulses often got the better of him, took offense, threw up a defensive encampment, and defiantly raised the American flag. Outraged at this display of contempt for Mexican sovereignty, Castro issued a proclamation calling on fellow Californios to join him in evicting Frémont's "band of robbers." Several hundred rancheros and vaqueros responded, besieging the Americans. "We will die, every man of us, under the flag of our country," Frémont declared melodramatically. But instead he retreated to Sutter's Fort, where American settlers greeted him as a conquering hero. That demonstration of sentiment worried the Californios far more than Frémont's bravado.

★

Not long after this confrontation, Comandante Castro convened a meeting of Californio officials to consider their options. Considerable rivalry and distrust existed between Castro and Governor Pío Pico in Los Angeles, and Pico refused to attend. But virtually all the prominent men of the north were present, including Castro's lifelong associates, Juan Bautista Alvarado and Mariano Guadalupe Vallejo.

Castro opened the proceedings with an address. "We find ourselves suddenly threatened by hordes of Yankee emigrants," he began.

> Already have the wagons of that perfidious people
> scaled the almost inaccessible summits of the Sierra
> Nevada, crossed the entire continent, and pene-

> trated the fruitful valley of the Sacramento. What
> that astonishing people will next undertake, I can-
> not say. . . . We cannot successfully oppose them
> by our own unaided power, and the swelling tide of
> emigration renders the odds against us more formi-
> dable every day.

Without troops and arms, or the ships to transport them, Mexico was powerless. Their only hope, Castro declared, was to request the protection of Great Britain or France. "Is it not better that one of them should be invited to send a fleet and an army to defend and protect California, rather than we should fall an easy prey to the lawless adventurers who are overrun-ning our beautiful country?"

Don Mariano rose in disagreement. "We are republicans," he declared, and would chafe under the rule of a foreign king. He dared his colleagues to consider a more radical alternative: "annexation to the United States."

> Why should we shrink from incorporating ourselves
> with the happiest and freest nation in the world,
> destined soon to be the most wealthy and power-
> ful? Why should we go abroad for protection when
> this great nation is our adjoining neighbor? When
> we join our fortunes to hers, we shall not become
> subjects, but fellow-citizens. . . . Look not, there-
> fore, with jealousy upon the hardy pioneers who
> scale our mountains and cultivate our unoccupied
> plains; but rather welcome them as brothers, who
> come to share with us a common destiny.

Vallejo had long admired the United States. His vision of a "common destiny" was a beautiful dream, but one that would depend on the good faith of the Americans. Consul Larkin promoted the idea of peaceful annexation with the Californios, and many of them shared Vallejo's hopes. But Castro viewed the Americans as perfidious actors who could not be trusted. The meeting adjourned with no consensus. Fearing that Frémont would return to Monterey reinforced by los rifleros americanos, Castro issued orders for his meager forces to assemble in defense of the capital.

★

While Californios were deliberating in Monterey, things were coming to a head in Washington, D.C. Envoy John Slidell reported from Mexico City that the Mexicans refused to sell California. "Depend upon it," he wrote President Polk, "we can never get along well with them until we have given them a good drubbing." Polk agreed. Achieving his goal of a continental nation would require a war. But he needed a *casus belli,* a justification. Mexico's refusal to surrender its national territory to the United States was not a defensible reason for war.

General Taylor's army was encamped along the Gulf coast, on the north bank of the Nueces River, the traditional southern boundary of the Mexican province of Tejas. The state of Texas, however, claimed jurisdiction over territory that extended another hundred miles south to the Río Grande, a region known as the "Nueces Strip." Polk decided to incite the Mexicans into a violent response by ordering Taylor to occupy this disputed territory. General Taylor marched his army south and built a rough fortification directly across the Río Grande from the Mexican town of Matamoros. The Mexicans denounced the move as an act of war and demanded Taylor's withdrawal, but he refused.

On April 25, 1846, a detachment of Mexican cavalry crossed the Río Grande and attacked an American patrol, killing sixteen dragoons. News of the deadly skirmish, which reached

Polk two weeks later, gave him the justification he needed. He sent a war message to Congress. "Mexico has passed the boundary of the United States, has invaded our territory and shed American blood upon the American soil," he declared. That was, of course, a matter of interpretation. But on May 13 Congress overwhelmingly declared war with Mexico.

Two weeks later Commodore Sloat, anchored with the Pacific Squadron at the Mexican Pacific port of Mazatlán, received a secondhand report of the fighting along the border. But had war been declared? Fearful of repeating the error of his predecessor, Commodore Jones, Sloat hesitated. Finally, after waiting a week, he received word that the American navy had blockaded the Mexican port of Vera Cruz, a clear act of war. With that, Sloat set sail for California.

★

That same day, June 7, 1846, William B. Ide, a pious fifty-year-old Mormon farmer with a wife and five children, received a copy of a letter circulating among American settlers on the Sacramento River. "Notice is hereby given," it read, "that a large body of armed Spaniards on horseback, amounting to 250 men, have been seen on their way to the Sacramento Valley, destroying the crops, burning the houses, and driving off the cattle. Capt. Frémont invites every freeman in the valley to come to his camp at the Buttes immediately." Those assertions were boldfaced lies. There was no large body of armed men approaching, no destruction of crops, no burning of houses, no driving off of livestock. But the claims made effective propaganda. Frémont's notice, wrote settler John Bidwell, "was simply a pretense to justify the premature beginning of the war."

Two days later, Ide joined several dozen settlers at Frémont's camp where the young officer addressed them. The danger was real, he said, lying through his teeth. They must not wait for Castro to attack, but should seize the initiative, striking at the presidio in Sonoma and taking General Vallejo hostage. Frémont hoped to provoke Castro into striking the first blow, providing him—as it had provided President Polk—with a justification for violence. Ide objected that the plan would tarnish American honor, but Frémont cut him off. He would not tolerate such talk. The die was cast and they must act decisively or be destroyed. Ide suddenly realized that none of the other Americans shared his reservations. We must all stand together, he resolved; "we are too few for division." He joined a band of several dozen men who set out for Sonoma to engage the enemy.

Most of these men had been in California for no more than a year or two, having come from Kentucky and Tennessee, Missouri and Arkansas. Two-thirds were under the age of thirty. "Some were settlers, some hunters," John Bidwell observed. "Some were good men, and some about as rough specimens of humanity as it would be possible to find anywhere." Virtually all believed in their God-given right to seize and settle lands occupied by others, be they Native, Mexican, or Californio. Bidwell himself had come across the plains and mountains with precisely that intention. "To take the country," wrote Bidwell, "that was what sent me to California." But after becoming acquainted with individual Californios, he had a change of heart. "I shudder," he wrote some years later, "that I ever entertained the idea of making a kill upon a people who have never done me any harm."

★

The Americans arrived at Sonoma at dawn on the morning of June 14. The town was undefended, most of the garrison having gone south in response to Castro's call to defend Monterey. They surrounded the Vallejo residence as a small delegation of the oldest men, including William Ide, pounded on the front door. Don Mariano and his wife were still in bed. "I looked out of my bedroom window and to my great surprise I made out groups of armed men," he later recalled. Doña Francisca urged him to flee by the back door, but he refused, fearing the consequences if he left her alone to face the Americans.

In dressing gown and slippers, he invited the delegation into his parlor and asked what he could do for them. They had risen in rebellion, they declared, fed up with Mexican domination and determined to establish a new regime based on "republican principles." They had come to take him prisoner. Struggling to keep his composure, Don Mariano asked to speak with their leader. We have no leader, they insisted; "we are all heads!" But he noted that they kept making reference to Captain Frémont and seemed to be operating under his instructions. Trusting that an American officer and gentleman would do the right thing, he agreed to submit to arrest, along with his brother Salvador, his brother-in-law, and his secretary.

Outside, the young Americans were passing a bottle and growing rowdy. Don Mariano heard them shouting, "Get the loot! Get the loot!" The older men attempted to restore order, addressing the group from the Vallejo veranda. "Choose ye this day what you will be!" shouted William Ide. "We are robbers, or we must be conquerors!" His curious turn of phrase seemed to calm the young men. While a small group escorted Don Mariano and the other prisoners back to Frémont's camp, the rest of the company secured control of Sonoma.

The men chose Ide to draft a statement laying out their justification for rebellion. American settlers, Ide wrote, had been "invited into this country by a promise of lands on which to settle themselves and families." Mexican officials had assured them that California enjoyed a "republican government." Instead, they had been oppressed by a "military despotism" and denied an opportunity to purchase land. They were determined "to overthrow a government which has ruined and shamefully oppressed the laboring people of California." Pure nonsense, every word. Since no such promises or assurances had been made by any Mexican or Californio official, they could not possibly have been broken.

The rebels decided they needed a banner. They did not have the authority to raise the stars and stripes, so they devised a crude flag of their own, featuring a lone star and a single stripe, the words "California Republic," and the silhouette of a grizzly bear. "The Mexicans said it looked more like a hog than a bear and laughed about it," recalled one of the rebels. The flag lent its name to their cause: the Bear Flag Rebellion. The rebels became known as the Bears. To Don Mariano, it was an ironic choice. Californios considered grizzlies a menace to livestock; by adopting the animal as their emblem, the Americans labeled themselves the party of "rapine and violence."

When Don Mariano arrived at Frémont's camp, he demanded to know by what authority he and his associates had been arrested. Frémont denied all responsibility, declaring that the rebels had acted on their own initiative. He refused to ensure the safety of the hostages, ordering them placed in the custody of Sutter, Don Mariano's bitter rival, who locked the prisoners in a dark chamber with neither beds nor blankets. "Sutter no doubt thought that since we had lost our liberty we had also ceased to retain our dignity," Don Mariano wrote in his memoirs. "God decreed that the month of June 1846 should be the blackest month of my life." But June stretched into July and then well into August, with the prisoners still confined at Sutter's Fort.

On July 2, Commodore Sloat arrived at Monterey Bay. Still concerned that he was repeating the mistake of his predecessor Jones, he refused to send his men ashore. Meanwhile, Consul Thomas Larkin attempted to persuade the Californios to voluntarily place their homeland under American authority.

But Don Mariano's imprisonment made a peaceful transfer impossible. "The North American nation can never be our friend," Governor Pío Pico declared when he received news of the rebellion. "She has stolen the Department of Texas and now wishes to do the same with California." All hope that California might join the United States through negotiation rather than war ended with the Bear Flag Rebellion. "Frémont, and he alone, is to be credited," wrote John Bidwell. "Upon him rests all the responsibility."

FRÉMONT + PICO SIGN THE TREATY

17

The Horrors of War

Commodore John Drake Sloat spent his sixty-fifth birthday, July 6, 1846, aboard his flagship, the frigate USS *Savannah,* anchored in Monterey. He had little to celebrate. Suffering from rheumatism and a problematic liver, he had several months before asked to be relieved of his command, and he now anxiously awaited the arrival of his replacement. In the meantime he was facing the most challenging situation of his long naval career. His instructions to seize California included the caution that he preserve "the most friendly relations with the inhabitants." Conquer and befriend. That combination would be difficult to pull off.

In the days following the invasion of Sonoma, the "Bears" under Frémont's command engaged in several skirmishes with the Californios. Lives were lost on both sides, and neither was in a mood to negotiate. Sloat, cautious by nature and lacking a clear understanding of the situation on the ground, followed the advice of Consul Larkin and kept his men aboard ship for several days after his arrival on July 2. But Larkin had no luck persuading Californio officials to surrender. They used the time to evacuate the capital and regroup in the interior.

Finally, under intense pressure from his own officers, who were eager for action, Sloat decided he could wait no longer. On the morning of July 7, a force of 250 sailors and Marines went ashore and raised the flag. "We must take the place," Sloat told Larkin. "I shall be blamed for doing too little or too much—I prefer the latter." In fact, Sloat's delay had already ruined his reputation. The secretary of the navy later characterized his caution as "shameful," and for the remainder of his career fellow officers ridiculed him as "Grandma Sloat."

Sloat issued a proclamation addressed to the Californios. He came in arms, he wrote, yet he hoped they would consider him their friend. He guaranteed the personal safety of all those who remained peacefully in their homes. He also promised the full benefits of United States citizenship for those who chose to remain in California, and the right to remove their families and personal property without hindrance for those who wished to leave for Mexico. Sloat wrote personal letters to Governor Pío Pico and Comandante José Castro in the same spirit, demanding their surrender but also inviting them to meet with him to negotiate articles of capitulation, promising to receive them "with all the respect due to your distinguished situation." Their compliance, he wrote, would "prevent the sacrifice of human life and the horrors of war, which I most anxiously desire to avoid."

Sloat said nothing about the hostile exploits of the Bears. He had yet to meet with Frémont and was reluctant to make any public declaration before he did so. Comandante Castro responded that he would not negotiate until Sloat assured him that Frémont's men were under his command and control. Former governor Juan Bautista Alvarado made the same point in a note to Consul Larkin, a friend for many years. While he joined in the hope that the conflict might be peacefully resolved, he wrote, national honor demanded that Frémont's underhanded insurrection in Sonoma be avenged.

In this moment of crisis, Alvarado continued, he could not help but reflect on his many years of public service to California. "The history of your country holds in remembrance the efforts of the immortal Washington," he told Larkin. "Although I know myself unworthy to compare with that hero, I would desire you to have the goodness to be the judge and decide what you would do in my case." By the time Larkin read those melancholy words, Alvarado and Castro had departed for the south with a small number of defenders, planning to join forces with Governor Pico. As they had in the past, the Californios would make their stand at Los Angeles, this time against the Americans.

★

Frémont arrived at Monterey on July 14 with more than two hundred Bears, a force he christened "the California Battalion." He found Sloat in a sour mood. "I want to know by what authority you are acting," the commodore demanded. He assumed the young captain had official instructions. Frémont, who may have been under orders not to reveal his private conversation with President Polk, responded defensively. "I acted on my own responsibility," he said, "without any authority from the government." Sloat's jaw dropped. American military officers simply did not conduct armed operations against foreign countries on their own hook. He angrily terminated the interview.

Frémont feared he would be sacked. But the following day, Captain Robert F. Stockton, Sloat's replacement, arrived in Monterey. The contrast between the two naval commanders could not have been more striking. Sloat felt his years;

Stockton flaunted his youthful energy. Sloat acted cautiously, Stockton impulsively. Sloat worried over doing the right thing with the Californios; Stockton believed "Americans should rule America." Sloat wished to leave California behind; Stockton itched to assume command. They quickly accomplished the transfer of power, and within days Sloat was homeward bound.

Stockton called Frémont to his quarters, listened sympathetically to his account, and offered an enthusiastic endorsement of everything the young officer had done. He mustered the California Battalion into service and enlisted Frémont as his second in command. Together they made plans to attack southern California. Stockton then issued a fire-breathing proclamation of his own. Sloat had addressed California's leaders with respect, but Stockton branded them as "criminals" whom he would hunt down and punish. Comandante Castro, he declared, had "violated every principle of international law and national hospitality by hunting and pursuing Captain Frémont." He warned Californios to remain in their homes or "be treated as enemies and suffer accordingly." Frémont gloated. As one of his subordinate officers put it, with Stockton in charge there would be no more of Sloat's "halfway measures."

★

In Los Angeles, Castro and Pico issued a public statement, boldly vowing to repel the invaders. But they understood their situation. "No matter how great our patriotism," Pico wrote to Mexico City, "we shall never be able to reconquer what is lost nor avoid losing the rest." He and Castro could count on no more than three hundred men, while Stockton commanded more than two thousand sailors and Marines, as well as the California Battalion. Frémont and the Bears sailed for San Diego, which they occupied without firing a shot. Commandeering horses from outlying ranchos, they headed north to Los Angeles. Meanwhile, Stockton landed at San Pedro with several hundred men. Castro, knowing his meager forces could not resist the onslaught, sent a delegation to Stockton under a flag of truce with a proposal for a cease-fire.

Stockton received Captain José María Flores, a Mexican officer on Castro's staff, with insulting disdain. He left the officer and his entourage standing on the beach in the hot summer sun while he retired to his tent to read Castro's message and compose a response. Reemerging, he handed Flores a sealed message. "I will either take the country or be licked out of it," he exclaimed, then dismissed the Mexican officer with a flick of his wrist. Flores was deeply offended, as was Castro when he read Stockton's reply. The commodore refused the request for a cease-fire. He would press the fight until California was no longer part of Mexico. The only alternative to war was unconditional surrender. "If you will agree to hoist the American flag in California, I will stop my forces and negotiate the treaty."

Castro replied in anger. "You offer me the most shameful of propositions, to hoist the American flag in this department. Never, never, never!" Stockton might succeed in raising his banner over Los Angeles, but "it will not be by my acquiescence, nor by that of my compatriots, but solely by force." Stockton's refusal to negotiate, Castro warned, "makes you responsible for all the evils and misfortunes that may result from a war so unjust." This exchange, Juan Bautista Alvarado later wrote, marked the point of no return. "If Stockton had sent a commission to confer with Castro, a treaty satisfactory to both sides might have been arranged."

Retreat, Castro and Pico concluded, was their only option. Better to withdraw honorably to Mexico than to accept defeat at Los Angeles. Pico delivered an impromptu farewell address to the legislature. "My friends, farewell," he said through bitter tears. "I abandon the country of my birth, my family, property, and everything that a man holds most dear." There would be hard days ahead, but he placed his trust in the courage and loyalty of his fellow Californios. "The Supreme Being that guards over the future destiny of nations will provide us the glorious day in which we shall again see our dear Fatherland free and happy." The legislature then adjourned what proved to be its final session. That night a stream of functionaries, officers, and common soldiers abandoned Los Angeles, leaving the residents to their fate.

★

Stockton and Frémont, leading several hundred Americans, occupied Los Angeles on August 13. "My word is at present the law of the land," Stockton wrote to President Polk, "my person is more than regal." He issued a proclamation declaring California a territory of the United States and placing it under martial law. All civil and military officials remaining in the department were required to swear an oath agreeing not to take up arms against the United States before being paroled on their honor. Stockton immediately began planning an assault on Mexico's Pacific ports. When he departed for that campaign, he told his subordinates, Frémont would become California's military governor. In early September both Stockton and Frémont, along with most of their men, returned to Monterey, leaving Los Angeles under the command of Marine Lieutenant Archibald Gillespie and a force of fifty Bears.

Los Angeles was the largest settlement in California, with about fifteen hundred residents in the pueblo and an equal number in the surrounding countryside, as well as three or four thousand Christian Natives living in their own communities. Gillespie's force was small and weak, but he administered martial law with a heavy hand, enforcing a sundown-to-sunset curfew, prohibiting all public gatherings, and arresting Californios for the most trivial of offenses. It did not take long for the simmering resentment of Angelenos to break out in full-scale revolt.

Before dawn on September 23, a group of young rowdies, fortified by a night of heavy drinking, attacked the American headquarters in the pueblo, provoking a firefight before fleeing into the darkness. Gillespie responded by arresting many paroled military officers, which resulted in an entirely spontaneous uprising. By the afternoon the Americans were surrounded by more than four hundred armed and angry Angelenos. They issued a proclamation. "Shall we permit ourselves to be subjugated and to accept in silence the heavy chain of slavery? No! A thousand times no! Countrymen, death rather than that!" As their commander they chose Captain José María Flores, the officer Stockton had insulted at San Pedro. Rather than fleeing to Mexico, Flores had chosen to remain in Los Angeles with his California-born wife and children.

Gillespie and the Bears withstood a four-day siege before finally surrendering. The Angelenos marched them under heavy guard to San Pedro, where they boarded an American merchant vessel. Los Angeles was back in Californio hands. Gillespie had already dispatched a mounted messenger to Stockton in Monterey, so instead of sailing away as he had promised to do, he remained anchored off the coast, awaiting the arrival of reinforcements. When Stockton received Gillespie's call for help, he vowed to crush the Los Angeles rebels. "We go this time to punish as well as to conquer," he declared. If he found that a single American had been harmed by the insurgents he would "wade knee-deep in his own blood to avenge it."

★

Stockton took a flotilla south with several hundred men, ordering Frémont to remain and secure the countryside surrounding Monterey. Resistance to the American occupiers came from ordinary rancheros and vaqueros. In early October, sixty or seventy of them turned back an assault from San Pedro by four hundred American sailors and Marines, an engagement that claimed the lives of several fighters on both sides. Stockton retreated to San Diego, where he prepared for another assault on Los Angeles. In the north, meanwhile, Californios attacked a detachment of the California Battalion near Monterey, killing three men and forcing Frémont onto the defensive.

For the Americans, the worst was yet to come. At the onset of the war with Mexico, President Polk had ordered an army under the command of General Stephen Watts Kearny to proceed across the plains to secure New Mexico. After successfully occupying Santa Fe, Kearny pressed on to California with an elite force of a hundred dragoons. Fording the Colorado at the Quechan crossing, they followed a trail across the desert and mountains. In early December, in a valley known as San Pasqual, about thirty miles northeast of San Diego, they challenged a force of mounted Californios under the command of Andrés Pico, Governor Pico's brother. In the ensuing fight, Californio lancers mauled the Americans, killing twenty-two dragoons, nearly a quarter of Kearny's force.

But while the Californios could win battles, they could not win the war. The American superiority in arms and men was simply too much for them. Kearny and his surviving dragoons made it to San Diego where they joined Stockton's "webfoot infantry" of sailors and Marines. The commodore and the general both aspired to overall command, but Stockton, with the larger force, prevailed for the moment. Finally, at the end of December, the motley army of more than five hundred men, hauling heavy artillery taken from the warships, began the march north to Los Angeles, following the old trail that linked the missions.

As they approached their destination they were met by a delegation with a message from Captain José María Flores requesting a cease-fire. He hoped to avoid "the useless effusion of human blood," Flores wrote. But once again Stockton refused to negotiate. Flores had violated his parole and "could not be treated as an honorable man," Stockton later recalled. "I had no answer to return to his communication but this— that if I caught him I should shoot him." The Americans triumphed in two final battles fought on the outskirts of Los Angeles, and on January 10 they retook possession of the pueblo.

★

In the meantime, Frémont's California Battalion was riding south from Monterey. Formerly an enthusiast of Stockton's blood-and-thunder style, Frémont now viewed his impending governorship as reason to adopt a more conciliatory approach, and he ordered his men "to abstain from any further offensive proceedings against the Californians." Nearing Los Angeles, they were met by a delegation bearing the same cease-fire request that Stockton had rejected. "We are ready to abandon this strife," the Californios told Frémont, "to submit and live peaceably under the laws." Stockton had refused to treat them as honorable men, they said, threatening to shoot their leaders on sight. If Frémont took the same approach, they were prepared "to take to the hills and make a guerrilla war of it." Sensing an opportunity for himself, Frémont agreed to negotiate.

Captain Flores and most of the Mexican officers had retreated to Mexico, leaving Californio Andrés Pico in charge. On January 13, Frémont and Pico met at Cahuenga Pass, a place of profound significance for Californios, the site where twice before they had succeeded in overthrowing Mexican governors. The Californios would lay down their arms, Pico agreed. Frémont in turn pledged protection of their lives and property, as well as the promise of equal rights with all American citizens—essentially the same terms offered by Commodore Sloat six months earlier, before all the bloodshed. Frémont was a consummate opportunist, but this was his finest hour.

He was, however, about to overplay his hand. Neither Stockton nor Kearny knew anything of the treaty until Frémont and the Bears rode into Los Angeles the following day. The audacity of this junior officer shocked them more than the liberal terms of the treaty. But realizing that the alternative to a cease-fire was a guerrilla insurgency, they endorsed it. In fact, both commanders were more preoccupied with the conflict between themselves over who was to rule California, and Frémont immediately became a pawn in their game.

General Kearny insisted that as an officer in the U.S. Army, Frémont take orders from him. But lured by Stockton's promise of the governorship, Frémont decided to cast his lot with the navy commodore. It proved a bad call. When instructions arrived from Washington, it was Kearny who won command of California. Stockton returned to Washington with his tail between his legs. Frémont's final bit of opportunism ended in court-martial, conviction, and a dishonorable exit from military service.

JENNIE WIMMER + HER SOAP KETTLE

18

Gold from the American River

On February 2, 1848, representatives of the United States and Mexico signed the Treaty of Guadalupe Hidalgo, ending the war. President Polk had predicted a short, easy struggle, but the conflict had worn on for nearly two years and cost the lives of 13,238 Americans and at least 25,000 Mexicans.

The previous September, an American army, having fought its way over two hundred miles of mountainous terrain, had captured Mexico City in hard fighting. The treaty negotiations then dragged on for months as Mexican authorities resisted the partition of their country. In the end, however, they reluctantly agreed to cede the northern half of their national domain to the United States, an area that included Texas as well as a huge region that would become the states of New Mexico, Arizona, Colorado, Utah, Nevada, and California. The United States paid Mexico $15 million and agreed to cover $5 million in Mexican debts to American creditors. The war itself cost the nation $75 million, the equivalent of about 4 percent of the output of the U.S. economy in 1848. A comparable figure in 2020 would be about $850 billion. That's real money, but nonetheless a bargain for all that land.

The treaty stipulated that Mexican residents who chose to remain in the ceded territory would automatically become citizens of the United States, "maintained and protected in the free enjoyment of their liberty and property, and secured in the free exercise of their religion." Until Congress established a territorial government, however, California would remain under military rule.

Soon the Californio officials who fled to Mexico during the war began returning to their ranchos, former governor Pío Pico and Comandante José Antonio Castro prominent among them. Juan Bautista Alvarado and Mariano Guadalupe Vallejo emerged from self-imposed seclusion. American authorities kept a close eye on them all. "The people dislike the change of flags," noted military governor Colonel Richard Mason; but "California seems to be as quiet as possible." Governor Mason commanded only fifteen hundred soldiers and sailors and his men were "pretty well stretched out," he acknowledged. But, he wrote, "we must keep up a show of troops, however small in numbers." Mason felt ready for any Californio unrest. For what was about to happen, however, he was completely unprepared.

★

On January 24, 1848, as Elizabeth "Jennie" Wimmer stirred a large kettle of boiling soap over an open fire, her eight-year-old son Martin came running. "Here, mama," he shouted, "here's something Mr. Marshall and Pa found." Jennie Wimmer did the cooking and laundering for a crew constructing a water-powered sawmill for Johann August Sutter. James Marshall and her husband, Peter Wimmer, supervised the operation, located on the South Fork of the American River, in the foothills of the Sierra Nevada, about forty miles northeast of Sutter's Fort. The Nisenans (NEE-sha-non), Native residents, knew the area as Coloma, meaning "beautiful valley." It remains one of the state's loveliest locations.

That morning, while inspecting the mill race, Marshall found several small nuggets of yellow metal. "Boys, I believe I've found a gold mine," he exclaimed. "I reckon not," one of the men replied, "no such luck." Wimmer suggested that Marshall show the nuggets to his wife. When she was a child in northern Georgia she had panned for gold during a short-lived mining rush there. She would know gold when she saw it.

Years later, Mrs. Wimmer recalled taking the nugget in hand. About the size of the tip of her thumb, it weighed less than an ounce and resembled, she said, "a piece of spruce gum just out of the mouth of a schoolgirl." She rubbed its indented surface. "I'll throw it into my kettle," she said. "If it's gold, it will be gold when it comes out." Later, when the soap had cooled and hardened, she scooped it out. Several men crowded around, eager to see. The nugget lay at the bottom of the kettle, "as bright as it could be." Marshall sent his excited crew back to work while he took the other samples to Sutter. He told Mrs. Wimmer she could keep the nugget.

Jennie Wimmer's soap kettle was the epicenter of the earthquake known as the California gold rush, one of those rare human events that fracture the flow of history, opening a chasm between what came before and what came after. As the news spread, gold seekers from all over the globe began to pour into California by the tens of thousands. California's population (excluding Natives) would explode from about 14,000 in 1848 to more than 120,000 in September 1850, when California entered the union of states. Miners would overrun Native homelands, with catastrophic consequences for thousands of people. Gold would thrust California into the speculative capitalist economy, producing boom, then bust. Some Californians would become fabulously wealthy. The vast majority would not.

★

Sutter gave his men permission to hunt for gold in their spare time, but soon they were doing nothing else. At first they simply gathered nuggets. But when the supply grew thin, they began digging in the sandbars along the river. From folks with some experience, like Jennie Wimmer, they learned how to use flat tin pans or waterproof Native baskets to "wash" the "pay dirt," swilling off the lighter sand and gravel, leaving the heavier gold fragments. It was no picnic, squatting for hours at the edge of a stream, ice-cold snowmelt up to your ankles and the California sun beating down on your shoulders. "I never knew what hard work was until I came here," said one miner. "No man can pick up gold, even here, without the very hardest labor, and that's a fact." Miners began using homemade "cradles," wooden sluice boxes on rockers, more efficient at sifting and separating the gold dust.

Soon, gold seekers spread out. Upstream, they found even richer deposits. Millions of years before, when tectonic forces lifted the granite slab of the Sierra Nevada, molten silica and heavy metals bubbled up from the earth's core, filling fractures and fissures in the rock and forming gold-laden veins of quartz. Over millennia, erosion washed the granite, quartz, and gold downstream, creating what Spanish-speakers called "placers" or sandbars. Prospectors were soon finding gold along nearly all the rivers and streams draining the western slope of the Sierras, as well as the Trinity River of the Klamath Range in the north.

Reports began filtering back to the coast. Governor Mason was shown a sample of gold nuggets, but he kept his attention focused on his assignment, suppressing all potential unrest among the Californios. In the town of San Francisco (formerly Yerba Buena), two weekly newspapers printed short notices of Marshall's discovery, but the news created little excitement among the several hundred seamen, ship captains, and merchant traders residing there.

Some men saw the potential, however. One was Samuel Brannan, a twenty-something son of Irish immigrants who had come to California by sailing ship in 1846, leading a group of Mormon settlers. Brannan soon left the church, preferring to devote himself to business, including a general store he operated near Sutter's Fort. Learning about the gold discovery when his customers began paying with gold nuggets, he quietly bought up all the digging tools, tin ware, and blankets he could find in San Francisco, then set out for Coloma to investigate. Astounded by the frenzied activity he found, he arranged for the construction of a warehouse and sent word to have his stock of goods sent upriver.

Brannan's return to San Francisco became the stuff of legend. Stepping off the ferry, he lifted a small bottle filled with gold dust in one hand and, swinging his hat with the other, walked down Market Street, shouting at the top of his voice: "Gold! Gold! Gold from the American River!" The effect was dramatic. Within days, throngs of men had left for "the diggings," and within weeks San Francisco was virtually deserted. Brannan's timing was perfect. "Within the last year," he wrote to relatives, "I have cleared over a hundred thousand dollars." Brannan became the first gold rush millionaire, setting the pattern for those who followed—making their pile not by mining gold but by selling goods at vastly inflated prices to those who did.

★

By early summer the news had spread to southern California. "Every seaport as far south as San Diego, and every interior town, and nearly every rancho has become suddenly drained of human beings," the *California Star* of San Francisco reported. Californios, Mexicans, and Americans all headed for the diggings. They found hundreds of miners already at work, many of them Natives from the surrounding area.

The gold region was located in the traditional homelands of a score of Native peoples, including Nisenans, Maidus, and Miwoks in the Sierras, Shastas, Hupas, and Yuroks in the north. Ranchers of the Sacramento Valley relied on Native laborers to tend livestock, harvest crops, and cook and clean, and putting them to work mining gold was relatively easy. Natives quickly caught on, and soon hundreds were working the streams for themselves.

American soldiers and sailors deserted their posts, making Governor Mason's mission all the more difficult. In late June of 1848 he toured the diggings and dispatched a report to Washington. He found the hillsides along the rivers and streams thick with canvas tents and brush huts. At least four thousand men, he estimated, were working the placers, half of them Native Californians. On average, each man collected two or three ounces of gold per day, valued at $16 an ounce ($550 in 2020 values). Provisions sold for outrageous prices. "The discovery of these vast deposits of gold," Mason concluded, "has entirely changed the character of Upper California."

First word of the discovery reached the eastern United States in late summer. Newspapers printed letters from California making claims that sounded so outrageous, most readers dismissed them. But in his annual message to Congress in December, President Polk confirmed the discovery. "The accounts of abundance of gold," he announced, "are of such an extraordinary character as would scarcely command belief were they not corroborated by the authentic reports of officers in the public service." Not long after, the first shipment of

California gold arrived in Washington and went on public display. The California gold rush was about to begin.

★

The "forty-niners" came from all over the globe. Over plains and mountains, around Cape Horn or across the Isthmus of Panama, some sixty thousand Americans traveled to California in the spring of 1849. Another twenty thousand individuals came from around the Pacific rim—Mexico, Peru, Chile, Hawai'i, the Philippines, China. Late in the year the first Europeans arrived. By 1854, three hundred thousand gold seekers were crowded into a relatively small portion of California.

In part, men were drawn by the opportunity to see the world, to break away from the ordinary and routine. In the parlance of the day, the gold rush offered a chance "to see the elephant," a phrase that originated in a popular American story. A farmer drives his wagon into town to see the circus, and on his way encounters the circus parade, led by the elephant. His terrified horses buck, pitch, and overturn the wagon. When the disheveled farmer returns home, his wife asks how he liked the show. "Didn't get there," he replies with a crooked smile, "but I've seen the elephant!" The analogy is revealing for what it suggests about expectations. The gold might prove elusive, but oh, the thrill of the rush!

Much more important, however, were the economic motives. The United States was awash with thousands of dislocated and unemployed men, including many veterans of the late war with Mexico. The prevailing wage for laborers was a dollar a day, and a twelve-hour day at that. Yet jobs were scarce. The economy had been on the skids since the panic of 1837. Low prices for cotton and other farm commodities made for hard times in the countryside. The California discovery offered hope that an ordinary man, possessing a few simple tools and a willingness to work, could accumulate a small fortune through his own effort, then buy a farm, open a shop, or purchase a small business.

But the notion of California as a paradise for the free worker ignored the reality on the ground. Hundreds of Native Californians labored under the harsh supervision of ranchers. "The Indians of California make as obedient and humble slaves as the Negroes in the South," wrote rancher Pierson Reading, who supervised a large contingent of Native miners. Southern masters dragged hundreds of enslaved African Americans to California. Men from Latin America, Hawai'i, and China came as indentured workers. There was plenty of unfree labor in gold rush California.

★

And there were relatively few women. Single men in their twenties made up the largest group of miners. Married men usually left their wives at home. Jennie Wimmer was the only White woman in Coloma until the arrival of several families in the summer of 1848. In 1850 the federal census enumerator listed 585 men and 46 women living there. That's thirteen males for every female, a typical sex ratio for the gold diggings.

Those women attracted a great deal of attention. A grizzled miner approached Luzena Wilson, one of the few married women to come overland with her husband and children, as she prepared a meal over the campfire. "I'll give you five dollars, ma'am, for them biscuit," he drawled. She hesitated, not knowing what to say, and he quickly upped the offer. "Ten dollars for bread made by a woman!" Another miner recorded in his diary how his heart "leaped with joy" one evening when he heard "the voice of a pretty girl raised in song."

Virtually every mining camp included prostitutes. The 1850 census found a total of eleven single women in Coloma, five in one dwelling, six in another a few doors away, both in the center of town, next to a saloon and restaurant. Brothels, surely. The women, ranging in age from seventeen to thirty, hailed from Canada, Ireland, Chile, Mexico, and the United States.

The Wimmers had migrated from rural Missouri in 1846 with their six children, crossing the Sierras only a few days ahead of the Donner Party. Her traveling companions described Jenny Wimmer as lively and pretty, with auburn hair and blue eyes. In a daguerreotype taken in the early 1850s, Peter Wimmer is dark and handsome, with a thick, full beard. Upon their arrival in California, he enlisted in Frémont's California Battalion, leaving his wife to fend for herself with the children. She was pregnant at the time. He returned just before the baby's birth, nursing an injury that left him permanently disabled. Fortunately, he found work with Sutter.

After the gold discovery, the Wimmers spent some time mining. But despite being among the very first on the ground, they failed to strike it rich—though they did gather gold enough to buy a little farm in Coloma where they lived for many years, raising hogs and orchard fruit. Mrs. Wimmer kept the original nugget in a tiny leather sack that hung from a chain she wore around her neck. But years later, approaching old age and down on their luck, the couple decided to sell it. The nugget eventually became part of the collection at the Bancroft Library of the University of California at Berkeley, where it is on display, as brilliant today as the morning Jennie Wimmer pulled it from her soap kettle.

DAME SHIRLEY AT THE DIGGINGS

19

A White Republic

The California gold rush drew thousands of men from dozens of nations and threw them together, cheek by jowl. Strolling among the tents and shacks of a mining camp called Indian Bar, Louise Smith Clappe overheard conversations in English, Spanish, French, German, Hawaiian, Cantonese, and Maidu. Indian Bar, she wrote, was "a living polyglot of languages, a perambulating picture-gallery illustrative of national variety." Clappe, a Yankee woman who resided in the diggings for several months with her physician husband, published an account of her observations under the pen name "Dame Shirley." The miners, she wrote, were "wanderers from the whole wide earth," assembled for "the golden harvest." White men from "the States" were in the majority, but just barely. How would they respond to such ethnic and racial diversity?

California had no government of any kind. Journalist Bayard Taylor expected to find "a state of things little short of anarchy." But instead, as he wrote in a best-selling account, he found the miners taking charge, holding meetings, and choosing representatives who adopted "rules for mutual security—rules adapted to their situation." With "fiery energy and impulsive spirit," Taylor wrote, they organized more than five hundred mining districts, each with its own codes for staking claims and arbitrating disputes. The United States was a democratic republic, and over the previous half century the individual states had lifted barriers to voting. American men had plenty of experience with self-government. California, Taylor believed, would become "the most democratic country in the world."

But most miners were transients. "Not one out of ten thousand then in California thought seriously of making the Pacific Coast his continual abiding place," wrote Cornelius Cole, who settled in the state and later became a U.S. senator. "All men were sojourners and everybody habitually talked about going home." Historian J. S. Holliday estimates that between 1849 and 1852, ninety thousand men returned to the eastern states by the Panama route. Many of those who remained demanded anonymity. As people later said about Las Vegas, what happened in California remained in California. "Nobody asks who you are or where you come from," said a Frenchman. "You take the name that suits you." Men who refuse to use their own names don't make the best citizens.

★

Absent the restraining influence of home and community, many miners drank to excess, consorted with prostitutes, brawled in public, and openly carried Bowie knives and Colt revolvers. Dame Shirley, who wrote affectionately about individual miners, was appalled by their general conduct. "The swearing, drinking, gambling and fighting," she complained, "is truly horrible."

Despite a good deal of sentimental nonsense about how well the miners got along, crime and violence were everyday occurrences. With no sheriffs, no courts, no jails, how did they administer justice? Small disagreements they settled among themselves, often with their fists. Serious wrongdoing—robbery, assault, homicide—they handled with what was known as "popular justice": the accused sometimes tried by a community-selected judge and jury, but more frequently by an assembly of miners, what Dame Shirley termed "their majesties the mob." Penalties were swiftly administered and often severe—confiscation of property, banishment, flogging, ear-cropping, or hanging. Things often got out of hand. As Dame Shirley put it, "justice in the hands of a mob is at best a fearful thing."

Consider an episode that took place in a mining camp a few miles from Coloma in January 1849. Five men were caught in the act of robbing a gambler. A crowd of two or three hundred men declared them guilty and sentenced them to thirty-nine lashes apiece. Journalist Edward Buffum arrived at the scene as the last of them received his punishment. "I found a large crowd collected around an oak tree," Buffum wrote, "to which was lashed a man with a bared back, while another was applying a raw cowhide to his already gored flesh."

Afterward, as the prisoners lay prostrate, recovering from their ordeal, a miner stepped forward to say that three of them—two Frenchmen and a Chileño—were wanted for robbery and attempted murder in another camp. A second trial immediately commenced, and despite nothing but hearsay evidence, the crowd found them guilty. "They were known to be bad men," wrote Buffum, "and a general sentiment seemed to prevail that they ought to be got rid of." The acting judge asked what punishment should be inflicted? "Hang them!" shouted the crowd.

Buffum was horrified by this miscarriage of justice. "I

mounted a stump, and in the name of God, humanity, and law, protested against such a course," he wrote. "But the crowd, by this time excited by frequent and deep potations of liquor from a neighboring groggery, would listen to nothing contrary to their brutal desires, and even threatened to hang me if I did not immediately desist from any further remarks." Buffum stepped down and watched in silence as several miners bound the prisoners and hoisted them onto the bed of a wagon, placed nooses around their necks, and tossed the ropes over the branch of an oak. The victims desperately protested their innocence in Spanish and French, but the crowd jeered. A rider spurred the horses, the wagon rolled, and the three men, as Buffum put it, "were launched into eternity." The camp became known as Hangtown. Later, in an effort to claim some respectability, residents renamed it Placerville.

★

As the supply of placer gold ran thin, the miners' take fell. In 1849 miners averaged $20 a day, two years later only $10. Gold production peaked in 1852. The mountains held plenty more, locked in veins of quartz, but releasing it required stamping mills or high-pressure jets of water, equipment well beyond the means of most miners. Wealthy investors bought up dozens of claims and organized mining companies. By 1855, the days of placer mining had passed, and independent miners became wage workers. Meanwhile, the cost of basic commodities remained sky high, and much of what workers earned ended up in the pockets of merchants, saloon keepers, and professional gamblers.

Dashed hopes led to rising frustration and anger. As the incident at Hangtown suggests, men perceived as outsiders made easy targets for misplaced blame. "The feeling is very general among the Americans that foreigners should not be allowed to dig for gold," reported the *Alta California,* a San

Francisco newspaper. Mining districts rewrote their rules, prohibiting claims by "foreigners," especially those from Mexico and Latin America. Dame Shirley condemned such measures as "selfish, cruel, and narrow-minded in the extreme." But the war with Mexico had just ended and Americans remained intensely hostile to "greasers," the epithet Americans used for Mexicans. White miners drove several hundred of them from the mines near Coloma. "The disposition to expel them," said the *Placer Times* of Sacramento, "seems to be extending throughout the whole mining community."

Resentful miners also targeted Natives. In 1848, when hundreds of Native miners worked the diggings, there was relatively little conflict with Americans, most of whom had been in California long enough to be familiar with local customs. But the situation changed in early 1849 when the first Americans arrived from Oregon, where violent conflict between settlers and Native communities prevailed. The "Oregon people," said a man who had been in California for several years, "regarded all Indians as their enemies."

The Nisenans, who lived along the American River where the rush for gold began, bore the brunt of the first racial violence. In February, a company of Oregonians attacked one of their villages and force-marched several dozen prisoners to Coloma. Following what a local newspaper described as "a sort of trial," the Whites summarily executed thirty of them. In April another group of Americans raped several Nisenan women, shooting and killing the husbands and brothers who came to their defense. The Nisenans retaliated by killing five Americans at a place afterward known as Murderer's Bar.

The White reaction was swift and deadly. A "posse" attacked an unoffending village, slaughtering residents and seizing several dozen more, who were again driven to Coloma. Witnesses identified seven Nisenan men as the likely perpetrators of the killings at Murderer's Bar. James Marshall, in charge at Sutter's Mill, spoke up for them. They were working for him at the time, he said, and "could not have had anything to do with the killing." Outraged that a White man would defend the Natives, a member of the posse waved a cocked revolver in Marshall's face and told him he had just five minutes to get out of town. Marshall did as he was told, just as Edward Buffum had at Hangtown. The accused Nisenans made a run for it, but the Americans shot and killed them in cold blood. The violence foreshadowed a coming catastrophe. White Americans, experienced in self-governance, put their talent for organization to work persecuting those from other cultures.

★

In 1849 a new military governor, Colonel Bennet C. Riley, arrived in California. To Americans who pressed him to organize a provisional representative government, he insisted that he had no authority to do so. But Congress was deadlocked over the question of slavery in the territory ceded by Mexico, and fearing that violence in the diggings might spread with further delay, Riley finally relented, authorizing a late summer election to choose delegates for a constitutional convention. In September the winners assembled in Monterey.

Only eight of the forty-eight delegates were Californios: five from sparsely populated southern California, where Spanish-speakers were still a majority, and three from the north, where the flood of miners turned them into a tiny minority. Mariano Guadalupe Vallejo was among them, but Juan Bautista Alvarado and José Antonio Castro, his old comrades, chose not to participate. Alvarado accepted American citizenship, but for the remainder of his life he avoided politics, devoting himself to the defense of his rancho from encroaching squatters. Castro, always the most militant of the three, retained his Mexican citizenship. Growing restive under American rule, he accepted an offer from Mexican authorities to become the territorial governor of Baja California. "Perhaps on the border," he wrote, "I can still be of use to my Californio countrymen." He relocated to Baja and served until 1860, when he was killed in a gun battle between opposing political factions.

The American delegates included a handful of long-term residents like Thomas Larkin and Johann August Sutter, men with deep if complicated relations with the Californios. Most delegates, however, had been in California for two years or less. For them, the Californios were an afterthought. Delegate William M. Gwin expressed the consensus at the opening session: "It is not for the native Californians that we are making this constitution," he declared, but "for the great American population, comprising four-fifths of this country." His remark elicited a sharp rebuke from José Antonio Carrillo of Los Angeles, who "begged leave to say that he considered himself as much an American citizen as the gentleman."

In their first debate, the delegates took up the question of statehood. California, the majority insisted, was already too populous and wealthy to be a mere territory and should immediately petition Congress for admission to the Union. The small contingent from southern California, Americans and Californios alike, argued against statehood, fearing domination by the much larger population in the north. Carrillo proposed splitting California in two, a state in the north, a territory in the south, but that idea went nowhere. The delegates voted overwhelmingly to write a state constitution and apply to Congress for immediate statehood. Most of their text they took from the constitutions of other states. There would be three branches of government—the executive, headed by a popularly elected governor; the legislative, with both an assembly

and a senate; and the judicial, capped by an elected supreme
court.

★

With two notable exceptions, the delegates ignored the policies and principles of the previous Mexican regime. The first
concerned women and property. According to English common law, husbands were sole owners of all family property.
That contrasted with the Spanish tradition, in which wives
maintained ownership of all the property they brought to the
marriage and joint ownership of everything acquired thereafter. Charles T. Botts, a Virginian who represented Monterey,
was in favor of adopting the common law approach. "The only
despotism on earth that I would advocate," he declared, "is the
despotism of the husband. There must be a head and there
must be a master in every household."

But since Californios held legal title to nearly all of California's real estate, with their property rights protected by international treaty, there were fears that changing the law and
dispossessing women would throw the state's property system
into chaos. "It will be remembered," one delegate reminded
the others, that this provision "always has been the law of *this*
country." Others argued that given the shortage of women in
gold rush California, the Spanish legal custom might attract
more. "I would call upon all the bachelors in this convention
to vote for it," said one delegate. "I do not think we can offer a
greater inducement for women of fortune to come to California. It is the very best provision to get us wives." It passed.

The other exception involved slavery, which Mexico had
formally outlawed in 1837. Miners strongly opposed the use of
slave labor in the diggings, not out of sympathy for slaves, but
because they believed it gave masters an unfair advantage. Following their lead, the delegates voted unanimously to maintain

Mexico's prohibition. Some wanted to go further, banning the entry of free African Americans to the state. "A free black population is one of the greatest evils that can afflict society," said Oliver M. Wozencraft, representing the town of Stockton (named for the American commodore), "a greater curse than the locusts of Egypt." In an initial vote, the delegates passed the ban. But before the convention concluded, they reconsidered. "I shall vote against," said Francis J. Lippitt, representing San Francisco, "on the ground that it may jeopardize the acceptance of this Constitution in Congress." Although a majority wanted to exclude all African Americans from the state, they listened to Lippitt and voted to remove the ban.

The delegates had come of age during a political era when the right to vote in the United States was being extended to all White men, regardless of wealth or class. They scorned the "aristocratic" limitations of the former Mexican regime, including the system of indirect election. But what about race? The delegates spent many hours debating a clause that would limit the suffrage to "white male citizens." Pablo de la Guerra y Noriega of Santa Barbara asked for a clarification about the meaning of the term *white*. "Many citizens of California have received from nature a very dark skin," he told the delegates, and "it would be very unjust to deprive them of the privilege of citizens merely because nature had not made them white." Delegate Botts from Monterey responded that skin color wasn't really the issue. He wanted language that unequivocally "excluded the African and Indian races" from voting.

If *white* was "intended to exclude the African race," said Guerra y Noriega, "then it was correct and satisfactory." But if it referred to Native ancestry, he objected. To delegates who "sneered at the Indian race," he wished to say that many Native Californians were "equally as rational and gifted as highly by nature as those who had depreciated them." If the conven-

tion voted to restrict the suffrage to Whites, he hoped they
would give the state legislature the latitude to make exceptions.
The delegates agreed to a compromise, providing the legislature with the authority to extend the suffrage to "Indians or the
descendants of Indians" in special cases. In point of fact, such
legislation was never passed. The state of California would be
a *White* democratic republic.

★

Voters ratified the new constitution in a special election held
in November 1849. At the same time, they cast ballots for state
officers, legislators, and supreme court justices, as well as two
representatives to Congress in Washington, D.C. A few weeks
later the new legislature convened for its first session in San
José.

In those days, before the adoption of the Seventeenth
Amendment to the Constitution in 1913, voters did not choose
U.S. senators, legislatures did. So that was the initial item on
their agenda. The first choice of the legislators was John C.
Frémont, the well-known instigator of the Bear Flag Rebellion,
who had returned to California following his court-martial. It
took two more rounds of voting before the legislators awarded
the second seat to William Gwin, a leader of the constitutional
convention. Both men were familiar with the ins and outs of
Washington politics. Frémont was the son-in-law of Senator
Thomas Hart Benton of Missouri; Gwin, who had previously
served as a congressman from Mississippi, was a protégé of
Senator John C. Calhoun of South Carolina. Because senators
from the same state serve staggered terms, one of the new California seats would extend for the entire six years, the other
would expire in 1851. The two men drew straws, and Gwin won
the long term.

The legislators then turned to the task of forming the first
state government, laying out the responsibilities of executive

California Counties

officers, defining the structure of the justice system, levying taxes, and issuing state bonds. Don Mariano, elected to the state senate, chaired the committee charged with laying out and naming California's counties. The legislators authorized the creation of twenty-seven, some the size of states. Over the next half century that number would rise to fifty-eight as the largest counties were gradually partitioned into smaller ones.

★

In its first session, the California legislature passed a series of acts doubling down on White supremacy. The state constitution limited the suffrage to White men. Now the legislature decreed that only Whites would be allowed to enjoy the full protection of the justice system. "No black or mulatto person, or Indian," read a law passed in 1850, "shall be permitted to give evidence in favor of, or against, any white person." That left people of color, for all intents and purposes, legally defenseless against Whites. A few years later, the state supreme court decided that the term *Indian* included "the whole Mongolian race," thus extending this exclusion to Chinese residents.

Legislators then turned to "An Act for the Government and Protection of Indians," codifying the forced labor system that had been in operation since the first days of Spanish colonization. The act purportedly provided for the care of homeless and orphaned Native children. But under this cover, thousands of young Natives were abducted and forced into "apprenticeship," laboring for ranchers and farmers throughout California. After the law was passed, federal agents apprehended three men with a group of nine Native children ranging in age from three to ten. The kidnappers insisted that they had taken possession of the children as "an act of charity," because their parents had been killed. The agent asked how they knew that. "I killed some of them myself," one of them replied. "This law works beautifully," wrote the editor of the *Humboldt Times*. "What a pity the provisions are not extended to Greasers, Kanakas, and Asiatics."

Legislators also enacted the Foreign Miners' Tax, levying a fine of $20 a month (about $500 in today's values) on every "alien miner" in the state. No ordinary worker could afford such a sum; it was simply a way to get rid of the competition.

There were as yet few Chinese in California, so the tax primarily affected Mexicans and other Latinos. After its passage, White mobs drove hundreds of Hispanic miners from the diggings. Ramón Jil Navarro, a Chileño working a valuable claim with a group of his countrymen, reported being attacked. The Americans "despoiled every man of everything of value he had on his person," he wrote, "then they demolished each house, not leaving a single wall standing, but taking care to steal the canvas that covered the roofs." The expelled miners included hundreds of Californios, all of them American citizens. Virtually no European nationals were required to pay the tax.

★

On January 1, 1850, Frémont, Gwin, and the two prospective congressmen left California for Washington. They arrived several weeks later to find Congress still deeply divided over slavery. Prohibiting slavery in California, Southerners worried, would be the first step toward outlawing it in all the territory acquired from Mexico. The South had sent its best young men to beat the Mexicans, but now it was being denied the prize.

The political fight continued through the spring and summer. Southern zealots talked of secession. The standoff finally ended with the adoption of a series of measures known as the "Compromise of 1850." California was admitted as a free state on September 8, 1850. The remainder of the Mexican cession was organized as the territories of Utah and New Mexico, each with the option of legalizing slavery, which both immediately did. Congress outlawed the slave trade in Washington, D.C., but also passed the infamous Fugitive Slave Act, which greatly increased the power of masters to force runaway slaves in the free states back into slavery in the South. California statehood was linked to White supremacy and slavery from the very beginning.

SAN FRANCISCO VIGILANTES

20

Popular Justice

Would the new state government succeed in calming the turmoil roiling gold rush California? The first decade of statehood was not promising. Even as the legislature met in its first session, events were spiraling out of control in Sacramento, the mining supply town at the confluence of the American and Sacramento rivers, which in 1854 would become the state capital.

In 1849 a group of speculators—led by entrepreneur Sam Brannan and lawyer Peter H. Burnett, who soon became California's first governor—made a deal with Johann August Sutter. By virtue of his 1840 grant from Governor Juan Bautista Alvarado, Sutter claimed ownership of land at the Sacramento-American river junction. In exchange for valuable riverside lots, Brannan and Burnett agreed to survey and grade the streets of the prospective town. They then offered the lots to merchants and wholesalers at top dollar. Many businessmen, however, balked at paying the high prices the speculators demanded.

Denying the legitimacy of Sutter's title, they simply staked out claims and conducted their business from tents and shacks along the waterfront. What was fair play in the diggings, they argued, was also fair play in Sacramento.

In the spring of 1850, Brannan and Governor Burnett hired a force of armed men to pull down the squatters' fences and shacks. "You touch this house at your peril!" a man cradling a shotgun shouted as they approached his place. "Cover that damned scoundrel," Brannan ordered his men, "and if he raises his gun, shoot hell out of him!" The squatters were sent packing, but they soon returned. Confronted by the new county sheriff, they ridiculed the "pretend" government that empowered him. The stalemate continued well into the summer.

It came to a head in August, when James McClatchy, a leader of the squatters, delivered a fiery speech at a public meeting. "Let us put up all the fences pulled down," he declared, "and also *put up* all the men who pull them down." McClatchy's allusion to lynch law was clear to everyone, and the sheriff arrested him for incitement. His supporters rushed the jail in an unsuccessful attempt to free him, precipitating a violent confrontation. Street fighting continued for two days and cost the lives of the county sheriff, a city official, and a half dozen squatters. Finally, Governor Burnett declared martial law and dispatched a militia company of five hundred men to occupy Sacramento. The squatters lost the battle, but the wider war over property continued.

★

Many settlers questioned the legitimacy of the land grants handed out by California's Mexican governors. Accustomed to open access to western land, Americans found it hard to accept the notion that the state's prime acreage should be monopolized by a few hundred Californio families. If the "old feudal system of landed monopoly" were allowed to continue, declared the Sacramento Settlers' League, "the homes of American freemen will become the huts of tenants and serfs." Yet in the treaty ending the war, the United States had solemnly pledged to protect the property of former Mexican citizens. The Settlers' League wanted congressional action.

Senator John C. Frémont argued that the property rights of Californios must be "inviolably respected," and he introduced legislation in Congress confirming the Mexican grants. But Frémont had a dog in the fight. He had purchased a large land grant in the southern Sierra Nevada that included one of the richest veins of gold-bearing quartz in the entire range. Frémont would have been the principal beneficiary of his own bill, and charges of self-dealing dashed his hopes for reelection.

Frémont's colleague Senator William Gwin introduced alternative legislation, the California Land Act, which Congress passed in 1851. The law steered a middle course, establishing a procedure for grantees to obtain clear title, but saddling them with the burden of proof. That required hiring lawyers to represent them before the land commissioners and judges, a difficult and expensive process given the poor record keeping of the Californio regime. Grantees filed more than eight hundred claims, and while three-quarters of them were eventually approved, court costs and attorneys' fees forced many Californio landowners into bankruptcy. With few courts and heavy caseloads, it took seventeen years before the last of the claims were confirmed, and in the meantime squatters overran many ranchos. The Californio elite was not spared. Squatters tore down Don Mariano's fences and stole his cattle, and he was forced into court to protect his property. "It was impossible for us to defend our rights," he lamented. He eventually lost nearly all of his vast holdings in the Napa and Sonoma valleys.

★

Land problems also bedeviled the city of San Francisco, squeezed between the bay on the east and a series of steep hills to the west. Eventually the grid of streets would ascend those hills with the city's famous fleet of cable cars. But in the 1850s developers chose instead to expand into the bay itself, extending wharves across shallow Yerba Buena Cove, scuttling abandoned sailing ships to serve as makeshift buildings, and filling the spaces between them with garbage, trash, and sand, creating real estate where none had previously existed.

According to existing federal law, such tidal lands were state property, but in 1847, before the state existed, military governor Richard Mason had granted ownership of those so-called "water lots" to San Francisco's town council, which auctioned them off to raise revenue. They were then sold and resold at ever higher prices. Once California was admitted to the Union, however, the state asserted its right and filed a legal claim, creating confusion and conflict over the title to water-front property that would continue for decades.

San Francisco's weak municipal government, inherited from Mexican California, collapsed when the multitudes began arriving in 1849. In desperate need of some method of polic-ing, local merchants pooled their resources and hired a group of discharged Mexican War veterans to act as a private secu-rity force. But the "Hounds," as they became known, quickly got out of hand, intimidating shopkeepers and harassing the city's foreign-born, especially Spanish speakers. In the sum-mer of 1849, following a brutal attack by the Hounds on a Chileño encampment, a volunteer force of citizens arrested the most prominent ruffians and turned them over to local courts for trial. A "Law and Order" party, voted into power at the next election, established a regular police force of seventy-five officers.

The gold rush made San Francisco into the mercantile capital of the Pacific Rim, exporting millions of dollars in gold and importing commodities of every description, sending them by steamboat to the expanding towns of Sacramento and Stockton, which supplied the mines of the northern and southern Sierras respectively. The booming commercial economy of San Francisco itself attracted thousands of migrants. By 1850 the population had grown from a few hundred residents to more than twenty-five thousand—only several hundred of whom were women—and it continued to surge, reaching nearly sixty thousand by 1860, when it ranked as the nation's fifteenth-largest metropolis.

San Francisco was an immigrant city, with foreign-born Latin Americans, Europeans, and Chinese greatly outnumbering Americans. Irish men and women, many of them former residents of New York City, made up the single largest group. In fact, more than half the native-born residents of San Francisco, including most of the merchants and lawyers, came from cities in the northeastern United States. The mercantile economy employed a large force of clerks, bookkeepers, and managers, perhaps a fifth of the city's residents. But the majority of San Franciscans worked as longshoremen and teamsters, artisans and construction workers, or simply as unskilled laborers.

In the early 1850s, the city boasted several dozen newspapers, a score of churches (including a Roman Catholic cathedral), theaters, and concert halls. But because the population was so overwhelmingly male, it resembled a huge mining camp, with hundreds of taverns, gambling parlors, and brothels. "There is nothing to turn to for recreation but the drinking-saloons and gambling-houses," wrote an English visitor. "The merchant and his clerk, and perhaps his cook, jostle in the crowd together, and stake their ounces at the same gaming table."

★

San Francisco politics resembled warfare. In the city's first election following statehood, Democrats won control of local government. They were led by David C. Broderick, an Irish politician from New York. Broderick, who served in the state senate, introduced machine-style urban politics to California, organizing working-class voters into ward clubs, building a party organization capable of getting them to the polls, and using patronage, payoffs, and ballot stuffing to win elections. Broderick and the Democrats built their political base among the foreign-born, assisting them in becoming naturalized citizens, which required two years of continuous residence and nothing more. Among his constituents, Broderick enjoyed a reputation as one of the boys (or "b'hoys," in Irish brogue), contributing to charitable causes, providing relief for the infirm and unemployed, and treating for drinks at his favorite watering hole.

The city's merchant and financial elites hated Broderick. They dreamed of overthrowing the Democrats and establishing a municipal regime based on conservative principles, a government that would resist the clamoring rabble. They found their issue in the public fear of crime and violence. San Francisco suffered a series of devastating fires, and conservatives declared they were the work of criminal arsonists, who used the conflagrations as a cover to rob and steal. They faulted city government for lax enforcement and accused Broderick's Democrats of criminal complicity. Examining the record, historians note that San Francisco's crime rate was no worse than that of other American cities of the era. What distinguished the place from others was its mining camp spirit, including an inordinate enthusiasm for "popular justice."

The tipping point came in June 1851, a few weeks after a massive fire that destroyed the city's downtown. A score of frustrated merchants assembled at Sam Brannan's office to discuss their options. Brannan, a law and order man during the squatter crisis in Sacramento, now argued the necessity of extralegal action. The men organized what they called a Committee of Vigilance, pledging to attack crime themselves. By the end of the day more than two hundred San Franciscans had signed on.

Their first test came that very evening. A hoodlum named John Jenkins, apprehended while burglarizing an office, was turned over to members of the committee. They conducted a sham trial, declared Jenkins guilty, and resolved to punish him immediately, before the established authorities could intervene. At two in the morning, they marched their prisoner to Portsmouth Square in the center of the city.

A large crowd had already gathered, including David Broderick with a contingent of Democrats. From atop a hay bale he delivered a passionate speech, urging the people to turn Jenkins over to the legal justice system. But the vigilantes absolutely refused. "To hell with the courts, we're going to take things into our own hands," one shouted. Broderick later testified that the man "seemed in favor of hanging everybody that didn't belong to his party."

A scene of wild confusion ensued, but the vigilantes prevailed. Pushing Broderick and his men back at gunpoint, they placed a noose around Jenkins's neck and threw the rope over the roof beam of an old adobe building. As Broderick's men attempted to rescue him, grabbing hold of his legs, Sam Brannan called out to the crowd: "Every lover of liberty and good order lay hold of the rope!" Several dozen men did as he said. Literally pulled at both ends by the competing factions, Jenkins was strangled to death.

An inquest concluded that John Jenkins had died by "violent means" and named Brannan and other leading citizens as the perpetrators. But the authorities were too intimidated to indict them, which sent membership in the Committee of Vigilance soaring. Over the next several weeks, the vigilantes replaced the city's criminal justice system, making nearly a hundred arrests, banishing several dozen opponents, and executing three more men before finally disbanding.

★

Over the next several years, every uptick in criminal activity set off calls for the return of the committee. In 1856, a year of economic hardship, it happened. With the transition to industrial mining well underway, hundreds of former miners crowded into the city. Owners and squatters clashed over city lots, while nativist politicians mounted inflammatory campaigns against the Irish and other immigrants, Broderick's political base. When a Democratic politician shot and killed a crusading newspaper editor on a public street, the merchant elite responded with a reorganized Committee of Vigilance that included several thousand members, many of them unemployed. Armed vigilantes forced their way into the jail and seized the assassin along with another accused murderer, and following a secret trial both men were hanged before a crowd of several thousand.

The Committee of Vigilance ruled San Francisco with strong-arm tactics through the summer of 1856, executing another two men and forcing two dozen Democratic politicians to leave the state. Governor J. Neely Johnson condemned the movement as an "insurrection," but he lacked the power to put it down. The committee became the nucleus of a new political organization, the so-called People's Party, which triumphed in the subsequent municipal election and continued in power for another decade. Merchants got the conservative government they wanted, and then some.

The seizure of power by the vigilantes was "a regular *coup d'état,*" said William Tecumseh Sherman, the manager of a San Francisco bank who later became a famous Civil War general. Sherman was a conservative who believed that regular law enforcement and the court system needed strengthening. But that would require more funding and higher taxes, adamantly opposed by the business community. Sherman's conclusion is worth remembering. "If one-tenth the money had been expended, or one-tenth the effort had been exerted, to sustain the courts as have been to overthrow them, our city would be as well governed as any in America."

★

Gold rush California, writes California historian Kevin Starr, was a place of "primitive and brutal conditions." His assessment can be supported with numbers. In December 1855, the *Sacramento Daily Union* published statewide homicide statistics for the year. Homicide, violence at its most extreme, offers the best measure of the general violence in a society. Authorities in different jurisdictions may have different ideas of what constitutes assault, battery, or rape, making comparison difficult. But death by violent means is universally considered a homicide. Moreover, as criminologists have repeatedly shown, the more murder there is, the more assault, battery, and rape as well. Consider the following numbers with that in mind. During 1855, when the state's population numbered some three hundred thousand, officials reported a total of 538 homicides in California. Using the standard calculation for the homicide rate—the number of violent deaths per 100,000 people—the state's rate for 1855 was 179. In 2020, the state of California reported a homicide rate of 4.2. That's a shocking contrast.

The rate of violent death varied greatly from county to county. San Francisco's rate of 30 was the lowest of all the state's counties, which puts vigilante claims of a violent city the following year into perspective. The mining counties, with little or no formal law enforcement, all ranked considerably higher than the state average. Mariposa County, including the mines of the southern Sierra Nevada, suffered the highest rate in the state, an astounding 580, the equivalent of low-scale warfare. Los Angeles County ranked a close second with a rate of 567. In places like those, nearly every resident was touched by violence, either as a perpetrator, a victim, or a witness.

What accounts for that kind of lethal mayhem? There were many causes: the legacy of violent conquest, ethnic antagonism and racial hatred; conflicts over land; deadly weapons readily at hand; and an oversupply of young, unattached males. Disaffected Californios and Mexicans sometimes turned to violent crime, and both Mariposa and Los Angeles counties were terrorized by outlaw gangs led by men who became legends in their own time. The exploits of bandits like Joaquin Murrieta actually conflated the activities of multiple criminals. With minimal law enforcement and weak courts, conflicts were often settled privately through violence. "Honorable men"—merchants, lawyers, and politicians—participated in hundreds of duels or "affairs of honor," many of which were reported in the press.

Such violence helps explain the frequency of "popular justice." During the 1850s, at least three hundred episodes of lynch law occurred in California, resulting in the extralegal execution of more than two hundred individuals, the majority of them people of color. About half those lynchings took place in mining camps, a third in towns like Los Angeles, Monterey, and Sacramento, the others scattered throughout the state. Vigilantism was the remedy of a frustrated people. But as William Tecumseh Sherman well understood, vigilantism itself was toxic, undermining the very rule of law it sought to enforce. Californians of the 1850s—from the streets of San Francisco to the diggings in the Sierra Nevada, to the ranchos surrounding Los Angeles—were addicted to violence.

NISENAN FUNERAL DANCE

21

My Little Sister's Heart in My Hands

After a long day herding sheep in April 1849, a young Nisenan named Konnick and his boss, Heinrich Lienhard, were relaxing around an open fire at their camp on a tributary of the American River, which the Nisenans knew as *kum mayo* or "roundhouse river," an allusion to the fact that it encompassed their homeland. Suddenly several men from Konnock's village, a short distance away, materialized out of the darkness. They huddled with the young man, whispering in worried tones, then departed. Lienhard asked if there was trouble. "Yes," Konnick said. "Some white men who were washing gold further up the river killed my uncle and another Indian, scalped them, and took their heads." His relatives had brought the bodies back to the village for cremation and burial.

After several years working for Johann August Sutter, the

proprietor of Sutter's Fort, Lienhard took pride in his relations with the indigenous Nisenans. "They had always been friendly," he later recalled, "and I did not care to see them harmed." The hundreds of Americans arriving each week in search of gold did not share his perspective. Several days earlier, Lienhard had encountered a heavily armed group of Americans on their way to the mines. The moment they saw Konnick, they went for their guns. "See that black devil? Look at his wild eye. Why not blow his brains out?" Lienhard considered them "scum," and he made no effort to hide his disgust. He would not allow them to hurt his friend, he declared, and they left cursing.

It was men like those, Lienhard knew, who had murdered Konnock's uncle and his companion. He attempted to comfort the young man, but also confessed his fear that in their desire for revenge the Nisenans might target Lienhard himself. He would not let that happen, Konnick assured him, but that night Lienhard slept with a cocked rifle by his side.

Konnick joined his community for the funeral ceremony. They built a pyre in the center of the village on which they placed the bodies and personal possessions of the murdered men. The fire was lit and the people began their death dance, singing and crying. The lamentations gradually grew louder, rousing Lienhard's dogs, who yelped and howled along with the chorus. "I listened to the periodic cries and the rhythmic tramping of many feet that continued all night long," Lienhard wrote. "Toward dawn the sounds became less audible. At intervals a broken voice could be heard singing the familiar song of death." At dawn he made his way to the village, where he found Konnock's mourning father sitting next to a mound of earth. "Is your brother there?" Lienhard asked, pointing to the mound. "*Sí, Señor,*" the grieving man replied. "Poor fellow," said Lienhard, "they were bad men to kill him." "*Sí, Señor, muy malo.*"

The Nisenans had their own funereal customs, but like most Native Californians they believed the dead ought to be interred near the home village, so their spirits could linger among friends. Ghosts angered easily, however, and the living feared their power. It was considered disrespectful, even dangerous, to speak of the dead or even to say their names. Eventually, in the fullness of time, the spirit would depart, "to be with Coyote, where the sun goes down."

Old Man Coyote spoke the truth when he declared that families and friends must make a great ceremony for the dead. But when people are killed by the hundreds, when they are slaughtered like pests, when their villages are torched and their lands seized, no funeral ceremony can restore order. Families are devastated, leadership decimated, and ancient life ways destroyed. Survival becomes the only thing that matters. In the quarter century following the discovery of gold, that is what happened to the Native peoples of California.

★

"There has been considerable difficulty in different portions of the mines between the whites and Indians," the *Alta California* newspaper of San Francisco reported in the spring of 1849. "The whites are becoming impressed with the belief that it will be absolutely necessary to *exterminate* the savages." For decades Spaniards, Mexicans, and Californios alike had mistreated and exploited Native Californians. Men like Don Mariano made their reputations and fortunes waging wars of expansion, driving Native people from their ancient homelands. But no Hispanic colonist had ever advocated *extermination*. Rancheros and farmers, like missionaries, needed Natives to herd their livestock, tend their crops, and prepare their meals. Sutter, who depended on Native labor, saw the change in real time as the Whites took over. The Americans, he told a visitor, "had commenced a war of extermination against the aborigines."

Americans brought a virulent form of racism to California. The Franciscans and the Spanish colonists certainly viewed Natives as different, even inferior. They were pagans, they were uncivilized, they were ignorant. But mid-nineteenth-century Americans brought with them a conviction of *racial* difference. Animated by nightmare visions of ambush, torture, and mutilation at the hands of ruthless savages—the stuff of frontier folklore, found in every part of the country—they armed themselves with rifles, handguns, and Bowie knives. Hundreds of miners posed for daguerreotypes proudly displaying the weapons meant to protect them from "the Indians."

In fact, warfare played a minor role in the life and culture of Native Californians. None practiced scalping, which Americans introduced to California. "They have only the rudest implements of war, and cannot successfully defend themselves against American rifles," the *Sacramento Transcript* reported. Fear of *the other* corroded into contempt. "What is lower in the scale of humanity than a California Indian?" asked the *Californian* of San Francisco. "They are a burden and pest to the country," echoed the *California Star.* "Gladly would I behold the exit of every one of these miserable creatures from our midst."

The *Alta California,* the state's leading newspaper during the 1850s, took a somewhat more humanitarian view. "The poor Indian has been robbed and fleeced of his birthright," the paper editorialized. "Could all the human gore that the discovery of America has cost the poor aborigines be rolled into one collective stream, Heaven itself would blush to look upon it." But this regret amounted to little more than crocodile tears. The destruction was horrible, the editorial continued, but unavoidable. Nothing could have prevented it. History showed that as civilization advanced upon them, Natives simply "faded or fled away like a dissipating mist before the morning sun."

This was the myth of the "vanishing Indian," offering cover to the man with a gun and comfort to the man with a conscience.

★

The state would soon launch a concerted campaign against the Native people of California, and Californians did not hesitate to call it by its real name, *extermination.* Today we use a different term. "It's called genocide," said California governor Gavin Newsom in 2019. "That's the way it needs to be described in the history books." The precipitating event was a cascade of violence that began in late 1849 at Clear Lake, a large body of fresh water in the rugged Coastal Range, some fifty miles north of Sonoma.

The Pomo people had lived along the shores of Clear Lake for several thousand years. In the 1830s, however, epidemic disease struck, devastating them and leaving them vulnerable to Californio expansion. In 1839, Salvador Vallejo, Don Mariano's brother, led his men north to Clear Lake, seeking grass for his cattle and Native workers to herd them. "I would rather die than be taken," one Pomo told Vallejo. But the Vallejos were willing to employ ruthless violence, and the Pomos eventually agreed to go to work for them. By the time of the Bear Flag Rebellion, the family had large herds grazing the grassland that bordered Clear Lake, under the care of Pomo vaqueros.

After the war, Charles Stone and Andrew Kelsey, former Bears, bought the Clear Lake herd from the Vallejos. Along with the animals came customary rights to both the grassland and Native labor. When the two White men arrived, the Pomos welcomed them as their new employers, but things quickly went off the tracks. Stone and Kelsey treated the Pomos as if they were slaves, working them unremittingly and providing scant provisions. The Natives objected and refused to work, but when word of their resistance reached Sonoma, an armed posse of Americans stormed north and thoroughly intimidated them.

Stone and Kelly might have taken Native resistance as a warning sign, but instead they doubled down. They surrounded the village with an enclosure of some sort and refused to allow anyone to leave for any reason other than ranch work. Unable to practice their traditional hunting and gathering economy, the people went hungry and a few elderly men and women starved. Anyone violating the rules suffered brutal punishment. "From severe whipping four died," one Pomo later recalled. "They murdered Indians without limits or mercy," said settler George Yount. What's more, Yount added, both Stone and Kelly pursued "their unbridled lusts among the youthful females."

Finally, after nearly two years of abuse, the Pomos reached their limit. A quarter century later, an old headman named Shuk, who claimed to be the leader of their revolt, told the story: "The Indians thought they might as well die one way as another," he said. "So they decided to take the final and fatal step." One night in December 1849, as Stone and Kelsey slept, a Native woman in the house—one of several being kept for their masters' pleasure—sabotaged their guns by pouring water down the barrels. When Stone emerged from the house early the next morning to light the breakfast fire, a large group of Pomos were waiting. "You came early," he said, looking around. "Is something wrong?" One man picked up his bow and threaded an arrow. "What are you doing?" Stone exclaimed. A second later the arrow pierced his stomach. Staring down at it in disbelief, he pulled it out, then hustled back inside, slammed the door, and fell dead at Kelsey's feet.

Kelsey went for his guns but found them useless. A few minutes later, he opened the door and came out. "Don't kill Kelsey," he said. "Kelsey *bueno hombre*—Kelsey good man."

The Pomos laughed. "Yes," one of them said, "good at killing many of us." Kelsey tried to run, but the Pomos slashed at him with their knives. He fell wounded beside a man and his wife. "This is the one who killed our son," said the man, handing his wife a spear. "Now you have the chance to take revenge." She plunged the weapon into Kelsey's heart.

When word of the revolt reached Sonoma, White residents panicked. A company of army dragoons marched north, but found the Pomo village abandoned. They spied a group of Natives on an island in the middle of the lake, but having no means of crossing the water, they returned to Sonoma. Over the next several weeks mobs of angry settlers rode roughshod over the region, indiscriminately shooting every Native ranch hand they could find, ultimately killing several dozen people. George Yount and other ranchers, who depended on the Native workforce, formed a posse, arrested the vigilantes, and turned them over to the authorities. But since state law did not allow Native testimony against Whites, there was no case to make, and the California Supreme Court released the vigilantes on bail. They were never tried.

Responding to demands that the Pomos be punished, the army dispatched another company in May 1850 with instructions to attack Natives wherever they might be found, "without attempting any parley or communication." This time the soldiers hauled a couple of whaleboats. Reaching Clear Lake, they launched their craft and attacked the Pomos on their island refuge. The soldiers "poured in a destructive fire indiscriminately upon men, women, and children," the *Alta California* reported. "Little or no resistance was encountered, and the work of butchery was of short duration." Years later a Pomo survivor, a young girl at the time of the massacre, described what she saw from her hiding place, high in the branches of a tree. "Two white men came with their guns up in the air, and on their [bayonets] hung a little girl. They brought her to the creek and threw her in the water. And a little while later two more men came in the same manner. This time they had a little boy on the end of their guns and also threw him in the water."

The official report of what was called the Bloody Island Massacre concluded that the soldiers killed no fewer than four hundred and perhaps as many as eight hundred Pomos, the majority women and children. A few days later the dragoons attacked another village near what is today the town of Ukiah, killing at least another hundred Natives. It was "a perfect slaughter pen," the commander of the operation boasted.

Over the course of four or five months as many as a thousand Natives were killed in retaliation for the death of two infamously sadistic White men. The editor of the *Alta California* deplored the violence. But, he wrote, the deed had been done and there could be no turning back. Angry Natives would seek retribution and they would have to be crushed. "There will be safety only in a war of *extermination,* waged with relentless fury far and near." It was all so inevitable, he sighed. "We cannot but yield to the conviction that such is the destiny of that miserable race."

★

In April 1850, during its first session, the state legislature passed an act authorizing volunteer militia companies to apply for state recognition and financial support. Within months, several militia operations commenced against Native communities in the mining region, including the Trinity and Klamath river country in the north. At a time when miners' earnings were falling drastically, legislators agreed to generous wages for militiamen, greatly stimulating enlistment. Over the course of the decade the state legislature allocated a total of $1.4 million for these killing campaigns, expecting that the federal government would reimburse the state, which it eventually did.

Thus did both the state and federal governments sponsor and fund the destruction of Native Californians. Governor Peter H. Burnett announced the policy in his annual message in January 1851. "A war of *extermination* will continue to be waged between the races until the Indian race becomes extinct," he declared. "The inevitable destiny of the race is beyond the power or wisdom of man to avert."

President Millard Fillmore had appointed three commissioners to negotiate treaties with the "various Indians tribes of the state." They assembled in San Francisco and were about to commence their work when Governor Burnett made his genocidal pronouncement. Their mission, they thought, offered an opportunity to prevent further bloodshed. "The people of California appear to have left but one alternative," they wrote. "*Extermination* or *domestication*." By "domestication" they meant good-faith negotiation, the cession of Native territory, the creation of reservations, and the guarantee of federal protection for Native peoples. The commissioners hoped that would be what Californians chose.

They canvassed the state, negotiating eighteen treaties with a total of 119 "tribes." The commissioners did not understand the lifeways of Native Californians, just as Native leaders had virtually no comprehension of the specific terms of the treaties. The whole process, concluded California anthropologist Robert Heizer, "was a farce from beginning to end." Nevertheless, dozens of headmen put their marks on treaties surrendering their homelands in exchange for reservations totaling some 7.5 million acres, about 7 percent of the state's land. "The Indians complained very much," said one commissioner, and only consented so "they might have a home in which they would be protected from the white man." That much, at least, was clear.

But most public officials, as well as every newspaper in California, condemned the treaties as a violation of White supremacy. An editorial in the *Los Angeles Star* exemplified public opinion. "To place upon our most fertile soil the most degraded race of aborigines upon the North American continent, to invest them with the rights of sovereignty, and to teach them that they are to be treated as powerful and independent nations, is planting the seeds of future disaster and ruin." The governor and the state legislature urged the United States Senate to reject the treaties, and in July 1852 the Senate agreed to table them with neither hearings, debate, nor vote. "The fate of the Indians is irrevocably sealed," declared California senator John Weller. "They must soon disappear before the onward march of our countrymen. Humanity may forbid, but the interest of the white man demands their extinction." California had chosen extermination.

★

From 1850 to 1861 the state of California mounted twenty-four extended military campaigns against Native communities. Vigilante mobs launched dozens of additional devastating attacks. Federal troops participated, often driving Native survivors onto "military reservations," another name for concentration camps. Historian Benjamin Madley provides documentary evidence of more than 370 separate outright massacres. The worst of the violence took place in the state's far north, where settlers pushed ever deeper into previously unconquered Native homelands. In many instances, armed companies surrounded Native villages at night and opened fire while the community slept, killing most of the inhabitants and enslaving the survivors.

In April 1852 a Wintu village on the Trinity River was targeted by a sheriff's posse, incensed over the murder of a White rancher. "When the day broke, the attack commenced," reported the *Shasta Courier.* "Each rifle marked its victim with unerring precision—the pistol and the knife completed the work of destruction and revenge, and in a few brief moments all was over. . . . Only two or three escaped, and those were supposed to be dangerously wounded." The attackers spared only a handful of young women and girls, who were carried back to the nearby town of Weaverville and parceled out to Whites as unpaid domestic servants and sex slaves. Blood lust drove much of it. "You can well imagine the wild excitement and joy at the extermination of this tribe," one settler wrote. "Indian scalps were nailed to many door posts in that town for quite a while."

Rampaging Whites decimated hundreds of villages. Very few Natives lived to recount what happened. Occasionally, however, there were survivor stories. Sally Bell, a Sinkyone (SINKY-own) woman from the northern coast, was ten years old when Whites attacked her village. "About ten o'clock in the morning some white men came," she recalled years later. "They killed my grandfather and my mother and my father, I saw them do it. . . . Then they killed my baby sister and cut her heart out and threw it in the brush where I ran and hid. My little sister was a baby, just crawling around. I didn't know what to do. I was so scared that I guess I just hid there a long time with my little sister's heart in my hands. I felt so bad and I was so scared that I just couldn't do anything else." She and a few others hid out in the woods for months, living on roots and berries. Eventually she reunited with several surviving members of her extended family.

Historical demographers believe that Native Californians numbered some 150,000 individuals in 1845, the eve of the American conquest. Fifteen years later that number had fallen to an estimated 35,000. The campaign of extermination claimed thousands of lives, while thousands more died of exposure and disease. Whole communities and entire peoples were obliterated. But like Sally Bell, some survived. They would not only endure, but make new lives for themselves in a very different kind of California.

ARCHY LEE IN COURT

22

I'll Never Be Carried into Slavery

On the evening of January 6, 1858, Officer Nathan Coon of the Sacramento police strode into Hackett House, a small hotel operated by free people of color, and presented the night clerk with a warrant for the arrest of Archy Lee, a Black man accused of being a fugitive slave by his alleged master, Charles Stovall of Mississippi. Lee surrendered and Coon hauled him off to jail. Later that night, one of the hotel's proprietors made a call on his attorney, and by two in the morning they had obtained a writ of habeas corpus from a county judge, ordering the city marshal to show cause why Lee should not be released.

A reporter interviewed Stovall. He had come to California with his bondsman Archy Lee several months before, he said, "with a view of recovering my health." Stovall hired Lee out and collected his wages while recuperating. Slavery might be illegal in California, but as a citizen of another state Stovall claimed the right to the continuing service of his slave. Lee had been happy and content, he said, until conniving men, "moved and seduced by the instigation of the devil," inspired him to run away.

Archy Lee told a different story. Stovall had come to California to settle, he said, purchasing land and opening a private elementary school. He had been Stovall's slave in Mississippi, but upon arriving in California he had, he insisted, become "a free person." He ran away after Stovall hired someone to escort him back to Mississippi. That man forced him aboard a riverboat docked at the K Street wharf in Sacramento, but Lee gave him the slip and raced up the thoroughfare to Third Street, a mixed neighborhood of Chinese, Mexicans, and Blacks. His friends at Hackett House hid him for several weeks, and now they were helping with the cost of the legal fight to secure his freedom.

Lee's supporters retained attorney Edwin Crocker, an antislavery Republican, to represent him in court. Charles Stovall chose James Hardy, a strong proslavery Democrat. *Ex parte Archy* was not the state's first fugitive slave case, but it would become the most famous, marking a turn in California's political history.

★

Controversy over slavery had agitated state politics for years, cleaving the dominant Democratic Party into two opposing factions. "The Chivalry," so named for its loyalty to the "chivalrous" slaveholding South, was led by Senator William Gwin, who represented the free state of California in Washington, D.C., while retaining ownership of a large plantation in Mississippi. The "Chivs," as they were known, enjoyed strong support in the state's mining and rural districts, including the "cow counties" of southern California. The weaker "Free Soil" faction of the Democrats, led by state senator David Broderick of San Francisco, found its support among working men of the cities and towns, especially Irish Catholics and other foreign-born citizens of San Francisco.

California's constitution addressed the slavery question without ambiguity. "Neither slavery nor involuntary servitude," it read, "shall ever be tolerated in this State." But what of the several hundred Black slaves who mined gold for their owners in 1849 and 1850? Many remained in California after statehood, continuing to toil for their masters. Free Soil Democrats argued that the slaves had become legally free once the constitution was ratified. But the Chivs—despite stiff parliamentary resistance from Broderick—enacted a state fugitive slave law authorizing masters to force Black men and women back into southern bondage. Upheld by California's Supreme Court in 1852, the law amounted to a flagrant suspension of a key portion of the state's constitution.

As the national controversy over slavery in the territories intensified, Free Soil Democrats gained public support. In 1855 they prevented the Chivs from renewing the fugitive slave law, and two years later succeeded in electing Broderick to a seat in the U.S. Senate, where he served alongside his archrival Gwin. Broderick went to Washington expecting to be treated as a loyal Democrat, but found himself shunned and isolated by the party's proslavery establishment, which deprived him of the patronage appointments he would otherwise have bestowed on his California followers.

At about the same time, a group of prominent lawyers and businessmen in Sacramento organized the California branch of the Republican Party, declaring that the "cardinal principle" of their politics was the prohibition of slavery in the nation's western territories. That was essentially the same position taken by Broderick's Free Soil Democrats. But rather than unite with the Republicans, in 1856 Broderick supported Democrat James Buchanan for president over Republican John C. Frémont.

Frémont, losing the national contest, did especially poorly in California, where he remained an unpopular figure. Antislavery Republicans did, however, capture several seats in the California legislature.

What distinguished the Republicans was their commitment to civil and political rights for African Americans. There were small Black communities in San Francisco and Sacramento, and they pressed for repeal of the law enacted by the California legislature prohibiting people of color from testifying in court, as well as the constitutional ban on Black suffrage. Republicans introduced a bill allowing Black testimony, but it failed when Broderick's Free Soil Democrats refused to support it. By taking up the defense of Archy Lee, Republicans sought to press the issue, and to build public support for the antislavery cause.

★

At Archy Lee's court hearing in January 1858, James Hardy, Stovall's attorney, blamed the whole affair on "outsiders." Lee loved his master, Hardy told the judge, and looked forward to returning home to Mississippi. Judge Robert Robinson turned to Lee and asked him directly whether that was true. Lee knew that Blacks were not allowed to testify in court, and it took some persuasion to get him to speak. "I want things to work out right," he finally replied, "but I *don't* want to go back to Mississippi." After hearing arguments from both sides, Judge Robinson announced his ruling. When Stovall relocated to the free state of California, he said, Lee became a free man. Robinson saw a larger issue at stake. "If one citizen of Mississippi could sojourn here with his slave, why not a thousand or ten thousand?"

Had the case ended there, it might have been forgotten. But the moment Lee walked out of Judge Robinson's court, he was rearrested. Attorney Hardy had persuaded Justice David Terry of the California Supreme Court to assume jurisdiction. Terry and one of his colleagues, former governor Peter H. Burnett, both proslavery Democrats from the South, considered the case in a special hearing in early February and announced their decision several days later. They could find no error in Judge Robinson's ruling, they said, but nevertheless ordered Lee returned to his master. While Stovall had made a mistake bringing Lee into a free state, they wrote, it would be unjust to "rigidly enforce" the law against a sick man who required the service of his bondsman. The decision shocked Californians of all political persuasions. The justices, declared the *Alta California,* "had rendered the Supreme Bench of California a laughingstock in the eyes of the world."

Stovall took Lee and went into hiding. The evidence suggests that he punished Lee with a terrible beating. African Americans and Republicans vowed to prevent him from removing Lee from the state. Black leaders in San Francisco obtained a new writ of habeas corpus as well as a warrant for Stovall's arrest on the charge of kidnapping. They placed lookouts on roads and ports, and finally, after nearly a month, a group of them caught Stovall trying to sneak Lee aboard a steamship in San Francisco Bay.

At Lee's second court hearing, held in San Francisco, he was represented by Republican Edward Baker, formerly a congressman from Illinois and a personal friend of Abraham Lincoln's. Attorney Hardy objected that the state supreme court had already ruled, but Baker argued that since Terry and Burnett had acted in a special proceeding and not on appeal, their decision was open to challenge. The judge agreed and, citing Judge Robinson's earlier ruling, ordered Lee released. But Hardy had another trick up his sleeve, filing a suit in federal court that charged Lee with running away from Stovall in Mississippi and coming to California as a fugitive. Lee was immediately rearrested by a federal marshal.

After being held against his will for more than three months, after having his hopes raised and dashed not once but twice, Lee was desperate. "I'm a free man. I'll never be carried into slavery," he cried. "I'll die first!" He resisted the marshal, who manhandled him. The courtroom, packed with African Americans, erupted in chaos. A group of White men formed a cordon around Lee and hustled him back to jail. Black men attempted to rescue him, there were fistfights, and the police made several arrests.

Lee spent another month in jail before the scheduled federal hearing. When the proceeding opened, attorney James Hardy objected that the terms of the Fugitive Slave Act did not entitle fugitives to legal counsel. "Archy is property and nothing more," he declared, "and he has no more right to be heard in this proceeding than a bale of goods or a horse." The court overruled him.

Renowned for his oratory, attorney Edward Baker didn't disappoint. He aimed his argument not at the court, but at the press and the public, for whom he summarized the long and tortuous history of Archy Lee's case. But this matter did not simply concern Lee, Baker declared. It raised the great question of "liberty and humanity." Slavery, he reminded the court, was "not recognized by the law of nations," but only by local law, and in California it was illegal. The case provided Californians with an opportunity to lay down a marker declaring freedom the rule and slavery the exception. "I abhor oppression and bondage," Baker told the court. Over the course of his legal career, he said, he had represented many clients. But never had he been prouder than he was arguing for Archy Lee. On Judgment Day, he concluded, "I shall be able to say confidently that

I met the trial of my fidelity to freedom." Baker's address, wrote a reporter for the *Alta California,* "was one of the most eloquent efforts that we have ever heard," leaving many an eye in the courtroom "moist with tears." The court ordered Lee released, this time for good.

That night several hundred African Americans, perhaps half of San Francisco's Black community, assembled at First African Methodist Episcopal Zion Church. "Sound the glad tiding o'er land and sea," they sang. "Our people have triumphed and Archy is free!" That was ample cause for celebration. The case, followed closely by the state's newspapers, was equally significant for its impact on White opinion. *Ex parte Archy* raised the moral stakes of the slavery debate in California.

★

The following year, California held an election for state offices. In 1856 Baker and Broderick had joined forces in opposing the San Francisco Vigilantes, and in the process had forged a close personal relationship, despite their loyalty to competing political parties. In 1859, there was much talk of a fusion between them, but that proved premature. Instead, Broderick's Free Soil Democrats bolted from the regular party and nominated their own slate of candidates. Broderick campaigned vigorously in all the state's major cities and towns, speaking to huge crowds. "Slavery is old, decrepit, and consumptive," he declared. "Freedom is young, strong, and vigorous." The Chivalry attacked Broderick with a campaign of personal vilification and verbal abuse, attempting to bait him into a duel. He would not fight during the campaign, Broderick said, but once it was over he would willingly defend his honor.

Republicans hoped the division among the Democrats would open a path to victory. Instead, they split the antislavery vote with Broderick's supporters, which gave the victory to the Chivs. Broderick had been crushed, but his opponents kept up their personal attacks. When Justice David Terry hurled a racist insult at him, Broderick responded by calling Terry a "damned miserable wretch." Terry demanded "satisfaction," Broderick obliged, and in the pistol duel that followed, Terry shot and killed him.

Political violence and dueling were commonplace in California, but Broderick's violent death shocked the state. At the public funeral, Edward Baker delivered the eulogy before thousands of San Franciscans who crowded into Portsmouth Square, where years before Broderick had attempted to prevent the city's first vigilante lynching. "His death was a political necessity," said Baker, "poorly veiled beneath the guise of a private quarrel. What was his public crime? The answer is in his own last words: 'I die because I was opposed to the extension of slavery.'" Baker turned Broderick into a martyr for the antislavery cause. The names of Archy Lee and David Broderick would be used to forge a realignment of California politics.

★

Not long after Broderick's funeral, Baker relocated to Oregon, where legislators named him to an open U.S. Senate seat. The leadership of the antislavery movement in California was taken up by Thomas Starr King, a Unitarian minister who came from New England to lead San Francisco's First Unitarian Church. During the months preceding the presidential election of 1860, King spoke to large crowds on the high moral issues at stake in the coming contest. "Christianity has no respect for rank, color, or sect," he preached. Californians must learn to accept and embrace people of all kinds. "The diversity of race in our country," he declared, revealed the "the broad purposes of Providential good." No prominent Californian had ever spoken like that before. King challenged White Californians to apply their democratic values to people unlike themselves.

The national Democratic Party was torn apart by the conflict over slavery. In the presidential campaign of 1860, Republican Abraham Lincoln ran against three candidates, all of them Democrats. In California, a majority of Broderick's followers voted for Lincoln, and the combined votes of Free Soil Democrats and Republicans succeeded in winning the state's electoral vote by a slim plurality.

With the looming crisis of southern secession and the opening shots of the Civil War, many of California's leading Chiv politicians, including Senator William Gwin and state supreme court justice David Terry, left the state and joined the secessionists. Their absence further consolidated Republican strength, and in 1861 Californians elected Sacramento businessman Leland Stanford as their first Republican governor. Not long after, California's antislavery Democrats formally joined the state's Republicans in a Unionist coalition that denounced slavery as "an institution condemned by God and abhorrent to humanity." The Unionists swept the midterms in 1862, and two years later captured nearly 60 percent of the vote for Lincoln's reelection.

For the duration of the war, Unionists governed the state. They endorsed the Emancipation Proclamation and the Thirteenth Amendment to the federal Constitution, which abolished slavery in the United States. In 1863, legislators repealed the legal prohibition of African American testimony as well as Native indentured servitude or "apprenticeship." They left in place, however, the restriction on testimony for Native Californians and Chinese, leaving them legally unprotected against assault from Whites. Even the most liberal and humane Californians placed limits on equality.

Thomas Starr King was a case in point. During his first months in California he paid a visit to the spectacular Yosemite Valley. It had been known to White Californians for only a few years, first discovered in 1851 by a militia company sent to root out the Native Awahnechee people, who made Yosemite their home. Those who survived the attack were removed, and within months Yosemite became a favorite stop for White tourists. Moved by its beauty and grandeur, King wrote a book about Yosemite that played an important role in convincing the federal government to conserve and protect the valley, which Congress and President Lincoln did in 1864. Bereft of its indigenous inhabitants, Yosemite later became a national park.

King loved Yosemite. Yet he had nothing but scorn for what he called "the lazy, good for nothing, Digger Indians" who drifted back to their former homeland from time to time. They were not only dirty and miserable, they got in the way of the inspiring scenery. King could not conceive that the Awahnechee people found both material and spiritual sustenance in the valley. Why? Because like most Americans, he thought Native people were "savages," and did not include them in his conception of civilization.

King was certainly not unique. Some sixteen thousand Californians enlisted to fight for the Union, but few left the state. Some performed garrison duty in southern California, where there was considerable support for the Confederacy. But the majority were pressed into service in the continuing genocide of Native Californians.

In September 1863, a company of Union volunteers was dispatched to the town of Chico in the Sacramento Valley, where several hundred Maidus awaited relocation to a reservation at Round Valley in Mendocino County, 120 miles away. The removal was hastily organized and horribly mismanaged. The Maidus were force marched across the Sacramento Valley and over the Coast Range. Many were sick with malaria, others suffered from malnutrition and exhaustion, and many perished along the way. Of the 461 Maidus who began the trek, only 277 survived the march. In the twenty-first century, descendants of those survivors reenact the Konkow Trail of Tears each September. That is the way they memorialize the Civil War in California.

CHINESE RAILROAD WORKERS

23

Bohemian Days

Bret Harte arrived in San Francisco in March 1860 after being run out of town at Humboldt Bay, in the state's far north, where he worked as a reporter for a weekly newspaper. His offense? Writing an account of the dreadful massacre of some two hundred and fifty Wiyot people by local vigilantes, enraged over the theft of cattle by Natives who were literally starving to death. Harte described what he saw. "Old women, wrinkled and decrepit, lay weltering in blood, their brains dashed out and dabbled with their long gray hair. Infants, scarce a span long, with their faces cloven with hatchets and their bodies ghastly with wounds." Harte was horrified. "We can conceive of no palliation [excuse] for woman and child slaughter," he wrote. "Perhaps we do not rightly understand the doctrine of 'extermination.'" That final bit of irony pointed to Harte's future as a writer. Threatened by a lynch mob, he fled south on a steamer.

Only twenty-three, Harte had spent several years drifting around California, panning for gold in mining camps, riding shotgun for Wells Fargo, and teaching school to ranchers' kids. In writing, though, he found his calling. He began contributing to the *Golden Era,* a San Francisco literary newspaper, publishing patriotic poems that Thomas Starr King read at pro-Union rallies.

> Today, old vows our hearts renew—
> These throes that shake the Earth
> Are but the pangs that usher in
> The Nation's newer birth!

But irony was Harte's specialty. Adopting "the Bohemian" as his *nom de plume,* he began publishing a weekly column of urban observations. Despite San Francisco's reputation as a wide-open town, he found it "sober, materialistic, and practical" in the extreme. He mocked the pro-vigilante People's Party with its "spectacle of several thousand black-coated, serious-minded business men in embattled procession." He preferred to focus on the city's discordant elements: the huge rats that "fearlessly crossed the wayfarer's path at every turn, and even invaded the gilded saloons of Montgomery Street"; the gambling parlors, where "people staked and lost their last dollar with a calm solemnity and a resignation that was almost Christian"; the bustle of "steamer night," preceding the departure of the mail packet for "the States," when the accounts of merchants and wholesalers were settled and people stayed up drinking and cavorting until dawn.

He wrote presciently about the city's ethnic enclaves, places about which San Franciscans "knew but little and cared less." The restaurants in Chinatown "with their quaint display of little dishes on which tidbits of food delicacies were exposed for sale." The dance halls and dives of the "Barbary Coast," the city's red-light district. The "Spanish Quarter" near the old mission, the men in colorful jackets and sashes, their fingers "steeped in cigarette stains," the women with their "caressing intonations, the one musical utterance of the whole hard-voiced city." He wrote stories about the forgotten Spanish colonial past. In one, a Franciscan missionary traversing California's wild country encounters Satan in the form of a grizzly, who taunts him with visions of California's future, including the destruction of the missions by the "pushing, bustling, panting, and swaggering" miners. The gold rush, Harte suggested, was a tragedy.

In 1864, Harte became editor of the *Californian,* one of the city's many newspapers. By then he was the acknowledged leader of San Francisco's cultural radicals, committed to ridiculing the "humbug" of conventional society and writing the truth as they saw it. He encouraged his correspondents to develop a voice much like his own, both cosmopolitan and countrified, literary and colloquial. One of the best of them was Samuel Clemens, a reporter from Missouri by way of Nevada. In 1865, writing under the pseudonym Mark Twain, Clemens published a tale that featured miners in all their vulgar coarseness. "Jim Smiley and His Jumping Frog" announced the arrival of a new kind of American literature and made Clemens, or rather Twain, famous. But in the glow of success he acknowledged Harte's leadership. "Though I am generally placed at the head of my breed of scribblers in this part of the country," Clemons wrote home from San Francisco, "the place properly belongs to Bret Harte."

★

In 1868 Harte became founding editor of the *Overland Monthly,* a literary journal introducing California writers and issues to a national audience. The publisher, San Francisco bookseller Anton Roman, chose the name in anticipation of the completion of the transcontinental railroad. For the cover image, he and Harte chose an engraving of a snarling grizzly standing astride the railroad tracks. "Take him, if you please, as the symbol of local primitive barbarism," Harte wrote in the first issue. "He is crossing the track of the Pacific Railroad, and has paused a moment to look at the coming engine of civilization and progress, which moves like a good many other engines of civilization and progress with a prodigious shrieking and puffing."

Californians waited in eager anticipation. A rail connection with the East had been high on the agenda since the gold rush, but sectional rivalry in Congress over the location of the route stymied the federal financial support considered essential. The stalemate ended with the secession of the South after the election of Abraham Lincoln.

In 1861, four Sacramento businessmen incorporated the Central Pacific Railroad. Corporate president Leland Stanford had accumulated a fortune in the grocery business. He was joined by Collis P. Huntington, co-owner of the largest hardware store in Sacramento; Huntington's partner, Mark Hopkins, who kept the books; and dry goods merchant Charles Crocker, brother of attorney Edwin Crocker, who first represented Archy Lee. The Associates, as they called themselves, were staunch Republicans, among the founders of the state party. In 1862, Stanford was elected California's first Republican governor, and that same year the Republican majority in Congress passed the Pacific Railroad Act. It authorized generous federal loans and land grants to two companies, the eastern-based Union Pacific heading west from Omaha and the Central Pacific pushing east from Sacramento.

The Associates invested assets totaling $100,000 in the Central Pacific. But most of the capital came from gigantic federal subsidies. Governor Stanford pressed the California legis-

lature for millions in state bonds, and local communities, eager
to be connected by rail, offered more. Despite putting up relatively little of their own capital, the Associates accumulated
vast personal fortunes. Within a decade their collective wealth
totaled more than $200 million, which exceeds $4 billion in
2020 values.

It took months to get the route surveyed, the financing
arranged, the iron rails and rolling stock transported by steamship from the East. A steady supply of labor proved the major
bottleneck. Charles Crocker, in charge of construction, decided to experiment with Chinese workers. It was a controversial decision, but as Crocker put it, "we can't get enough
white labor to build this railroad, and build it we must, so
we're forced to hire them." To a certain extent, acceptance of
the Chinese by the Associates was in line with their commitment to racial equality. As they grew wealthy, they continued
to contribute to African American causes and churches. But
they also ruthlessly exploited their workers, paying them as
little as possible. As historian Dennis Drabelle writes, the apparent contradiction "speaks to the complexity of the human
heart, even a robber baron's."

By April 1865, more than two thousand Chinese workers
were blasting their way through Sierra granite. Ultimately the
Central Pacific employed more than fifteen thousand Chinese,
many recruited directly from China. Some continued to work
on the railroad, building modest lives for themselves along
with the first rail lines throughout the Far West.

★

The Chinese made up the largest group of California's foreign-
born, approximately fifty thousand individuals, about 10 percent of the state's population. Most intended to return home
once they accumulated their pile of California gold, and about

half did exactly that. That was not unusual. Polish, Italian, and Greek immigrants to the United States had similar rates of return. The Chinese who came to California were not "coolies," the name given to bound Asian workers, but they were not exactly free either. Migrants borrowed the cost of passage—about $70—from brokers, who retained control of their services until the debt was repaid in full (some $200 with interest). Most were married, but virtually none brought their wives, who remained at home. Of the several thousand Chinese women who did come to California during the gold rush, the majority were prostitutes, most of them victims of human trafficking.

At first the Chinese were welcomed. "Scarcely a ship arrives that does not bring an increase to this worthy integer of our population," the *Alta California* opined in 1852. "The China boys will yet vote at the same polls, study at the same schools, and bow at the same altar as our own countrymen." Governor John McDougal, a Democrat, praised them as among "the most worthy classes of our newly adopted citizens." But many Californians considered them a threat. "When I first came," one Chinese migrant later recalled, "Chinese treated worse than dog. . . . Hoodlums, roughnecks, young boys pull your queue, slap your face, throw all kind of old vegetable and rotten egg at you. All you could do was run and get out of the way."

Miners from the town of Sonora in the southern Sierra petitioned the authorities to "drive the coolies from our mining districts." McDougal's successor, Governor John Bigler, another Democrat, urged the legislature to adopt restrictive measures. Otherwise, he argued, California would be overwhelmed with a flood of "Chinese cheap labor" that would drive down the wages of White workers. Exclusion, he admitted, contradicted the nation's "long cherished" policy of welcoming "the oppressed of all nations." But the Chinese, he argued, were different. They would "endanger the public tranquility and injuriously affect the interests of our people."

A Chinese merchant in San Francisco responded to Governor Bigler in an open letter, printed in the *Alta California.* "We are not the degraded race you would make us," wrote Sang Yuen, who went by the Christian name of Norman Assing. A resident of the United States since 1820, Assing became a naturalized American citizen before coming to San Francisco, where he opened the city's first Chinese restaurant. "When your nation was a wilderness, and the nation from which you sprung barbarous," he reminded Bigler, the Chinese had already invented "most of the arts and virtues of civilized life."

Deaf to such appeals, the state legislature enacted a head tax on every Chinese miner in the state. But most of the Chinese chose to pay the tax and remain. State and county governments, which shared the tax revenue, came to depend on it. Before it was finally voided by national civil rights legislation following the Civil War, the Chinese tax generated nearly $60 million in revenue.

★

The *Overland Monthly* rarely addressed politics directly. But Harte published many essays challenging anti-Chinese prejudice. Augustus Loomis, who had served as a Presbyterian missionary in China, debunked claims made about the "Six Companies," the council of Chinese merchants that many Californians considered a sinister cabal controlling the "coolies." In fact, Loomis pointed out, the companies were benevolent societies, providing helpful information and refuge to strangers in a strange land. In another fascinating essay, Loomis translated the "sign-board literature" that hung outside places of business in San Francisco's Chinatown. The signs, written in Chinese characters, were "full of poetry," he wrote, like the restaurant named "Odors of Distant Lands" or the gambling parlor named "Get Rich, Please Come In."

Not only were the Chinese building the Pacific railroad, Loomis argued, they were helping to transform California agriculture, reclaiming Delta wetlands, erecting levees, and introducing intensive horticultural techniques for growing fruit and vegetables. Loomis urged his readers to consider the benefits. Californians were profiting from the accumulated experience of the world's oldest civilization. And when the migrants returned home, they would in turn transform China with what they had learned about American enterprise. It was a relationship of mutual benefit.

Such cosmopolitan thinking was in striking contrast to the ugly clamor of California politics. As an essential part of its plan for Reconstruction following the conclusion of the Civil War, the Republican Congress in Washington passed the Fourteenth Amendment to the Constitution—guaranteeing all persons residing in the United States "the equal protection of the laws" and establishing the principle of birthright citizenship. Sent to the states for ratification, the amendment became the focus of California's 1867 gubernatorial election.

Civil rights for African Americans, Democrats pointed out, would apply to the Chinese as well. But while the state's small Black community presented little danger, the Chinese population was large and growing. At stake, declared the *Sonoma Democrat,* was "the great principle of White Supremacy." California Republicans defended African American rights, but on the Chinese question they equivocated, refusing to take a principled stand. Because the Chinese were "sojourners," Republicans argued, their civil rights were not up for debate. But anti-Chinese politics proved to be the issue that revived the California Democratic Party. In the 1867 election they crushed the Republicans, winning both the governorship and control of the legislature. The short period of Republican dominance during the Civil War gave way to a quarter century of close competition between the two parties.

The Democratic majority in the legislature refused to bring the Fourteenth Amendment up for a vote, making California the only "northern" state that failed to ratify the most important constitutional reform of the Civil War era. When Congress passed the Fifteenth Amendment in 1869, guaranteeing the suffrage to all American citizens regardless of "race, color, or previous condition of servitude," California legislators voted it down. "I believe this country of ours was destined for the Caucasians, our own white race," one state senator declared. California's government went on record in opposition to multicultural democracy.

★

Despite the remaining bitterness of the late war, despite the divisive politics, San Francisco prospered as the center of a flourishing empire. In 1859 an enormous deposit of silver and gold, the Comstock Lode, was discovered in western Nevada, near the California border. San Francisco capitalists exploited the discovery on an industrial scale, extracting precious metal worth more than $400 million. Comstock silver provided the capital for San Francisco banking and finance, as well as the capital for the city's industrial development—foundries, machine shops, and metal-working plants.

The state was connected by telegraph to the rest of the nation in 1861, but distance continued to insulate it from competition with the nation's industrial heartland, allowing local industry to thrive. A great drought in the early sixties had decimated cattle ranching in much of the state, a disaster for old-time rancheros. But it cleared the way for the expansion of agriculture, particularly the production of wheat. Wheat became part of a triangular trade in British vessels: English manufactured goods to Australia, Australian coal to San Francisco, California wheat around Cape Horn to Liverpool. Getting the grain to San Francisco Bay greatly stimulated river shipping. The California economy was in full bloom.

That prosperity was the context for the literary flowering of San Francisco. At the *Overland Monthly,* Bret Harte shared editorial duties with two close friends, Charles Warren Stoddard and Ina Donna Coolbrith. With a good eye for talent, they cooperated in reading manuscripts and laying out the individual issues, publishing a crowd of first-rate writers. Often, after their working day, the three friends walked from the office on Portsmouth Square to Coolbrith's apartment on Russian Hill, where they dined together. The three editors became known as "The Overland Trinity."

Charles Warren Stoddard had grown up in San Francisco. Although he experimented with other occupations, writing was his passion, and like Harte he concluded early on that he was "fit for nothing else." He met Harte when he submitted a poem to the *Golden Era* and they became fast friends. Stoddard's poetry may strike modern readers as wordy and tedious, but his essays remain lively. He was a homosexual, although during his lifetime that term had yet to be coined. On an extended visit to the Hawaiian islands, where same-sex relations were an accepted cultural tradition, he fell in love with a young Kānaka. "For the first time," he wrote to a friend, "I act as my nature prompts me."

He published an essay on his experience in the *Overland.* Reading it today, Stoddard's words seem clear enough. "We two lay upon an enormous old-fashioned bed," he wrote. "He lay close by me. His sleek figure, supple and graceful in repose, was the embodiment of free, untrammeled youth." Stoddard is celebrated today as a pioneer of gay American literature. He wrote several more essays about his visits to Pacific islands and collected them in an 1873 book. Surprisingly, they raised few eyebrows. Reviewers appreciated or disparaged them as "Bohemian" musings. He loved his Kānaka friend, Stoddard wrote, "because he hates business, and so do I."

★

Ida Coolbrith was an equally fascinating character. Born Josephine Donna Smith, a niece of Mormon prophet Joseph Smith, she grew up in the frontier town of Los Angeles. While still in high school she was celebrated for poems she published in the local newspaper. Beautiful, charming, and talented, she married young, as many did in those days. But her husband turned out to be a jealous bully who threatened her with violence. She divorced him in 1861 when she was only twenty, then fled to San Francisco. She never remarried, and for the rest of her life she went by her mother's maiden name. She submitted poems anonymously to Harte, who published a dozen of them before they met. Her "full throated songs," said Stoddard, were "touched with a gentle melancholy."

At first Coolbrith supported herself as a teacher. But she longed for a literary career, and chafed at the limited opportunities for women. In an essay published by Harte in the *Californian,* she ridiculed "model wives" who passed their lives in meek devotion to their "lord and master." She would never accept the idea, she wrote, that women were intended for "making puddings rather than poetry." She struck the same theme in a poem that appeared in the *Overland's* inaugural issue:

> O aimless fret of household tasks!
> O chains that bind the hand and mind—
> A fuller life my spirit asks. . . .
> For Eden's life within me stirs,
> And scorns the shackles that I wear.

Such personal writing spoke to the *Overland*'s many female readers. Coolbrith also provided the emotional support that kept the Trinity working together effectively. Although poetry and editing paid very little, it was enough to allow her to pursue creative work.

But then the responsibility of family intruded. By 1874 she was supporting her aging mother as well as her niece and nephew, the children of her late sister, and was compelled to take a job as librarian of the Oakland Public Library, across the bay. "I entered my library prison," she later wrote, "a daily grind from 8 am to 9 pm for twenty years." Her creative output plummeted. Nevertheless, in her new role she nurtured the talent of dozens of young, creative Californians. "You were the first one who ever complimented me on my choice of reading," best-selling author Jack London, an Oakland native, wrote to her. "You are a goddess to me."

★

Like his friends, Harte not only edited, but he also frequently published in the *Overland*. "The Luck of Roaring Camp," a story that appeared in the second issue, made him a national celebrity. It is a tale told in the vulgar, humorous vernacular of the common men that Harte got to know during his youthful wanderings through California. The story is short but not at all sweet. In a Sierra mining camp a lone Native woman, a prostitute, dies in childbirth. The hard-bitten miners adopt the baby as their own and name him "Luck." They try to raise him, but their efforts amount to an absurd caricature of parenting. The story, rich in heart-tugging pathos, ends ironically with what Mark Twain called "the snapper." Torrential rains come and a flood carries off the camp, killing Luck. Miners were famous for believing that, come what may, life was all about "luck." Harte's story recognizes their dreams and acknowledges their tragedy, but his ending amounts to a very dark joke.

Reviewers were universal in their acclaim. "Out of its roughness," wrote a critic in the *Sacramento Daily Union,* "flash piquant gleams of gentle and imaginative feeling, like light from an uncut diamond." A reviewer in the *Nation* magazine called it the best American short story in many years. "It comes nearer than almost anything else that we know to being at once good literature and American literature." Harte followed this story with many more—"The Outcasts of Poker Flat" and "Tennessee's Partner" among the best—and in 1871 he collected them in a best-selling volume.

By then Harte had left California for the East, lured away by a lucrative offer to write for the *Atlantic Monthly.* But cut off from the culture that inspired his art and separated from his dear friends, he never regained the creative summit he conquered in San Francisco. Before leaving town, however, he published a poem that became one of the most famous, or perhaps infamous, things he ever wrote. "Plain Language from Truthful James" was a parody, written in first-person miner's doggerel, recounting a card game played by a Chinese man named Ah Sing and two White men, one of whom narrates. All three of the players cheat, but Ah Sing cheats better and wins the game. The White men are outraged. "We are ruined by Chinese *cheap labor,*" they exclaim, using the ubiquitous anti-Chinese phrase recognized by all Californians. And the poem ends:

> Which is why I remark,
> And my language is plain,
> That for ways that are dark
> And for tricks that are vain,
> The heathen Chinee is peculiar,
> Which the same I am free to maintain.

In the *Overland,* where the poem originally appeared, Harte's intention was clearly ironic, exposing the hypocrisy of White racism. He had ridiculed anti-Chinese prejudice in the pages of the *Overland* for years. The Chinese "did as the Caucasian did in all respects," he wrote, except, "being more patient and frugal, they did it a little better." Like Ah Sing, they learned the White man's game and beat him at it. However, ripped from its context and published in dozens of newspapers and magazines around the country, the poem took on a different meaning. Harte intended it as satire, but his maneuver backfired and the phrase "the heathen Chinee" entered American lingo as an ugly racist epithet. Harte came to loathe his own creation. "The worst poem I ever wrote," he said, "possibly the worst poem anyone ever wrote."

DENIS KEARNY ON NOB HILL

24

The Terrible Seventies

In late 1868 a young San Francisco journalist named Henry George published an essay in the *Overland Monthly* on the nearly completed Pacific railroad. George asked a pressing question: "What is the railroad to do for us?" Surveying the prospects, he was pessimistic. "The completion of the railroad and the consequent great increase of business and population," he wrote, "will not be a benefit to all of us, but only to a portion." The rich would get richer, that much was clear. But "those who have only their own labor will become poorer and find it harder to get ahead."

George saw an analogy in California's experience with mining. The gold rush, he wrote, had fostered "a reckless, generous, independent spirit," encouraging "general hopefulness and self-reliance, a certain large-heartedness and open-handedness." This description willfully ignored the racial hatred fueling the extermination of Native Californians, but that is not surprising, since George, like most White Californians, was himself a racist. His point, though, was that the days of the hopeful, independent miner were long gone. "The Chinaman, the millionaire and his laborers, the mine superintendent and his gang, are his successors," George wrote. "This crowding of people into immense cities, this aggregation of wealth into large lumps, this marshalling of men into big gangs under the control of the great 'captains of industry,' does not tend to foster personal independence—the basis of all virtues—nor will it tend to preserve the characteristics which particularly have made Californians proud of their state."

Henry George was a lonely critic in 1868. The following year, enthusiastic celebrations throughout California greeted the driving of the "golden spike." But it wasn't long before George began to seem prophetic. The transcontinental railroad did not begin an era of great prosperity but rather one of unemployment and depression. The subsequent decade—which became known as the "Terrible Seventies"—would test Californians like nothing since the conquest.

★

The transcontinental railroad promised efficient transport of passengers and freight to and from the eastern states at lower cost. But northern California already enjoyed a relatively efficient system of short-haul railroads and river steamboats, linking mines, ranches, and farms to ports on San Francisco Bay. The newly completed Central Pacific was unable to compete with those carriers on price. Farmers in the Central Valley were producing vast quantities of wheat, virtually all of which went to Great Britain via ocean transport. It cost more to ship a bushel of California wheat by rail over the mountains to Nevada than to England by vessel. Not until the invention of the refrigerated boxcar and shipments of fresh fruit and vegetables to eastern markets later in the century would the transcontinental business itself begin to turn a profit.

The Associates of the Central Pacific overcame this disadvantage by using their capital—generated by the sale of federally guaranteed construction bonds—to buy up local railroad and steamship lines. By the mid-1870s they had established a monopoly over California's transportation system, allowing them to arbitrarily set the highest rates in the nation for shipping exports to port and distributing imports to the state's interior.

Through the seventies and the eighties they extended their system throughout the state, coercing local communities into providing them with construction subsidies. Some resisted. When the town of Stockton rejected their demands, corporate president Leland Stanford vowed "to make the grass grow in the streets." On his order, the city was bypassed and a new rail center built ten miles away. Fearing the same thing would happen to them, voters in Los Angeles not only approved a large subsidy but also agreed to hand over the local railroad connecting their town to the port at San Pedro, which had been constructed at public expense.

★

The extension of rail lines played a role in the final episode in the state's merciless campaign against Native Californians. In 1872, the Central Pacific reached the town of Redding in the northern Sacramento Valley. This new connection to market inspired ranchers to make plans for a large cattle grazing operation in the state's far northeastern corner, an isolated region of flowing rivers, pristine lakes, and rich grasslands—and the traditional homeland of the Modoc people. In the mid-1860s, after repeated attacks by militia and vigilantes, the Modocs agreed to remove to a reservation in Oregon. But in 1870, finding conditions there intolerable, a band of fifty or sixty families returned to their homeland. With the completion of the rail line into their country, these Modocs stood in the way of development.

"God gave me this country," declared Kintpuash, their headman, called Captain Jack by the press. Army captain Reuben Bernard, well acquainted with the Modocs, argued for allowing the band to remain. "The only thing they claim or ask," he said, "is a home where they were born and raised," and he suggested granting them a reservation in the Lava Beds, a rugged landscape produced by ancient volcanic action, with little productive value as grazing land. "Nobody will ever want these rocks," said Kintpuash. "Give me a home there." But "avaricious land-grabbers," in Captain Bernard's description, continued to demand the band's removal.

In late 1872, shortly after the completion of the rail line, the army attempted to drive the Modocs out. A violent confrontation claimed lives on both sides, and the Modocs fled to the nearly inaccessible Lava Beds. Using the railroad, the army brass dispatched artillery and infantry companies from San Francisco, accompanied by a scrum of journalists covering the conflict for the national press. The nation followed news reports that chronicled the standoff between more than a thousand well-armed troops and several dozen Modoc fighters in their rocky stronghold.

By the early spring of 1873, their supplies running short, Kintpuash and his band concocted a desperate plan that they hoped would give them an opportunity to escape. During a negotiating session in April—Good Friday, as it happened—the Modocs shot and killed two peace commissioners, then led their people further into the rugged backcountry. Frightened reporters filed shrill stories calling for "extermination." The Modocs held out for several more weeks, but were finally forced to surrender.

Kintpuash and three of his lieutenants were tried for murder by a military court and hanged in October. Soldiers hauled surviving band members, 155 people, to the railroad depot in Redding, where they boarded a train that took them two thousand miles east to a forsaken corner of Indian Territory, in today's state of Oklahoma. "It makes sick heart," one Modoc told a reporter, to "go 'way off from lakes, 'way off."

★

White Californians had reasons of their own to fear the railroad. The Central Pacific was a classic monopoly, and Americans had long held the belief that such monopolies threatened the republic. Representative government, they believed, required independent citizens with minds of their own, and in turn an economy that enabled an ordinary American to own a farm, a shop, or a small business, or earn wages sufficient for the support of a family. This ideal had taken shape earlier in the century before the advent of industrial capitalism, but it remained powerful in the decades after the Civil War.

Antimonopoly candidates triumphed in the statewide election of 1871. Newton Booth, the newly elected governor, had made a fortune in the wholesale liquor business. Romulado Pacheco, the new lieutenant governor, was a Californio, the son and namesake of Captain Romulado Pacheco, killed in the violent encounter between Californios and Governor Victoria forty years before. Both men were outspoken opponents of the Central Pacific. Booth denounced what he claimed were attempts by the Associates to bribe him. "My goods have always been for sale," he declared, "my principles never." Both he and Pacheco were determined to rein in the railroad's power. "There is imminent danger," Booth warned, "that we will become enslaved in spirit and lose that sense of manly independence which is the essence of freedom."

The Associates were not intimidated. As Charles Crocker

once put it, they were experts in knowing how "to manage men after the election." Governor Booth may have been incorruptible, but he headed a corruptible administration, and despite talk of reform he got very little accomplished. In 1875 the legislature kicked him upstairs to the United States Senate and Pacheco became governor, the only Californio following the American conquest to hold the state's highest office. But like Booth, Pacheco had no success at confronting the railroad monopoly.

The Associates had numerous techniques for getting their way, and nearly all of them involved money. The most common form of graft was the railroad pass, which over the years provided free passage for hundreds of legislators. When required, more extravagant measures were employed, such as when Collis Huntington wrote privately to Leland Stanford asking him to grease the palm of an influential politician. "Arrange something out of which he could make some money (something handsome)," Huntington wrote. "Like the rest of us, he has to eat and drink." The Associates skimmed tremendous profits from their enterprise, and they willingly shared a portion of the cream. An official investigation later concluded that over some two decades they had distributed nearly $5 million in bribes to government officials.

So Californians had cause to fear and loathe the railroad, but they often misdirected their hostility. Just as the opponents of slavery focused their ire on Black people, so the opponents of railroad monopoly frequently targeted the Chinese who worked for the Central Pacific. "What the Blacks of the African coast were to the great land lords of the Southern states," declared Henry George, "the Chinese coolies are to the great lords of our Pacific slope." The Chinese, George wrote, were "utter heathens, treacherous, sensual, cowardly, and cruel."

★

With the completion of the transcontinental railroad, thousands of construction workers lost their jobs. Unemployment rose and wages fell. Many blamed the Chinese, who made up nearly a quarter of the general workforce and were willing to work for less pay than White men. Protesting "Chinese cheap labor," White Californians joined "anti-coolie clubs" and mobs attacked Chinese workers.

The most horrific episode of violence took place in Los Angeles, home to a small community of a few hundred Chinese who worked as laundrymen, cooks, domestics, and field hands. For years, Los Angeles had been one of the most violent towns in the nation, and the Chinese adopted the local custom of carrying handguns and using them to settle disputes. In October 1871, rival Chinese companies got into a gunfight on a street near the central plaza, hitting and killing a White man in the crossfire. Within minutes an angry crowd of several hundred men—Americans, Californios, and European immigrants alike—surrounded the Chinese quarter, firing indiscriminately into houses, then setting them afire. Residents fled from the flames and into the hands of the mob. Eighteen Chinese men were lynched. "The cheap labor was done away with and the sons of bitches hanged," one rioter exclaimed. A grand jury indicted several dozen men, nine of them stood trial, and seven were convicted and sentenced to terms in the state penitentiary at San Quentin. But after a few months of incarceration, the state supreme court released them on a legal technicality.

The anti-Chinese rage continued during the national economic depression that began when a speculative bubble in railroad stocks burst and the stock market crashed in 1873, freezing the nation's banking system. For a time, California was spared the worst. Silver from the Comstock Lode kept the state's economy afloat. The mine owners, known as the "Bonanza Kings," built extravagant mansions next to the palaces of the Associates of the Central Pacific on San Francisco's Nob Hill. But frantic speculation in silver mining stock created California's own speculative bubble, which burst in 1875, taking down the Bank of California, the state's largest financial institution. With the economy on the slide, a third of San Francisco's workers lost their jobs.

Many Chinese workers found employment in the countryside as field hands. They cleared land, dug and maintained irrigation ditches, worked in the fields and orchards. But small farmers and rural laborers saw them as a threat. A secretive organization of White supremacists—calling themselves the Caucasian League and mimicking the tactics of the Ku Klux Klan—launched a campaign of terror. The worst of several dozen violent incidents took place at a ranch outside the town of Chico in the Sacramento Valley when vigilantes attacked a bunkhouse full of Chinese workers, killing five men. Several White men were convicted of murder and sentenced to terms in San Quentin, but were soon pardoned by Governor William Irwin on purely racist grounds. The Chinese, the governor declared, were "the enemy of American civilization."

★

In the summer of 1877, following a series of crippling wage cuts, railroad workers staged a walkout that shut down the nation's entire rail system. President Rutherford B. Hayes mobilized federal troops to break the strike. In San Francisco, supporters held a rally attended by more than eight thousand people, many of them unemployed. Once again, righteous anger turned to racist rage. Several hundred men—chanting "On to Chinatown!"—surged into the city's Chinese quarter, smashing windows, torching buildings, and beating residents. After two nights of rioting, order was restored by city police and state militia, augmented by veterans of the old Vigilance Committee.

The riot of 1877 spawned a new political organization, the Workingmen's Party of California, an anticapitalist, prolabor organization led by a charismatic and pugnacious Irish immigrant named Denis Kearney, the "sand lot orator," who rallied crowds of unemployed men in the vacant lots near San Francisco's City Hall. Kearney burst into prominence that autumn when he led two thousand up Nob Hill for a mass rally in front of the mansions of the Associates. "The Central Pacific railroad men are thieves and will soon feel the power of workingmen," Kearney roared. He urged every worker in San Francisco to buy a gun. "We will march through the city and compel the thieves to give up their plunder!" That threat got Kearney arrested, but it also made his reputation. The Workingmen's Party promised "to wrest the government from the hands of the rich and place it in those of the people, where it properly belongs." The party advocated timely reforms like the public regulation of corporations, the eight-hour day for all workers, and the direct election of U.S. senators and the elimination of the electoral college.

These proposals, however, came attached to an ugly and potent racism. "We declare that the Chinese must leave our shores," Kearney told a rally of his supporters. "Are you ready to march down to the wharf and stop the leprous Chinese from landing?" That got Kearney arrested again, making him even more notorious. "The Chinese Must Go!" Kearney exclaimed. Organizing under that mantra, the Workingmen's Party became the most potent political force in San Francisco. "When the Chinese Question is settled," Kearney declared, "we can discuss whether it would be better to hang, shoot, or cut the capitalists to pieces." The party dispatched organizers throughout the state, and soon it had active branches in nearly all of California's counties.

★

Many Californians had lost faith in a political process corrupted by corporate graft. In September 1877, voters approved a ballot measure mandating a revision of the state's constitution. In the ensuing campaign for delegates to the state's second constitutional convention, the most pressing issues were railroad regulation and Chinese exclusion. Candidates for the Workingmen's Party outpolled both Republicans and Democrats, but failed to win an absolute majority. The convention took several months to produce a lengthy document, which voters ratified in 1879.

The new constitution was by no means a radical document, but it included several notable features. One clause, for example, prohibited discrimination against women in employment: "No person shall, on account of sex, be disqualified from entering upon or pursuing any lawful business, vocation, or profession." Women were also declared eligible for admission to the University of California.

But public attention focused on more controversial sections. The constitution created two new regulatory bodies, an elected Railroad Commission empowered to set fair shipping rates, and an elected Board of Equalization to ensure that taxes on corporate (that is to say, railroad) property were fairly apportioned and equally applied by all the state's counties. The Associates had plenty of experience corrupting elected officials, and over the subsequent three decades they had little difficulty eliciting favorable decisions from the Railroad Commission.

The Board of Equalization, however, proved somewhat more difficult to control. When it ruled against the sweetheart deals that several counties had made with the Central Pacific, for example, the Associates sued. The case was eventually settled by the U.S. Supreme Court in 1886, when it ruled that corporations were "legal persons" and that the due process and equal protection clauses of the Fourteenth Amendment made it illegal to tax them differently than other individuals. Measures intended to guarantee the rights of African Americans were thus deployed to protect corporate wealth and power.

Regarding the "Chinese Question," the new constitution banned government agencies from employing Chinese workers and legalized discrimination, authorizing cities and towns to segregate Chinese residents in prescribed districts or forcibly evict them from their jurisdictions. Chinese leaders challenged those provisions, and a federal court struck them down as violations of the Fourteenth Amendment, which guaranteed the equal protection of law to all *persons* residing in the United States. Nevertheless, the court suggested where anti-Chinese activists might turn to achieve their aims. "The remedy is not with the state," the judge advised, "but with the general government."

★

"Chinese exclusion" became a national topic when the national Republican and Democratic parties both endorsed restriction in the presidential campaign of 1880. The next year Congress debated and passed the Chinese Exclusion Act, and it became law in 1882. The nation abandoned the traditional policy of open borders and for the first time proscribed the entry of an entire ethnic or national group. Denis Kearney went on a national tour to promote his party and himself. In New York City, an outspoken Chinese American writer named Wong Ching Foo invited him to debate. When Kearney refused, Wong challenged him to a duel, giving his opponent the choice of weapons: chopsticks, Irish potatoes, or heavy artillery. The incident made headlines around the country. "Wong Ching Foo succeeds," observed the *New York Tribune,* "in making the sand-lot agitator look ridiculous." Kearney's hour in the spotlight had passed.

In California, newspaper editors complained that despite

the new law, Chinese migrants continued to cross the unprotected borders with Canada and Mexico. The time had come, anti-Chinese activists declared, for White Californians to take the law into their own hands. This new vigilante campaign commenced in 1885 in the northern town of Eureka on Humboldt Bay when a White man was shot and killed by a Chinese gangster. Chanting "Burn the devils out," a White mob rounded up eight hundred Chinese residents, forced them onto steamboats bound for San Francisco, then burned Eureka's Chinatown to the ground. The expulsion, declared the editor of the *Stockton Mail,* "conveys a lesson which other communities might learn to their advantage."

Over the next few years, in a campaign of violence the Chinese called "the driving out," Whites forced them from dozens of California towns. In response, Congress strengthened the Exclusion Act, effectively ending all Chinese immigration. "The experiment of blending the social habits and mutual race idiosyncrasies of the Chinese laboring classes with those of the great body of people of the United States," President Grover Cleveland announced, had been "unwise, impolitic, and injurious to both nations."

In the farming regions of the state, meanwhile, agriculture was booming as growers expanded the range of market crops, adding vegetables, nuts, fruit, and wine to the former staples of beef and wheat. The demand for rural workers grew, intensified by Chinese exclusion. "Chinese labor is rapidly becoming scarcer," the editor of the *Watsonville Pajaronian* wrote. "The Exclusion Act has kept out immigration of young Chinese, and most of those who remain have reached an age where they are unable to give a full day's work." Farmers began looking elsewhere for "cheap labor."

ELIZA TIBBETS + HER ORANGE TREE

25

The Cow Counties

In 1870, southern California remained undeveloped. The four huge counties south of the Tehachapi Range contained a total of thirty-five thousand residents, only 6 percent of the state's population. Spanish speakers remained in the majority, and a visitor described Los Angeles as "a Mexican town." Several thousand Natives, mostly former mission converts and their descendants, lived in their own rural communities scattered across the region, supplying labor for cattle ranchers and farmers. Winemaking was an important business in Los Angeles, but hardly the foundation for a regional economy. Southern California accounted for less than 4 percent of the state's agricultural production.

Northerners disparagingly referred to the south as "the cow counties," although the cattle grazing business was a thing of the past, destroyed by the devastating drought of the 1860s. Some ranchers shifted to sheep, but others began to sell off their holdings. "One of the best signs of the times is the subdivision of large ranches into farms and small parcels of land," wrote J. Ross Browne, a frequent commentator on California topics. "The owners are beginning to see that men and women are more profitable than cattle." The Central Pacific extended its rails to southern California, part of a second transcontinental line across the desert Southwest known as the Southern Pacific, for which the Associates received federal land grants amounting to a huge portion of the public domain. Those lands first went on the market in the late 1870s.

Serious agricultural settlement in the southern counties began with what was called the "colony system." In 1857, a company of German immigrants, pooling their resources, had purchased land and water rights to land southeast of Los Angeles, dividing it into individual farms, laying out roads, and establishing a town center. They called their development the "Anaheim Colony." The colonists depended on the hired labor of the Luiseños, formerly the Native Christians of Mission San Luis Rey, who had a reputation as "sprightly, skillful, and handy workers," in the words of one Anaheim farmer. The Luiseños constructed a canal to bring water from the lower Santa Ana River, dug an extensive system of irrigation ditches, planted vineyards and orchards, and provided the colonists with field labor. By the 1870s the Anaheim Colony was producing fruit and wine in commercial quantities and the market value of its farms had more than tripled.

★

Anaheim's success became a model for further development. The town of Riverside was founded in 1871 on the upper Santa Ana River by the "Southern California Colony Association," a group of "free thinkers" from the eastern states. Eliza Tibbets, a married woman of middle age who was associated with the Riverside colony, played a key role in developing the industry that would soon drive regional growth.

Mrs. Tibbets and her husband, Luther, were something of an odd couple. Both were avid supporters of equal rights for African Americans and women, but they possessed contrasting personalities. He was a cantankerous individualist with a talent for picking fights. She was a gregarious spiritualist who made friends easily and often held séances in her home for friends and neighbors.

The couple were living in Washington, D.C., when they first learned of the Riverside colony. Mr. Tibbets traveled to California by rail to investigate. He liked what he saw, but balked at coughing up the several-hundred-dollar fee required to join. So instead, he filed a homestead claim on government land nearby. He built a small house, prepared the land, and began experimenting with crops. Some colonists were having luck with oranges, but the local variety, introduced to California by the Franciscans, was small, seedy, and easily bruised.

Mrs. Tibbets, still in Washington, asked one of her neighbors, a botanist working for the Agriculture Department, if he had any advice on growing oranges. He informed her that the department had obtained samples of a promising new variety, a sweet, seedless, thick-skinned orange from Brazil, and she talked him into sending a few samples to Riverside. The orange trees arrived there in 1873, not long after she did. Mrs. Tibbets planted them near her kitchen door and made a point of hand watering them every day with her dirty dishwater. It took a couple of years before they bore their first golden fruit, which had a curious indentation on one end that looked something like a human bellybutton. The "navels," as they became known, were both delicious and impervious to bruising. She entered them in a local competition and won first prize.

Soon other Riverside colonists were clamoring for cuttings. Because they are seedless, navel oranges must be propagated from cuttings grafted onto citrus root stock, and for several years Mrs. Tibbets made a good living selling them. Navel orange groves spread through the foothills of the San Gabriel and San Bernardino mountains, watered by irrigation, sweetened by crisp, cool winter nights. By the late 1880s a "golden rim" of commercial orange groves extended for seventy miles along the rail line from Los Angeles to Riverside.

Native workers supplied much of the labor. The federal government established a boarding school in Riverside—the Sherman Indian Institute—that provided a supply of cheap, abundant labor for growers. They were supplemented by Chinese workers. In 1885, Charles Warren Stoddard found hundreds of them working in the groves at Riverside, "picking and washing and sorting oranges, chattering and laughing as they worked." The Chinese perfected what became known as the "China pack," each piece of fruit individually wrapped in tissue paper then carefully arranged in a crate, tighter at the edges than at the center, creating a fecund and appealing bulge. It was like a work of art, one grower remembered, "every wrapper smooth, not a wrinkle, and the tissue triangled to a point on top so that when the box was opened it was something to display in a grocer's window."

Some colonists made a fortune growing oranges, but Luther and Eliza Tibbets were not among them. Inexplicably, Mr. Tibbets scorned his wife's oranges, refused to grow them commercially, and instead experimented with less successful crops. He also continued his quarrelsome ways. "He had suits about stray stock, land, water, and every conceivable subject," wrote a neighbor. Litigation drained the family finances, forcing the couple to mortgage their property, which they eventually lost. Although Eliza Tibbets died poor and unacknowledged in 1898, she is now credited as the individual most responsible for introducing naval oranges and transforming the economy of southern California. One of her original trees

survives, still standing where she planted it and still producing delicious fruit.

★

Southern Californians saw a boom coming. Eager horticulturalists scrambled to obtain irrigated land. Oranges and other
orchard crops were planted where cattle and sheep had formerly grazed. California citrus growers organized themselves
into an association, marketing their product under what would
become the Sunkist brand, shipping their bounty to eastern
markets in refrigerated railroad boxcars.

Ranchers relocated their livestock to the interior, where
they frequently encroached on the lands of Native communities. "Real estate in that section is much sought after," a federal
inspector reported. "It is hardly expected that the Indians can
retain their old homes much longer unless something is done
by the government to protect them." The Native people at risk
included several thousand Luiseños, who lived in a handful
of rural villages, including a place they called Temecula, about
fifty miles south of Riverside.

The Luiseños of Temecula traced their village back "to
time immemorial," long before the arrival of the Franciscans.
Following the secularization of Mission San Luis Rey, many
returned to the village, where they farmed and grazed livestock. In 1852, along with other "Mission Indians" of southern
California, they signed a treaty with the United States that
would have protected their land. But Congress refused to con-
firm the treaty, leaving the Luiseños without legal title. In the
early 1870s, a group of investors purchased the land encompassing Temecula, and in 1875 they obtained a court order evicting the Luiseños. When the two hundred residents refused to
vacate, the county sheriff and his deputies forcibly removed
them, then released a flock of sheep that quickly devoured the
crops they depended on for the winter. "The Indians see in this

Temecula ejectment what is soon to follow all over," a federal official wrote. "It will be but a short time when scarcely an acre of tillable land will be left to them in all southern California."

★

The eviction at Temecula is the central event in Helen Hunt Jackson's 1884 novel *Ramona*. A popular travel writer, Jackson had previously published *A Century of Dishonor*, an indictment of the treatment of Natives by the United States. When that book failed to have the impact on public opinion she had hoped for, Jackson vowed to find another way to communicate her message. Learning of the Luiseño eviction, she decided to write a book that would appeal to the conscience of her readers by breaking their hearts.

Ramona narrates California history as a family story. The title character, the daughter of a Native mother and a White father, is raised as a foster child in the household of a land-owning Californio family. But when Ramona falls in love with Alessandro, a Luiseño from Temecula, she is cast out of her childhood home. Ramona and Alessandro hope to relocate in Temecula, but the eviction intervenes. "These Americans will destroy us all," says Alessandro. "They will . . . shoot us and poison us to get us all out of the country, as they do the rabbits and the gophers." The couple searches in vain for a place to live in peace, finally retreating to a mountain hideout. But Alessandro is stalked by a White racist and murdered. Ramona nearly dies of grief before being rescued by her foster brother.

Ramona became a national best-seller. Readers were swept up by the struggle of the lovers, and shed many tears over their cruel fate. "How pretty and tender and complete it all is," wrote a reviewer in the *Overland Monthly*. But, he added, "the poet has, perhaps, been a little stronger than the reformer." This comment foretold the book's fate—to be read as romance rather than tragedy. She was "much cast down" by this reception, Jackson wrote to a friend, "sick of hearing" of her readers' infatuation with the young lovers, without "even an allusion to the ejectment of the Temecula band from their homes."

Just as irony failed Bret Hart when it came to the Chinese, sentimentality kept Helen Hunt Jackson from making her point about the Luiseños. She portrayed Ramona and Alessandro as buoyant lovers but fatalistic historical actors. "There is no hope," says Ramona, and Alessandro nods his head. "Hide," he says, "that is all we can do." The novel dwells on dispossession, impoverishment, and disappearance: the myth of the vanishing Indian all over again.

But unlike the novel's lovers, the Luiseños of Temecula did not retreat to a mountain hideout. Unwilling to abandon the graves of their ancestors, they relocated several miles away to the arid Pechanga Valley. Their leader, Olegario Calac, hired an attorney. For years, Calac had worked as a labor contractor in Los Angeles, supplying Luiseño workers for vineyards and wineries, and he enjoyed solid working relationships with several notable businessmen. The eviction was illegal, Calac argued, because the Luiseños had never officially ceded legal title of their land to the United States.

With the financial assistance of his business associates, Calac purchased a round-trip ticket to Washington, D.C., where his friends arranged for an audience with President Ulysses S. Grant. The president promised assistance, and not long after Calac's visit he issued an executive order creating nine small reservations for several communities of "Mission Indians," including the Luiseños. Calac returned with an American flag presented to him by the president, which the Luiseños preserved as an *aide-mémoire,* displaying it on special occasions. Regrettably, the injustice suffered by the Native people of southern California did not end there. Many struggles lay ahead. But unlike the tragic characters in *Ramona,* the Luiseños never lost their determination to resist and survive.

★

Until the end of the nineteenth century wheat was California's most important export. Central Valley farmers grew it on an unprecedented scale, working huge fields with gang plows, mechanical harvesters, combines, and other farm machinery powered by dozens of horses or mules. A handful of "Wheat Kings" ran their farms like little fiefdoms. The fields of rancher Hugh Glenn of Colusa County in the Sacramento Valley, for example, covered more than thirty-five thousand acres, fifty square miles. By 1890 California had become the nation's second-largest wheat-exporting state, right behind Minnesota.

Workers in the wheat fields were overwhelmingly White. Most were migrants, coming and going with the seasons, drifting between districts with the ripening of the grain. Tramping harvesters were known as "bindlestiffs," for the bedrolls or "bindles" that hung from their shoulders. They slept in overcrowded bunkhouses on piles of straw. "Oh, we were always scratching," one wheat thresher recalled. "We ate burned beef. We drank filthy water. . . . We lived with the chickens and the cows. We were always dirty. We never had any money. We stank to hell." They were also poorly paid. "Fleas were more easily acquired than money," said one man, "and indeed cling to a person longer and far more pertinaciously than dollars."

The future of California agriculture, however, was not in wheat but in fruit and vegetables. In the 1870s, the well-watered Santa Clara Valley, south of San Francisco, became the state's leading producer of orchard crops and site of the state's first fruit and vegetable canneries. In the eighties, when Los Angeles County rapidly converted to citrus, wine production shifted north to the valleys of Napa and Sonoma. Fresno County, in the arid San Joaquin Valley, diversified from wheat to the production of table grapes and raisins.

Vineyards require hot summers and an abundance of water, a combination difficult to find. But the Fresno region offered both, with the water supplied by irrigation from the Kings River, which tumbled down the western slope of the southern Sierra Nevada only twenty miles to the east. Fresno attracted numerous settlement colonies. One of the first, the "Central California Colony," included many middle-class San Franciscans. One group of four Bay Area school teachers, all single women, combined their resources and purchased a hundred-acre plot they called Hedgerow Vineyard. Minnie Austin, who managed the operation, began marketing raisins in small, colorful packages for extra consumer appeal.

Austin promoted horticulture as the ideal profession for women. Indeed, in the late nineteenth century at least seven hundred California women ran their own horticultural operations. Kate Sessions, a native San Franciscan who graduated from the University of California at Berkeley with a science degree in the late 1870s, opened a commercial nursery in San Diego. She popularized dozens of exotic species, including bougainvillea, bird of paradise, oleander, and jacaranda with their distinctive blue blossoms. Sessions, who continued in business until her death in 1940, did more to invent the color palette of the southern California landscape than any other individual.

★

Joining a colony, however, required an investment beyond the means of most settlers. Like Luther Tibbets, most farmers filed a claim under the Homestead Act, or purchased a parcel of the public domain at the government price of $2.50 an acre for unimproved land. In addition to the price of the land, there were high startup costs, especially for irrigation. Lacking capital, many settlers continued the old American tradition of simply squatting on the land, cutting a ditch to the nearest water-course, and planting crops. This was known as a "preemption claim." By law, preemptors on the public domain were given the opportunity to purchase their claims at the government price. But private landowners like the railroad had no obligation to honor the claims of squatters. Often, that led to trouble.

Along the Kings River in Tulare County, south of Fresno, several hundred squatters staked out claims on land owned by the Southern Pacific (popularly known as the SP), a holding company organized by the Associates to consolidate all their railroad operations. When the SP put their San Joaquin Valley holdings on the market in 1878, they offered parcels at prices eight to ten times higher than unimproved government land. The land, of course, was no longer unimproved; there were irrigation ditches, fences, barns, and homes, improvements put in by the squatters, and they protested that the railroad was charging them for their own labor. A group of farmers sued in federal court but lost. Some settled with the SP, but others formed a vigilante organization and vowed to resist any and all attempts at eviction. Much of their anger was directed at neighbors who had paid the railroad's price. Hooded night-riders terrorized farm families, a number of whom were burned out of their homes.

On May 11, 1880, near a watercourse called Mussel Slough, a federal marshal, a corporate official, and two land buyers attempted to evict a squatter family. Fifty armed vigilantes tried to prevent them. There was pushing and shoving, and when someone accidentally fired a rifle, a gunfight ensued that left the two buyers and five squatters dead. Vigilante leaders were convicted of resisting a federal official but were sentenced to relatively short prison terms. The press and the public held the Associates responsible. A San Francisco magazine published a political cartoon titled "The Curse of California," depicting a huge octopus labeled "Railroad Monopoly" squeezing the life out of miners, farmers, fruit growers, and vineyardists. In the foreground a graveyard labeled "Mussel Slough" featured a tombstone inscribed "Killed by the Railroad Monster." The SP became known throughout California as "the Octopus."

★

The Southern Pacific didn't want trouble. It wanted productive farmers settled along its lines, shipping produce to market in its boxcars, and it did everything it could to encourage migration to California. This included running dozens of "emigrant cars" on its transcontinental service. They were crowded and uncomfortable, with hard wooden bench seats, a coal-burning stove at one end, a lavatory stall at the other. Often they were attached to slow-moving freight trains. Still, the ten-day railroad journey was far better than six months in a covered wagon along a dusty, dangerous trail.

Nevertheless, California's population grew slowly. Farmers, whether Americans or immigrants, greatly preferred the Midwest to California. During the 1880s more than a quarter million people moved to Dakota Territory (which entered the Union as the states of North and South Dakota in 1889). Over the same decade, California attracted less than half that number.

An average of approximately sixty thousand people came by rail to California each year. But most were well-to-do tourists, traveling in plush Pullman sleeping cars. Touring California had become fashionable. In addition to making the rounds of San Francisco—exclusive Nob Hill, exotic Chinatown, Cliff House overlooking the Pacific, and perhaps a little late-night slumming on the Barbary Coast—visitors marveled at the redwood groves of Marin County and the spectacular vistas of Yosemite. Following the completion of the rail line to Los Angeles in 1876, many tourists added a side trip to southern California, famous for the healing benefits of its sunshine and aridity. Thousands of affluent easterners, suffering from tuberculosis and other bronchial disorders, spent time recovering in this "asthmatic's paradise." After the publication of *Ramona,* many eagerly visited the sites mentioned in the book. Enthralled by the imaginary world of caring missionaries and grateful Natives, tourists began seeking out the old missions, which local residents mostly ignored. The crumbling ruins of California's past became destinations of romance.

★

In late 1885 the Atchison, Topeka, and Santa Fe Railroad opened a through line to Los Angeles across the desert Southwest, breaking the Southern Pacific monopoly. A rate war broke out between the two companies, and for a time the one-way fare to Los Angeles from St. Louis dropped to less than $15. Passenger traffic exploded. An estimated 150,000 passengers came to Los Angeles by the southern route in 1887, eager to see a region previously accessible only to the wealthy.

With the shift to citrus well underway, real estate sold briskly. Middle-class migrants wanted in on the action, and a full-fledged land rush ensued. Land that had formerly sold at $100 per acre went for ten times that amount. The logic of a boom is to buy immediately, then sell at a profit as quickly as possible, and during the height of the frenzy in 1887 properties with an accumulated value of a million dollars were changing hands every day. County officials could not keep up with title searches and deed registrations. Eventually nervous local bankers stopped lending, and the bubble burst. By 1888 the boom had ended.

But there were lasting effects. Developers laid out plans for sixty new towns. Most failed to materialize, but a number thrived, especially in the San Gabriel Valley, crossed by the rails of both the Southern Pacific and the Santa Fe. The city of Los Angeles itself went from eleven thousand residents in 1880 to more than fifty thousand ten years later. For the first time, Spanish-speaking Angelenos became a minority, mostly segregated in "Sonoratown," the city's oldest neighborhood. By 1890 southern California included more than two hundred thousand predominantly White residents. The region greatly outdistanced the rest of the state in its rate of growth, a trend that would continue well into the future.

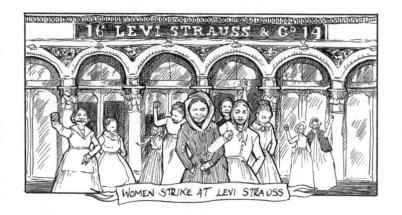

WOMEN STRIKE AT LEVI STRAUSS

26

A Cosmopolitan City

California's growth bottomed out in the last decade of the nineteenth century. The economy stalled and a financial panic in 1893 plunged the state and the nation into a severe depression that continued for five years. Over the decade, the state's population increased by less than 25 percent, the lowest rate since statehood. Southern California proved an exception. The city of Los Angeles doubled in size, slightly exceeding one hundred thousand residents in 1900.

San Francisco, with a population approaching four hundred thousand, remained California's unrivaled metropolis. Residents and visitors alike paid it loving tribute. It was "the gayest, lightest hearted, most pleasure loving city of the western continent," wrote newspaperman Will Irwin, "a city of romance and a gateway to adventure." San Francisco remains one of America's most fabled cities. "I left my heart in San Francisco," in the words of the song, "where little cable cars climb halfway to the stars." It's a wonderful image, but great cities are made of sterner stuff. San Francisco was the premier Pacific port of North America, and the pulsing heart of the economy of the Far West, a region that included California, Nevada, Alaska, Hawai'i, and Arizona as well as northern Mexico. The city imported goods from the eastern states and distributed them throughout the region, collected raw material from mines, farms, and forests and exported them to the world. San Francisco was headquarters for the West's largest banking, insurance, transportation, and manufacturing companies.

The city ran on the labor of more than 150,000 workers, the majority connected in one way or another with maritime commerce. The waterfront swarmed with seamen, longshoremen, and teamsters; downtown sidewalks bustled with clerks and merchants. Industrial development may have been hampered by the lack of substantial coal and iron ore deposits in the state, but in the manufacturing district south of Market Street, foundry workers produced iron and steel for railroad cars, steamships, and mine and farm equipment, while factory hands turned out consumer goods of all sorts. In half a century, San Francisco had gone from trading village to capitalist metropolis.

★

Levi Strauss & Co.—maker of Levi's, the original American blue jeans—opened for business in 1853. Corporate headquarters remain in San Francisco today, making it the city's oldest manufacturing firm. Founder Levi Strauss left Bavaria in 1848 and worked with his brothers in a New York City dry goods business before heading west. His career paralleled the economic development of the city. He first operated as a wholesaler, importing textiles and ready-to-wear clothing, supplying retail establishments. His business prospered and grew, with a customer base that ranged throughout the Far West. Strauss never married—"My entire life is my business," he once told a reporter—but extended family joined him in San Francisco and filled key management positions in the company.

Strauss was one of several thousand middle-class German Jews who migrated to the city during the gold rush. Encountering very little anti-Semitism, they assimilated into the business community, helping to construct the city's capitalist economy from the ground up. By 1900 San Francisco was home to a Jewish community of some twenty-five thousand. As a group, they were remarkably secular. Despite a half dozen synagogues, religion played a relatively minor role for most of them. Isaac Meyer Wise, the most notable rabbi in the United States, visited the city and was shocked to find Jewish businesses operating on the Sabbath. He sharply questioned several prominent Jews about it. "I take no interest in Jewish affairs," one of them told him. That was typical. Levi Strauss participated actively in the city's civic life, but he rarely attended temple.

In 1873, Strauss made a business deal with one of his customers, Jacob Davis, a Jewish tailor in Reno, Nevada, who made work clothes for miners and cowboys. In response to complaints of torn pockets, Davis began reinforcing the seams with copper rivets. His innovation proved popular, and he approached Strauss about increasing his manufacturing capacity. Strauss was intrigued, and the two men jointly patented Davis's design, the prototype for today's Levi's. Strauss opened a garment factory in San Francisco, with Davis managing production.

Within months they were doing a booming business. Strauss reorganized his company, focusing exclusively on the manufacture of workwear, especially the "waist overalls" we now know as jeans. The company produced a quality product and expertly branded it, not only with the shiny copper rivets, but with distinctive stitching on the back pockets and a visible leather patch featuring their trademark. Within a few years

Levi Strauss had become the largest apparel manufacturer in San Francisco. The *New York Times* included him on a list of the city's ten wealthiest men, alongside the Associates of the Southern Pacific, the Bonanza Kings of the Comstock Lode, and the directors of the Bank of California.

★

Garment production was low-skill, low-wage labor, often performed by Chinese workers. But following the anti-Chinese riots of 1877, Strauss dismissed his Chinese hands and began advertising that his jeans and jackets were "The Only Kind Made with White Labor." The company now relied exclusively on young working women. "GIRLS! GIRLS! GIRLS!" barked a "Help Wanted" ad placed in the local papers. "Highest wages paid to good sewing machine operators." In fact, the company had for years been waging a concerted campaign to drive wages down.

Occasionally the women workers pushed back. "Three hundred and sixty spunky young ladies employed in the overall department of Levi Strauss & Co.'s factory sailed out on strike yesterday morning," the *San Francisco Examiner* reported in 1890. Stimulated by the insurgency of the Workingmen's Party, unions had surged during the eighties. But labor leaders refused to organize women workers, who made up nearly 20 percent of the labor force, so the women in Strauss's factory acted on their own. Management had reduced piecework rates from $1.05 to 95 cents per dozen pair, the fourth such reduction in as many months. Only a year before the rate had been $1.25.

Manager Jacob Davis met with the strikers. A young woman named Lulu Lindsay spoke up for them. "You're trying to cut us down to Chinese wages," she told Davis. "We work hard and we're entitled to fair pay. That ten cents on a dozen means a great deal to us. There's girls who can only make eight pairs a day." The strikers cheered in agreement. Like most workers at the time, they labored six days a week, ten hours a day, taking home five or six dollars a week (less than $10,000 a year in 2020 values). "Not enough for a chicken!" one of the women shouted at Davis. "We're willing to go back at the old pay," Lindsay said, "but we will not do another stich if we're reduced." The company withdrew the cut and the women went back to work. But a few days later, Davis fired Lulu Lindsay and other "ringleaders" and reinstated the wage reduction.

The decade's most significant labor struggle took place in 1894 when a national rail strike against the Pullman Palace Car Company shut down the nation's rail system. Workers in Sacramento, Los Angeles, and Oakland occupied the railroad depots and fought with the police and state militia that sought to evict them. Union workers in San Francisco walked off the job in sympathy. President Grover Cleveland called out federal troops and broke the strike. Employers then launched an offensive, cutting wages and dismissing "troublemakers." It took organized labor several years to recover.

★

The Spanish-American War of 1898 ended the depression. Admiral George Dewey of the U.S. Navy triumphed over the Spanish fleet in Manila Bay, while Filipino nationalists pushed the Spanish from the countryside and declared independence. The Spanish refused to negotiate with the nationalists and instead handed possession of the colony to the United States. Intent on establishing a chain of coaling stations for the Pacific fleet, Congress annexed the Philippines and the island of Guam, betraying a promise to recognize Filipino independence. The U.S. Army subsequently waged a fierce three-year struggle against nationalist forces that cost the lives of thousands of Filipinos. San Francisco was the training center and embarkation point for that counterinsurgency. Some eighty thousand soldiers and sailors passed through the Bay Area on their way across the Pacific, and the influx of federal dollars revived the economy. In gratitude, the city erected a towering monument memorializing the conflict in downtown Union Square.

During the war, Congress also annexed the Hawaiian Islands—with important consequences for California. Over the years, by means fair and foul, Americans had taken possession of most of the fertile land in the islands, which they converted to sugar plantations. San Franciscan Claus Spreckels, a German immigrant who prospered as a brewer, built the first California refinery for processing Hawaiian sugar cane. To ensure a steady supply he began purchasing land on the islands, eventually establishing the largest sugar plantation in the world, worked by thousands of Japanese immigrants.

Japanese workers began migrating to Hawaiʻi in the 1880s, and to California in the 1890s. "As the Exclusion Act crowds out the Chinese," one grower wrote, "the Japs seem to come in to take their places." By 1900 some thirteen thousand Japanese resided in the state. With Hawaiian annexation those numbers rapidly increased, reaching thirty thousand by 1910. "Immigration officials are unable to deny the Asiatics landing because of their coming from a port of the United States," the *Sacramento Bee* reported. Similarly, the annexation of the Philippines opened the door for the migration of thousands of Filipinos.

★

With the economy on a roll and unemployment down, organized labor in San Francisco launched a drive to recover lost ground. Unionization was particularly successful in the city's manufacturing sector, including the garment trade, and by 1900 several large textile manufacturers had agreed to union contracts. Levi Strauss & Co., however, stubbornly held out, despite a union-led boycott of its apparel.

The resurgence of organized labor took place during the administration of Mayor James Phelan, the son of an Irish immigrant who made a fortune in the grocery business. Phelan was an elite reformer who argued for "scientific, systematic, and responsible government," supported the municipal ownership of utilities (water, gas, electricity, streetcars), and advocated an expanded municipal civil service. He was also an incorrigible racist, always willing to employ ethnic prejudice for political purposes. "The Chinese and Japanese," he declared, "are not the stuff of which American citizens can be made."

Like many elite San Franciscans, Phelan feared that worker militancy "foreshadowed the possibility of revolution." As mayor, he encouraged the city's largest employers to band together in opposition to unionization. Levi Strauss was among the first to join the newly formed Employers' Association, and he proved to be "an uncompromising member," in the words of the pro-labor *Examiner*. Spoiling for a fight, in the spring of 1901 the Employers' Association encouraged waterfront hauling companies to dismiss their union employees.

In response, the unions representing sailors and longshoremen went on strike, closing the port of San Francisco at a net loss of more than a million dollars a day. The Employers' Association refused to negotiate, making it clear that its goal was breaking the unions, so workers in other industries struck in sympathy. The entire city was crippled. Next the Employers' Association imported hundreds of strikebreakers. When strikers attacked them, Mayor Phelan ordered the police to clear the streets of picketers. "If you don't want to be clubbed," he told union leaders, "go back to work." In subsequent violent clashes, five men were killed and more than three hundred seriously injured. The strike dragged on for months. Fearing economic calamity, California's governor finally pressured the hauling companies into negotiations. They refused to give in to demands for a "union shop"—union membership required as a condition of employment—but agreed to rehire the strikers, a stinging defeat for the Employers' Association.

Organized labor then launched a campaign of boycotts and strikes that succeeded in winning union contracts with the city's largest employers. San Francisco soon became one of the nation's most unionized cities, with the highest wages for workers in the Far West. A few firms continued to hold out, Levi Strauss & Co. prominent among them. Strauss died in 1902 at the age of seventy-three, but the company continued his policy of resisting unionization.

★

Disgusted with Mayor Phelan, labor leaders decided to enter politics directly, pulling together a coalition they called the Union Labor Party and running their own candidates in the municipal elections of 1901. Enjoying the overwhelming support of the city's working class, Eugene Schmitz, president of the Musicians' Union, won election as mayor, and Union Labor candidates won a majority on the board of supervisors.

Handsome and well-spoken, Mayor Schmitz was popular not only among the working class but also in the middle-class neighborhoods on the city's west side. But his administration soon became mired in corruption. Abraham Ruef, a dapper lawyer who grew up in San Francisco's Jewish community, became the administration's fixer. As a young man in the 1880s Ruef had learned the ropes from the city's political bosses. They employed gangs of thugs, known as "rockrollers," to intimidate voters, illegally stuff ballot boxes, and steal elections. Ruef favored more refined tactics. He no longer needed the rockrollers because organized labor assumed the responsibility for getting voters to the polls. Ruef took care of the sordid behind-the-scene details, like accepting bribes from business leaders and brothel owners and distributing the "boodle" to elected officials in exchange for political favors.

The corruption was relatively open, but nevertheless Mayor Schmitz was handily reelected in 1903, then again in 1905 when he overwhelmed John Partridge, a "fusion" candidate nominated by both the Republican and Democratic parties. With the exception of elite enclaves like Nob Hill, Schmitz carried all the city's electoral districts. "Thousands of men voted for Schmitz because their employers favored Partridge," said a Republican politician. "It was a class movement. Partridge was the candidate of the rich and Schmitz was the champion of the poor."

★

One afternoon in early April 1906, shortly after Schmitz began his third term, a filmmaker strapped a hand-cranked movie camera to the front of a cable car and filmed the thirteen-minute trip from midtown San Francisco to the waterfront. "A Trip Down Market Street," which survives today in remarkably good condition, offers a rare moving picture of ordinary San Francisco life at the turn of the twentieth century. Cable cars, horse-drawn vehicles, bicycles, and a few new-fangled automobiles fill Market Street. People crowd the sidewalks and amble into the thoroughfare, carrying bags and packages, crossing against traffic, the women in long skirts that skim the pavement, the men in sack coats. All the boys wear knickers and the girls dresses, some fancy, some plain. Everyone, without exception, wears a hat.

Little vignettes stand out. A worker sweeps the street with a large push broom. A policeman walks his beat, billy club in hand, warily surveying the crowd. A group of well-dressed women and girls wait for a streetcar. A man hurries across the street with a baby in his arms. A burly teamster in a large wagon drawn by two horses makes a lumbering left turn. Newsboys carrying bundles of papers cavort for the camera. It's all wonderfully ordinary, yet also terribly poignant when we realize what was about to happen.

A few days later, at 5:12 a.m. on the morning of April 18, 1906, the Pacific Plate suddenly jerked ten feet northwest along the San Andreas Fault. The earth shook violently for forty-five seconds. Scientists today estimate the intensity as 7.9 on the Richter scale, which would make the San Francisco earthquake the largest in the state's recorded history. San Francisco had previously suffered quakes that destroyed buildings and took lives, but nothing compared to this. Warnings had gone unheeded. Dennis Sullivan, the city's fire chief, had argued in vain for a new high-pressure water system with backup reservoirs inside the city limits. "The Town is in an earthquake belt," said Sullivan. "One of these fine mornings, we will get a shake that will put this little water system out, and then we'll have a fire. What will we do then?" Sullivan was in bed the morning the earthquake struck and his house collapsed, killing him.

Thousands of buildings were immediately destroyed, killing or trapping people under fallen walls, roofs, and chimneys. Downed electrical lines ignited ruptured city gas lines, and fires swept across the city. The water delivery system was destroyed, so the helpless fire department attempted to limit the fires by dynamiting whole blocks to create firebreaks. But the explosions threw off embers that only spread the conflagration. As first responders worked frantically to free victims from the rubble, hundreds of trapped people perished in the flames. On the third day firefighters succeeded in creating a firebreak at Van Ness Avenue, saving the western sections of the city. Virtually everything to the east, three-quarters of the metropolis, was incinerated, including the entire south-of-Market industrial district and the adjacent working-class neighborhoods, the civic center and downtown core, Chinatown and Nob Hill.

At least three thousand people were killed and three hundred thousand left homeless. Dr. Margaret Mahoney, a physician treating victims at a makeshift clinic, watched as thousands of refugees silently filed down Market Street. "All that day and all that night they passed," she wrote, "the inhabitants of a cosmopolitan city: French, Spanish, Italians, the dark children of African origin; Oriental, Chinese, and Japanese. They came pushing trunks, wheeling baby carriages full of household goods, carrying babies, carrying canaries in cages, carrying parrots; pushing sewing machines and trunks until the sickening sound of grating on the concrete entered so deep into my brain that I think it will never leave it."

★

Mayor Schmitz led the city through the first days of the crisis. But lacking confidence in the ability of his own corrupt officials to manage the recovery, he appointed a "Citizens' Committee" of prominent capitalists, businessmen, and lawyers to oversee relief and reconstruction. The group included the city's most prominent critics of the Union Labor Party, former mayor James Phelan among them. In effect, Schmitz handed the reins of city government over to the Employers' Association.

Operating behind closed doors, the Citizens' Committee took charge. They pressed insurance companies to pay out $250 million, covering damage estimated at $400 million. The rebuilding, which began immediately, included many obvious inequities. Upper-class neighborhoods were quickly reconstructed, but thousands of working-class San Franciscans remained homeless for years. Even so, the committee's emphasis on economic recovery enjoyed enormous popular support, in large part because the massive effort created thousands of jobs at good union wages.

Newspapers reported on the plans of individual companies and businesses. Ten days after the disaster, Levi Strauss & Co. announced that it would rebuild its headquarters and factory "on an extensive scale and in a strictly fireproof manner." In the meantime, the company declared, it would continue to pay its workers, a public-spirited act that did it great credit. A new factory was soon up and running, and before year's end the women were back at work, sewing those new blue jeans.

San Francisco's elite handled the rebuilding well and with very little controversy. But they got their pound of flesh by bringing down the city's labor government. Phelan and other wealthy capitalists funded a private investigation of the Schmitz administration, and in 1907, as details were leaked to the press, Mayor Schmitz resigned. A grand jury handed down several dozen indictments. Abraham Ruef confessed to accepting bribes and implicated a score of business and corporate executives. But in the end, he was the only one to take the fall.

A few San Franciscans wondered aloud if Ruef was a victim of anti-Semitism. One of his principal accusers labeled him a man of "low cunning" and suggested that the Jewish character was "terribly at variance with the rest of mankind." Rabbi Jacob Nieto, the man who had convinced Ruef to come clean, believed he was a scapegoat. But Miriam Michelson, a reporter for one of the city's newspapers and a prominent member of the city's Jewish community, objected. It was, she wrote, a "contest between Right and Wrong. All of us will suffer if San Francisco does not punish her thieves."

★

There are historic events that change everything. The gold rush was such an event. Many people believed the great earthquake and fire would prove to be another. "San Francisco is gone," wrote novelist Jack London. "Nothing remains of it but memories." He was wrong. Though one of the worst natural calamities in American history, the earthquake and fire had relatively few enduring effects.

Certainly there were changes. The old city was gray, its buildings stained dark by the smoke that belched from the foundries and factories south of Mission. The new city would remain white and sparkling, powered for the most part by electricity and natural gas. San Francisco continued to grow, although at a much slower pace than rival Los Angeles. Many displaced San Franciscans moved to Oakland, across the bay, which doubled in size in the five years after the disaster. By 1920 Oakland had overtaken San Francisco as the region's principal port. Likewise, people and industry gradually dispersed to neighboring towns and cities. Those trends were accelerated by the earthquake, but they would have taken place without it. Rising from the ashes, however, San Francisco would for another century maintain its reputation among Californians as "the City."

HIRAM JOHNSON BARNSTORMS

27

The Remedy Is More Democracy

In the spring of 1901 a young San Francisco writer named Frank Norris published *The Octopus,* a novel focused on the struggle between Californians and the railroad. In the book's first chapter, a locomotive speeds across the countryside at night, "filling the air with the reek of hot oil, vomiting smoke and sparks." A wayward herd of sheep has wandered onto the rails and the engine charges into it, tossing the animals like bowling pins and leaving the tracks drenched in gore. The novel's shocked narrator sees the carnage as the "symbol of a vast power, huge, terrible, flinging the echo of its thunder over all the reaches of the valley, leaving blood and destruction in its path; the leviathan, with tentacles of steel clutching into the soil, the soulless Force, the iron-hearted Power, the monster, the Colossus, the Octopus."

An immediate best-seller, *The Octopus* remains on the short list of the most important California novels. In its day, everyone knew that the title referred to the Southern Pacific.

The novel's central event was a violent clash between wheat farmers facing eviction and the railroad's hired guns, a fictionalized account of the Mussel Slough shootout of 1880. Norris misrepresented that affair—but he was writing a political allegory, not a history.

The Southern Pacific amassed its power through crony capitalism, the mutually self-serving relationship between the economic and the political elites. The company maintained an army of lobbyists who employed bribery and graft to maintain control over the legislature and the regulatory commission. In 1885, former California governor and SP corporate president Leland Stanford "opened the sack," as he put it, and distributed some $700,000 among California's legislators, buying himself a seat in the United States Senate.

To be sure, the railroad was not the state's only corrupt player. The year following Stanford's election to the Senate, George Hearst, a ruthless Bonanza King and one of America's richest men, also bought himself a Senate seat. To publicize his campaign he purchased the *San Francisco Examiner* and put his son, William Randolph Hearst, in charge. The Senate "will be worth a million to you," the son wrote to his father. "That will allow us to sit back and watch the coffers swell."

Men like Hearst and Stanford attributed their success to the "natural" working of the free market. "You are dealing with forces," says the fictional president of the railroad in *The Octopus*. "The Wheat is one force, the Railroad another, and there is the law that governs them—supply and demand. . . . No man can stop or control it." Norris was simply rephrasing what he read in the newspapers. "All those who throw themselves in the way of the wheels of progress will be crushed sooner or later," a railroad man declared to a state legislative committee.

★

A broad movement for economic and social change arose at the end of the nineteenth century. Farmers joined the Farmers' Alliance, a national organization that advocated a series of economic reforms, including government ownership of the railroads. Workers joined trade unions to improve working conditions and wages. Advocates of "good government" challenged political bosses who practiced corruption. Women mobilized to win the vote.

Many reformers professed their commitment to socialism, which put the emphasis on community and cooperation rather than competition and individualism. In 1890, a wealthy Los Angeles real estate speculator named Gaylord Wilshire became the first self-proclaimed socialist in the nation to campaign for a seat in the U.S. Congress. Ignored by his Republican and Democratic opponents, Wilshire offered a dollar a minute to the opponent who would "dare to face me in debate." When neither took up his offer, Wilshire was scornful. "I classify men into two classes," he said, "fools and socialists." Despite being badly beaten by men he considered fools, Wilshire remained a lifelong socialist. His name is still familiar in Los Angeles, not for his politics, which is a shame, but for the commercial thoroughfare he developed linking Los Angeles with westside Santa Monica: Wilshire Boulevard.

The agenda of these reform groups was lengthy. At the top of the list was the public ownership of utilities—water and power, telegraph and telephone, railroads and streetcars. Next came workplace reforms—the eight-hour day, workman's compensation to cover accident and injury, and regulations protecting health and safety. Then political reform, including the popular election of U.S. Senators and state-supervised party primaries. Wealthy physician Dr. John Randolph Haynes of Los Angeles, another socialist, headed a statewide campaign promoting "direct democracy," amendments to the state constitution that would allow citizens to place measures of public interest on the ballot, including the *initiative* (a vote to enact a new law), the *referendum* (a vote to approve or reject a bill passed by the legislature and signed by the governor before it becomes law), and the *recall* (a vote to remove and replace elected officials in the midst of their terms). "The remedy for the evils of democracy," said Haynes, "is more democracy."

★

The most sweeping reform was woman suffrage, which would have doubled the size of the electorate by simply eliminating the word *male* from the state constitution. The cause went back to California's founding decades. In the late 1860s, feminist Laura de Force Gordon toured the state lecturing on women's rights. "The most chaste, elegant and forcible words in the language poured from her lips like a stream of liquid fire," wrote one observer, and "the whole audience became electrified." Gordon was a founding member of the California Woman Suffrage Society, and in 1871 she made history by becoming the first woman in California to run for the legislature. She lost, receiving only 116 votes in a district of several thousand registered voters. Afterward, she purchased a Stockton newspaper and made a point of covering "women's news," including regular reports on the progress of the women's rights movement.

In 1877 Gordon joined another California feminist, Clara Shortridge Foltz, in a successful campaign to persuade legislators to open the practice of law to women. Both Gordon and Foltz then attempted to enroll at the law school of the University of California, but were denied admission. By charter, the university was coeducational, so the two women sued. Administrators of the law school argued that attending class with men would "make women less womanly." But Foltz countered that "knowledge enlarges and improves" and would make women "better mothers, better wives, and better citizens." The women won their case and both of them became attorneys. Gordon later argued before the United States Supreme Court.

The Women's Christian Temperance Union (WCTU), a powerful evangelical Protestant organization that sought to protect wives from abusive husbands by prohibiting the sale of alcoholic beverages, also backed woman suffrage. "Without women this state would still be a mining camp, the law would be mob law, and the chief executive Judge Lynch," declared Sarah M. Severance, a leader of the California WCTU, which launched a major effort to lobby the state legislature. "The franchise is the symbol of freedom," Severance declared, "and half the members of the republic are deprived of that right." The WCTU succeeded in getting a bill passed by the senate, but it failed in the assembly.

In the nineties, women's clubs in California's cities joined the struggle. In contrast to the WCTU, which drew most of its members from the working and middle classes, club women came from the elite. But they too believed women to be the moral guardians of society. "If women believe in peace and not war, justice and not injustice, virtue and not vice, right and not wrong," said club woman Harriet Strong, "they must take their part in public life."

In 1894 the state federation of women's clubs organized a "Woman's Congress," bringing affluent suffrage activists together in San Francisco. They lobbied a meeting of the state Republican Party, which passed a resolution endorsing votes for women, and the following year the legislature narrowly approved the necessary amendment. But constitutional amendments required approval by voters, so it went on the 1896 ballot. Several western states had already adopted the reform. "Women vote for president in Wyoming, Colorado, Utah, and Idaho," the suffragists reminded voters. "Why not in California?" Women of the WTCU rallied to the campaign, provoking brewers, liquor dealers, and saloon keepers to join the opposition. If women got the vote, they claimed, no man would be able to buy a glass of beer. The state Democratic Party, with its working-class base, came out in opposition. Club women campaigned energetically, but the amendment went down to defeat. It was a demoralizing loss, but reformers pressed ahead.

★

In the early nineties, many radical farmers, socialists, and feminists joined forces in what they called the "People's Party." Running under the banner of "equal rights for all, special privileges to none," they succeeded in electing a handful of state legislators who joined with Democrats in electing Stephen M. White of Los Angeles to the U.S. Senate. White had come up through the Workingmen's Party, campaigning for Chinese exclusion. But he was also a reformer, best known for his longtime opposition to the Southern Pacific.

Senator White's principal concern was the economic progress of his hometown, particularly legislation authorizing the Army Corps of Engineers to improve the harbor at San Pedro. If Los Angeles was to become a great city, it required a deepwater port. But the Southern Pacific opposed the measure, arguing that federal dollars should go instead to improving the harbor at Santa Monica, where it controlled most of the waterfront. Collis P. Huntington, president of the Southern Pacific and last surviving member of the Associates, pulled out all the stops to win congressional support for this project. Senator White went on the offensive, lambasting Huntington for his attempt to postpone repayment of the federally guaranteed bonds that had filled the coffers of the Associates. The struggle was long and hard-fought, but in 1897 Senator White and Los Angeles prevailed. It was a significant political defeat for the Southern Pacific and a key development in the transformation of Los Angeles into an urban metropolis.

Huntington died in 1900, but under new management the Southern Pacific doubled down on its control of California. When Republican governor George Pardee, the former mayor of Oakland, challenged the company's stranglehold of his hometown port, the Southern Pacific once again "opened the sack." Offering railroad passes, free booze, and more, its lobbyists persuaded a majority of delegates at the 1906 Republican state-nominating convention to dump Pardee in favor of a reliable "Railroad Republican." Reformers lambasted this infamous backroom deal as "the Shame of California," but the Southern Pacific remained in control.

★

The first decade of the twentieth century was a politically polarizing time in California as well as the nation. Industrial capitalism produced a flood of goods, but also a society of growing economic and political inequality. Many elected officials, Democrat and Republican alike, were beholden to corporate power. Frustrated advocates of change moved to the left. Some joined the newly organized Socialist Party, which advocated the nationalization of industry. Others were drawn to even more radical groups like the Industrial Workers of the World (IWW), which not only advocated state ownership of the means of production, but rejected electoral politics in favor of "direct action," including strikes, protests, even sabotage.

Moderate reformers feared that unless they succeeded in smoothing capitalism's rough edges, Californians might be seduced by the "wild craze for government ownership of everything," as one of them put it. Inspired by the politics of Theodore Roosevelt, who became president after the assassination of President William McKinley in 1901, a movement for moderate reform arose within the ranks of California Republicans. The movement attracted many people in the professional and managerial classes—lawyers, doctors, ministers, newspaper editors, and small businessmen, most of them urban and middle class. They called themselves "Progressives."

At first the Progressives agreed on little more than opposition to the Southern Pacific. But pushed by savvy reformers like John Randolph Haynes, they adopted a more general agenda, calling for the strict regulation of public utilities, essential labor legislation, and electoral reform. Progressives won a number of legislative seats in the contentious state elections of 1908. That momentum provided them with the boost they needed to pass a bill providing for primary elections supervised by the state. It turned out to be sufficient to begin a process of real change.

★

Hiram Johnson first came to statewide attention as the victorious prosecuting attorney in the corruption trial of San Francisco political boss Abraham Ruef. A prosperous lawyer in his early forties, he was the son of a Railroad Republican who served as a California legislator and congressman. But Johnson broke with his father, denouncing "the concentration of the wealth of this country in few hands and the alarming increase of poverty in our midst." Without fundamental change, he feared, desperate men and women would rise in a rebellion "that will eclipse in its bloodshed and its fierceness, in its lawlessness and its slaughter, any the world has ever seen." In 1910 the Progressives recruited Johnson as their candidate for governor of California.

Avoiding the hated railroad, Johnson barnstormed the state by automobile—the first politician to do so. With his son at the wheel, he traveled more than eight thousand miles over rough dirt roads in an open roadster, delivering nearly a thousand stump speeches. The election, he told Californians, was "a contest for freedom from the Southern Pacific, which has debauched, polluted, and corrupted our state." In the first ever state-run Republican primary, held in August 1910, he over-whelmed his opponents, handing control of the party to the Progressives. In the general election Johnson appealed for the votes of all reformers. Running against Democratic and So-cialist candidates, he won the governorship handily, carrying with him healthy Progressive majorities in both houses of the legislature.

★

The 1911 session of the state legislature ranks as the most impor-tant in California history. In his inaugural address, Governor Johnson again denounced the Southern Pacific. But he went further, indicting "special interests" of all kinds for treating state government "as a mere thing for exploitation and private gain." Following the governor's lead, legislators strengthened the Railroad Commission, which for the first time was able to curb the power of the Southern Pacific. They created a new public utilities commission with broad regulatory power. They enacted labor laws setting standards for workplace health and safety, mandating the eight-hour day for women, and regulat-ing child labor. They expanded the state's authority over public education, providing free textbooks for students and pensions for teachers. They strengthened the electoral laws, and adopted a plan for the popular election of U.S. senators.

What was to prevent special interests from undoing these reforms? "The first step in our design to preserve and per-petuate popular government," Governor Johnson announced, "shall be the adoption of the initiative, the referendum, and the recall." The Southern Pacific or other corporations might bribe state legislators or party delegates, but it could not bribe the people. The legislature complied, passing a constitutional amendment enacting "direct democracy." That required voter approval, so it went on the 1911 ballot along with measures for

workman's compensation insurance, public ownership of utilities, and woman suffrage.

Governor Johnson campaigned vigorously for most of
these measures but declined to endorse votes for women. On
that issue, he was old school. "The more I think of woman suffrage," he wrote a friend, "the more I think it's something that
will ultimately destroy us." Without the governor's support,
feminists feared another defeat. This time, however, the cause
was taken up by trade union women, who argued that workers
needed all the votes they could get if they were to protect their
own interests. Voters approved a total of twenty-two reform
amendments, transforming state government overnight. Direct
democracy measures passed overwhelmingly. Woman suffrage
squeaked through, thanks to strong support in working-class
precincts.

With these developments, Californians for the first time
had a state government that accepted a measure of responsibility for the inequities of industrial capitalism. Governor
Johnson was thrust into the national limelight as a progressive
champion. His reforms set a benchmark for other states. In
1912, when Theodore Roosevelt mounted a campaign for a
third presidential term as the candidate of the newly formed
national Progressive Party, he chose Johnson as his running
mate. Roosevelt lost to Democrat Woodrow Wilson and retired from politics. But Johnson was just beginning one of the
longest political careers in California history.

★

The reforms of the Progressives amounted to a major victory
for the workers' movement in California. Organized labor became a powerful political force and one of Governor Johnson's
strongest supporters. It enjoyed great success in San Francisco,
the nation's most unionized city. But workers suffered a major

defeat in Los Angeles, where the Merchants and Manufacturers Association, representing the majority of large employers, fought unionization tooth and nail. Leading the group were two prominent local capitalists, Harrison Gray Otis, owner and publisher of the *Los Angeles Times,* and Henry E. Huntington, the streetcar magnate of southern California, heir to the huge fortune of his uncle, Collis P. Huntington, the last of the Associates. If Los Angeles was to have any chance of competing with San Francisco, these industrial barons believed, employers had to maintain a plentiful supply of cheap labor. Preventing unions from gaining a foothold, they believed, offered the best way of accomplishing that goal.

For Otis, whose newspaper had been locked in battle with the printers' union since the early nineties, it amounted to a holy crusade. He seethed when union organizers from San Francisco came to Los Angeles to lend support to his workers. "If the San Francisco gorillas succeed," he declared, "the brilliant future of Los Angeles will end." For his part, Huntington pursued the antiunion policies he had learned from his uncle. If any of his streetcar workers joined a union, or was even seen talking to a union organizer, he lost his job and was blacklisted. But the workers had a blacklist of their own. "In the city of Los Angeles are gathered some of the most notable and powerful enemies of organized labor in the United States," the city's Central Labor Council declared, "and the most wealthy and vindictive among them all is Henry E. Huntington."

Northern California Progressives like Hiram Johnson had made their peace with labor. But southern California reformers were infected with antilabor bias. Progressives won control of Los Angeles city government in 1909, but when organized labor launched a citywide campaign for the union shop, Mayor George Alexander passed an antipicketing ordinance and arrested union activists. Following the example of union leaders in San Francisco, Los Angeles activists forged an alliance with the local Socialist Party, choosing labor lawyer Job Harriman to run against Alexander. Everyone expected a close race.

The campaign coincided with another bitter strike at the *Los Angeles Times*. In the autumn of 1910, saboteurs dynamited the *Times* building, killing twenty-one people. Police arrested two labor activists, the brothers James and John McNamara, who Harriman's supporters claimed were innocent. Shortly before the election in 1911, however, the McNamaras confessed to the crime and cut a deal saving them from the hangman's noose, indelibly staining the city's union movement. Harriman's campaign collapsed and he lost the election. Los Angeles maintained its status as a notoriously "open shop" town.

★

Two steps forward, one step back. Anti-Asian racism continued as a force to be reckoned with. In 1905, the San Francisco Board of Education ordered the small number of Japanese students in the city segregated into schools of their own. When the government of Japan complained, President Roosevelt negotiated what was called the "Gentleman's Agreement." He convinced the San Franciscans to end the policy in exchange for a pledge from the Japanese that they would voluntarily limit the migration of Japanese workers. The Japanese population continued to grow, however, because of an exemption allowing Japanese wives and children to join husbands and fathers in the United States.

Anti-Asian racism had been the leading edge of reform politics since the era of the Workingmen's Party, and Progressives proved no exception to the rule. "A white population and a brown population can never occupy the same soil together," declared an editorial in the newsletter of the state's Progressive movement. "Our legislature should limit Mongolian ownership of the soil to a space four feet by six." A grave, in other words. "Progressive" did not necessarily mean "enlightened."

Japanese workers made up a growing proportion of the state's agricultural workforce, and a growing number of them were leasing or buying farmland of their own, pioneering the production of "row crops"—vegetables, melons, strawberries, and flowers. By 1910 Japanese farmers owned or leased 200,000 acres in the state, accounting for more than a fifth of the dollar value of the state's crops. But instead of seeing this as a benefit, many Californians considered it a threat. In 1913, with Governor Johnson's enthusiastic support, the legislature passed an "Alien Land Law," prohibiting the ownership of land by Japanese. To comply with this racist law, Japanese farmers deeded their land to their American-born children, citizens by birthright. A few years later, in 1920, California growers placed an initiative on the ballot strengthening the law and further restricting the ability of Japanese farmers to cultivate their own land. The measure passed after an overtly racist campaign.

By that time, many reformers began to wonder about the wisdom of the direct democracy reforms. It turned out the provisions were most effectively used by well-organized and well-funded organizations that could finance the collection of voter signatures required to place measures on the ballot. Progressives passed a series of economic reforms, but big corporations spent millions to have them overturned at the ballot box through the referendum process. Perhaps Hiram Johnson was right, perhaps California voters could not be bribed by special interests. But they certainly could be influenced. Despite the corner turned in 1911, these were warning signs of things to come.

MUIR + ROOSEVELT AT YOSEMITE

28

Bounty of the Mountains

When thirty-year-old John Muir arrived in San Francisco in 1868, he did not linger in the city but headed directly for Yosemite, a place he had read about. Born in Scotland, then raised on a hardscrabble farm in Wisconsin, Muir was the son of a strict Protestant father who preached hellfire and damnation. That turned the young man against organized religion, but throughout his life he remained a spiritual seeker. He found his church in the wild nature of California.

An avid reader with an inquiring mind, Muir studied natural science at the University of Wisconsin until 1864, when he fled to Canada to avoid the draft and military service. He returned to the United States after the Civil War and found work as a farm and factory hand. He led a vagabond life, traveling hither and yon, exploring his surroundings and keeping a detailed journal of his observations. After an industrial accident that nearly blinded him in one eye, he quit work altogether and hit the road, tramping across the country, determined to take "the wildest, leafiest, and least trodden way I could find." That trail eventually led him to Yosemite.

Several years before Muir arrived, Congress had given the state of California responsibility for protecting the soaring granite slabs, lofty waterfalls, and verdant meadows of that spectacular site. Hearty tourists were already trekking there on foot or by mule. Muir found work in the valley herding sheep and running a sawmill. He spent all the time he could exploring and writing in his journal. His time at Yosemite awakened the deepest and most intense passion of his life.

The forest groves of the Sierra Nevada, Muir wrote in his journal, were "God's first temples." He often quoted from the Bible, and Christian teachings formed the basis of his moral code. Muir's faith, however, was not Christian but rather a version of pantheism, the belief that God is embodied in nature. "It is a blessed thing to go free in the light of this beautiful world," he wrote, "to see God playing upon everything, as a man would play on an instrument, his fingers upon the lightning and torrent, on every wave of sea and sky, and every living thing, making all together sing and shine in sweet accord, the one love-harmony of the Universe." Immersion in wild nature, Muir believed, offered a direct relationship with the divine. "In God's wildness lies the hope of the world," he wrote. "The galling harness of civilization drops off and wounds heal."

After more than five years in the Sierras, Muir relocated to San Francisco. Inspired by the American Transcendentalists— the likes of Emerson, Thoreau, and Whitman—he wanted to write and be read. He joined the city's community of creative bohemians, including Charles Warren Stoddard and Ina Coolbrith. Although barely forty years old, Muir cultivated an image as the "old man of the mountains," allowing his hair and beard to go untrimmed. Coolbrith took him under her wing, as she often did with aspiring writers, helped him polish his style, and published a score of his essays in the *Overland Monthly*. He became a "roving correspondent" for a San Francisco newspaper.

Writing was always a slow and painful process for Muir. But his prose captivated readers. "Looking eastward from the summit of Pacheco Pass one shining morning," he wrote in a famous passage,

> a landscape was displayed that after all my wanderings still appears as the most beautiful I have ever beheld. At my feet lay the Great Central Valley of California, level and flowery, like a lake of pure sunshine, forty or fifty miles wide, five hundred miles long, one rich furred garden of yellow.... And from the eastern boundary of this vast golden flower-bed rose the mighty Sierra, miles in height, and so gloriously colored and so radiant, it seemed not clothed with light but wholly composed of it, ... the Range of Light.

In 1875, *Harper's*, a magazine of national renown, published one of Muir's essays. Following that breakthrough, his naturalist writing appeared regularly in the nation's most prestigious magazines and journals. He collected them in a series of popular books, beginning with *The Mountains of California* (1894). By then Muir had become America's best-known naturalist and California's most celebrated author.

★

Admirers often describe Muir as a "preservationist," but that term did not come into use until well after his death. The land, he wrote, "must be, and will be, not only preserved, but used." The nation's forests, "like perennial fountains, may be made to yield a sure harvest of timber, while at the same time all their far-reaching beneficent uses may be maintained unimpaired." He advocated a policy of multiple use that included the protection of wild beauty.

But wherever Muir looked, he saw destruction. The picks and shovels of the forty-niners had turned the once-verdant valleys and canyons on the western flank of the Sierra Nevada into featureless moonscapes. The high-pressure hoses of hydraulic mining had washed away entire mountainsides. "It is impossible to conceive of anything more desolate, more utterly forbidding," wrote one observer. Mud mixed with the toxic tailings of the mines polluted streams and raised river channels, resulting in flooded farms and towns. In 1884, a federal court declared hydraulic mining a public nuisance and issued a permanent injunction against washing earth and debris into flowing streams. By then, however, an estimated twelve billion tons of the eroded mountains had been sent downstream, and many portions of the once luxuriant landscape had become virtual wastelands.

Along the northern California coast, loggers cut old-growth redwoods for construction lumber. In the Sierras, thousands of acres of ponderosa pine fell to provide timbers to shore up the silver mines of the Comstock Lode. In the southern Sierra, loggers threatened the groves of giant sequoias, among the world's oldest and tallest trees. Mountain deforestation, Muir warned, would lead to soil erosion of "a vastly more destructive degree than all the washings from hydraulic mines."

Muir was an idealist and a romantic, but also an advocate and an activist. In 1892 he became founding president of the Sierra Club, a watchdog organization determined to save wilderness areas in California and the wider West. The federal government had established America's first national park at

Yellowstone, and the Sierra Club successfully lobbied for the creation of a half dozen more, including one at Lassen Peak in remote northeastern California. The club's top priority was persuading California's government to return Yosemite Valley to federal control so it could become part of a large national park protecting the southern Sierra. Muir presented the case in *Our National Parks* (1901).

One of his most enthusiastic readers was President Theodore Roosevelt. In 1903, the president invited Muir to join him on a camping trip to Yosemite. "I want to drop politics absolutely and just be out in the open with you," he wrote. Muir accepted. "I might be able to do some forest good in freely talking around the campfire," he told a friend. The two men, accompanied by Roosevelt's large entourage, spent three days "roughing it" at Yosemite. After rides, hikes, and climbs they talked well into the night. "I stuffed him pretty well regarding the timber thieves, the destructive work of the lumberman, and other spoilers of the forest," said Muir. "It was bully," Roosevelt told reporters. "I had the time of my life!"

Thanks in large part to Muir's influence, Roosevelt became one of the most environmentally conscious of all the nation's presidents, convincing California to return Yosemite to federal control in 1906, whereupon it was included as part of the national park system. He used his presidential influence and authority as well to establish dozens of other national parks, national monuments, and national forests in the state, protecting land from California's remote northeast to the mountain ranges and seashores of the south. The camping trip with Roosevelt represented the high point of Muir's political influence.

★

In 1880 Muir had married the daughter of a prosperous fruit grower with a large farm outside the town of Martinez, twenty-five miles northeast of San Francisco on the Carquinez Strait, which connects San Francisco Bay to the Delta. Well before his father-in-law died in 1890, Muir assumed management of the place. He occasionally complained about being tied down by the responsibility. "I, who have breathed the mountain air, who have really lived a life of freedom, condemned to penal servitude," he grumbled. "And for money! Man, I'm like to die of the shame of it!" But his writing produced only sporadic income, while the farm supported his family handsomely. The Muirs and their two daughters resided on the property in a three-story mansion topped with a cupola looking out on a lush landscape of orchards and vineyards.

Several hundred yards away, tucked in among the orchards, was a cluster of one-room cabins the Muir family called "China house," quarters for the men who labored in their orchards. Work on the Muir place was seasonal, requiring as many as forty hands at harvest, and Muir found supervising their work a vexing task. Like most Californians, he was a racist. He found the Awahnechees, the Native people of Yosemite, "filthy," "uncouth," and "absolutely hideous." When they returned to their homeland to visit, he found their presence bothersome, writing that they distracted him from experiencing the "solemn calm" of the wilderness. He felt equally uncomfortable around his farm workers. "We should live in Christian sympathy and charity with our Chinese," he wrote. "But we should not try to flock together too closely, for they are birds with feathers so unlike our own they seem to have been hatched on some other planet." Muir's disdain for other cultures was palpable.

Muir's orchards were watered by diversions from a creek that flowed through the property. Many California horticulturalists required more complex irrigation systems. Muir once wrote of an encounter he had with farmers in the Central Valley. "Water's what we want," they told him, "and there's water aplenty in the rivers." Muir endorsed their views and anticipated a day when the waters of the Sierra Nevada, what he called the "bounty of the mountains," transformed the valley into a landscape of farms. That would require harnessing the swift-flowing rivers with dams and reservoirs.

In making such an endorsement, Muir overlooked red flags signaling caution. There was the case of Lake Tulare in the southern San Joaquin Valley, which farmers drained dry to provide irrigation for their adjacent farms, spoiling a sanctuary for millions of birds migrating along the Pacific flyway. An even more spectacular irrigation calamity occurred in the state's far south, where the Colorado River was diverted to irrigate agricultural fields in a portion of the desert that developers promoted as the "Imperial Valley." In 1905, after particularly heavy winter snows in the Rockies, the surging Colorado broke through a poorly constructed diversion gate and poured unchecked into a sink in the desert, creating a vast inland lake that became known as the Salton Sea. It required two years of effort and millions of dollars to restore the Colorado to its old channel. Muir came late to the realization that the development and diversion of rivers could threaten his beloved wilderness.

★

Los Angeles had been built on the banks of a river that at the turn of the twentieth century supplied sufficient water to support the city's hundred thousand residents. But the metropolitan population was growing, doubling in size by 1905. Would the river be sufficient? "The time has come," announced William Mulholland, superintendent of the city's water system, "when we shall have to supplement its flow from some other source."

Mulholland, a gruff, self-taught engineer, set his sights on the Owens River, which drained the eastern flank of the southern Sierra Nevada. That was 235 miles away, but Mulholland developed a plan to construct a gravity-flow aqueduct from the Owens Valley to the city. The farmers of the valley had already won federal approval for a project to provide irrigation and hydroelectric power for their farms and homes, so Mulholland knew he needed to act with dispatch. In secret, agents for the city purchased land and water rights along the river, and in 1905 Mulholland publicly announced the plan. City voters authorized nearly $25 million in bonds to finance the project. The farmers of the Owens Valley, about to lose their access to irrigation water, appealed to President Roosevelt to protect their river for local use.

Roosevelt announced his decision the following year. "It is a hundred or a thousand fold more important to the state and more valuable to the people as a whole," he wrote, "if used by the city than if used by the people of Owens Valley." When asked about the project, Muir went on record in favor of tapping the "pure and sparkling flow" of the Sierras "for the future water supply of Los Angeles." Los Angeles authorities reacted with jubilation. "John Muir approves the Owen River enterprise," the *Los Angeles Herald* crowed. "And no man can question the knowledge, loyalty and truthfulness of John Muir."

Construction of the Los Angeles Aqueduct, an engineering feat comparable to the building of the transcontinental railroad, began in 1908 and was completed in just five years. At the opening ceremony, engineer Mulholland was asked to say a few words. "There it is," he pronounced, pointing to the flowing water. "Take it!"

★

San Francisco also thirsted for the bounty of the mountains. The city's Board of Public Works announced a plan to tap the Tuolumne River, which tumbles down the western flank of the mountains to meet the San Joaquin a few miles west of the town of Modesto. The city's engineers planned a dam at the lower end of the Hetch Hetchy Valley, creating a large reservoir from which the water would flow to the city by aqueduct. The only obstacle was that Hetch Hetchy sat in the northern portion of Yosemite National Park.

Muir vehemently opposed the plan. Like Yosemite Valley itself, Hetch Hetchy was a glacially carved canyon with spectacular granite walls. "There is not in all the wonderful Sierra," Muir wrote to President Roosevelt, "so grand and wonderful a block in Nature's handiwork." But to San Franciscans, Hetch Hetchy was simply a giant tub waiting to be filled with water. Roosevelt hesitated, reluctant to disappoint Muir. But in the end his administration approved San Francisco's plan. Muir and the Sierra Club lobbied untiringly against the required congressional legislation. The *San Francisco Chronicle* castigated club members as "mushy esthetes"—the equivalent of the "tree hugger" epithet of today. The reservoir, the newspaper argued, would "add charm to the landscape of the Sierra" while simultaneously supplying the city's need for water.

Muir went ballistic. "These temple-destroyers, devotees of ravaging commercialism, seem to have a perfect contempt for Nature," he wrote. "Instead of lifting their eyes to the God of the Mountains, [they] lift them to the Almighty Dollar. Dam Hetch Hetchy! As well dam for water-tanks the people's cathedrals and churches, for no holier temple has ever been consecrated by the heart of man."

Hetch Hetchy would be Muir's last stand. In 1910 San Francisco voters approved a bond issue financing the project. The Sierra Club succeeded in delaying congressional consideration for several years, but in 1913, pressured by President Woodrow Wilson, Congress finally voted approval. "It's hard to bear," said Muir, as he imagined the dam and the waters rising to fill the canyon. "The destruction goes to my heart." He died the next year at the age of seventy-six, crushed by his defeat.

★

Muir opposed the flooding of his beautiful, uninhabited mountain canyons. But by blessing the Los Angeles Aqueduct he had sanctioned the sacrifice of the arid Owens Valley, populated by several thousand farm families. That was a great disappointment to Mary Austin, an Owens Valley resident and the author of *The Land of Little Rain* (1905), a moving testimonial to California's arid places. Like Muir, Austin wrote a naturalist's account of the land, but unlike him she also paid close attention to the people who made their living from it, Natives and settlers, miners and farmers, women and children alike. Life in arid places was hard, she wrote. But "the rawness of the land favors the sense of personal relation to the supernatural." Austin knew that the diversion of Owens River water spelled the destruction of her neighbors' fields and orchards. "Is all this worthwhile," she wondered, "in order that Los Angeles should be just so big?"

She was right. Los Angeles took far more water from the Owens River than it actually needed. It used the excess to entice surrounding communities to surrender their municipal independence and incorporate with the city, allowing Los Angeles to expand to ten times its original size. San Francisco, too, was greedy. When completed in 1934, the aqueduct delivered much more water than the city required. Isolated at the head of a peninsula, San Francisco could not use water to expand its boundaries like Los Angeles; instead it sold the excess to neighboring communities, collecting millions in tribute.

There were other outrages. In a blatant case of insider trading, Moses Sherman, a member of the Los Angeles Board of Water Commissioners, shared advance knowledge of the

Owens River diversion with a group of wealthy investors, who bought up a great deal of land in the arid San Fernando Valley, north of Los Angeles. Those investors included streetcar magnate Henry E. Huntington and Harrison Gray Otis, owner and publisher of the *Los Angeles Times,* who pushed for the project in his paper without revealing his own financial interest. When the water arrived in the valley, the group reaped windfall profits in the millions.

Mulholland was not implicated in those dealings. He did not gain a fortune from Owens Valley water. Instead, the self-made water engineer suffered a cruel fate. To hold the excess mountain water, his Department of Water and Power constructed numerous reservoirs on the outskirts of the city. The largest of them was squeezed into San Francisquito Canyon, north of Los Angeles, contained by the Saint Francis Dam, which rose 185 feet above the canyon floor. In March 1928, shortly after the reservoir had been filled to capacity for the first time, the dam failed spectacularly, sending a hundred-foot wall of water surging toward the sea, destroying everything in its path. Four hundred people were killed, making the collapse the worst man-made disaster in California's history. An investigation concluded that the culprit was faulty engineering. Mulholland resigned in disgrace, a ruined man. "I envy the ones who are dead," he said.

LITTLE TOKYO, LOS ANGELES

29

Invisible Walls of Steel

In the summer of 1923, Fred and Maude Burkett, a young married couple with a baby daughter in arms, arrived at the Santa Fe railroad station in Los Angeles after a journey from southeastern Colorado. Both had grown up on the High Plains, but the metropolis called to them. Fred Burkett aspired to a career in music. Folks called him an "Irish tenor," although he didn't have a drop of Irish blood. In L.A., he found a day job and joined a choral group. His wife had a tougher time. Within months she was pregnant again and in 1924 she bore a son. While her husband was at work or out with his singing friends, she cared for the kids in their apartment. Lonely and bitter, she wrote home, and some months later her parents, Marcellus and Dora McFarlin, came to Los Angeles to lend assistance, followed by a sister and two brothers. Maude and Fred Burkett separated, then divorced. She moved in with her parents. He enlisted in the army.

Maude McFarlin was my maternal grandmother. Growing up, I heard her story of coming to Los Angeles many times. It was personal, but it also exemplified the experience of thousands of folks who relocated to California during the first third of the twentieth century. Over those years the state's population quadrupled, reaching nearly six million. The growth centered in southern California, which by 1930 claimed more than half the state's residents. Los Angeles exploded from a medium-sized city of 100,000 to a metropolis of more than 1.2 million— the nation's fifth largest, nearly twice the size of San Francisco.

★

A robust economy pulled migrants to California. That had not always been the case. The economy had grown slowly in the last quarter of the nineteenth century, held back in part by the absence of coal deposits on the Pacific coast. In the 1890s, however, Californians began exploiting other forms of energy that would power a takeoff into sustained economic development.

They first harnessed the power of the water that coursed down the watercourses draining the state's many mountain ranges. In 1893, utilizing technology developed for the mining industry, the first modern hydroelectric plant in the nation began operation on a fast-flowing creek near the southern California town of Redlands. Local orange growers needed a source of power that would enable them to pump water up into the hills, where they wanted to lay out more groves. The Redlands generating station became the model for dozens of others, many in the Sierra Nevada, designed to provide power for both domestic and industrial use.

Alternating current could be transmitted on high-voltage lines over long distances, crossing hundreds of miles of rugged terrain to reach users. Building this infrastructure required a large capital investment. Local power companies gave way to large conglomerates, including Pacific Gas and Electric (PG&E,

organized in 1905), serving the northern two-thirds of the state, and Southern California Edison (1909). By 1915, California boasted the world's most extensive electric grid, with transmission lines stretching for hundreds of miles, providing cheap, abundant power. To service and extend this network, the University of California established programs to train a generation of scientists and engineers, the beginnings of California's high technology sector.

Meanwhile, prospectors discovered extensive petroleum reserves in the Los Angeles basin, along the southern California coast, and in the southern San Joaquin Valley. Petroleum had been a big business in the United States since the 1870s, refined to produce kerosene for oil lamps, but the adoption of electrical illumination made that business model obsolete. With Californians leading the way, refiners shifted to fuel oil, used to power engines of all kinds. Natural gas became the standard fuel for heating and cooking. By 1910, the state was one of the world's leading fossil fuel producers. California's industrial revolution would be powered by electricity, fuel oil, and natural gas.

Refiners also produced gasoline to power internal combustion engines. With the availability of locally produced, relatively cheap gasoline, California in general and Los Angeles in particular led the world in the mass adoption of the automobile. At first motorcars were merely expensive toys for the wealthy, but all doubts about their utility ended after the San Francisco earthquake, when authorities pressed hundreds of private vehicles into service for rescue and relief. "I was skeptical about the automobile previous to the disaster," said a San Francisco fire chief, "but now give it my hearty endorsement." Registration statistics tell the story. In 1915, for every thousand Americans, there were 23 registered motor vehicles—but in California there were 55, and in Los Angeles 122. Gradually rates of automobile ownership across the nation converged, but in 1930 Angelenos were still twice as likely as other Americans to own a car.

★

New sources of energy provided a foundation for economic growth. The petroleum and electric power industries created thousands of jobs, the sale, repair, and service of automobiles thousands more. Roads required improvement, bridges needed construction. Bay Area shipbuilders turned out hundreds of steel vessels, including battleships and destroyers for the U.S. Navy. Several major automobile manufacturers opened assembly plants in Oakland, which became known as the "Detroit of the West."

Los Angeles boomed. With the completion of federally sponsored improvements to the port at San Pedro in 1911, and the opening of the Panama Canal in 1914, Los Angeles County became the nation's most important distribution point for petroleum products. Big automakers, tire manufacturers, and glass companies opened branch plants, and new factories and warehouses sprawled along the floodplain of the Los Angeles River and spread south toward the harbor. The city, boasted the *Los Angeles Times,* would soon be "a combination of Gary, Pittsburgh, and Chicago, minus the smoke and soot." No one considered the pollution produced by thousands of automobiles—the "smog" that became a major problem by the 1940s.

The nation's first air show, held on the plains south of Los Angeles in 1910, drew a quarter million spectators. Impressed with the year-round flying weather, a number of aircraft manufacturers set up shop in the region. They benefited from research and technical support from the California Institute of Technology, or Caltech (1920), and a new University of California campus in L.A. (1925). Another attraction was the "open shop" policy enforced by southern California's employers, which

crippled unionization efforts. In 1920, wages in heavily unionized San Francisco were 30 percent higher than they were in
Los Angeles. By the late twenties, southern California was the
national center of the emerging aircraft industry, with twenty
manufacturers operating within thirty miles of L.A.'s City Hall.

The climate, as well as the variety of accessible locations—
mountains, deserts, and seashores—also drew filmmakers, and
by 1915 Hollywood, formerly a quiet semirural suburb, was
home to the nation's motion picture industry. During the early
twenties the movie studios produced 80 percent of the world's
films, generating revenue four times the combined total of the
nation's live theater and professional sports exhibitions.

★

Some four million men and women relocated to California
during the first third of the century. Individuals born in the
state fell from a third of all residents in 1900 to less than a
quarter thirty years later. "In a population of a million and a
quarter," wrote a visitor to Los Angeles, "every other person
you see has been here less than five years." The newcomers
came mostly from midwestern states like Iowa, Illinois, and
Missouri. "Retired farmers, grocers, Ford agents, hardware and
shoe merchants sold out their farms and businesses in the Middle West," wrote journalist Louis Adamic, "and now they are
here in California—sunny California—to rest and regain their
vigor, enjoy the climate, look at pretty scenery, live in little
bungalows with a palm tree or banana plant in front, and eat
in cafeterias."

Most settled in southern California, a majority in Los
Angeles County. Many were retirees, some skilled craftsmen,
others opened small businesses and shops. Long Beach and
Glendale became midwestern enclaves, strongly Protestant and
Republican. Many homesick migrants joined "state societies."
During the twenties and thirties the annual Iowa Society pic-

nic in Long Beach drew more than a hundred thousand participants each year.

Another half million people came from Europe. San Francisco, a human magnet since the gold rush, remained the favored destination for immigrants. "Foreign-born whites," the term used by the Census Bureau, made up a quarter of San Francisco's population in 1930. Italians settled in North Beach, the city's "Little Italy." Amadeo Peter Giannini, the child of immigrant parents, got his start in the wholesale produce business, then went into banking, opening the Banca d'Italia in North Beach. In the hours after the 1906 earthquake, he fled the burning city with $80,000 hidden under fruit crates. Giannini was the first of the city's bankers to reopen for full operations. He invented the idea of consumer banking, making loans to small businessmen or ordinary people, and opening branch banks in urban neighborhoods. In 1930 he renamed his institution the Bank of America.

Fewer Europeans settled in Los Angeles. But prior to the passage by Congress of a restrictive immigration law in 1924, the county attracted a large migration of eastern European Jews. Why didn't they join the well-established Jewish community of San Francisco? In part because highly assimilated Jewish community leaders there feared that thousands of Yiddish-speaking, orthodox Jews would provoke anti-Semitism. "We are confronted by an invasion from the East that threatens to undo the work of two generations," declared Jacob Voorsanger, San Francisco's most prominent rabbi. So Jews from eastern Europe headed instead to Los Angeles, particularly the neighborhood of Boyle Heights east of the Los Angeles River, which by 1930 boasted the largest Jewish community west of Chicago.

★

In 1930 the federal census enumerator found my grandmother, Maude McFarlin, living with her two children (one of them my mother) and her parents on the 1200 block of West Sixty-Eighth Street in southwest Los Angeles. This neighborhood of tidy two- and three-bedroom bungalows had been carved out of raw farmland a few years before by the Los Angeles Investment Company, one of the area's largest property developers and home builders. Two-thirds of the twenty-six householders on my grandmother's block reported owning the homes in which they lived—a high rate even for Los Angeles, where home ownership was more common than elsewhere in the country.

Three-quarters of the neighborhood's residents came from other states, the majority from the Midwest. A quarter had been born in foreign countries, including Italy, Germany, Russia, and England. A Jewish Rumanian had a wife and child born in Canada. Only one head of household had been born and raised in California, a divorced woman in her early forties living with her children and a brother, the descendants of a once-prominent Californio family.

The neighborhood was working class. One man held a job at the Firestone tire factory, another at the Ford assembly plant. A number worked in skilled trades, including a carpenter employed at the Fox movie studio in Hollywood. The residents included a postal clerk, a cafeteria chef, two truck drivers, and a federal immigration inspector. One man operated a gas station and another managed a specialty food shop. One wife worked as a nurse, but the census taker listed all the others as "homemakers." Two adult daughters had jobs as stenographers. My grandmother Maude was a waitress in a coffee shop.

★

According to the census, all the residents of West Sixty-Eighth Street were White. But Los Angeles was far from being an all-White city. During the first third of the twentieth century more than a quarter million Japanese, Mexicans, and African Americans relocated to Los Angeles County. From 1900 to 1930 the proportion of residents from those three groups jumped from 4 to more than 12 percent. Yet not a single person of color could be found on West Sixty-Eighth Street.

My first encounter with racism took place at my grandmother's house when I was about ten years old. By that time she was living in the city of Long Beach, south of L.A. While staying with her one summer, two of my brothers and I wandered home with a friend we'd made during swimming lessons at a nearby high school pool. "He can't come in here," my grandmother said forcefully as she stood in the doorway. Our friend was Black. I was confused, and it was some time before I was able to sort it out. Over the next two decades, as my brothers and sisters made Black and Hispanic friends, our grandmother would be forced to confront her own prejudices.

Racism and de facto segregation divided the residents of Los Angeles. Most hotels and restaurants banned people of color, and theaters restricted them to balcony seating. In a region known for its beautiful beaches, they enjoyed access to only a few small patches of sand. Yet L.A. attracted far more migrants of color than San Francisco, where the powerful labor movement had for decades enforced racial restrictions. National civil rights leader W. E. B. DuBois advised African Americans interested in moving to California to choose Los Angeles over San Francisco, where "white trade unions held the Negro out and down." Los Angeles also included the nation's largest community of Japanese.

Good jobs in petroleum, manufacturing, or the movie studios, however, were reserved for White workers. People of color, though essential to the economy, were shunted into low-paying work. Mexicans took jobs as *traqueros,* poorly paid section hands for Henry Huntington's streetcar system. African Americans worked as waiters and porters, janitors and manual laborers. The Japanese excelled as gardeners, urban farmers, vegetable and flower merchants.

People of color lived on the city's Eastside, kept out of Westside neighborhoods by "restrictive covenants," provisions in deeds specifying that the property could not be sold, leased, or rented "to any persons other than of the Caucasian race." Los Angeles home builders and real estate agents had introduced this method of segregation around the turn of the century. In 1919, an African American named Alfred Gary challenged its legality. Gary had purchased a home in a Westside subdivision constructed by the Los Angeles Investment Company—the same firm that built the houses in my grandmother's neighborhood. But when Gary and his family moved in, White neighbors objected, and the company sued to evict him. The case eventually reached the state supreme court, which ruled that while a restrictive covenant could not prevent people of color from *buying* a house, it could prevent them from *living* in it. Restrictive covenants proved far more effective than outright harassment or intimidation, creating what one African American leader called "invisible walls of steel."

★

Those walls divided the White Westside from the ethnically diverse Eastside. Some Eastside neighborhoods were ramshackle, run through with railroad tracks, factories, and warehouses. But many were indistinguishable from working-class neighborhoods on the Westside—modest single-family bungalows with little front yards and garages. Home ownership was almost as common on the Eastside as the Westside. The Japanese concentrated in a district east of downtown L.A. that became known as "Little Tokyo." Many African Americans lived along South Central Avenue, where middle-class Black families purchased homes and opened businesses. Migrants from Mexico first located in "Sonoratown," the neighborhood north of the city's old plaza, but as their numbers grew many settled across the Los Angeles River in the Boyle Heights neighborhood, already home to L.A.'s large Jewish community.

In fact, all these Eastside neighborhoods were multicultural. Boyle Heights struck sociologist Pauline Young as "a strange conglomerate of immigrant peoples living side by side though speaking a veritable babble of tongues.... Negro workmen, Jewish merchants, Armenian truck drivers, Japanese gardeners have succeeded in accommodating themselves to each other to a certain degree." Emilia Castañeda de Valenciana later remembered her block as a "United Nations of Mexicans, Chinese, Japanese, African Americans, Filipinos, Jews, and Greeks." Jewish and Mexican children played together in the streets. "The Jewish kids would come over, and we'd go to their house," Margarita Salazar told an interviewer. "We didn't think anything of eating sour cream and fish, the same as eating beans and tortillas. We blended in." Segregation in Los Angeles had the ironic effect of producing some of the most diverse and multicultural neighborhoods in the United States.

The 1930 graduating class of Thomas Jefferson High School in South Central—so called because the area was bisected by South Central Avenue—included 43 African Americans, 17 Mexican Americans, 13 Asian Americans, and 125 Whites, most from immigrant families, many of them Jewish. "Our school is one of the most cosmopolitan in Los Angeles," a proud student wrote in the Jefferson yearbook. "We have in attendance here representatives of five races and as many nationalities, and almost all of the religious faiths." South Central was an "integrated neighborhood," remembered Edythe Espree, an African American who grew up there. "There were Jews, Germans, Chinese, Japanese, and Blacks. We were friends with all of our neighbors."

CAHUILLAS AT PALM CANYON

30

Human Rights and Home Rule

On May 2, 1912, the morning after the annual fiesta of the Mountain Cahuillas, Indian Agent William Stanley met with a group of angry residents of the reservation, located in the southern foothills of the rugged San Jacinto Range in southern California. Without consulting them, Stanley had leased a portion of their grazing land to White ranchers, and the Cahuillas blocked access by closing the road. Stanley demanded they reopen it. "I am the boss and will not follow your advice," Leonicio Lugo, the Cahuillas' leader, told Stanley. "You are nothing," said Stanley. "I am Captain," Lugo shot back.

Some months before, Stanley had removed Lugo from office, citing his uncooperative attitude. But in the eyes of the Cahuillas, Lugo remained their leader. "The government does not recognize you," Stanley fumed. "I'm not appointed by the government," Lugo replied. "The people here at the reservation voted." And with that, he turned heel and walked toward the door, followed by the other Cahuillas. Outraged at this display of insolence, Stanley ordered the reservation policemen at his side to bring them back. There was a struggle and pistols were drawn. "Shoot that goddamn Indian," Stanley shouted as gunfire erupted. But when the smoke cleared, it was Stanley who lay mortally wounded.

This fight had been brewing for several years. Lugo, born to a family of hereditary leaders, was in his fifties when his people elected him captain in a vote administered by Stanley in 1908. The agent had orders from his superiors to assume more control over reservation governance, but Lugo resisted. "We are not asking very much," he appealed. "Only to be allowed to elect our own Captains and our own Judges, and remain on the land that our forefathers lived on for generations past." When Stanley ordered him to step down, Lugo sought support among other Cahuilla bands as well as from their Luiseño neighbors. Passing the hat, he raised sufficient funds to purchase a railroad ticket and take his cause to Washington, just as Luiseño leader Olegario Calac had done a generation before. At the time of the melee that took Stanley's life, Lugo had returned and was still awaiting an official response.

The Native people of southern California had just cause for concern. A few years before, federal authorities had forcibly removed the Cupeño people from their ancient homeland in northern San Diego County after their land fell into the hands of a real estate speculator. Cupa, their principal village, included a hot mineral spring that the people used to leach the bitterness from their acorns, soften the grasses for their baskets, and irrigate their fields and orchards. The Cupeños constructed a bathhouse with soaking pools and charged admission to health-seekers, producing a little revenue for the band. "The hot spring is a valuable property," said a San Diego businessman, "or would be in the hands of men who could develop it."

The Cupeños appealed when they received notice of eviction, but the U.S. Supreme Court ruled against them. In 1903 several hundred residents were loaded onto wagons and relocated to a Luiseño reservation thirty miles away. "They threw us out," said Rosinda Nolasquez, a member of the band. "We lost everything. We went away from there just cleaned out." Contractors razed the village of Cupa and built a resort in its place. The Mountain Cahuillas vowed that they would not allow the same thing to happen to them. They would defend their homeland to the death.

Nine Cahuilla men were indicted on a charge of conspiracy to commit murder and stood trial in Los Angeles. The all-White jury announced the verdict to a courtroom packed with Cahuilla kith and kin. Six men, including Lugo, were found guilty, each sentenced to ten years in prison. They appealed, arguing that they were not subject to federal jurisdiction because the United States had never confirmed the treaty they signed in 1851. But the U.S. Supreme Court upheld the verdict, ruling that the Cahuillas were "under the control of the United States." One of the men died in prison and another four won paroles after six years. But Lugo served his entire sentence. When he finally returned to the reservation in the mid-1920s, his people elected him to be their tribal judge.

★

Native Californians had suffered through a horrific ordeal. Forcibly missionized, decimated by infectious diseases, slaughtered by marauding vigilantes, they had fallen in number to less than 20,000 by the turn of the twentieth century, down from an estimated 150,000 at the time of the American conquest. "We are almost at the end of the road," said Robert Spott, a Yurok from the Klamath River region in the state's far north. "Today, when we go back to where we used to go for berries, there is a sign, 'Keep Out.' Then, again, we go to where we used to go to hunt. You see the sign, 'Keep Out. No Shooting Allowed.' All right. We go away. Then, again, we go down to where we used to fish. That is taken by the white man. What are we going to do?"

Californians were largely ignorant of this history. Most accepted the myth of the "vanishing Indian." Natives, they believed, unable to cope with change, had simply withered away. But the shocking removal of the Cupeños, widely reported in the state's newspapers, made it clear that Native Californians were still alive and very much present. The same year, the California Indian Association, an organization of reform-minded women dedicated to securing the human rights of Native Californians, petitioned Congress. In all of the other states and territories, they noted, the federal government had made treaties with Native tribes who agreed to cede their homelands in exchange for protected reservations. But not in California.

Put aside for the moment the inherently oppressive and exploitative nature of conquest and colonization. For most Native Americans, there was at least a pretense of legal process. "The utmost good faith shall always be observed towards the Indians," declared the nation's founders; "their lands and property shall never be taken from them without their consent." But because the California treaties had been rejected out of hand by the Senate, the state's Native peoples received nothing in return for what the women of the California Indian Association described as "the most beautiful and valuable country in the world."

Various presidents had created a dozen small executive-order reservations in the state, and several hundred individual Natives filed claims for allotments of public land, but there were no guarantees of ownership or permanence: they were merely "tenants at will." Most Native Californians remained landless squatters, many of them living from hand to mouth. "We therefore earnestly petition and pray," the women of the

California Indian Association petitioned the federal government, "that lands be granted to the landless Indians."

The immediate result of their petition was a revival of interest in the forgotten California treaties, which were retrieved from the Senate archive and published for the first time. An embarrassed Congress responded with an appropriation for the creation of several dozen new reservations. More important, the treaties became a powerful symbol for Native Californians, a reminder of their historic suffering and their continuing struggle for justice.

★

In 1911, the state's newspapers reported another Native story that received wide attention. An emaciated man, clothed in rags, was apprehended while rummaging through the garbage behind a slaughterhouse in the Sacramento Valley town of Oroville. He spoke neither English nor Spanish, nor the language of local Maidus, a few of whom were summoned to the jail where the man was incarcerated. Learning about him from newspaper stories, anthropologists from the University of California at Berkeley took charge. They identified him as a Yahi, a mountain people wiped out during the state's genocidal campaign of "extermination" in the 1860s. Gradually they learned enough of his language to communicate. The man would not reveal his given name—his culture forbade him from speaking it aloud—so the anthropologists called him Ishi, meaning "man" in his native tongue.

Ishi told them that when he was a child, White men had attacked and killed nearly all his band. He managed to escape with several members of his family, and for more than forty years they lived together deep in the Sierra Nevada Range. In 1908, however, a surveying party for a hydroelectric company stumbled upon them. Ishi's family scattered as the White men ruthlessly ransacked their camp. His mother died, and he lost contact with the others. For three years he survived alone, until a forest fire drove him out, leading to his arrest.

The anthropologists gave Ishi a job as janitor for the University of California's Museum of Anthropology in San Francisco. He became a kind of living exhibit, demonstrating his skill at making stone tools and his accuracy with a bow and arrow. He provided anthropologists with invaluable information about the culture of his people before his death from tuberculosis in 1916. The astounding story of Ishi, "the last Yahi," the victim of a rapacious civilization, shocked the moral conscience of many Californians.

★

Because of their desert location, the Cahuillas—several distinct bands, each with its own territory—were spared the trauma of missionization. Like the Yokuts of the Central Valley, they responded to colonial invasion by developing the capacity to act in common under powerful warrior chiefs. During the rancho era, including the first decades of American control, several hundred Cahuilla fighters made up the most powerful military force in southern California. Those days were long since past by the early twentieth century, but the Cahuillas remained proud and indomitable. If federal agents pushed them too hard, one official predicted, "friction is sure to come."

By presidential order, each of the Cahuilla bands was granted a small reservation in the Coachella Valley or the surrounding mountains, arid patches of land that federal authorities considered unsuitable for development. In the fullness of time, however, that assumption proved shortsighted. That was especially true for the Agua Calientes, who for a thousand years or more had inhabited the canyons on the northern slope of towering Mount San Jacinto, a hundred miles east of Los Angeles. Water from the mountainside nourished lush groves of native palms and fed a hot mineral spring they called *Sec-he*.

"We are the People of the Water," says Jeff Grubbe, who in 2012 became chairman of the Agua Caliente Band of Cahuilla Indians.

By the time the Agua Caliente reservation was created by executive order in the 1870s, the federal government had already rewarded the Southern Pacific Railroad with alternate sections of the Coachella Valley for constructing a rail line across the desert. The band got what remained, a checkerboard of square-mile sections that by mere luck included the palm canyons and *Sec-he,* which Americans named Palm Springs.

The Agua Caliente band, like the Cupeños, recognized the economic potential of the springs. They built a bathhouse and soaking pools and set up toll gates at the entrance to their beautiful canyons. "We do not allow any white person to go up to the canyons without our consent," they declared in 1892, and warned that trespassers "shall be removed immediately from our country." Tolls and fees provided them with a modest source of revenue. Several inns and hotels sprouted on private land adjoining the reservation, and by the 1910s, as automobiles became the dominant mode of transportation, Palm Springs became a popular winter resort for wealthy Angelenos, especially the Hollywood elite. Inevitably, developers began to lust after control of the hot springs itself.

"It is much to be desired," wrote the author of a tourist guide, "that some square miles of this locality, with Palm Canyon as a center, should be set aside as a national park." Like Yosemite, where the Awahnechee people had been chased out, *Sec-he* and the palm groves would cease to be a Native homeland and become a tourist destination. The proposal was embraced by the Palm Springs Chamber of Commerce, but the Agua Caliente band refused to consider it. "We do not want to sell our land for any money," declared Francisco Patencio, the band's hereditary leader. "Everybody can use it just the same as a park, if they get our permission." But businessmen didn't like the idea of following rules written by Native people. "Injuns Won't Sell Canyon," complained a headline in the *Los Angeles Times*. It was a crying shame that the beautiful desert views were spoiled by the "pitifully squalid" reservation next door. Perhaps the Cahuillas should receive the Cupeño treatment.

★

Like the Mountain Cahuillas, the Agua Caliente band found support among their Cahuilla kindred as well as other Native communities in southern California. In 1919 they helped found the Mission Indian Federation (MIF), an organization that soon counted more than two thousand members from thirty southern California reservations. They adopted "Human Rights and Home Rule" as their slogan. How did they hope to accomplish it? By winning full U.S. citizenship for Natives while at the same time maintaining their limited political sovereignty. This platform was prescient, anticipating the political course of Native American history through the remainder of the twentieth century, not only in California but throughout the nation.

The MIF built on a tradition of indigenous pride. At the organization's annual convention, held at Riverside in 1924, the Luiseño delegation proudly unfurled the American flag President Grant had presented to their leader, Olegario Calac, a half century before. Rehearsing their history of struggle provided them with the strength to move forward.

That same year, Congress adopted the MIF's key demand and passed the Indian Citizenship Act, granting birthright citizenship to all Native Americans born within U.S. territorial limits. The demand for full citizenship rights was simply too powerful to ignore. Thousands of Native men had served during World War I, many of them heroically. The MIF celebrated the legislation as a great victory: not only did it promise constitutional protection, but it also provided the legal standing to challenge the arbitrary rule of federal Indian agents who often ran roughshod over reservation residents. In 1927 the MIF won another important victory when, after an intense lobbying effort, the California legislature authorized the state's attorney general to seek compensation from the federal government for its unlawful seizure of Native homelands. That case was not resolved until the 1960s, however, and the settlement resulted in the payment of a measly few hundred dollars to individual Natives, most of whom considered the settlement insulting.

Over those thirty years, the Agua Caliente band found itself in the vanguard of the struggle. By the thirties, well-to-do White visitors were coming by the thousands to Palm Springs each winter. People of color staffed the hotels and restaurants, but restrictive covenants prevented them from living in the city's residential section. The Agua Caliente band did not have the capital to develop their section, nor would the federal Indian Bureau allow them to lease it for long-term development. So to supplement the revenue they received from bathhouse fees and canyon tolls, they began renting small plots to workers, who constructed low-cost homes and trailer courts. "It was a community where it wasn't just Indians," recalled band member Lois Segundo-Workman. "It was Blacks, it was Mexicans. It was like a family unit there, because they all were in the same situation and they all leaned on each other."

The ramshackle multicultural neighborhood within sight of the posh resorts infuriated the Palm Springs Chamber of Commerce. Acting together, the federal government and the business community went on the offensive, demanding that the Agua Caliente band allow White authorities to collect the revenue and hold it "in trust" for the band. When the Cahuillas resisted, federal authorities seized the band's assets, including the hot springs and bathhouse, the palm canyons, and the downtown section of the reservation.

"White people want your land," warned MIF leader Adam Castillo, "and they are not going to stop until they get it." Protests by band members led to the arrest and incarceration of several elected leaders, whom federal officials charged with "rebellion against constituted authority." They included band leader Francisco Patencio, eighty-one years old and in frail health. His jailing outraged Native people throughout southern California. Realizing they had gone too far, the Indian Bureau ordered the prisoners released and returned control of the reservation to the band. It was an important, if temporary, victory.

Federal authorities had a difficult time understanding the Agua Caliente perspective. "Palm Springs lays the golden eggs for you," declared one frustrated official. "The better you can learn to get along with the people who have the money, the bigger your golden eggs." But for Francisco Patencio and his people, more than money was at stake. "My people could not live without their homes, their gardens, their lands," he said shortly before his death at the age of ninety. "No matter how far away, . . . when they know it is near the time for them to go, they always come back to the homes where they were born to die. They always come back." For them, land was far more than real estate.

CENTRAL VALLEY COTTON STRIKERS

31

The Man with the Hoe

Despite the rapid development of manufacturing, agriculture remained the most productive sector of the California economy. By 1930, the state was supplying more than half of the nation's fresh fruit and vegetables and nearly three-quarters of its canned food. The expansion of production increased the need for farmhands. An estimated 250,000 workers labored in California's fields, most of them transient and seasonal. Bindlestiffs continued to travel from harvest to harvest, and thousands of immigrant Portuguese, Greeks, and Italians worked in the fields.

But as the industrial economy surged, many White workers found jobs in manufacturing or other urban enterprises, and people of color, who had always supplied much of the state's field labor, became increasingly important. Native Californians, the state's first agricultural workforce, had been succeeded by the Chinese, who made up more than a third of farm laborers at their peak in the 1880s, before the full implementation of the Exclusion Act. The Chinese in turn were succeeded by the Japanese, about 40 percent of the workforce in 1910. Then, as the Japanese became growers or took up urban occupations, they were replaced by Mexicans, who made up close to half the state's farm workers by 1930. They were joined in the fields by Filipinos, Sikhs, Armenians, Basques, and other ethnic minorities. "Growers prefer a mixture of laborers of various races speaking diverse languages and not accustomed to mingling with each other," noted a state official. Why? Because their cultural differences prevented them from arriving "at a mutual understanding which would lead to strikes and other labor troubles." Divide and conquer.

Crops around the state matured at different times, so most farm workers migrated from place to place. That made it difficult for them to act collectively. Growers, on the other hand, united in trade associations to keep wages low. They provided migrants with few amenities, often little more than an open field for a tent encampment. For most workers, arriving with empty pockets and growling stomachs, it was a case of "take it or leave it." The wages and living conditions of California's rural poor had always been deplorable.

As the state grew increasingly urban, it became easier for most Californians to ignore the miserable living and working conditions of the countryside. At the turn of the century, however, they were given a glimpse when an Oakland school teacher named Edward Markham published, to considerable acclaim, a poem titled "The Man with the Hoe":

> Bowed by the weight of centuries he leans
> Upon his hoe and gazes on the ground,
> The emptiness of ages in his face,
> And on his back the burden of the world.

The rural worker, Markham wrote, was "humanity betrayed, plundered, profaned, and disinherited."

★

Upset by low wages or poor working and living conditions, Chinese and Japanese farm workers of the late nineteenth century often left the fields in spontaneous strikes. Sometimes the strikes were called by labor contractors, who bargained with growers directly and pulled workers from the fields when they didn't get what they wanted. The first farm strike by a labor union took place in 1903, after sugar beet growers in Ventura County, determined to break the power of labor contractors, organized a trade association and began hiring workers directly. Feeling confident of their power, they enacted a deep wage cut.

In response, labor contractors Kosaburo Baba and J. M. Lizarras founded a union they called the Japanese-Mexican Labor Association, sent organizers into the fields, and succeeded in convincing the workers to walk off the job. Shocked growers cracked down in what would prove a typical response. During a confrontation on the streets of Oxnard, police fired into a crowd of striking workers, killing one man and wounding three. But the men refused to be intimidated and faced their bosses down. With the beets rotting in the field, growers rescinded the cut.

The Labor Council of Los Angeles endorsed the strike and petitioned the American Federation of Labor (AFL) to support the multiethnic union. As the *San Francisco Examiner* noted, it was the first time in living memory that a California labor organization had "put itself on record as in any way favoring Asiatic labor." But the White supremacist leadership of the AFL declared they would charter the fledgling union only if it expelled its Japanese members. That was something they would not do, responded union president Lizarras. "Our Japanese brothers were the first to recognize the importance of cooperating and uniting in demanding a fair wage scale," he said. "We will refuse any kind of charter except one which will wipe out race prejudice and recognize our fellow workers as being as good as ourselves." That was not just a noble sentiment. It was the only practical strategy for uniting farm workers from many ethnic backgrounds. Migrants had no means of sustaining a union on their own, however, and the Japanese-Mexican Labor Association soon disappeared. Spontaneous strikes by labor contractors and frustrated farm workers continued to break out around the state, but they had only local and immediate effects.

★

The Exclusion Act and the Gentleman's Agreement put enormous pressure on growers to find other sources of cheap labor. One response was to recruit families, promoting work in the orchards and fields as the opportunity for a working summer vacation. "Before the early part of the twentieth century," writes historian Richard Steven Street, "children were never seen in farm labor camps or in the fields. . . . Yet, very slowly, as the agricultural industry grew, married couples began drifting with the crops, their children in tow."

Hop farmers, especially, aimed at attracting family labor. Hops, which provide the bitter flavor in the brewing of beer, needed to be harvested at precisely the right moment, and the work was considered appropriate for women and children as well as men. In 1913, Ralph Durst, owner of the largest hop farm in the state, located near the rural town of Wheatland, thirty miles northeast of Sacramento, advertised widely for pickers. Nearly three thousand people showed up, twice as many as Durst needed. But that was his plan, allowing him to cut wage rates in this take-it-or-leave-it system. "The competition of destitute work-seekers," a state investigator later testified, "insured enough pickers even at the reduced rate." The workers included

Whites and many ethnic minorities, most with their families. There were said to be four or five hundred children in the encampment, an open field without any permanent shelter, little drinking water, and appalling sanitation. People soon began falling sick with dysentery and other intestinal disorders.

Among the crowd were several activists of the Industrial Workers of the World, a labor union committed to organizing among California's farm workers. The strategy of the "Wobblies," as they were known, was to bring all industrial and agricultural workers, regardless of race or ethnicity, into "one big union." One Saturday evening several days into the harvest, the Wobblies circulated through the crowded encampment, encouraging people to discuss their plight. Veteran organizer Richard "Blackie" Ford assisted a group to draw up a list of demands, and Sunday morning he presented it to Durst, who angrily rejected it. A few hours later, speaking from the bed of a wagon to fifteen hundred men and women, Ford urged the workers to strike. As the crowd cheered, Ford reached down and took a sick baby from the arms of its mother. Then, hoisting the child above his head, he cried: "It's for the life of the kids we're doing this!" For those who were there, it was an unforgettable moment.

A few minutes later a contingent of armed sheriff's deputies, summoned by Durst, invaded the encampment. Greeted by jeers from the crowd, one of the deputies fired a shot in the air, as he later said, to "sober the mob." Not surprisingly, it had the opposite effect. Most people scattered in panic, but others counterattacked. In the resulting melee four men were killed— a deputy, a county official, and two workers. Governor Hiram Johnson called out the National Guard, and the authorities arrested dozens of Wobblies. Although they had nothing to do with the shooting, Blackie Ford and another organizer were convicted of murder and sentenced to prison terms of twenty years.

★

There were no more than a few hundred card-carrying Wobblies in California, but they enjoyed an outsized influence. Activists of the Agricultural Workers Organization, affiliated with the IWW, earned the admiration of farm workers for their audacity and commitment. Over the next several years a wave of strikes threatened harvests and closed canneries. Nothing frightened growers more than the possibility of a broad-based union of many different ethnic groups.

With the nation's entry into the European war in 1917, officials saw an opportunity to crack down. Like other groups on the left, the IWW vigorously opposed what they characterized as "the capitalist war." Congress clamped down on antiwar protestors, who were labeled "German sympathizers," by passing legislation that made it a felony to use "disloyal, profane, scurrilous, or abusive language" concerning the draft, the army, or the flag. A national roundup of Wobblies soon began, and no state pursued them more aggressively than California. "The IWW must be put completely out of existence," declared Republican governor William Stephens, who succeeded Hiram Johnson when he was elected to the U.S. Senate. "Every person that preaches its doctrines must be dealt with summarily."

After the Bolshevik revolution in Russia, fear of Germans mutated into a fear of "Reds." The California legislature passed the Criminal Syndicalism Act, which made the advocacy of overthrowing the government by violent means a felony, punishable by up to fourteen years in prison. What constituted violent means? Strikes and boycotts, according to growers. During the Red Scare that followed the war, more than five hundred Californians were arrested for the expression of left-wing political opinions, in a crackdown that effectively destroyed the IWW. The Criminal Syndicalism law remained a bulwark against union organizing for decades to come, not repealed until 1991.

★

California agriculture boomed with wartime demand, but following the armistice the price of farm commodities collapsed and remained depressed throughout the twenties. Thousands of small farmers went bust, resulting in more consolidated ownership by corporations and banks. Growers cut wages, using the threat of criminal prosecution to keep workers in line. But militancy gradually reemerged, this time among Mexican migrants. A social and political revolution had shaken Mexico during the 1910s, and many migrants were militant veterans of that struggle. In the spring of 1928, Mexican cantaloupe pickers in the Imperial Valley struck for better wages and working conditions. Growers crushed the strike with brute force, but it was a portent of things to come.

The next year the stock market crash of 1929 began the slide of the economy into the Great Depression, the worst economic calamity in American history, affecting people of every class and station. California agriculture was hit especially hard. With falling demand and plunging prices, growers slashed wages, which fell to their lowest level since the turn of the century. The average California farm worker of the 1930s made less than $300 a year ($6,000 in 2020 dollars), starvation wages.

Industrial labor struggles intensified throughout the nation during the Depression. Elsewhere the action took place on urban streets or the factory floor, but in California the struggle centered on rural areas. The countryside erupted in an epidemic of strikes. At least 160 major strikes took place in California's fields and canneries during the thirties, many of them organized by activists affiliated with the American Communist Party. During the tumultuous year of 1933 alone, thirty-seven strikes involving forty-eight thousand farm workers threatened two-thirds of the state's agricultural production.

The walkouts began in April among pea pickers in the Bay Area, spread to the berry fields of southern California in June, then to the fruit orchards and vineyards of the Santa Clara Valley, finally concluding with a massive strike of fifteen thousand cotton pickers in the San Joaquin Valley in October. The majority of the cotton strikers were Mexican. Forcibly evicted from grower-owned migrant camps, with the aid of Communist Party organizers they set up their own encampments on unoccupied land, including a huge compound housing some three thousand people near the dusty San Joaquin Valley town of Corcoran.

The cotton fields of the valley stretched nearly one hundred miles along U.S. Highway 99. Labor organizers formed truck brigades, transporting strikers from one site to another, keeping up the pressure. Deputy sheriffs, backed by armed vigilantes, used tear gas, beatings, and arrests to intimidate law-abiding picketers. In separate attacks on the same day, three men were killed and several others wounded. "A small army of ranchers fired point blank into a crowd of striking cotton pickers," a correspondent reported. "I saw eleven unarmed persons shot down in cold blood," wrote another. News accounts compared the attacks to the violence at Mussel Slough fifty years before.

Public opinion shifted dramatically in favor of the workers, and state authorities responded with a fact-finding commission. "Without question," the commissioners concluded, "the civil rights of strikers have been violated." Under intense pressure, growers agreed to a modest increase in wages, but they refused to recognize the union. Strikers debated what to do. Although many wanted to hold out, in the end a majority voted to accept the partial victory and return to work.

Determined to avoid future concessions, prominent growers around the state banded together as the Associated Farmers of California. Despite its name, the organization was run by corporations like Del Monte, the nation's largest distributor of canned fruit and vegetables, the Bank of America, the Southern Pacific Railroad, and even PG&E. With a huge budget and a large paid staff, the group coordinated a statewide campaign against what they claimed was a Communist revolution taking place in the countryside.

The following year, in an action coordinated with county sheriffs, local police, and groups of armed vigilantes, the Associated Farmers cracked down on union leaders. Vigilantes "ranged through a dozen cities," reported the *Fresno Bee,* "smashing windows, wrecking Communist headquarters, beating the men they found there, and sending warning notes to Red sympathizers." Several hundred of those "sympathizers" were jailed. The state charged the Communist organizers of the cotton strike with violating the Criminal Syndicalism statute. Eight were found guilty and sentenced to terms in the state penitentiary.

Progressive Republican Simon J. Lubin, chief of the state Bureau of Commerce, condemned the repression. "We have little or nothing to fear from radicals and agitators," he told the press. "But there is genuine ground for fear—great fear—in the greed and selfishness, the intellectual sterility, the social injustice, the economic blindness, the lack of political sagacity, and the mock heroics and hooliganism among ourselves." Lubin's views, though widely reported, had little impact.

★

In 1936 California novelist John Steinbeck published *In Dubious Battle,* a fictional depiction of an apple pickers' strike. The novel focuses on two Communist organizers and their efforts to mobilize the workers after growers announce a steep pay cut. The pickers were "sore as hell," the veteran organizer Mac tells his young associate Jim, "but they don't know what to do about it." The two men labor in the orchards, earning the respect of fellow workers and providing practical advice. Mac cautions patience. "Leadership has got to come from the men," he tells Jim. "We can teach them method, but they've got to do the job themselves." Finally, when an elderly picker falls from a faulty ladder and breaks his hip, the workers walk off the job. Mac and Jim help channel their anger into action.

The growers employ Red Scare tactics in an attempt to fracture the strikers' unity. "Your red pals here can't help you," a foreman warns London, the strikers' elected leader. "They don't give a damn about you." London doesn't buy it. "They may be reds," he responds, "but they're good guys." Yet London wonders. "You always hear about reds is a bunch of sons-of-bitches," he says to Mac. "Depends on how you look at it," Mac replies. "If you was to own thirty thousand acres of land and a million dollars, they'd be a bunch of sons-of-bitches. But if you're just London, a workin' stiff, why they're a bunch of guys that want to help you live like a man, and not like a pig, see?"

Mac views the strike as a small battle in a larger war. "Raising wages isn't all we're after," he says. "You've got to look at the whole thing." That makes London nervous. "That's kind of reva—revolution, ain't it?" he asks. "Sure it is," Mac says. "It's a revolution against hunger and cold." But Mac warns young Jim that the strike will fail. The growers are too well organized. The strikers will be attacked, beaten, and arrested. Some may be killed. But individuals are expendable. "For every man they kill, ten new ones come over to us." He advises Jim not to worry. "The thing will carry on and on. It'll spread, and some day—it'll work. Some day we'll win. . . . If we didn't believe that, we wouldn't be here."

★

Steinbeck wrote the novel after meeting some of the leaders of the cotton strike. Pat Chambers, who inspired the character of Mac, was a slender, soft-spoken man in his mid-thirties. A Wobbly before joining the Communist Party in the twenties, he had a long record of arrests for organizing, and was busted again during the cotton strike. While Chambers languished in jail the leadership of the strike fell to his associate, a young woman named Caroline Decker. In the novel, Steinbeck transformed her into the character of Jim. All the book's main characters are men, although in actual fact many women played an active role in the cotton strike.

Decker grew up in the American South, the daughter of Jewish immigrants from Ukraine. Despite being just twenty-two, she was a veteran organizer. "I considered myself a Communist from the time I was sixteen," she later told an interviewer. "I was very idealistic. If you weren't a radical in those days, you were just a blob of protoplasm." She worked with striking coal miners in Kentucky and steelworkers in Pittsburgh before the Communist Party dispatched her to California to organize farm workers. An electrifying speaker, she impressed even her enemies. "Besides being the Joan of Arc of the cotton pickers," wrote the editor of the conservative *Visalia Times-Delta,* "Miss Decker is a blonde. The combination is too great to withstand."

Decker read *In Dubious Battle* while serving her prison term. She didn't like it. Steinbeck, she thought, misunderstood how things really went down. The strikers acted spontaneously. She and Chambers helped when they could. "We were involved with realities," she said. "Raising wages, bettering working conditions. Basic concerns. We helped write leaflets and get them out. We helped raise demands. We helped pull stuff together. We cared and were on the scene. That's called leadership." She did not share the cold-blooded strategy voiced by Mac in the book, although she acknowledged that many Communist Party leaders did. For her, the tactical victory in the cotton strike was sufficient reward. "We felt we had made tremendous strides," she said. "The mere fact of arbitration was a huge step forward." Indeed, the 1933 strikes forced growers all over the state to raise farm worker wages.

The organizers appealed their conviction, which was based on concocted evidence, and in 1938 it was overturned by the state supreme court. Chambers, who remained a union activist, turned to organizing dockworkers in San Pedro. Decker went to work in the office of San Francisco labor lawyer Richard Gladstein, who had won the appeal that got them released. She and Gladstein later married. He continued to defend workers, union leaders, and Communists, while she devoted herself to raising their four children. She and Chambers both left the Communist Party. "Human beings didn't mean all that much to the Communists," Decker told an interviewer years later. "They were only instruments to serve their goals." For her, the struggle was not ideological but about securing a better life. "If number one is not to bring better conditions to the people of the United States," she insisted, "I'm not interested."

CAPITALISM HAS SERVED ITS TIME AND IS PASSING FROM THE EARTH. A NEW SYSTEM MUST BE FOUND TO TAKE ITS PLACE

UPTON SINCLAIR SPEAKS ON KHJ

32

End Poverty in California

On an August evening in 1934, following his impressive victory in the Democratic primary, gubernatorial candidate Upton Sinclair spoke to Californians from the studio of Los Angeles radio station KHJ. "We confront today the collapse of an institution which is worldwide and age-old," he told his listeners. "Capitalism has served its time and is passing from the earth. A new system must be found to take its place." The Great Depression was in its fourth year. California's economic output, the value of all the goods and services produced in the state, had dropped by 50 percent from its highpoint in 1929. More than a quarter of the state's workers were unemployed. Crowds joined in "hunger marches" organized by radical leaders. Reformers of all kinds proposed a myriad of schemes and strategies to end the crisis. Socialism—public ownership of vital industries—had been part of California's political discourse since the late nineteenth century, and in 1934 it seemed more relevant than ever.

Sinclair offered a plan to "End Poverty in California," EPIC for short. When he became governor, he pledged, the state government would acquire the idle factories and farms and put unemployed Californians to work for themselves. "That is the simple proposition," Sinclair told his radio audience. "There can be no valid objection to it." His program also included pensions for widows, the disabled, and the elderly. The state's political and economic elite, he told his listeners, were opposed to his candidacy for a simple reason: "They are afraid my plan will succeed and show the unemployed how to produce for use instead of for profit."

Harry Chandler, son-in-law of the late Harrison Gray Otis and his successor as publisher of the *Los Angeles Times*, responded in an editorial the following morning. He spoke for a Republican Party that had turned away from Hiram Johnson's Progressivism and embraced unregulated capitalism. Sinclair's ill-considered scheme, wrote Chandler, might sound good to some. But it would open the gate for a "maggot-like horde of Reds," determined to destroy the American way of life. "We are standing at a fatal crossing of the roads," Chandler warned. "There can be no turning back. Either we take the Red path, or we close that gate right now—forever."

Two years before, California Republicans had been shocked by the landslide victory of Democrat Franklin Delano Roosevelt over incumbent Republican Herbert Hoover, who claimed California as his home state. Educated as an engineer at Stanford University in the 1890s, Hoover had made a fortune in the mining industry, then won universal acclaim as the leader of an effort to feed starving Europeans during the First World War. But as president, Hoover did little to assist fellow Americans hit hard by the Depression, which began in the first year of his term. He vetoed legislation providing direct relief to unemployed workers, declaring that "prosperity cannot be restored by raids upon the public Treasury." A true laissez-faire capitalist, he trusted the economy to correct itself.

When it didn't, Roosevelt promised action. During his celebrated first hundred days, he collaborated with Congress on legislation designed to mitigate the disaster. New federal agencies provided funds for relief and put nearly a hundred thousand Californians to work on dozens of public works projects. Another thirty thousand men joined the California branch of the Civilian Conservation Corps, doing much-needed work on public lands, clearing fire breaks, planting trees, and constructing campgrounds. These programs reduced unemployment, but they did not cure the problem of a broken economic system. Sinclair promised that his plan would.

★

Sinclair had been converted to socialism at the turn of the century by H. Gaylord Wilshire of Los Angeles, dubbed the "millionaire socialist" by the press. In hopes of recruiting readers to the cause, Sinclair wrote *The Jungle,* an exposé of the nation's meatpacking industry. Published in 1906, it became a best seller and a popular sensation—more for its shocking revelations of unsanitary practices than for its politics. "I aimed at the public's heart," Sinclair joked, "and by accident I hit it in the stomach." Over the next quarter century, from his home in Pasadena, he published more than sixty books. Twice he ran for governor and once for the U.S. Senate as the nominee of the Socialist Party, badly losing each time.

Republicans dominated California politics in the twenties. The party comprised two wings, which pulled in opposite directions. Establishment conservatives, representing the state's business interests, wanted to preserve the state's low tax rates and keep regulation of economic activity to a minimum. Senator Hiram Johnson's Progressives, in contrast, believed in selective state supervision to keep capitalism in check. What united the two factions was their mutual hatred of Democrats, who drew support from the working class, organized labor, and ethnic and immigrant voters.

In 1931, the vast majority of the 120 seats in the state legislature were held by Republicans of both stripes. Not a single Democrat held statewide office. These Republicans responded to the economic crisis in the manner of President Hoover, by cutting spending. They also sponsored a successful ballot initiative that instituted a supermajority requirement—a two-thirds vote of the legislature—to approve the state budget. But Roosevelt's victory revived the Democratic Party in California. Riding on FDR's coattails, Democrats captured a majority of the state's congressional delegation as well as a U.S. Senate seat. The Democratic Party, Sinclair concluded, might be a vehicle for real social change.

California was awash in alternative political movements seeking to address the economic crisis. A group called Technocracy, which promoted the idea of turning government over to scientific experts, claimed a half million California members. It spawned another organization, the Utopian Society of America, which proposed to "free the skillful hands of modern man to produce wealth for consumption and use rather than for hoarding and the shackles of debt." A Utopian rally in the spring of 1934 drew twenty-five thousand people to the Hollywood Bowl. Meanwhile, Dr. Francis E. Townsend of Long Beach proposed a system of pensions for all Americans over the age of sixty financed by a national sales tax, declaring: "Youth for work and age for leisure." By early 1934 there were hundreds of "Townsend Clubs" in California.

Sinclair's program was part of this political mix. It generated enormous enthusiasm and led to the organization of nearly a thousand EPIC clubs throughout the state. Sinclair and his followers conducted a voter registration drive that added

350,000 new Democrats to the rolls. For the first time in half a century, registered Democrats outnumbered Republicans in California. The chances for a Sinclair victory looked good.

★

In 1931, the Hoover administration began rounding up and deporting Mexican nationals. Growers considered them radical troublemakers, county officials worried they would strain welfare rolls, and racists promoted the myth that they carried disease. Immigration agents went door to door in ethnic neighborhoods throughout California, demanding that Spanish-speaking residents provide proof of legal residency. Those unable to do so were summarily arrested. "It was for us the day of judgment," a Mexican woman told a reporter. "The *marciales,* deputy sheriffs, arrived in late afternoon when the men were returning home from the lemon groves. They rode around the neighborhood with the sirens wailing and advising people to surrender themselves to the authorities. They barricaded all the exits to the *colonia* so that no one could escape."

In this climate of fear, many Mexicans "voluntarily" joined repatriation programs organized by county welfare agencies. Thousands boarded buses and trains transporting them to the border. "The men were pensive and the majority of the children and mothers were crying," one deportee recalled. "Some sang with guitars trying to forget their sadness."

> Goodbye dear countrymen
> They are going to deport us
> But we are not bandits
> We came to toil.

The exodus peaked in 1933, but the deportations continued through the end of the decade. The Mexican population of Los Angeles, estimated at 170,000 in 1930, fell by nearly a third.

Although no government agency kept comprehensive statistics, historians estimate that as many as a million people went to Mexico, half of them from California. A large proportion of the deportees had been born in the United States and were American citizens.

★

Getting rid of Mexicans did not put an end to labor militancy. The National Industrial Recovery Act, passed by Congress in 1933, included a section guaranteeing the right of workers "to organize and bargain collectively through representatives of their own choosing." As a concession to growers, farm laborers were explicitly excluded from this protection, but the new law inspired a great deal of organizing in the cities. In the late spring of 1934, the International Longshoreman's Association, representing thousands of dockworkers on the Pacific coast, went on strike for union recognition and better pay. The walkout, which closed ports from San Diego to Seattle, lasted several weeks.

"This is war," declared the *Los Angeles Times*. "On the one side are the forces of law and order; on the other a group of Red-directed insurrectionists who, in their bloody defiance of authority, disgrace the name of honest and patriotic American labor." Republican governor Frank Merriam condemned what he called "Communistic and radical agitators." San Francisco employers attempted to crush the strike. During a confrontation known as "Bloody Thursday," police used tear gas and live ammunition to disperse picketers blocking access to the waterfront. Two men were killed and thirty wounded. Governor Merriam sent the National Guard to occupy the city and reopen the docks, and in response longshoremen called a general strike.

One hundred and fifty thousand workers from sixty-three unions walked off the job, halting almost all economic activity and turning San Francisco into a virtual ghost town. Employers finally agreed to recognize the longshoremen's union, a victory celebrated by workers all over the state. In the aftermath of the victory, union organizers in "open shop" Los Angeles began successful membership drives in several important local industries, including food processing, garment manufacture, aircraft assembly, and motion picture production.

Republicans argued that Sinclair's candidacy was part of an effort by Communists to seize control of the state. Determined to defeat him, they mounted one of the first mass-media political campaigns in American history, a barrage of negative advertising. Newspapers published a daily diet of "Sinclair-isms," passages culled from the candidate's many muckraking books. Bankers, he had written, were "legalized counterfeit-ers," the Boy Scouts were "warmongers," the Bible was a story of "slavery, rape and wholesale murder, committed by priests and rulers under the direct orders of God." Such quotes, most taken out of context, took their toll.

Hollywood executives raised a campaign fund of half a million dollars. Metro-Goldwyn-Mayer, the town's largest film studio, produced a series of fake newsreels in which actors playing ordinary citizens explained who they were voting for. A rough-looking man, speaking directly to the camera, declared that he would vote for Sinclair "because his system worked so well in Russia." A demure grandmother rocking on her front porch explained that she was voting for Merriam "because I want to have my little home. It's all I have left in the world."

The November election was a three-way contest between Merriam, Sinclair, and a moderate nominee of the Progres-sives, who split the reform vote, allowing Merriam to eke out a victory. Sinclair lost the election, but he transformed the po-litical landscape. For the first time in half a century, California had a two-party system. "Upton Sinclair has re-founded the

Democrats in this state," declared Culbert Olson, a state senator from Los Angeles, chosen as the Democrats' new state
chairman. "We will take up where he left off."

★

Four years later, Olson ran against incumbent governor Merriam under the banner "Bring the New Deal to California." He
excoriated Merriam for backing growers and employers against
striking workers, and campaigned on an extensive platform
of reforms, including labor rights, unemployment insurance,
public ownership of utilities, and progressive taxation. A soft-
spoken attorney, Olson was not encumbered with Sinclair's
baggage.

Many of Olson's supporters were also in favor of a political movement known as "Ham 'n' Eggs," yet another pension
scheme which proposed to pay every Californian over the age
of fifty "$30 Every Thursday." President Roosevelt had already
signed the Social Security Act, but its pension program was
still being put together (the first Social Security checks were
not issued until 1940), and there was a great deal of popular
support for immediate state action. "Ham 'n' Eggs" activists
circulated petitions and got their proposal on the November
ballot. President Roosevelt opposed their plan, though, which
put Olson in a difficult spot. He declined to take a position on
the initiative.

Olson defeated Merriam decisively, becoming the first
Democratic governor of the state in forty years. The opposition of conservative legislators from rural counties, however,
frustrated his plans for a reform administration. Olson needed
the solid backing of the left. But the "Ham and Eggs" initiative
had failed to pass, and when the governor refused to endorse
a second try, many former supporters turned on him and organized a recall campaign. They were unsuccessful, but the
struggle kept Olson on the defensive. In 1940 California voters

overwhelmingly voted for Roosevelt's third presidential term. But they also reelected the legislative opponents of the president's most vigorous California supporter, the lonely and embattled Democratic governor.

★

The New Deal, writes historian Kevin Starr, was responsible for "an epic of construction without precedent in the history of the state." A flood of federal funds financed dozens of public infrastructure projects supervised by private contractors, who in turn hired tens of thousands of workers. They built schools, courthouses, hospitals, and other public buildings, and labored on immense construction projects like the Bay Bridge, connecting Oakland and San Francisco, and the Arroyo Seco Parkway between Pasadena and downtown L.A., the first installment of what would become California's freeway system.

The most ambitious plans focused on water and power. The Colorado River Project began with legislation introduced by Senator Hiram Johnson. Approved by Congress in 1928, the project got off to a slow start under President Hoover but was pushed to completion by the New Deal. Massive Hoover Dam, dedicated in 1935, provided flood control, hydroelectric power, irrigation for the Imperial Valley, and drinking water for southern California. The Central Valley Project was the northern California counterpart. The plan, adopted by the state legislature in 1933, envisioned a series of major dams on the rivers draining the western slope of the Sierra Nevada, providing flood control, abundant hydropower, and irrigation for San Joaquin Valley growers.

When the state proved unable to market the bonds financing the project, the New Deal stepped in and took over. In 1937 construction began on Shasta Dam on the upper Sacramento, the second-largest in the world, after Hoover Dam. When completed in the early sixties, the Central Valley Project boasted twenty dams and reservoirs, eleven power plants, and five hundred miles of canals serving three million acres of farmland.

Most of California's big growers opposed the New Deal, but they enthusiastically embraced these projects. Because the federal government financed them, they were subject to congressional regulations that attempted to encourage family farms by placing a limit of 160 acres on the amount of land that could be irrigated. Intensive cultivation of fruit, nut, and vegetable crops can be quite profitably accomplished on an irrigated farm of that size. But by the 1930s, 70 percent of the state's farms were a thousand acres or larger, and the corporate owners of these large operations opposed this restriction. Rather than enforcing the limitations, federal authorities allowed these growers to exploit legal loopholes. "By nearly all measures," writes historian Norris Hundley, California growers "transformed the Central Valley Project into a vehicle of great corporate aggrandizement."

★

In the mid-thirties, economic refugees from drought-ravaged farms in the central United States began a mass migration to California. Many were former tenant farmers, displaced by labor-saving machinery and the environmental catastrophe known as the Dust Bowl. They came from a vast region, stretching from Texas and Oklahoma in the south to the Dakotas in the north.

One of those migrants was my father, Alvin Robert Faragher, a young man of twenty-one from Watertown, South Dakota. His mother had been dead for several years, and in the autumn of 1937 he and his sister buried their father, a tenant farmer. The two of them managed to plant a crop of flax the following spring, but the rains failed and it withered in the field. That was it. My father put his sister on a bus bound for southern California, where they had an aunt. Then he and three friends headed west in an old jalopy, earning food and gas money any way they could, working in fields, orchards, and lumber camps as they crossed the country. He reached his aunt's house in the town of Bellflower, southeast of Los Angeles, in January 1939. A small-town farm boy, the first thing he did was attend the midwinter reunion of former South Dakotans in Sycamore Grove Park in Highland Park.

My father was done with farming. But many rural migrants headed straight for California's Central Valley, taking farm labor jobs vacated by departing Mexicans, as the Joad family does in John Steinbeck's vivid 1939 novel *The Grapes of Wrath*. The Joads hope for a new promised land in California. "By God, they's grapes out there, just a-hangin' over inta the road," says Grandpa Joad. "I'm gonna pick me a wash tub full a grapes, an' I'm gonna set in 'em, an' scrooge aroun', an' let the juice run down my pants." Instead of an agrarian dream, however, they find an industrial nightmare, what California journalist Carey McWilliams called "factories in the fields." An estimated four hundred thousand migrants from the American heartland relocated to California during the second half of the decade.

Steinbeck's humanitarian concern was echoed by the work of other California artists, scholars, and activists. Feeling the urgency of the economic crisis in agriculture, Paul Schuster Taylor, a professor of economics at Berkeley, conducted firsthand field research and published a pathbreaking study of Mexican migrant farm workers. But Taylor felt that scholarship alone was insufficient. "I wanted to produce reports that would bring action as well as information," he later recalled. In 1934 he took a leave of absence from teaching and accepted an investigative position with a state agency. He assembled a modest staff and hired a photographer, a young woman named Dorothea Lange, to help document his findings.

Taylor and Lange, who soon fell in love and married, worked together preparing reports intended to convince state officials to provide assistance and enact reforms. Lange's photographs offer a powerful visual record of Californians during the Depression. They include "Migrant Mother," which over the years has become one of the world's most famous photographs. The mother is Florence Owens, a Cherokee woman from Oklahoma. Although that fact was not known at the time, it underlines the diversity of the migration. "Migrant Mother" and Lange's other photographs supported the argument that farm workers needed assistance and support.

In the mid-thirties, the federal government began the construction of a chain of model camps providing sanitary housing and social services for farm workers and their families. By 1939, ten camps were sheltering 45,000 people. That was indeed a positive accomplishment, but there were at least 250,000 migrant farm workers in California. Keep that in mind, for it puts the accomplishments of the New Deal in perspective. Farm laborers gained a small program that kept some from living in squalid misery. Growers benefited from a massive program that provided cheap water and electricity to expand their "factories in the fields."

HOLLENBECK JR. HIGH NINTH GRADE

33

Unite to Win

In mid-December 1941, student journalists at Hollenbeck Junior High, in the Boyle Heights district of Los Angeles, published a holiday edition of their school newspaper, the *Siren*. "This Christmas season has come, but not as we foresaw it," wrote assistant editor Marilyn Greene. A few days before, on December 7, Japan had attacked the U.S. Pacific Fleet as it lay anchored at Pearl Harbor, on the Hawaiian island of Oahu, killing 2,400 Americans. Los Angeles was home to the largest Japanese community in the United States, and many lived in Boyle Heights. "We have a special concern for our loyal American citizens of Japanese descent, who are as truly American as any of us," the ninth-grader wrote. "We Americans of all colors, races, and creeds must unite to win, so that freedom for all people may be possible."

Marilyn Greene grew up in a Jewish household in a multicultural neighborhood, one described by a sociologist at the University of Southern California as "cosmopolitan." The curriculum at Hollenbeck—indeed, at all Los Angeles public schools—encouraged an appreciation of diverse cultures. Green's upbringing shaped her understanding of "liberty and justice for all."

The Great Depression was over. With the outbreak of war in Europe in 1939, federal spending for the production of warships, aircraft, and other weaponry accelerated. Within months, California's factories were operating at full capacity. Construction at shipyards surged. The aircraft industry expanded rapidly. Good jobs put money in people's pockets. Then, with the attack on Pearl Harbor, America was suddenly at war. Thousands of Californians enlisted in the armed forces and shipped out for the duration. Lives were disrupted, families separated.

Many Californians felt particularly vulnerable because of the Japanese living among them. Were they loyal to the United States or to Japan? A rational response to this question was clouded by racist rhetoric going back half a century. The Japanese were "not the stuff of which American citizens are made" former San Francisco mayor James D. Phelan had insisted during his campaign for reelection to the U.S. Senate in 1920. "Keep California White," demanded the Phelan campaign—an update of the Workingmen's Party slogan "The Chinese Must Go." Japanese immigrants and their offspring were "a tributary colony of Japan," Phelan insisted. "In time of trial they will not fight for Uncle Sam, but betray him to the enemy."

Phelan died in 1930, but such racist thinking lived on. Not long after Marilyn Greene's sympathetic editorial in the *Siren,* veteran news reporter Henry McLemore, whose syndicated column appeared in the *Los Angeles Times,* called for drastic action against Japanese Americans. "I know this is the melting pot of the world and all men are created equal," McLemore sneered, almost as if he was responding directly to young Miss Greene,

> but do those things go when a country is fighting for its life? Not in my book. I am for immediate removal of every Japanese on the West Coast to a point deep in the interior. I don't mean a nice part of the interior either. Herd 'em up, pack 'em off, and give 'em the inside room in the badlands. Let 'em be pinched, hurt, hungry, and dead up against it. Personally, I hate the Japanese. And that goes for all of them.

★

As soon as war was declared, FBI agents began arresting hundreds of prominent "enemy aliens," including leaders of German, Italian, and Japanese ethnic associations, ministers and priests, newspaper editors, and teachers. The federal government incarcerated more than four thousand individuals, including nearly 1,300 immigrant Japanese, or *Issei* ("first generation"). All of them were held incommunicado during the war.

But what about the majority of the Japanese who were *Nisei* ("second generation"), American citizens by birthright? Many of them made public expressions of their patriotism. "We affirm our absolute allegiance to the United States of America, pledge all-out energy to defeat Japan, and appeal to you to call upon us that we may do our part for our country," a group of Nisei in Los Angeles wrote to President Roosevelt. Koichi Kido, a freshman at L.A. City College who lived with his family in Boyle Heights, was interviewed by a reporter. "We Americans of Japanese blood have confidence in the fairness of white Americans," he said. "There will be no trouble."

Kido was wrong. Several weeks after the attack on Pearl Harbor, Governor Culbert Olson and Attorney General Earl

Warren jointly announced their support for the removal of the entire Japanese American population from the Pacific coast. California's congressional delegation, led by Senator Hiram Johnson, issued its own call for the incarceration of "all persons of Japanese lineage, aliens and citizens alike." Congressman Alfred James Elliott of Tulare County put it bluntly: "We must move the Japanese into a concentration camp somewhere, and do it damn quick. Don't let anyone tell you there are good Japs." There was plenty of such talk. "A Japanese-American, born of Japanese parents, grows up to be a Japanese, not an American," declared a prominent local attorney in the *Los Angeles Times*. "A viper is nonetheless a viper wherever the egg is hatched."

Californians were spooked. During the early months of 1942, Japanese submarines prowled the coast, torpedoing American transport vessels and even shelling a petroleum refinery near Santa Barbara, fortunately causing little damage. Air raid drills and blackouts were commonplace, including a frightening false alarm in Los Angeles late one night, with sirens wailing and anti-aircraft guns firing into searchlight-swept skies. An opinion poll indicated that a majority of Californians considered Japanese residents a threat to national security.

But the concern was overblown. In a confidential memo to the president, FBI Director J. Edgar Hoover reported that there was no evidence of Japanese Americans consorting with the enemy. The calls for removal, he wrote, were "based primarily upon public and political pressure rather than on factual data." During the course of the war, not a single person of Japanese ancestry, whether Issei or Nisei, was formally charged with espionage or conspiracy.

Nevertheless, on February 19, 1942, Roosevelt signed Executive Order 9066, authorizing military authorities to remove any and all persons considered a threat to national security. Lieutenant General John DeWitt, commander of the San Francisco Presidio, announced the government's intention to remove and incarcerate all ethnic Japanese residents of the Pacific Coast states. The status of alien Germans and Italians, on the other hand, would be considered on a case-by-case basis. "We believe that we can, in dealing with the Germans and the Italians, arrive at some fairly sound conclusions," explained Attorney General Warren. "But when we deal with the Japanese, we cannot form any opinion that we believe to be sound. Their method of living, their language, make for this difficulty."

The roundup of Japanese families began in late March. By June, federal authorities had relocated some 120,000 people— two-thirds of them American citizens—to what President Roosevelt called "concentration camps" in the interior. It was the most overt violation of constitutional rights in American history. "A Jap's a Jap," declared General DeWitt. "It makes no difference whether he is an American citizen or not."

★

The removal of their neighbors shocked many of the young residents of Boyle Heights. "All of a sudden, the Japanese friends we had just disappeared," recalled Leo Frumkin, another student at Hollenbeck Junior High. Authorities first took them to Santa Anita Park, a racetrack about twenty miles to the east. Families resided in horse stables while the federal government constructed permanent camps. A steady stream of classmates from Hollenbeck went to visit their incarcerated friends. Joe Portnoy bicycled out to visit Touru Yenari with a load of fresh laundry for the family.

By summer, the Japanese residents of the Pacific Coast had been moved to ten "internment camps" scattered across seven western states. Many of those from Los Angeles went to Manzanar, a barren military-style facility in the arid Owens Valley. "This place is virtually a concentration camp," wrote

Yoneo Bepp, incarcerated at Manzanar with his wife, daughter, and elderly parents. "Life as we have lived and enjoyed it in the past was beautiful compared to the circumstances in which we now find ourselves. We try to be philosophic about the whole thing, for after all, this is war, and this is the sacrifice we have been called upon to make."

★

Powered by federal wartime spending, California's economy went into overdrive. The expansion was built on the industrial foundation laid down in the twenties. Aircraft manufacturers, concentrated in the Los Angeles area, turned out three hundred thousand bombers and fighters, 70 percent of the nation's air power. Shipyards in the Bay Area, San Pedro, and San Diego launched nearly fifteen hundred ships, a third of the nation's wartime total. Those industries spawned others producing and fabricating essential materials—steel and aluminum, industrial chemicals, and synthetic rubber. Petroleum refining and electric generation set new records. The state's manufacturing output more than tripled during the war.

The economic expansion created a voracious demand for labor at the very moment the military was sweeping up new recruits. Eight hundred thousand Californians served in uniform during the war. To replace them in the factories, tens of thousands of men and women poured into California each month. In the history of California's many migrations, this one brought more people over the shortest period of time than any other, the gold rush included. From 1940 to 1945 the state gained more than two million new residents.

Thousands of farm workers left the fields for better-paying, more reliable factory jobs, creating a dire labor shortage in the countryside. California's growers turned again to Mexico. Despite having denounced Mexican workers as troublemaking "Reds" only a few years before, growers now wanted them back, but on more favorable terms. "A large supply of labor is available in Mexico," said an executive of Sunkist. "But they must be brought into the states and handled in a way that is workable and practicable." That was corporate-speak for making sure there would be no unions or strikes. In 1942, the United States and Mexico agreed to the terms of a guest worker program. Mexican laborers were promised a minimum wage of thirty cents an hour (about $5 in today's values) but prohibited from organizing or striking. During the course of the war, as part of what was known as the Bracero Program (*bracero* means "laborer" in Spanish), more than two hundred thousand Mexicans labored in the fields of California and other Southwestern states. Thousands more crossed the border illegally.

★

In the late thirties, the majority of migrants to California were White. But during the war a third of new Californians were African American, part of what historians term the "Great Migration" of Black people out of the South. The African American community of Los Angeles, the state's largest, more than doubled in size, reaching approximately 130,000 residents by 1946.

Before the war, Black people had been channeled into the lowest-paying, dirtiest jobs. These new migrants hoped for something better. In 1941, pressured by African American civil rights leaders, President Roosevelt issued an executive order that prohibited discrimination by "race, creed, color, or national origin" in all industries operating under federal contracts, and established a Fair Employment Practices Commission (FEPC) to enforce it. Investigating compliance in Los Angeles County, the commission reported that defense contractors had refused to hire Blacks, Mexicans, and Native Americans, as well as Jews, Catholics, and Seventh-Day Adventists.

"Here, in the midst of around-the-clock appeals for national unity," the FEPC chairman declared, "we found unfair employment practices only slightly removed from the Hitler pattern."

Determined to change that, Black civil rights leaders in Los Angeles organized the Negro Victory Committee, part of the national "Double V" campaign determined to defeat racism both at home and abroad. Using direct action, including rallies, picket lines, and marches, activists protested discrimination in employment. Under intense pressure, defense contractors began to hire and train a growing number of African Americans for skilled work, and by 1943 thousands of Black workers were employed at aircraft plants and shipyards throughout the state.

The struggle against racism was an everyday matter for African Americans. Chester Himes, a writer with a number of short stories to his credit, relocated to Los Angeles in 1941 with high hopes of finding work as a screenwriter. But he found the studios closed to Blacks. Himes landed a supervisor's job at a shipyard, but had to endure constant ridicule and harassment from White subordinates. "It was the lying hypocrisy that hurt me," he wrote. "Black people were treated much the same as they were in any industrial city of the South. . . . The difference was that the white people of Los Angeles seemed to be saying, 'Nigger, ain't we good to you?'" Himes's searing 1945 novel *If He Hollers Let Him Go* tells the semiautobiographical story of a proud Black man whose spirit is crushed by his encounters with racism in wartime Los Angeles.

★

The most important factor in easing the war's severe "manpower" shortage was the employment of women. Help Wanted ads for women filled the classified section of the newspapers. "LOOK!! WOMEN!!" shouted a full-column ad for an aircraft company in January 1942. "We Need 200 Women Right Now!!

BIG PAY JOBS. REGULAR MEN'S WAGES." The industry had employed virtually no women before 1942, but by 1944, with hundreds of thousands of American men fighting in Europe and the Pacific, women accounted for 42 percent of the aircraft workers in Los Angeles County.

Supervisors frequently assigned them to jobs requiring dexterity. Many women became riveters in the cramped interiors of the aircraft. "A lot of them guys at the time resented the women," recalled Beatrice Morales. Her first day on the job she was assigned to work with an experienced male riveter. "I messed up something and made a ding," and the man rolled his eyes. "You're not worth the money Lockheed pays you," he snarled. "He couldn't have hurt me more if he'd slapped me," said Morales. Another woman worker found her crying. "Don't worry," she told Morales, "I'll take care of it." She confronted the guy and cussed him out. "You had to hold your head high," remembered Helen Studer, a married woman who worked as a riveter. "You learned to swear like they did."

The resilient woman worker became an icon during the war. "Rosie the Riveter" appeared on recruitment posters and magazine covers and inspired a popular hit song of 1943: "She's making history, / Working for victory, / Rosie the Riveter." Working for victory, Beatrice Morales and Helen Studer both became expert riveters. "I wasn't working 'cause I wanted to," Studer remembered. "I was working 'cause I thought it was necessary." Laid off at the end of the war, she happily went back to being a housewife. "But I felt I had accomplished quite a feat." Morales was also proud of her war work. "I felt I was doing my part," she said. In two years she went from sixty-five cents an hour, the starting wage, to $1.05 (the equivalent of $31 in 2020). "That was top pay," Morales recalled. "And it was my own money. I started feeling a little more independent." After the war, she continued to hold down a paying job.

★

People had money to burn and, with wartime rationing, relatively little to spend it on. Some indulged in clothing and entertainment. "Half these fine mamas never wore an evening gown before," a Los Angeles bartender told a reporter, gesturing toward a group of well-dressed women. "But now that their husbands are making ninety, a hundred, maybe a hundred fifty bucks a week with overtime, what's a dollar? And if mama is on the assembly line too, it's like a chicken in every pot, all white meat." After the late shift at the factories, people hung out at all-night bowling alleys and drive-ins. They danced to the big bands of Bob Wills and the Texas Playboys, Woody Herman, and Cab Calloway. They went to after-hours clubs where the music, drinking, and pursuit of happiness went on till dawn.

Men, too, splurged on clothing. In their off hours many young workers, especially men of color, wore "zoot suits"—long draped jackets with pegged pants that ballooned at the knee—a fashion statement intentionally outré and rebellious. Teenager Cesar Chavez loved his zoot suit. "It was the style, and I wasn't going to be square," he later recalled. He willingly faced the scorn of elders and the harassment of the police. "We needed a lot of guts to wear those pants, and we had to be rebellious to do it. But I was prepared for any sacrifice to be able to dress the way I wanted." As Chavez's comment suggests, zoot-suiters often wore an attitude of defiance along with the clothes.

Violent crime dropped during the war. But unsettled conditions, separated families, and overcrowded housing produced an uptick in juvenile delinquency. Los Angeles newspapers railed against "zoot suit hoodlums." During the summer of 1942, the trial and conviction of a dozen young Mexican American men for a murder committed at an Eastside Los Angeles reservoir known as "Sleepy Lagoon" received sensational press coverage. The press portrayed the zoot suits of the young men as the symbol of criminality.

The thousands of soldiers and sailors stationed in the Los Angeles area frequently clashed with young men of color. Locals accused servicemen of paying improper attention to their sisters and girlfriends, and enlisted men complained of attacks by gangs of zoot-suited Mexicans. On the night of June 4, 1943, following an altercation on a downtown street, fifty sailors in a fleet of taxis invaded Boyle Heights and indiscriminately attacked young men on the streets. "We're out to do what the police have failed to do," a navy petty officer bragged to a reporter. "Tonight the sailors may have the Marines along!"

Over the following three nights, disorder and violence engulfed downtown Los Angeles. Hundreds of servicemen, reinforced by local White vigilantes, swarmed the streets, attacking Mexicans and other men of color, dragging them from streetcars, restaurants, and theaters, beating them bloody and stripping off their clothes. No one was killed, but many men suffered serious injury and ethnic neighborhoods were terrorized. Rather than arresting the attacking servicemen and turning them over to military authorities, cops arrested the victims. The name the press bestowed on this violent episode—the "Zoot Suit Riots"—reflected this same "blame the victim" sentiment. Zoot-suiters came from "the lowest dregs of our society," declared the *Long Beach Independent* in a front-page editorial. "They should be handled ruthlessly, just as you would handle a mad dog or a snake."

A special state investigative commission placed the blame for the riots on precisely that kind of newspaper coverage. "The press has created a false impression that any individual who wears a zoot-suit is a criminal and a gangster," the commission reported. In fact, it was the soldiers and sailors who had rioted, not the zoot-suiters. The violence ended as soon as military authorities canceled leaves and declared downtown L.A. off-limits. What motivated the attacks? "Most of the persons mistreated during the recent incidents in Los Angeles were either of Mexican descent or Negroes," the commissioners noted. "The existence of race prejudice cannot be ignored."

★

During the war thousands of men and women passed through Los Angeles, a city of intimate strangers. "The friends you made, even though you didn't really know them very well, you were connected," recalled Juanita Loveless, a young Texan who worked at an aircraft plant. She dated servicemen who, without notice, shipped out and disappeared. "Next thing," Loveless recalled, "you'd get a letter with just a PO number." Some men she never heard from again, some she caught up with later. "I get off a bus," she recalled, "and I'm walking home, and I hear, 'tap, tap, tap.'" She turned to see who it was. "My God, it's Dick. Still in uniform. He came home blind, totally blind—at twenty-three!"

Gold stars, signaling the loss of a family member, appeared in the front windows of homes in every California neighborhood. One of those stars long remained in the corner of my grandmother's window, commemorating the death of her twenty-one-year-old son, Frederick Marion Burkett Jr., in combat in Europe. My father, a bombardier in a B-17, was hit by antiaircraft fire during a run over Germany; the pilot successfully flew the plane to neutral Sweden, where the crew was interned in a POW camp, although it was several weeks before my mother knew her husband had survived. More than 400,000 Americans, including 17,022 Californians, lost their lives while serving in World War II. Faced with such staggering losses, said Juanita Loveless, "people just clung together."

But wartime Los Angeles could be an exciting place for

young people. "L.A. was just a beehive, twenty-four hours a day," one resident recalled. "Any time would be Saturday night." Marilyn Greene, the teenage journalist who wrote the idealistic editorial in the Hollenbeck Junior High newspaper, graduated high school in 1945. Many years later she spoke about those days with one of her grandsons. "She told me of working at a department store in downtown L.A.," he said, "exploring a city that had not quite established itself on the global stage. She told me how she met my grandfather." In 1946, at the age of nineteen, Marilyn Greene began dating a young Marine veteran from the Westside named Leonard Herman Smith. They fell in love, married, and made a life together in postwar Los Angeles.

GOVERNOR EARL WARREN

34

Make No Small Plan
for California

Governor Earl Warren delivered his first inaugural address before a joint session of the California legislature
on January 4, 1943. "We meet here in an hour of crisis," he began. On far-flung battlefields, America's enlisted men
were fighting for democracy and freedom, and Warren had
no doubt they would prevail. But overcoming tyranny and intolerance, he said, would require "a double victory." Warren
was borrowing the "Double V" language of Black civil rights
leaders. "Confronting us here on the home front is an equally
imperative challenge," he told the legislators, "perfecting the
machinery of democracy. This state has never been afraid to
be progressive. It has never been afraid to try new things."
What new things might Californians expect from their new
governor?

Earl Warren was born in Los Angeles in 1891 and raised

in the raw San Joaquin Valley town of Bakersfield. His father worked for the Southern Pacific and had once been blacklisted by the company for participating in a strike. Warren remembered him railing against "monopolistic power, political dominance, corruption in government, and their effects on the people of a community." When Hiram Johnson embarked on his crusade against the hated SP, Warren was a sophomore at Berkeley. Although not yet old enough to vote, he volunteered for Johnson's campaign.

After earning a law degree and serving as a junior officer during the First World War, Warren became a prosecutor in the Oakland office of the Alameda County district attorney. Personable yet forceful, he rose through the ranks and in 1926 won the election to succeed his retiring boss. Warren built a record as a crusading DA, battling vice and corruption. He was also an active Republican, serving as chair of the party's state central committee during the thirties. "I was a Republican simply because California was then an overwhelmingly Republican state," Warren wrote in his memoirs. That was disingenuous. In fact, he often engaged in hyperbolic partisan attacks, warning in 1936, for example, that the New Deal threatened to turn "the greatest free government of all time into a totalitarian state."

When Warren ran to become California's attorney general in 1938, registered Democrats outnumbered registered Republicans in the state for the first time in many years. Warren appealed directly to Democratic voters, pledging to protect civil liberties and distancing himself from Republican governor Frank Merriam, who had come down hard on striking workers. California had a "cross-filing" primary system, a legacy of Governor Hiram Johnson's electoral reforms. Only registered party members could vote, but candidates were allowed to run in any party primary. Warren ran for the nomination of three parties—Republican, Democratic, and Progressive—and won them all. He was a shoo-in at the general election in the fall, and assumed office along with newly elected Democratic governor Culbert Olson.

Warren professionalized the attorney general's office, and generated headlines with a crackdown on political corruption and dramatic raids on offshore gambling ships. But his term was characterized by simmering conflict with Governor Olson, who consistently undercut the attorney general, expecting that Warren would be his opponent in the next election. "I felt thwarted at every turn," Warren said later, and "it finally reached the point at which I could no longer stand it." As Olson feared, Warren challenged him in 1942, pledging to "take the bitterness out of Sacramento" and work with legislators "whether they be Republicans or Democrats." He defeated the incumbent in a landslide.

★

Governor Warren immediately turned to the wartime emergency, reorganizing the state's civil defense and streamlining the executive branch of government. But his attention was fixed on bigger things. The booming wartime economy was generating enormous tax revenue for the state, providing Warren with the wherewithal to set aside a huge "rainy day" fund for later use. "It was not easy to protect these accumulated funds," Warren wrote years later. "Business groups, through their lobbyists, were constantly pressuring the legislature to use savings in order to reduce the budget and taxes." Many Californians were anxious that when wartime spending ended, economic depression would return. The state needed a postwar strategy, and Warren seized the opportunity.

He proposed strengthening the social safety net by restructuring the state's welfare and hospital systems, expanding unemployment benefits, and introducing government-sponsored health insurance. Warren was a skilled consensus builder, appealing to businessmen, labor leaders, and the general public. He got much of what he wanted, although conservatives succeeded in killing his health insurance plan by claiming it was "socialized medicine."

The Republican governor consistently confounded liberals. "He's trying to out–New Deal the New Deal," a San Francisco Democrat complained. Conservatives were equally dismayed. "The Republican Old Guard are shocked and alarmed over the progressive character of the measures Warren recommended," reported the *Sacramento Bee*. The ideological confusion suited Warren. "The right wing called it a surrender to the New Deal," he recalled, "but the vast majority of the voters approved. . . . I would like to believe it was a progressive administration."

With the war's end in August 1945, men began returning from the front. At the same moment, demand for wartime production fell and manufacturers began laying off workers. The unemployment rate soared to 1939 levels. But Warren had prepared voters for a rough transition and they didn't blame him. In fact, the downturn proved to be temporary. As the wartime alliance between the United States and the Soviet Union fractured and the Cold War began, new contracts for military production soon had the economy operating on all cylinders once again. Up for reelection, Warren repeated his remarkable feat of 1938, running in the Republican and Democratic primaries and winning them both. Unopposed in November, he swept into a second term.

"My battle cry," Warren later recalled, "was to make no small plan for California." He laid out an ambitious agenda to deal with the enormous influx of migrants. "The stampede has visited us with unprecedented civic problems," he said. "We have an appalling housing shortage, our schools are packed to suffocation, and our highways are inadequate and dangerous.

We are short of water and short of power and our sanitation and transportation systems are overtaxed." To meet these pressing needs, he increased the size of the annual state budget, which topped a billion dollars for the first time. The number of state civil service employees exploded, from 24,000 in 1943 to nearly 60,000 ten years later. Warren transformed California's state government, committing it to the project of creating opportunity so that its residents could thrive.

A key feature was increased funding for public education, which Warren considered essential for future development. He expanded state support for local schools. He strengthened the higher education system with the addition of eighteen new junior colleges and three new four-year state colleges, raising the number to a total of twelve. He supported bringing the University of California branch at Los Angeles up to the world-class standard of Berkeley, and opened three new university campuses at Santa Barbara, Davis, and Riverside.

A second priority was the improvement and expansion of the state's notoriously poor highway system, which Warren proposed financing with a gasoline tax. When the petroleum industry opposed the bill, he appealed directly to the public, lambasting "special interests" in a series of statewide radio broadcasts. His program included massive investment in an innovative system of limited-access "freeways." By the time Warren left office in 1953, the state had completed several hundred miles of the new system.

Those freeways more easily linked metropolitan areas to the expanding suburbs. In Los Angeles County alone, builders constructed half a million new single-family homes during the eight years following the war. With mortgage financing provided by federal and state programs, most veterans could purchase homes with little or no down payment and low interest rates. In a few short years, the population of the San Fernando

Valley doubled. Southeast of Los Angeles, the planned community of Lakewood, the nation's largest housing tract, provided modest homes for seventy thousand working-class residents. Similar development took place in the suburbs surrounding San Francisco, Oakland, San Jose, Sacramento, and San Diego.

★

What returning veterans most needed, Governor Warren declared, was "the peace that comes from the elimination of racial prejudice, religious bigotry, and political intolerance." Those bold sentiments, however, were belied by Warren's tepid support for the struggle against discrimination. When, shortly after the war, Congress refused to extend the life of the federal Fair Employment Practices Commission—the agency that had overseen the hiring of people of color in defense industries— Warren endorsed a bill establishing a California equivalent. But when his fellow Republicans refused to support it, he allowed the legislation to die. Democrats placed a stronger proposal on the ballot as an initiative, but Warren denounced it as a "radical" measure and it went down to defeat. Progressive leadership would have to come from others.

In the summer of 1943, the *Manzanar Free Press,* a newspaper produced by the Japanese American inmates of the Manzanar relocation camp, published an editorial responding to the attacks on zoot-suiters in Los Angeles. "The Negro, the Mexican, and the Japanese have one thing in common," the editor noted. "They are all minority groups and face the same economic persecution and discrimination. This is the bond of sympathy." Many civil rights groups came to the same conclusion. An umbrella organization, the California Federation of Civil Unity, sought to turn those connections into political change. The goal, the group's executive director declared, was to establish "the most advanced democracy in the world" in "the most multiracial state in the union." During the last months of the war and for several years following, civil rights groups representing African Americans, Mexican Americans, and Japanese Americans collaborated in advancing several important court challenges to discrimination in California. Taken together, these precedent-shattering cases would dismantle the legal edifice of racial and ethnic discrimination in California.

They originated in the actions of ordinary people. Incarcerated Japanese Americans challenged the legality of state and federal actions during the war. Fred Korematsu, a Nisei born and raised in Oakland, contended that the United States did not have the constitutional authority to arrest and jail him for refusing to report for deportation. Mitsuye Endo, a young professional woman from Sacramento, argued that her internment without trial and conviction was unconstitutional. Fred Oyama of San Diego sued for the return of farmland seized by the state of California under the provisions of the Alien Land Law.

Blacks and Mexican Americans challenged legal segregation. Hattie McDaniel, an actress who won an Academy Award for her depiction of "Mammy" in *Gone with the Wind,* joined a group of African American homeowners defending their right to live in a Westside Los Angeles neighborhood despite restrictive racial covenants. Gonzalo and Felicitas Méndez of Orange County challenged the placement of their children in a segregated "Mexican school." And Andrea Pérez sued Los Angeles County for refusing to issue a license for her marriage to Sylvester Davis, a Black man she met while working at an aircraft plant.

Not all these cases were successful. In December 1944, a divided United States Supreme Court ruled in *Korematsu v. U.S.* that expulsion in the name of military necessity was legal, legitimizing the removal of Japanese Americans from their homes and communities. But in *Ex parte Mitsuye Endo,* announced the same day, the Court unanimously ruled that the government had no authority to incarcerate citizens "who are concededly loyal." The two decisions were difficult to reconcile. But with tens of thousands of loyal Japanese Americans still being held in relocation camps, the Roosevelt administration decided to immediately begin making preparations for their release. Governor Warren quickly pivoted, announcing that "all Americans will join in protecting the constitutional rights of the individuals involved."

The verdicts in the other cases were clearer. In *Oyama v. California,* the U.S. Supreme Court ruled that California's Alien Land Law violated the Fourteenth Amendment. That law, wrote Associate Justice Frank Murphy, was "a disheartening reminder of the racial policy pursued by those forces of evil whose destruction recently necessitated a devastating war. It is racism in one of its most malignant forms." The eviction suit against Hattie McDaniel and her co-defendants was dismissed by Judge Thurman Clark of Los Angeles Superior Court, who ruled that restrictive covenants violated the equal protection of the laws. "It is time," Judge Clark declared, "that members of the Negro race are accorded, without reservation and evasion, the full rights guaranteed them under the Fourteenth Amendment." Those two decisions overthrew hardline discriminatory policies that had been in place in California for decades.

Méndez v. Westminster, the school desegregation case, was decided by a federal district court judge who ruled that separate schools for Mexican Americans were illegal. Governor Warren embraced the decision and signed legislation outlawing overt segregation in California education. Finally, in *Pérez v. Sharp,* the California Supreme Court ruled unconstitutional the state's ban on interracial marriage. Although Warren declined to support a legislative repeal of the law, he would later have the opportunity to correct his mistake.

★

Civil rights groups worked cooperatively to achieve these results, supporting each other by filing supporting briefs and supplying experienced attorneys. But rising fears of the Soviet Union provided conservatives with an opportunity to attack progressive political groups with charges of "communism" and "fellow traveling." Although there were never more than a few hundred Communist Party organizers in California, they were among the most dedicated, working tirelessly for every progressive cause. "Unfortunately," said one California activist, "it is becoming increasingly difficult to undertake any kind of activity in the area of civil rights of minorities without being forced to face the charge of Communism." Many organizations were torn apart by internal conflict, and many activists hunkered down in an attempt to survive.

Republicans had long used anticommunism as a weapon, and Earl Warren was no exception. His first case as a deputy district attorney in the early 1920s was a prosecution under California's Criminal Syndicalism Act, which made it a felony to advocate the violent overthrow of the government. "I never liked this statute," Warren later wrote. "It is easy for some people to be carried away by an ideological approval of violence without their having any intention of inciting or participating in such action." Even so, Warren often dished anticommunist dirt. "We must fortify ourselves against a resolute effort to overwhelm California with Communism," he declared in 1934, during Upton Sinclair's campaign for governor. As attorney general, he accused Governor Olson of "cozying up" to Communists.

But anticommunism backfired on Warren when conservative legislators attacked the University of California as a breeding ground for commies and spies, demanding that tenured faculty be required to take a loyalty oath on pain of dismissal. Warren, a graduate of Berkeley and an active participant in alumni affairs, opposed such an oath, knowing that the faculty would treat it as a violation of academic freedom. But the governing Board of Regents voted that all professors swear that they did not advocate "the overthrow of the United States government by force or violence."

Thirty-one university professors refused to take the oath and were fired. They sued, and the California Supreme Court reinstated them with back pay, ruling that professors could not be compelled to take an oath not required of other state employees. The scandal humiliated Warren and weakened his support among Republicans. In 1950 he came out in favor of a loyalty oath for all California public employees, an act of political expediency that shored up his support from the right. Warren was a politician of rare agility, shifting with the political winds.

★

Governor Earl Warren, the political face of postwar California, the most dynamic state in the nation, grew nationally famous. In 1948 he joined the Republican presidential ticket as running mate of Governor Thomas Dewey of New York. They were defeated in a close contest by incumbent Harry S. Truman, who had become president upon Roosevelt's death in 1945. Warren won an unprecedented third consecutive term in 1950, overwhelming his liberal Democratic opponent, James Roosevelt, FDR's eldest son and a decorated Marine combat veteran. With that, Warren became a leading contender for the Republican presidential nomination in 1952. But after winning just a handful of delegates in primaries outside California, he threw his support to General Dwight D. Eisenhower, who repaid the favor by promising to appoint Warren to the first vacancy on the United States Supreme Court. In October 1953,

President Eisenhower honored that promise, and Warren became the new chief justice.

His first case was *Brown v. Board of Education,* which challenged the legality of segregation in public education in the United States. Warren wrote the unanimous opinion, declaring that "separate educational facilities are inherently unequal." This explosive decision launched the era of the "Warren Court," which over the following fifteen years issued a series of controversial rulings expanding civil rights, civil liberties, and democratic governance. Among the multitude of cases, Warren revisited several issues from his time as governor, overturning laws that banned interracial marriage or required college professors to sign loyalty oaths.

Conservatives reacted with outrage. President Eisenhower privately complained that appointing Warren was "the biggest damn fool thing I ever did." In his memoirs, however, Warren disputed the notion that as chief justice he suddenly became more liberal. His critics, he wrote, failed to understand the critical distinction between politics and justice. Politics was the art of the possible. Progress, he wrote, "most often was made by compromising and taking half a loaf where a whole loaf could not be obtained." Justice, however, was anchored in principle. "If the principle is sound and constitutional, it is the birthright of every American, not to be accorded begrudgingly or piecemeal or to special groups only, but to everyone in its entirety."

Plenty of times during Warren's career, politics rather than justice determined his course, but most striking was his public support for Japanese incarceration. At an event on the Berkeley campus in 1969, soon after his retirement from the court, a group of Japanese American students confronted him, demanding an apology. They caught Warren off guard. "I never apologize for a past act," he mumbled. "Besides, that's just a matter of history now." But in his memoirs, published shortly after his death in 1974, he attempted to make amends. "I have deeply regretted the removal order and my own testimony advocating it," Warren wrote. "It was not in keeping with our American concept of freedom and the rights of citizens."

STANDOFF IN WATTS

35

Rebels and Forerunners

In the spring of 1958, San Francisco newspapers reported the discovery of an eccentric new community of city dwellers. The North Beach district, adjacent to Chinatown and Telegraph Hill, had become, in the words of Herb Caen, popular columnist for the *San Francisco Chronicle*, a "hangout for the bearded *beatnik* generation." Caen invented the term, a mashup of *beat* and *-nik*, in the linguistic style of American Yiddish. Another reporter at the *Chronicle* offered an explanation of *beat*, a term North Beach bohemians used to describe themselves: "They are beat because they feel battered by life," he wrote. "They have lost faith in nearly everything, and they refuse to conform to ideals in which they no longer believe."

The beatnik meme went viral. Over the next few years, bearded, bongo-playing, poetry-spouting bohemians popped up in cartoons, comic strips, and TV sitcoms. Department stores promoted the "beatnik-look" in women's fashion: "Use light base so that you look pale and world-weary," a stylist recommended. "Punctuate with dark shadow and plenty of mascara. Result: beauty the 'beat' way."

The beatnik was a stereotype, of course, but the bohemian community of North Beach was the real deal. Since the time of Bret Harte San Francisco had been a mecca for eccentric, artistic types who lived and associated together in cheap-rent districts of the city. "Bohemian atmosphere demands a cosmopolitan population," a San Franciscan familiar with the scene wrote during the 1950s. "Different colors of skin, kinds of religion, domestic and foreign languages, restaurants, bars, bawdy houses, and a history in the arts."

The San Francisco bohemians were mostly young, White, and middle class. A majority of them held down "straight" jobs, but rejected what they called the "rat race"; they were contemptuous of bureaucracy, disillusioned by politics, and horrified by atomic weapons. During an era when most Americans dressed up to go downtown, the bohemians of North Beach made a point of dressing down—men in faded Levi's or war-surplus khakis, tattered sport coats over t-shirts; women in leotards topped with bulky sweaters or sweatshirts. They drank California wine and smoked Mexican marijuana. They enjoyed cool jazz and stand-up comedy. They held liberal attitudes about race and sexual orientation. In many ways, they were cultural rebels and forerunners.

The best-known North Beach bohemian was a New Yorker named Allen Ginsberg who relocated to San Francisco in the early fifties, where he worked for a marketing company, writing copy for toothpaste advertisements. Ginsberg loathed his job, and inspired by the North Beach scene, he turned to poetry. One evening in 1955, he and several other young poets presented their work at a small gallery in a run-down section of the city. Ginsberg read "Howl," a long poem with what became a very famous first line: "I saw the best minds of my gen-

eration destroyed by madness. . . ." Ginsberg delivered his vulgar, angry indictment of modern American civilization at fever
pitch, like an evangelical preacher at a camp meeting. When
Lawrence Ferlinghetti, owner of a North Beach bookshop, published it, San Francisco authorities arrested him on a charge
of obscenity. But in a path-breaking ruling, a municipal judge
dismissed the case, and Ferlinghetti went on to sell thousands
of copies. People were paying attention.

★

Between 1950 and 1970 California's population nearly doubled. Everyone, it seemed, wanted to live there. And why
not? Californians were enjoying the good life—grilling steaks
on the patio behind the ranch house, cruising the freeways in
a convertible, surfing Pacific breakers. A hit tune of 1961 said
it all: "They're out there having fun / In the warm California
sun."

Notwithstanding the state's many charms, however, most
migrants were drawn by the prospect of good-paying jobs in
the booming California economy. Industry surged, led by aerospace and electronics. The Cold War and the space program
demanded high-tech equipment and weaponry—communications, radar, jet aircraft, guided missiles, atomic bombs—
and California maintained the commanding lead it established
during World War II. From 1948 to 1991 the federal government spent $47 trillion (in 2020 dollars) on defense, nearly a
fifth of which went to California contractors. One in four of the
state's manufacturing workers held jobs in defense-related industries. The demand for labor pushed up wages and salaries
for everyone, with California median household income running 15 or 20 percent ahead of the national average.

Some economists worried over what would happen with
an "outbreak of peace," but there didn't seem much chance of
that. Most people were untroubled by a permanent war econ-

omy producing weapons for global annihilation. The story was told of a couple living in the desert, not far from the atomic testing grounds in Nevada, jolted awake one early morning by a loud blast. "What's that?" the man exclaimed, bolting out of bed. "Go back to sleep," said his wife. "It's only an atomic bomb."

Adults might be good at denial, but anxiety was more common among children who practiced "duck and cover" drills at school and watched film clips of the bomb's destructive power on TV. During the 1962 Cuban Missile Crisis, an elementary school in a southern California suburb received a "yellow alert," indicating imminent nuclear attack. The principal ordered an immediate evacuation. Younger students burst into tears. "Are we going to live?" they cried. Some time later, authorities called to apologize for the false alarm.

Teenagers resorted to dark humor. When you see the flash, went the joke, bend over and kiss your ass goodbye. "Listen up!" a history teacher in the early sixties admonished the rowdy boys in the back row during a lecture on the simmering conflict in Vietnam. "Soon enough some of you will be slogging through those rice paddies, and you ought to know why." When young men turned eighteen they were required to register for the draft; fearful of being sent halfway around the world to fight for a cause they barely understood, many joined the ranks of the disaffected.

★

There were, in fact, plenty of Golden State skeptics. Consider California's people of color. By the mid-sixties, African Americans, Mexican Americans, Asian Americans, and other ethnic minorities made up a fifth of the state's population. To be sure, they had made real progress over the previous quarter century. Many men found good industrial jobs. Women took positions as sales clerks and clerical workers. Unlocking the potential of these workers provided a significant boost to the economy.

Historians suggest that as much as 40 percent of economic growth during the immediate postwar period came from tapping the energy of people of color. There was also a significant generational effect as their children became better educated and set their sights on a middle-class future. It was a time of rising expectations.

But the legacy of racism continued to limit their options. California employers still channeled people of color into the least desirable and lowest-paid positions. For every dollar earned by White Californians in 1960, workers of color made sixty-five cents. According to state and federal guidelines, about a quarter of Black and Mexican American households lived below the poverty line. They found housing discrimination even more frustrating. The courts had declared racial covenants unenforceable, yet residential segregation remained a prominent feature of California life, enforced by an unspoken collusion among developers, real estate agents, and lending institutions. A Los Angeles survey of 1964 found four out of five Black families eager to move to the suburbs, but those who dared to buy or rent homes in White neighborhoods were often confronted with threats, vandalism, and sometimes violence.

African Americans made up 13 percent of L.A. County's population, but two-thirds of the cities and towns were exclusively White. Civil rights attorney Loren Miller, who led the legal fight against restrictive covenants, pointed to the new suburb of Lakewood, made White and kept White with the implicit consent of the Federal Housing Authority. As a result, most African Americans remained in the central city. Rather than looking to the suburbs, families with the means to purchase better homes pushed through the "invisible wall" into adjacent White neighborhoods, provoking what was known as "White flight."

The postwar period was similarly mixed for Mexican Americans in California, whose population grew to 1.5 million in 1960, the result of increased immigration and large family size. Boyle Heights became almost exclusively Spanish-speaking as the descendants of European immigrants moved elsewhere. The construction of L.A.'s freeway system, deliberately routed through the city's poorest neighborhoods, resulted in what one reporter described as "the eradication, obliteration, razing, moving, ripping asunder, and demolishing of Eastside homes." Minority communities found themselves cut off from the rest of the city by a wall of elevated roadways. Neighborhoods deteriorated and crime increased.

The Bracero Program, begun during the war, continued to bring thousands of guest workers to California's fields. Only about a third of farm laborers were citizens or permanent residents. In the late forties, the American Federation of Labor launched a campaign to organize agriculture in California, but when farm laborers struck, growers gave them a stark choice: "Go back to work or go back to Mexico." California agriculture was a source of great wealth, but the men and women laboring in the fields remained the state's poorest and most exploited workers.

People of color wanted the same things as other Californians—good jobs, nice homes, and quality education for their children. They wanted access to the state's amenities, the beaches and parks, the shopping centers and movie theaters. But when they joined the crowds in these public spaces they were often confronted by police. "You're way out of your district," a cop told one young man. "You don't belong in this part of town." A survey of L.A.'s minority residents in the early sixties found that nearly half the respondents reported being stopped, frisked, and publicly humiliated by the Los Angeles Police Department (LAPD). Even in their own neighborhoods, people of color suffered pervasive police harassment. "We can't tell the good Mexicans from the bad," one cop told a reporter, "so we have to treat them all alike."

★

After languishing during the Warren years, California Democrats rebuilt their party during the 1950s. They focused on extending the safety net, strengthening the state's infrastructure, and overcoming racial discrimination. They built strong alliances with labor unions and civil rights organizations. The payoff came in the statewide election of 1958 when Edmund G. "Pat" Brown won the governorship in a landslide and his party took control of the legislature, the first time in the twentieth century that Democrats had enjoyed complete control of state government.

They went to work immediately on a progressive overhaul of California's priorities, strengthening social insurance for workers and the needy, adopting multiyear master plans for California's higher education and freeway systems, and approving a new State Water Project, which they successfully financed in a special election. They enacted legislation prohibiting discrimination in public accommodations and established a state Fair Employment Practices Commission, something Governor Warren had failed to accomplish. They succeeded in enacting nearly the whole of their liberal agenda.

Governor Brown, a voluble and enthusiastic politician, stood for a second term in 1962. His opponent was Californian Richard Nixon, former congressman, U.S. senator, and vice-president of the United States. Nixon had narrowly lost the presidential election of 1960 to John F. Kennedy, but he carried his home state and was considered the odds-on favorite to defeat Brown. A notorious anticommunist, Nixon claimed that left-wing extremists controlled the Democratic Party. Brown, however, running on his record, won by a comfortable margin, joining Hiram Johnson and Earl Warren as only the third of California's governors to be returned for a second four-year term.

Shortly after the election, the Census Bureau announced that California had surpassed New York as the state with the largest population. Along with great size, Brown declared in his second inaugural address, came great responsibility. California must lead the nation. "Through the turmoil of change, and sometimes chaos," he said, "Californians have pressed on toward the good society, not for the few, not for the many, but for all." The national civil rights movement was approaching high tide and Brown took notice. The top priority for his second term, he proclaimed, would be legislation ensuring that all Californians, regardless of race, could live wherever they chose. "Fair housing," he said, was "the key element in the antidiscrimination struggle."

Democrats in the state assembly passed a bill prohibiting discrimination in sales or rentals by race, creed, or color. When conservative Democrats in the state senate refused to take it up, civil rights demonstrators occupied the capitol rotunda. Using parliamentary maneuvers, liberals finally succeeded in passing the bill in September 1963. The new law established a state commission to hear and resolve complaints of discrimination.

★

But the status quo had powerful defenders. The California Association of Realtors, vowing to fight "the threat of occupancy by Negroes," launched a campaign to repeal the law. Within months they had secured a sufficient number of signatures to place an initiative on the ballot amending the state constitution granting property owners the "absolute discretion" to sell, lease, or rent to whomever they chose. Conservatives argued that Proposition 14, as the measure was labeled on the ballot, simply protected private property rights. Liberals countered that it would enshrine discrimination, violating the constitutional guarantee of equal protection.

When opinion polls indicated that a clear majority of

California voters supported the initiative, liberals mounted a shrill "No on 14" campaign, denouncing all those in favor as racists, bigots, and "opponents of democracy." But as veteran California political reporter Bill Boyarsky noted, much of the support came from "white union members, an essential component of the liberal coalition." In November 1964, the liberal coalition triumphed in the presidential contest, giving Lyndon Johnson 60 percent of the California vote. But it fractured over Proposition 14, which passed by an even greater margin.

"The two-to-one victory struck minority group Californians like a smashing blow to the teeth," said Edward Howden, chair of California's Fair Employment Practices Commission. "Once again, in a vital test, the white man had resoundingly and cruelly rejected the legitimate needs and aspirations of nonwhite fellow citizens."

The frustration and anger of Black Californians was acutely felt in Watts, a neighborhood in the southern section of L.A.'s African American community, one of the most impoverished districts in the state. In 1965, average annual income for Californians stood at $7,300, but it was only $3,800 in Watts. Unemployment in L.A. County was 5 percent, but in Watts more than 30 percent. Watts was the epicenter for the policy failures of the postwar period.

In August 1965, the drunk driving arrest of a young African American man named Marquette Frye on a street in Watts escalated into a pitched battle between police and local residents, then exploded into six nights of rioting, looting, and burning. Thirty-four people were killed, most of them Black and most shot by police. "I been kicked and called 'nigger' for the last time," said one resident. "There's lots worse things than dying." Governor Brown dispatched the National Guard. Thirty-five hundred people were arrested. Property damage exceeded $40 million. This dreadful episode became known as the "Watts Riot." Marquette Frye objected to the name. "I don't like to use the word 'riot,'" he told a reporter. "That's a bunch of folks going crazy without reason. There was a reason."

An investigative commission concluded that the reasons included poverty, inferior housing, and police brutality. One of the commissioners, attorney Loren Miller, pointed out that a map of the violence aligned with the "invisible wall" of residential exclusion imposed on the city's Black residents. The passage of Proposition 14, the commission concluded, had been an "aggravating event." It recommended a long list of reforms, few of which were implemented. Instead, the LAPD intensified its policing of South Los Angeles.

★

The Watts Riot was one of a cascade of calamities that ended the political career of Governor Pat Brown, who took a stunning fall from the peak of popularity. Another contributing cause was the growing unrest among college students. In the fall of 1964, student activists at Berkeley organized a Free Speech Movement protesting university rules that prohibited political advocacy on campus. When several hundred students occupied an administration building, Governor Brown struck back. "This will not be tolerated," he declared, and ordered the protestors forcibly removed and arrested. But after the crackdown, the protests grew more shrill, including a notorious "filthy speech" episode, with students shouting obscene words and carrying signs announcing a "Fuck Rally." Many Californians were outraged.

But students were undeterred. "We cared about the problems of the world," recalled Berkeley student Sara Davidson. "No longer would we be apathetic." As President Lyndon B. Johnson escalated the war in Vietnam and the number of casualties rose, student protest became more widespread. Twenty thousand Berkeley students joined a Vietnam "teach-in." Gov-

ernor Brown, like most Democratic politicians, supported Johnson's Vietnam policy, so he became a target of protestors.

Brown also found himself squeezed by a growing conflict
in California's fields. Under intense pressure from organized
labor, Congress voted to end the Bracero Program after the
harvest season of 1964. Growers panicked, insisting that without imported Mexican labor, crops would rot in the fields. But
farm workers knew better. "Employ us at a decent wage and
better working conditions, and there will be enough workers
to harvest any and all crops," one of them declared. "We farm
workers want to live like human beings."

A new labor union, the United Farm Workers (UFW),
launched an organizing campaign. For the first time in a generation, the majority of farm laborers were American citizens
who could not be intimidated by threats of deportation. Governor Brown tried to craft a compromise, but growers and the
union were miles apart. When the grape growers of the San
Joaquin Valley absolutely refused to negotiate, union president Cesar Chavez declared a national boycott of table grapes,
which soon was cutting deeply into grower profits. In the
spring of 1966 Chavez conducted a highly publicized march
of several hundred miles from the vineyards to Sacramento,
where he demanded a meeting with Governor Brown. In a
ham-handed move, the governor refused, infuriating liberal
Democrats.

When Brown ran for a third term that year, Democrats
were bitterly divided. Brown's opponent, Ronald Reagan, a
Hollywood actor turned conservative politician, ran against
"forced housing" and the grape boycott, Watts rioters and
unruly students. Handsome and well-spoken, Reagan warned
against the danger of "beatniks, radicals, and filthy speech." The
streets of California's cities, he warned, "have become jungle
paths"—"a racially laden reference to Watts that no one could

possibly misconstrue," as historian Ethan Rarick puts it. Reagan defeated Brown with nearly 60 percent of the vote and became governor on January 2, 1967.

★

Twelve days later, on a beautiful Saturday morning, thirty thousand people gathered in San Francisco's Golden Gate Park for what was billed as the first "Human Be-In." Over the previous couple of years San Francisco reporters had noted a striking change in the character of the city's bohemians. The center of gravity had shifted from North Beach to the low-rent neighborhood of Haight-Ashbury, and cool jazz gave way to rock and roll. These new bohemians still smoked a lot of pot, and many were also "tripping" on LSD and other psychedelic drugs. The scene was considerably more colorful and quite a bit younger, including many teenagers. Reporter Michael Fallon of the *Examiner* christened this new breed of bohemian the "hippies."

Hippies made up most of the crowd at the Be-In. Wearing colorful shirts, bell-bottom pants, "granny gowns," and flower tiaras, they tripped to local rock bands like the Jefferson Airplane and the Grateful Dead. "I guess it doesn't matter anyway," sang Jerry Garcia as his electric guitar wailed. Allen Ginsberg and others of the beat generation chanted peace songs.

Ginsberg loathed the term *beatnik,* and he told reporters he didn't like *hippie* any better. A reporter asked an older participant, a long-haired man in his thirties, what he preferred to call himself. "A peacenik," the man said. The reporter hadn't heard that term before, and asked what it meant. "A beatnik with politics," the man replied. The torch was being passed to a new generation of skeptics.

Image contains signs reading: "KIDS DON'T HAVE BLUE EYES BUT THEY GO OVERSEAS TO DIE GIVE THEM A FAIR CHANCE EDUCA...", "NOT CONTEM...", and a banner reading "L.A. CHICANO BLOWOUT"

36

A Cyclone in a Wind Tunnel

Ronald Reagan served two terms as governor of California, from 1967 to 1975, one of the most turbulent periods in California's history. Those years, writes Todd Gitlin, a Berkeley graduate student at the time, felt like "a cyclone in a wind tunnel." Cold War consensus gave way to antiwar resistance as the armed conflict in Vietnam became a full-scale war and the draft swept up thousands of young men. People of color demanded political power. Students challenged authority. Women fought for empowerment and liberation. A veritable "tumult of movements," wrote Gitlin, sought "to remake virtually every social arrangement America had settled into after World War II."

According to Michael Deaver, one of Reagan's closest advisors, the governor "viewed what was going on as revolutionary and counter to what he thought America was about." But Reagan, too, wanted to remake the political world. "A lot has been written about college students and other young people who rebelled against society," he wrote in his memoirs. "But there was another, quieter revolution sweeping across the land during the same decade." A revolution in conservatism.

It began in the suburbs—places like Orange County, south of Los Angeles—with local fights over sex education in public schools or "filthy" books in public libraries. The aerospace industry, the region's largest employer, drew a highly educated workforce that skewed conservative and Republican. Some conservative activists were evangelical Christians who believed the American nation was uniquely favored by God. Others were members of the right-wing John Birch Society, which campaigned for the impeachment of Chief Justice Earl Warren, the architect of California's welfare state. Movement conservatives rejected Warren's concept of positive government. The former governor's plummeting reputation among California Republicans was a telling sign of things to come.

Ronald Reagan championed this movement. Big government, he asserted in his first inaugural address in 1967, destroyed "self-reliance, dignity, and self-respect—the very substance of moral fiber." The welfare state encouraged dependence, confining Blacks and other ethnic minorities "behind the bars of ghetto poverty." All Californians would thrive with less government, freer markets, and lower taxes. Government, according to Reagan, had a single responsibility: law and order. Remove the constraints on police so they can do their job. Require students to obey campus rules. Demand swift punishment for lawlessness. "We will act firmly and quickly," Reagan warned, "to put down riot or insurrection wherever and whenever the situation requires." The stage had been set for a long confrontation between two polarized political positions.

★

In 1967, President Lyndon B. Johnson, determined to contain international communist expansion, increased American troop strength in Vietnam to a half million men. "If we don't stop the Reds in South Vietnam," he warned, "tomorrow they will be in Hawaii, and next week they will be in San Francisco." In truth, the struggle in Vietnam was a civil war, transformed by American intervention into an international conflict of shocking human cost, including the deaths of 3.5 million Vietnamese.

U.S. aircraft dropped nearly eight million tons of explosives on Vietnam, Laos, and Cambodia—twice the destructive power of all the bombs dropped during World War II—wreaking destruction on small nations struggling to free themselves from colonialism. Chemical defoliants destroyed five million acres of fields and forests, leaving a legacy of poverty and disease. Americans, too, paid a heavy price. By 1973, when the last U.S. troops left Vietnam, 58,150 Americans had been killed in action and another 153,372 wounded, many of them grievously. Consider the emotional cost, the post-traumatic consequences. Some 350,000 Californians served in Vietnam; 5,575 died there.

Thousands of Californians protested. The nation's first mass demonstrations against the war took place in April 1967 in New York City and San Francisco. On a beautiful, breezy Bay Area day, some sixty thousand people from all over the state—families with children, union members, students, beats and hippies—marched five miles across the city to a rally at Kezar Stadium in Golden Gate Park, where they cheered antiwar leaders and rocked to local bands. Country Joe and the Fish performed a number that soon became an antiwar anthem: "And it's one, two, three, what are we fighting for? / Don't ask me, I don't give a damn, / Next stop is Vietnam."

In June, a coalition of antiwar groups drew a large and diverse crowd of fifteen thousand to protest President Johnson's appearance at a fund-raiser in the ballroom of the Century Plaza Hotel on L.A.'s Westside. After assembling at a nearby park, the marchers set off along a previously approved route.

As they approached the hotel, they found the street constricted by 1,300 police wearing riot gear. The march slowed to a crawl and marchers began piling up.

"People were packed so tightly that at times both my feet were off the ground," one young protestor later recalled. Nervous authorities declared the demonstration an "illegal assembly" and ordered the police to disperse it. Cops waded into the crowd with nightsticks. The young protestor heard "high-pitched shrieks of terror and screams of pain" and, craning his neck, saw "a phalanx of white helmets just a few yards away, and alongside each helmet was a swinging baton. We were under attack!" Several hundred people—men, women, even children—were beaten, many seriously. Protestors fled in terror.

In the aftermath of this debacle, antiwar activists debated how to proceed. "Many of us in Berkeley talked incessantly about our political impotence," said student activist Frank Bardacke. If protestors were going to be attacked, no matter how peaceful they were, shouldn't they at least aim to accomplish something? Berkeley activists organized a demonstration they called "Stop the Draft Week." During several days in mid-October, thousands of students surrounded the army induction center in Oakland, south of the university campus, in an attempt to close it down. Police attacked, swinging nightsticks and spraying chemical Mace, but this time protestors broke into smaller groups and surged through downtown Oakland, overturning cars and blocking intersections. It required several hundred police to restore order and keep the induction center open.

The organizers were tried for criminal conspiracy and acquitted by an Oakland jury. But many Californians, including opponents of the war, deplored their tactics. Bardacke was unrepentant. "As long as the war continues there are going to be major disruptions by young people," he predicted. Berkeley remained a center of protest. To quell demonstrators in 1969, sheriff's deputies lobbed tear gas canisters and fired shotguns loaded with buckshot. A bystander was killed and dozens were treated at local hospitals. Governor Reagan sent the National Guard to occupy Berkeley. Low-flying helicopters gassed the campus. "If it takes a bloodbath," said Reagan, "let's get it over with."

★

The civil rights movement also took a radical turn. In 1966, in the city of Oakland, a group of young Black community organizers led by Bobby Seale and Huey P. Newton founded the Black Panther Party for Self-Defense. "We want freedom," the party declared in its Ten Point Program. "We want power to determine the destiny of our Black community." This marked a significant shift from the political goals of the civil rights movement—from integration to self-determination. The demand reflected the failure to remedy deep racial inequities. The Black Panthers rejected nonviolence and, in the tradition of Malcolm X, called on people of color to defend themselves against police brutality "by any means necessary." Small groups of armed Panthers conducted "cop-watching" patrols, monitoring police activity in the Black community.

The Party burst into the news with a bit of guerrilla theater in the spring of 1967. When the Oakland police complained to legislators about the cop-watching patrols, the state assembly took up a bill that would restrict the right to carry loaded firearms. In protest, thirty Panthers, shouldering rifles and shotguns, marched into the capitol in Sacramento. They broke no law, but the action was extraordinarily provocative. Bobby Seale read a short statement opposing the legislation, which, he said, "aimed at keeping Black people disarmed and powerless." Governor Reagan, who by chance was meeting a group of school children nearby, held an impromptu press conference. "There's no reason," he told reporters, "why a citizen should be carrying loaded weapons on the streets today."

Film of the encounter led the evening news. Many White Californians were deeply disturbed by images of armed Black men, in black leather jackets and black berets. But young people of color, especially streetwise kids from the inner city, found it thrilling. Party membership soared, and within a year the Black Panther Party had offices in African American communities throughout the state and across the nation.

The Panthers inspired other political groups. In Los Angeles young Mexican Americans, calling themselves "Chicanos" (street slang for *Mexicano*), came together to form the Brown Berets, proclaiming their right to bear arms "against the racist police." They organized among students who complained of dilapidated schools and a curriculum that ignored their history, maligned their language, and channeled them into low-status jobs rather than local colleges. In the spring of 1968, thousands of high school students in East L.A. staged what they called the "Chicano Blowout," leaving their classes and marching for self-determination and "community control."

The Panthers put an emphasis on community organizing. They founded a host of "survival programs," including free breakfasts for school children that inspired a federal program that today feeds millions of students. But the focus on violence proved the Panthers' undoing. They recruited members from urban street gangs and tolerated a kind of gangster culture within the organization, leaving themselves vulnerable to infiltration by provocateurs working for law enforcement. The FBI, a congressional investigative committee later concluded, "engaged in lawless tactics and responded to deep-seated social problems by fomenting violence and unrest." Without warrants, police attacked and opened fire on Panther offices in Oakland, Los Angeles, San Diego, and other cities across the state and nation, taking the lives of many members and eventually all but destroying the organization.

★

It was a violent time. President Johnson and his military advisors said they could see "the light at the end of the tunnel" in Vietnam. But the Tet Offensive, mounted by North Vietnam in January 1968, said otherwise. American public opinion turned against the war. Johnson was up for reelection, and antiwar senators Eugene McCarthy of Minnesota and Robert F. Kennedy of New York both announced their intention of challenging the president. On March 31, after performing poorly in the nation's first primary in New Hampshire, Johnson stunned the nation by announcing he would not seek a second full term. Protestors were ebullient. Perhaps the times *were* changing. But four days later an assassin shot and killed Dr. Martin Luther King Jr. and everything turned dark. Rioting erupted in dozens of American cities. Robert Kennedy asked Americans "to say a prayer for our own country—which all of us love—a prayer for understanding and compassion."

The California Democratic primary, held in June, climaxed the battle for the nomination. Kennedy received the endorsement of Cesar Chavez, greatly admired by Mexican Americans. He met with Black Panthers in Oakland and sat quietly as they vented their anger. "This is between them and me," Kennedy told a nervous aide. Both the Black and Mexican American vote went overwhelmingly for Kennedy, helping him win the primary by a convincing margin. The key to their victory, he told supporters gathered that evening at the Ambassador Hotel in Los Angeles, was their multicultural coalition. Despite "the division, the violence, and the disenchantment with our society," he assured them, "we can work together." A few minutes later, as he and his entourage left the hotel, a deranged gunman, upset over Kennedy's support for

Israel, shot and killed him. The hopes of millions died with him. After more than fifty years, many people still wonder what might have been.

Two months later, antiwar protests rocked the Democratic national convention in Chicago, where delegates nominated Vice President Hubert Humphrey, a supporter of the war. Police attacked and beat antiwar protestors on live television. The Republican Party nominated Richard Nixon, who claimed to have a "secret plan" for bringing the troops home. He didn't. Following his election—a stunning political comeback for the native-born Californian—the fighting continued for five more years, claiming the lives of another 19,000 Americans.

When the war drags on and nothing changes, what do you do? "You take drugs, you turn up the music very loud, you dance around," said Country Joe McDonald, southern California native and leader of the eponymous rock band. "You build yourself a fantasy world where everything is beautiful."

★

A movement for social and political change also swept through Native communities, which by the sixties included migrants from reservations all over the United States, who, like many others, came to California in search of opportunity. In 1956, Congress passed the Relocation Act, which provided funding to help Native families relocate to urban areas, and some seventy thousand settled in greater Los Angeles and the Bay Area. The Native American population of L.A. was larger than that of any other city in the country. Although they hailed from dozens of distinct cultures, Native people came together at churches, cultural centers, community picnics, and "powwows." Like other people of color, many young Natives took inspiration from the decolonization struggle of "Third World" peoples, the civil rights movement, and especially the Black Panthers.

In 1969, students of color at San Francisco State College—

including Blacks, Mexican Americans, Asians, and Natives—joined forces in what they called the Third World Liberation Front (TWLF), demanding "ethnic studies" courses that would directly address their history and place in the world. When administrators balked, the TWLF at San Francisco State and Berkeley called a strike, which many students and faculty honored. After months of disruption, administrators at both institutions finally agreed to create ethnic studies programs and recruit more students of color.

Later that year, the Indian Center of San Francisco, an important gathering place for the city's Native community, was destroyed by an accidental blaze. The Bay Area Council of American Indians sought the assistance of city government in finding a new location, but when officials dragged their heels, they turned to activist students from the TWLF. The young people came up with an attention-grabbing idea. The infamous penitentiary on Alcatraz Island in San Francisco Bay had recently closed, and the federal government considered donating the island to a private developer. Why shouldn't the Native people of the Bay Area claim it for themselves? In a telling instance of the temper of the times, the leaders of the Bay Area Council, men and women at least a generation older than the students, endorsed a plan to occupy the island. Students and community leaders formed a group they called Indians of All Tribes and began organizing.

In November 1969, eighty-nine people, mostly Native students from San Francisco State, Berkeley, UCLA, and other college campuses around the state, occupied Alcatraz Island. They were led by two dynamic young people, Richard Oakes, a Mohawk from New York, and LaNada Means, a Bannock from Idaho. Oakes read a statement approved by Indians of All Tribes. "We, the Native Americans, reclaim the land known as Alcatraz Island in the name of all American Indians by the right of discovery," it proclaimed, tongue-in-cheek. They were prepared to pay $24 worth of glass beads and red cloth, the price the Dutch had paid for Manhattan Island. "We know that land values have risen over the years," the statement continued, but their offer was more generous than the 47 cents per acre the federal government had paid Native Californians in compensation for their lost homelands. They planned to turn Alcatraz into an educational and cultural center for all Native American people.

The Nixon administration, with jurisdiction over federal property, decided to go slow, wary about a needless confrontation with radical students. During the occupation, which continued for eighteen months, some ten thousand Native people visited the island, entering their names and tribal affiliation in a makeshift register. "Alcatraz was a good thing," said Tom Knifechief, a young Pawnee who lived in Los Angeles. "It got a lot of attention and shocked a lot of people because it told them we're tired of being pushed around, we're tired of being made fun of, and we're here!"

Eventually, with a decline in both the number and the spirit of the occupiers, federal marshals evicted them. But by then the occupation had roused Native people across the nation, and particularly in California. "Alcatraz was a great awakening," Adam Fortunate Eagle, one of the leaders of the Bay Area Council, wrote in 1992, "one which even to this day changes our lives and stirs our souls." Native Californians look back on the occupation of Alcatraz Island as a turning point in their struggle for justice.

★

"We are about to be engulfed in a tidal wave of feminism," wrote *Los Angeles Times* columnist Jack Smith in December 1969. Women, who had participated in all the political events of the decade, were now organizing for gender equality, and

Smith declared his support. He wanted to see women "stand free in society—equal and unafraid," But, he confessed, "it does unsettle my nerves a bit."

Feminism invariably made men uncomfortable. Simmering throughout the sixties, it boiled over at the end of the decade. Betty Friedan, president of the National Organization of Women (NOW), characterized by the *Times* as "an angry woman," led a picket line in front of the newspaper's downtown headquarters demanding "an end to segregated want ads" for men and women. NOW focused its attention on women in the public world. In Los Angeles it organized a campaign protesting discrimination in hiring and promotion by the phone company AT&T, at the time the largest employer of women in the country.

Friedan may have been angry, but other feminists were more radical. In November, several weeks before Smith's column appeared, the *Times* published a profile of Vicki Temkin, a student activist at San Fernando Valley State College who had been arrested during a campus demonstration. The "women's liberation movement," said Temkin, would overthrow the entire system of male dominance. Most fundamental was women's absolute right to control their own bodies. "Why should legislators decide whether or not a woman should have a child?" she asked. "We favor total abortion law repeal." NOW did its best to avoid the issue of abortion, but movement feminists embraced it. "The personal is political," they declared, a slogan coined in 1969 that would resound for decades.

The women's rights and women's liberation movements were responses to the rapidly changing position of women in society. Women made up a growing share of California's labor force. In 1969, 40 percent of California women worked outside the home, up from 30 percent twenty years before. Women were also limiting their childbearing as never before. Easily available contraception, especially the birth control pill, provided them with the means. In 1969 the fertility rate stood at 2.4 live births per woman, down by a third from the "baby boom" high of 3.6 in 1960, an astounding pace of change. Both those trends continued. By the turn of the twenty-first century, women made up nearly half of California's labor force, and the fertility rate had fallen below 2.0. Feminism—another name for women's empowerment—was made for those times.

THE SANTA BARBARA OIL SPILL

37

A Complicated Ecosystem

D riving across the San Francisco Bay Bridge one day late in 1962, Raymond Dasmann, a professor of wildlife management at Humboldt State College in the state's far north, passed a large billboard with a digital tally of California's expanding population under the banner "Watch Us Grow." Dasmann saw little to celebrate. The ever-growing number reminded him of the unwanted changes overtaking the state. More people, more houses, more cars, more pollution. "No one seriously wants to turn back the clock," Dasmann wrote in *The Destruction of California,* published three years later. "But one can request, seriously, that in the headlong dash through the last half of the twentieth century we stop for a moment and make sure that the world we are building in the West will be one worth living in."

A San Franciscan born and raised, Dasmann fell in love with wild California during summers spent with country cousins in rural Sonoma and Monterey counties. Following service in the Pacific during World War II, he attended Berkeley on the GI Bill, earned a doctorate in field biology, and became an enthusiastic disciple in the interdisciplinary practice of ecology. "The world is a complicated ecosystem and it doesn't fit a single discipline," he later explained. "You've got to have the whole spectrum of human knowledge applied to the problems that we face almost on a daily basis now."

From an ecological perspective, growth threatened the state. "We are making major environmental changes," Dasmann wrote, and "everything that lives in California will feel the effects." At Humboldt State, he conducted field research on the ecology of the state's northwest region. "It was inevitable that wildlife had to go," he wrote. "Grizzly bears cannot be raised in sheep pastures, nor are wolves welcome in the suburbs." Douglas fir and redwood forests were clear-cut to build those suburbs. Foresters set out young saplings to replenish the old growth, but with predators eliminated, exploding deer populations grazed the hillsides bare, causing erosion that choked watercourses with silt and crippled vital fish populations. Change in one area led to transformation in another. Dasmann applied that lesson to the state as a whole. "We pave over farmlands that are in production," he wrote, "then spend millions to make arid lands suitable for farming." It didn't make much sense.

The Destruction of California created quite a splash. Dasmann spoke at bookstores and appeared on radio and television throughout the state. He made calm, objective arguments, although he could not hide his bias against southern California. "It is difficult to find any really good reason why the city of Los Angeles should have come into existence," he wrote, willfully ignoring the fact that L.A. sat on a floodplain next to a river, while his beloved hometown of San Francisco occupied a barren peninsula with no access to drinking water. But even Los Angeles reviewers praised Dasmann's book, which for

many Californians served as an introduction to the environmental impact of the state's unprecedented growth.

★

California's environmental movement was born four years later
in the aftermath of an environmental catastrophe. On January
28, 1969, workers for the Union Oil Company drilling in deep
water on a platform six miles off the Santa Barbara coast punc-
tured a zone of highly pressurized natural gas. The resulting
explosion literally cracked open the sea floor, spewing petroleum at an alarming rate. By the time the breach was closed, a
month later, an estimated hundred thousand barrels of crude
had formed a huge slick enveloping Santa Barbara Channel
and blackening forty miles of coastline. It was up to that time
the worst oil spill in the nation's history, though it has now
been exceeded by the 1989 Exxon Valdez disaster in Alaska's
Prince William Sound and the 2010 British Petroleum blowout in the Gulf of Mexico.

Television news featured heartbreaking video of oil-cov-
ered sea birds and the desperate attempts to rescue them. The
president of Union Oil objected to the coverage. "I am amazed
at the publicity for the loss of a few birds," he told a reporter.
In fact, sea birds and mammals were dying by the tens of thousands, and his comment sparked public outrage. The Santa
Barbara spill became a flashpoint for activism. Membership
in the Sierra Club and other conservation groups surged. Citizens pressed legislators for action.

Later that year, President Richard Nixon signed the National Environmental Policy Act, the nation's founding environmental law, and several months later the California legislature
passed the California Environmental Quality Act (CEQA),
establishing the legal procedure for assessing and preventing
the adverse environmental impact of all significant construction projects in the state. In the twenty-first century, CEQA

remains California's most important defense against environmental damage.

Many Californians joined Dasmann in questioning the state's continued rapid growth. "Not since the first week of the Creation has so much physical change taken place in so short a time," declared Richard Lillard, a professor at Los Angeles State and author of *Eden in Jeopardy* (1966), a jeremiad protesting overdevelopment in southern California. Lillard advocated "slow growth": a deliberate deceleration of the pace of change. A survey of Los Angeles residents in 1972 found a healthy majority favoring that approach. Lillard organized a homeowner association in his Beverly Glen neighborhood in the foothills of L.A.'s Westside that actively sought to preserve open space. By the early 1970s, dozens of similar associations around the state had become skilled at using CEQA to stymie development.

The population of Los Angeles County grew by 35 percent over the last three decades of the twentieth century. But homeowner associations in the city's affluent, White neighborhoods successfully prevented the construction of new housing, and the residential population of the Westside actually fell slightly. Multifamily conversions and new apartment construction were concentrated on the city's multicultural Eastside, greatly increasing residential density there. Meanwhile, the construction of new single-family homes migrated to outlying areas, worsening sprawl and traffic congestion. The slow growth movement did not prevent growth; it simply forced it elsewhere, usually with adverse effects for communities of the less powerful.

Restricting the supply of housing helped fuel a steep rise in home prices. All Americans suffered runaway inflation during the 1970s, but in California median housing prices shot up at twice the national rate. As property values rose, so did assessments and property taxes, triggering a tax revolt. In 1978, California voters approved Proposition 13, an initiative that amended the state constitution, placing caps on property assessments and requiring a legislative supermajority of two-thirds to pass any state tax increase. Though considered a significant political triumph for conservatives, instead of limiting the growth of state government Prop 13 crippled the local financing of school districts, cities, and counties, which relied on the property tax to fund public education and basic services. Meanwhile, the median cost of California housing continued its upward climb, increasing another 150 percent by the end of the century.

★

Shortly after he published *The Destruction of California,* Raymond Dasmann left Humboldt State and went to work for an international environmental organization, a job that took him and his family all over the world. By the mid-seventies, Dasmann and his wife Elizabeth had grown homesick, and they decided to build a rural retreat in California. "We were interested in moving to the country," he recalled some years later, "dropping out of everything and just going and living in the woods." They bought several acres near the town of Nevada City in the Sierras, where they put up a cabin.

One of their neighbors was the distinguished California poet Gary Snyder. Snyder grew up in rural Washington State and, like Dasmann, had been drawn to the great outdoors as a boy. Working as a logger during high school summers, Snyder encountered and became intimately acquainted with Native people. At Reed College in Oregon he studied anthropology and literature, completed a senior thesis on Native myths, and began writing poetry. After graduating in 1951, Snyder relocated to San Francisco, determined "to sink or swim as a poet," hanging out in North Beach with Allen Ginsberg and other bohemians. He participated in the famous poetry reading where Ginsberg first performed "Howl." Snyder read a poem titled "A Berry Feast," which features the wry voice of Old Man Coyote ruminating on the self-destruction of modern civilization. Snyder spent several years in Japan studying Zen Buddhism, but returned to California in the mid-sixties and joined his friend Ginsberg at the "Human Be-In" in Golden Gate Park.

When Dasmann met him, Snyder had just published *Turtle Island* (1974), a collection of poems and essays inspired by Native Californians, "who have been living here for millennia." During his work in Africa and Asia, Dasmann had come to understand that the removal of indigenous people from their homelands was an event that often preceded environmental destruction. Snyder helped him to see that California's story was part of the larger history of colonialism. Native practices had shaped the character of the state's environment, and the fundamental principle of ecology demanded that Native people be incorporated into any plan for sustained management. The way forward had to be the Native way: never take it all, always leave some behind. "These people have been living here for thousands of years," Dasmann realized. "Let's let them be the stewards."

★

Thousands of Native Californians still lived in California's remote deserts and mountains. As with Ishi, the famous Native man who survived alone in the Sierras for many years, the wilderness offered isolation and some protection from White people. At the turn of the twentieth century, federal authorities had created several small reservations and encouraged individual Natives to file for allotments of public domain land. "These Indians have lived in the same general locality for generations, and so far as we know, it was their original Native home," noted a federal Indian agent in the Sierras. "They have taken up homes on the public domain, where they could get a little water to irrigate a garden and orchard and do some agricultural work." Natives, however, did not own these allotments; they were merely "tenants at will," at risk of eviction at any time.

In the early twentieth century, for example, Ole and Rose Salem, a Maidu couple, received an allotment of land near Fredoyner Pass, high in the Sierra Nevada, which they improved with a cabin, a fenced garden, and a wagon road. They owned six horses and grazed forty head of cattle, but they also practiced the old ways, gathering acorns for meal and grasses for baskets. The Salems were proud of their independence and their traditional way of life. But when a relative fell sick and they left their place for several months to care for him, their allotment was terminated. "When you left you relinquished it," the agent told them. The land went to a "more important" user, a power company that was amassing timber and water rights in anticipation of constructing a dam, reservoir, and hydroelectric station. Over the years, federal officials similarly terminated hundreds of Native allotments, handing the land over to developers. Ole Salem filed a claim to another parcel. "Hurry up and have my land surveyed," he wrote the agent, "so no white people can take it away from me again."

The loss of homelands was a wound that would not heal. The Pit River Tribe, several associated bands in Siskiyou and Modoc counties in the far north, lost their homeland to White ranchers in the 1860s, leaving them desperately poor, wanderers in their own country. A century later they remained impoverished. "Not more than one or two families have running water or plumbing in the homes," wrote an investigator. "Families live in makeshift cabins with as many as eight, ten, and twelve people crowded into two, three, or four tiny rooms." Few had electric service, which galled them, since PG&E generated many megawatts of hydropower on rivers they considered their own.

Inspired by the occupation of Alcatraz, and assisted by student activist Richard Oakes, a group of Pit River Natives took over a PG&E facility and a ranger station on national forest land northeast of the city of Redding in 1970. Sheriff's deputies, state troopers, and federal marshals evicted them. "Officers and sheriff's deputies swung billy clubs and sprayed Mace," reported a local newspaper. "Indians, both men and women, fought with bare fists, tree limbs, and planks of lumber." Two dozen occupiers were tried on charges of criminal conspiracy but acquitted after a lengthy trial. Despite unfriendly coverage in the press, Native Californians applauded the occupations. "This was a big statement," said Cindy La Marr, a Pit River Native. "This was a tribe who stood up for what it believed in."

Native people remained in the crosshairs of economic development. The State Water Project (SWP), approved by California voters in 1960, aimed to dam virtually every remaining wild river in northern California, generating hydropower and diverting water for urban consumers and rural growers. The Feather River was the first to be harnessed, with the largest earth-filled dam in the nation at Oroville. The state had even more audacious goals for the free-flowing rivers of the Klamath Mountain region in the far north. Engineers planned to divert most of their waters eastward toward Sacramento Valley agriculture rather than westward to the Pacific. The first project was a dam on the Eel River, creating a reservoir that would inundate Round Valley in Mendocino County, the site of a reservation for the descendants of the Yuki, Pomo, Maidu, and other peoples relocated there in the 1860s. After more than a century, reservation residents had laid down deep roots, but the project would force them to relocate again.

Natives joined with ranchers and other local opponents

of the dam. Norman Whipple, elected leader of the Round Valley Reservation, met with Governor Reagan. "How many times will the United States break the solemn treaties they have made with us?" he asked. "Where will we go and where will we find work if the same government who pushed us into the valley now decides to push us out?" Reagan, reportedly moved to tears, announced his opposition to the project several days later. "We've broken too damn many treaties," he said. In 1972 he signed legislation protecting the wild rivers of the north.

★

Governor Reagan expressed no such sympathy for California's farm laborers, another group living and working directly with nature. Reagan denounced the national grape boycott organized by the United Farm Workers as "illegal and immoral" and encouraged consumers to ignore it, underlining his message by happily eating grapes on camera. Big growers were among Reagan's most enthusiastic supporters and he was not about to alienate them.

But Democrats also attended to the interests of agribusiness. After all, the New Deal had financed the Central Valley Project (CVP), designed to provide irrigation for San Joaquin Valley growers, and it was Governor Brown who championed the SWP, which unlike the CVP made no attempt to limit the irrigation used by big growers. Governor Brown's water program, declared the California Grange, an organization of family farmers, amounted to a "shameful" subsidy of big corporate growers.

Despite Reagan's opposition, consumers throughout the nation honored the grape boycott, and the consumption of table grapes fell by 25 percent. Buckling under pressure, grape growers agreed to negotiate. UFW membership surged, and by 1973 it had signed contracts representing forty thousand farm laborers. When the contracts came up for renewal, growers

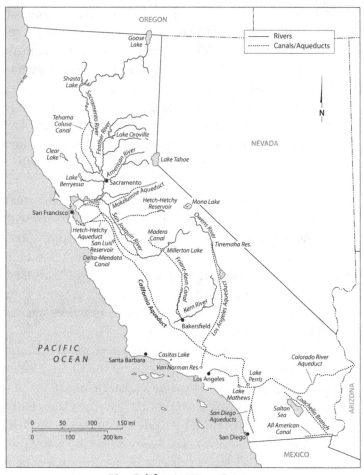

The California Water System

invited the maverick Teamsters Union to compete with the UFW. Violence in the fields marked a serious setback for the UFW.

In 1975, Jerry Brown, son of former governor Pat Brown, succeeded Reagan as governor of California. Rather than emulating his father, Brown followed the conservative trend toward limited government, squeezing social programs and limiting funding for the state's higher education system. But he also advocated a more harmonious relationship with the environment as well as greater social equality. He enthusiastically supported the UFW and backed legislation protecting the right of farm workers to organize, declaring he would "extend the rule of law to the agricultural sector." The UFW organized a march of thousands in support of the California Agricultural Labor Relations Act, which Brown signed into law in 1975. "This is the only state that has provided the farm worker with the right to elections, representation, and collective bargaining," said union president Cesar Chavez. "It means a whole new life for farm workers."

Reformers hoped the long history of farm worker exploitation in California was about to enter a new era. Economists expected union workers to win higher wages, providing growers with an incentive to mechanize their fields. Everyone would be better off with fewer, higher-wage workers operating high-tech equipment. Once again, it would not be that easy.

★

By the 1950s, California was the nation's most productive agricultural state and the third-largest producer of lumber. California's forest and farm operations have always been large-scale, a pattern that goes back to the huge land grants of the Californio era. Bigness became even more pronounced in the late twentieth century. Farms of 10,000 acres or more accounted for 31 percent of the state's total cropland in 1970. By 2007 that proportion had grown to 49 percent. These were corporate agribusiness operations, and they contributed to California's growing inequality in land ownership, the highest of all the states. Indeed, the pattern of land ownership in the state's leading agricultural regions—the San Joaquin, Salinas, and Imperial valleys—looked very similar to that in Central America, where the countryside is dominated by large holdings called latifundia.

The 1980s were the worst decade for American agriculture since the Great Depression. Federal banking authorities raised interest rates to fight inflation, contributing to a steep decline in the price of farmland. Meanwhile, record production led to a fall in commodity prices. Farm foreclosures rose dramatically. "The move toward latifundia is inevitable," wrote Victor Davis Hanson, speaking from his own experience as a fifth-generation raisin producer on a family farm near Fresno. "The American yeoman is doomed."

Yet Hanson fiercely defended the culture of his region. The urban residents of the coast, he argued, could not understand interior Californians—farmers, lumbermen, rural residents— because they lacked any real understanding of nature. They believed in a benign natural order that simply did not exist. In response, the residents of the interior, Hanson wrote, expressed "a blanket distaste for fashion, affluence, and leisure." The writer Joan Didion, who grew up in the Sacramento Valley, drew a similar distinction, albeit from the point of view of a cosmopolitan. The divide between residents of the coast and the interior, she wrote, "was profound," fueled by "rancorous differences in attitude and culture." Rural Californians, Didion claimed, considered environmentalists "a threat to the life of absolute personal freedom its citizens believe they lead."

★

In 1977, Raymond Dasmann became a professor of environmental studies at UC Santa Cruz, leading an interdisciplinary program that inspired many students to become field biologists, ecologists, and environmental activists. Twelve years later, turning seventy, he retired from the faculty. He and his wife Elizabeth were inseparable, and when she died in 1996, he was devastated.

In an interview conducted at the turn of the century, Dasmann confessed to being pessimistic about the future. "All the problems I wrote about in *The Destruction of California* are still here," he said. "We are still rebuilding on flood plains so that things will get washed away in the next flood. We are still rebuilding in chaparral hillsides where things will get burned out in the next drought. We're still thinking all we need is some dams and wells and we will have all the water we need forever." The accumulating effects of rampant growth frightened him. Climate change was even more horrifying. "Global warming is enough to make your hair stand on end." The interviewer asked him why he thought reform was so difficult. "Human greed is the driving factor," Dasmann replied. "We're in denial. We can't look at the reality because it's too horrible, so we say it doesn't exist."

In 2002, shortly before Dasmann's death, Bill Allayaud, director of the California branch of the Sierra Club, paid him a visit at his nursing home. As they talked, Dasmann grew distraught. "So many struggles, so many struggles," he said, as tears rolled down his cheeks. "It was hitting him," said Allayaud, "the really long, hard road we have to fight." He comforted the old man. "I know why you're crying," Allayaud said. "Don't worry, we will continue to fight."

'Can we all just get along?'

RODNEY KING SPEAKS

38

The Impossible Dream

"We want Bradley! We want Bradley!" the crowd chanted as Tom Bradley, his wife, and their two adult daughters made their way across the crowded stage to the podium in the ballroom of the Los Angeles Hilton. It was the evening of election day, May 29, 1973, and the press had just called it, making Bradley the first Black mayor of a major American city with a White majority. "Tonight was the fulfillment of a dream, the impossible dream," Bradley told his supporters. "We will make Los Angeles the jewel of the Pacific Basin and one of the great cities of the world."

It had been nearly fifty years since Bradley arrived in L.A., the seven-year-old son of sharecroppers from Texas. His father found a job as a railroad porter, his mother cleaned houses. His family may have been poor, but young Bradley was rich in talent and ambition. "I grew up under the system that said you can't do this, you can't go there, you can't achieve," he later recalled. Eager for "a clean break" from all that, he gained admission to the city's premier public high school, where he excelled as honors student, all-city track and football star, and president of Boys League. Tall, lithe, and strikingly handsome, Bradley won an athletic scholarship to UCLA. But following his junior year, eager to get on with life, he joined the Los Angeles Police Department (LAPD) and married his sweetheart from New Hope Baptist Church.

The LAPD was segregated by race. Bradley had been one of only four African Americans in a police academy class of seventy-two. "Blacks and whites were not permitted to work together," he told an interviewer years later. Working out of a predominantly Black precinct in South Central L.A., Bradley organized a successful program for juvenile offenders and won promotion to sergeant. He possessed a remarkable capacity for getting along with people. "He was always so notably calm and in control," said a fellow officer. Bradley himself put it plainly: "When a man angers you, he conquers you." Assigned to community relations in an ethnically mixed district straddling Eastside and Westside, he developed close connections with Black, Asian, and Jewish civic leaders.

Though always in the top tier for promotion, it nevertheless took eighteen years before Bradley became a lieutenant—and the department made it clear to him that neither he nor any other Black officer would ever be permitted to rise to the rank of captain or commander. "I did not see that it was worth the investment of time with so little promise of success," Bradley recalled. He began taking law classes at night, earned a degree, passed the bar, and in 1961, after twenty-one years of service, retired from the force and went into private practice.

But he hankered after a political career. A liberal Democrat, Bradley was first exposed to politics when he campaigned for Edward Roybal, who in 1949 put together a successful multicultural coalition and became the first Mexican American in the twentieth century to win election to the Los Angeles City Council. In 1963, building on relationships he had developed as a police officer, Bradley assembled a similar coalition and won a council seat representing his multiethnic district, becoming the city's first Black councilman. He quickly gained a reputation as a leading critic of the LAPD, directly confronting his old boss, Police Chief William Parker, during council meetings and warning of the corrosive effect police harassment had on the Black community. "There was unrest developing," Bradley said later, "and I thought we ought to deal with it."

After the Watts uprising, his criticism grew sharper. "Unrest among the poor, the young, and the minorities," Bradley declared, "cannot be dealt with by the traditional techniques of catching crooks." In 1969 he ran for mayor against the conservative Democratic incumbent, Sam Yorty. Thousands of idealistic young people went to work for Bradley, knocking on doors throughout the city. But Yorty prevailed by playing on White fears of "Black power." In a rematch four years later, Bradley carefully portrayed himself as an experienced cop, committed to both law-and-order policing and liberal reform. He built a coalition of Blacks, Mexicans, Japanese, and liberal Whites, including many Jews. He won over the downtown political establishment by committing himself to the redevelopment of the city's blighted central business district. This time he cruised to a comfortable victory.

Bradley won five successive terms as mayor and led the city of Los Angeles for twenty years. He changed the face of municipal government, greatly increasing the number of women and people of color employed by the city. Under his leadership, L.A. indeed became a "world city," a center of international finance. But despite his best intentions, the Eastside remained mired in poverty. He never mastered the LAPD, never developed an alternative to the department's aggressive policing of communities of color. Year by year, Los Angeles crept ever closer to calamity.

★

Bradley's election showcased the remarkable electoral success of men and women long excluded from political office by gender, race, and ethnicity. The transformation began in municipal government. In 1953 Clarissa Shortall McMahon, a Republican lawyer, joined the Board of Supervisors in San Francisco, where city and county government are consolidated. That same year, liberal Democrat Rosalind Weiner Wyman won a seat on the L.A. City Council. McMahon and Wyman served through the mid-sixties and blazed a trail for more women in government, including young Dianne Feinstein, who won election as a San Francisco supervisor in 1969.

Through the fifties and early sixties, only two African Americans held seats in the California legislature: Augustus Hawkins, representing L.A.'s Eastside, who first won his seat as a supporter of Upton Sinclair in 1934, and W. Byron Rumford from Berkeley, elected in 1948. In 1962 voters sent Hawkins to Congress, along with councilman Edward Roybal, the first Black and Mexican American representatives, respectively, from California. African American Mervyn Dymally was elected to fill Hawkins's seat in the assembly. Over the next ten years, during the apex of the civil rights movement in California, nearly two dozen people of color won seats in the state legislature, including Willie Brown of San Francisco, who in 1980 became assembly speaker, the second most powerful position in state government.

In 1973, the year Bradley was elected mayor, a total of seventeen women and people of color served in the state legislature, another five in Congress. Twenty years later, during Bradley's final year in office, that number had risen to thirty-eight legislators and twelve representatives.

★

Those victories relied on local organizing and multicultural coalitions. Consider the gay community of San Francisco, long a city of refuge for homosexuals. In the fifties, gays and lesbians hung out at taverns and bars catering to them, most famously a North Beach dive called the Black Cat. After repeated raids by city police, the owner sued and won a state supreme court case affirming the right of homosexuals to peacefully assemble, the first such ruling in the nation's history. But police harassment continued in both San Francisco and Los Angeles. In 1967, gays and lesbians participated in a protest against police harassment at the Black Cat in L.A., named for its famous North Beach counterpart. Historians consider it the first public demonstration of homosexuals in the United States.

During the early seventies, a gay residential neighborhood took shape along Castro Street in mid-city San Francisco. Gay businessman Harvey Milk, who owned a camera shop in the Castro, ran for a seat on the board of supervisors in 1973. Milk, a veteran of the civil rights and antiwar movements in New York, had deliberately relocated to San Francisco to join its gay counterculture. In a day when most homosexuals remained closeted, Milk was audaciously conspicuous. "You're never given power," he told supporters; "you have to take it."

Although Milk lost that election, he did much better than expected, and he continued to organize, pulling together an unlikely coalition of homosexuals, people of color, union workers, and small business owners. Milk reframed the issue of gay rights as support for urbanism. "The American Dream starts with neighborhoods," he declared, and "if we wish to rebuild our cities, we must first rebuild our neighborhoods." He argued against the overdevelopment of the city and its transformation into a high-rise corporate center, focusing instead on livability. Milk's position appealed to many San Franciscans, regardless of their sexual orientation.

Recognizing the growing importance of Milk's movement, other San Francisco politicians came aboard. In 1975 assemblyman Willie Brown and state senator George Moscone convinced their colleagues to repeal the state law criminalizing sexual acts between consenting adults. Then, with support from Milk's coalition, Moscone waged a successful grassroots campaign for mayor. Like Bradley in Los Angeles, Moscone sought to open city hall to many diverse constituencies. With his support, the city switched from at-large to district-based elections for supervisor, with impressive results: Gordon Lau became the first Chinese American on the board, Ella Hill Hutch the first Black woman, and Harvey Milk the first openly homosexual man. "If a gay can win," Milk ebulliently asserted, "it means there is hope that the system can work for all minorities."

But there was backlash. Conservatives placed an initiative on the statewide ballot banning homosexuals from teaching public school. Milk jumped into the fight, traveling across the state, engaging in debates and participating in rallies. In June, he led more than 350,000 marchers on a "Gay Freedom Day" parade through the streets of San Francisco. Milk's campaign turned California voters against the measure, which went down to defeat in November 1978, an early sign of changing views about sexual orientation.

The taste of victory turned to ashes a few weeks later when an emotionally disturbed San Francisco supervisor confronted Mayor George Moscone and Supervisor Harvey Milk in their city hall offices, shooting and killing them both. Supervisor Diane Feinstein heard the shots and discovered the bodies. Moments later, her voice shaking, she announced the murders to stunned reporters. Milk became a gay martyr. The board of supervisors named Feinstein to complete Moscone's term.

★

In Los Angeles, Mayor Tom Bradley focused on corporate investment in the downtown business district, precisely the approach Harvey Milk scorned. "With a major city like Los Angeles," Bradley argued, "you have to start at its heart." Bradley and his liberal supporters hoped to use increased tax revenue from the rising value of downtown property to lift up hardpressed neighborhoods. In the meantime the mayor deployed state and federal funds to increase public services—food stamps, rent assistance, day care—for the poor.

Bradley succeeded in attracting global capital investment, and during his years in office, high-rise office towers reshaped the downtown skyline. He led the expansion of the international airport, and the Port of Los Angeles and Long Beach became the biggest and busiest in the country. In car-crazy L.A., Bradley also won voter support for a light-rail rapid transit system. With the increase in defense spending after Ronald Reagan became president in 1981, the aerospace industries of southern California boomed, employing nearly half a million workers. Touting this success, in 1982 Bradley ran for governor against Republican George Deukmejian. Despite polling strongly in most coastal counties, he did poorly in the state's interior and in populous Orange and San Diego counties, losing a close contest. In a return match four years later, Deukmejian prevailed in a landslide.

By then it was clear that Bradley's strategy of focusing on downtown development had produced few positive results for L.A.'s poorest sections. During the seventies and eighties, "smokestack" manufacturing began shifting elsewhere, to take advantage of much lower wages. Aluminum and steel mills, auto assembly plants, and tire factories closed. Los Angeles lost a quarter-million industrial jobs, with people of color taking the biggest hit. With the passage of Proposition 13 and the administration of President Ronald Reagan, poor communities were left high and dry by cuts in state and federal antipoverty programs for job training, housing, and income assistance.

★

Millions of new migrants came to California during the seventies and eighties. In 1965, Congress passed a comprehensive revision of the nation's immigration laws, removing all limitations on Asian migration, a process that had begun in the postwar years. The new law capped immigration from Mexico and the rest of Latin America for the first time, but millions of Mexicans and Central Americans crossed the border illegally, pushed by economic depression and civil war. In 1986, Congress approved a path to legal status for unauthorized immigrants living in the United States, and more than two million Californians applied for resident status. Meanwhile, the surge in immigration continued. An estimated 6.5 million international migrants, mostly from Asia, Mexico, and Central America, settled in California during the quarter century from 1965 to 1990. Over the same period, the proportion of non-Hispanic Whites in the state fell from 79 percent to 56 percent.

This wave of migration played a decisive role in reshaping the state's economy. In agriculture, foreign-born once again displaced native-born. New labor contracting systems enabled growers to bypass the United Farm Workers and even the Teamsters. Other international migrants took low-wage jobs in domestic service, the hospitality industry, or a new low-tech manufacturing sector that took shape in southern California. These smaller, more dispersed factories relied almost exclusively on migrants to produce clothing, furniture, and other consumer goods, often in poorly ventilated sweatshops. By

1988, low-tech manufacturing in southern California employed nearly four hundred thousand men and women.

Average wages for the state's poorest-paid workers stagnated or fell. The poverty rate in L.A.'s Black and Hispanic neighborhoods rose as high as 40 percent. Unemployed and underemployed young men joined street gangs trafficking in drugs and weapons. The rate of violent crime doubled from 1970 to 1990. The LAPD responded with militarized crackdowns in ethnic neighborhoods, sweeping up and incarcerating hundreds of young men. During the eighties the population of the state's prisons and jails more than tripled.

Many Black and Hispanic Angelenos condemned the LAPD as an army of occupation. A 1991 survey of young men of color in Los Angeles found that nearly a third had been arrested one or more times that year. Most police officers lived in the suburbs, often far from the inner city, and many of them adopted an "us versus them" approach to policing. "Racism was expected, part of the group persona," said a former cop. "Race hatred was a dominating force." Complaints of abuse and brutality overwhelmed the Police Commission. As a councilman during the sixties, Bradley had lambasted that kind of policing. But as the mayor during the eighties, concerned with L.A.'s international image and the support of White voters, he sent a different message. "We are engaged in a war against the criminals of this city," Bradley declared in 1985.

★

In the summer of 1990, three African American social scientists from UCLA published an op-ed in the *Los Angeles Times* titled "A Quarter-Century of Slipping Backward." Despite an African American mayor and a liberal city council, the city's Black and Hispanic neighborhoods continued to suffer from unemployment, inadequate housing, underfunded schools, violent gangs, rampant drug use, and military policing. These were the preconditions of urban rebellion, they warned. "Watts is at more risk today than it was 25 years ago. The more things have changed, the worse they have become."

Six months later, late on an evening in March 1991, police pulled over Black motorist Rodney King in the San Fernando Valley after a high-speed freeway chase. Officers later claimed that King had resisted arrest, which he denied. But no one disputed the horrific beating he received, because a bystander videotaped it. When the police expressed no interest in the tape, the witness gave it to a local television station. Aired nationally on cable news, the shocking video stunned the city, the state, and the nation.

People of color had long complained of police brutality, and there it was for everyone to see. The officers would be punished, Mayor Bradley vowed, and he called for the resignation of Chief Daryl Gates of the LAPD. But Gates, who enjoyed civil service protection, refused to go. "I will leave when I choose," he declared, highlighting the fact that the LAPD was an authority unto itself. Four officers were charged with felonious assault by the district attorney of Los Angeles County. Because of extensive media coverage and concern over seating an impartial jury, a judge approved a change of venue and transferred the case to neighboring Ventura County. Finally, on April 29, 1992, a jury in a suburban section of that county found the officers not guilty. Mayor Bradley appealed for calm, but within hours Los Angeles was aflame.

The looting and burning went on for five days and nights, ending only after the deployment of the National Guard and U.S. Marines. Fifty-five people were killed, and sixteen thousand men and women arrested, half of them Hispanic, a third Black, a fifth White. The rebellion was multicultural. Although it began in Southeast Los Angeles, the riot spread throughout the city. Especially hard hit was Koreatown, the commercial and residential center of L.A.'s large Korean community. Korean merchants owned many small grocery and liquor stores in Black and Hispanic neighborhoods, and their relations with customers were fraught. A few weeks before the uprising, a Korean merchant had received a light sentence after being found guilty of shooting and killing a young Black schoolgirl wrongly accused of shoplifting. Angry rioters torched seven hundred Korean establishments. The estimate of overall property damage in the city ran to more than a billion dollars.

Tom Bradley's impossible dream, his vision of a fair and decent city for everyone, ended in a nightmare of destructive violence. Top-down liberal reform literally went up in flames. Crushed and demoralized, the mayor had relatively little to say. "It was a tragedy in his life that you can't overestimate," said a close friend. "It was like he was hit in the stomach with a two-by-four." Bradley quietly retired from the public stage. The rebellion's most enduring words came from beating victim Rodney King himself. At an impromptu news conference held while Los Angeles still burned, King spoke in a halting, unsteady voice: "People, I just want to say, you know, can we all just get along? Can we get along?"

MARÍA ELENA DURAZO + MIGUEL CONTRERAS

39

E Pluribus Unum

In 1990, California's State Board of Education approved a series of history and social studies textbooks for the public schools. The new books adhered closely to the board's "framework," calling for a "multicultural perspective" on American history emphasizing "the complex story of many peoples" and "the unfinished struggle to realize the ideals of the Declaration of Independence and the Constitution." Bill Honig, California superintendent of public instruction, praised the new approach. "Our kids for the first time are going to get history that's exciting, history that's interesting, history that's fair," he told reporters.

Honig expected parents and teachers to agree. But at a public hearing in Sacramento, individuals from many ethnic, racial, and religious groups denounced the books as Eurocentric and demeaning to people of color. A Black teacher objected that they paid insufficient attention to her culture. "Why can't my African American students have all the information about themselves available?" The president of the Associated Chinese Teachers of San Francisco complained of the "token" treatment of Asian Americans. One parent protested that the series caricatured fundamentalist Christians, while another argued that they ignored atheists. The books were "better than what we had," said the Black president of the Oakland school board, "but they are not good enough." Oakland refused to adopt the series, leaving its students without any history textbooks.

Professor Gary C. Nash of UCLA, one of the authors of the series, responded to the critics. A prominent historian whose published work on early America was praised by Black and Native American scholars, Nash was sympathetic to the demand for more ethnic history. But "if multiculturalism is to get beyond a promiscuous pluralism that gives everything equal weight," he warned, "it must reach some agreement on what is at the core of American culture." He pointed to the nation's Latin motto, *E pluribus unum,* "out of many, one." *Pluribus,* the diverse peoples of the United States, could flourish only within *unum,* a nation committed to democratic values. Nash insisted that students needed to understand both.

In the wake of this controversy, the U.S. Department of Education enlisted Professor Nash to develop a set of National History Standards with the assistance of scholars and teachers from around the country. When his group circulated a preliminary draft in 1994, it, too, was greeted with harsh criticism, this time from conservatives. The federal official who had funded the project didn't like the result and attacked the new standards for "multicultural excess." Prominent historian Alfred Schlesinger Jr. objected that they portrayed the nation as a "quarrelsome splatter of enclaves." The United States Senate rejected the standards by a vote of ninety-nine to one, the lone dissenter protesting that the resolution of condemnation was not strong enough.

According to Laurie Olsen, director of California Tomorrow, a nonprofit educational reform organization, the controversy wasn't really over textbooks or standards. It was about "how polarized we are and how much fear there is about diversity." The firestorm over history suggested that Americans and Californians had yet to come to grips with what it meant to be a multicultural society.

★

In the early 1990s, after two decades of record-breaking immigration, California had become one of the world's most culturally diverse societies. Hispanic, Black, and Asian residents made up 44 percent of the population. In Los Angeles, the state's most diverse city, six of every ten residents were people of color. Those broad categories masked an even greater diversity. Although Spanish-speaking migrants came predominantly from Mexico, they also included many people from war-torn El Salvador, Guatemala, and Honduras. Migrants from Asia included hundreds of thousands of Chinese, Filipinos, Vietnamese, and Koreans as well as substantial groups of Taiwanese, Cambodians, Thais, and Hmongs. Ethiopians, Eritreans, and West Indians diversified the state's Black community. Immigrants came as well from India and Pakistan, Israel and Iran, Armenia and Azerbaijan.

Ethnic restaurants flourished. Californians had long enjoyed Chinese and Mexican food. Chop suey, a Chinese-American amalgam, originated during the gold rush. In the 1950s, taco stands went head-to-head with the state's many hamburger joints. But by the 1980s, Californians were sampling cuisines from all over the globe. "There may be as many as five hundred Salvadoran restaurants in central Los Angeles, and at least half of them are pretty good," wrote Jonathan Gold, L.A.'s beloved food critic. "Los Angeles is the best place in the country to eat the cooking of Thailand and Burma, Guatemala and

Ethiopia, Taiwan and any of a dozen states of Mexico." Culinary traditions collided, resulting in all kinds of mashups—at fast-food stands (kosher burritos, chorizo burgers, kimchi tacos) as well as in upscale restaurant kitchens, where chefs experimented with ingredients like miso, ginger, and cilantro.

Food often served as a metaphor for diversity. "The United States isn't so much a melting pot as a salad bowl," immigration attorney Carl M. Shusterman wrote in the *Los Angeles Times* in 1978. "Instead of being melted down into a common type, Americans are mixed together and yet remain distinct." By the early nineties, the "salad bowl" metaphor had become commonplace, although it didn't provide much guidance about the unifying dressing that holds the multicultural salad together. As Professor Nash pointed out, a common commitment to core values is the most effective bond for a multicultural society. Vibrant, diverse California could thrive only when its citizens committed themselves to a multicultural democracy.

But after the violent events in Los Angeles—the endlessly looping video clips of White cops beating a Black man, Black rioters attacking a White truck driver, Korean merchants shooting at looters—the focus remained on diversity's dark side. Conservatives had long warned of such chaos. "A multicultural nation probably won't last long," columnist Guy Wright wrote in the *San Francisco Examiner.* "Either it will fly apart, or the dominant group will impose its culture on the minority, with nothing but trouble till the process is completed."

★

With the collapse of the Soviet Union and the end of the Cold War in the early 1990s, the federal government cut defense spending and California's aerospace industry went into a tailspin. "The bottom fell out," said aerospace engineer Bonnie Triezenberg. "We tanked." Several hundred thousand jobs evaporated, plunging the state into the worst economic recession since the Great Depression. Tax revenue fell drastically, producing the largest budget deficit in the state's history. Republican governor Pete Wilson argued for drastic cuts in state benefits and services, but the Democratic majority in the legislature refused to comply. Legislators were stymied by the constitutional requirement of a two-thirds supermajority to raise taxes or approve the state budget, so the government ran out of money, forcing Controller Gray Davis to issue IOUs to state employees, something that had not happened since the 1930s.

Approaching reelection in 1994, Governor Wilson found his poll numbers falling precipitously. He faced a challenge by State Treasurer Kathleen Brown, daughter and sister of former Democratic governors. With the state's middle-class voters in a foul mood, Wilson decided to hitch his campaign to the so-called Save Our State initiative, a xenophobic proposal authored by anti-immigrant groups.

Proposition 187, as it was numbered on the November ballot, would ban the estimated two million undocumented foreign immigrants in California from using government services, including schools and hospitals. It would also require all public officials, including teachers and doctors, to report suspected offenders to federal authorities. Republicans produced a series of incendiary television spots. "They keep coming," intoned a narrator over grainy footage of people dashing through traffic at the Mexican border. "Two million illegal immigrants in California. The federal government won't stop them at the border, yet requires us to pay billions to take care of them."

The campaign outraged the Hispanic community, which focused its anger on Governor Wilson. "He was saying we don't work hard," recalled L.A. businessman José Legaspi. "People felt they were being maligned as a group. We were being called lazy and loafers." Shortly before the election, a hundred thousand Mexicans and Mexican Americans marched from the East-side to Los Angeles City Hall in protest.

The proposition passed, winning 59 percent of the vote. Exit polls revealed a wide split between Whites (63 percent in favor) and people of color (75 percent opposed). Wilson trounced his liberal opponent. Republicans won five of seven statewide contests and took control of the state assembly. Within days a federal judge issued a temporary restraining order suspending enforcement of the proposition, and a federal appeals court later declared it unconstitutional, but the Republicans kept up their assault.

In 1996, Governor Wilson endorsed an initiative banning state government from using affirmative action to remedy discrimination based on sex, race, or ethnicity. Again, people of color voted solidly against the measure, but it passed with overwhelming support from Whites. Two years later Wilson supported yet another initiative, this one ending bilingual education programs that served nearly 1.5 million Hispanic and Asian students. It also passed, despite strong opposition from voters of color. The ballot initiative, a reform introduced in the early twentieth century as a way of strengthening democracy, was being used to smother it.

★

California's Hispanic community responded to these "racial propositions," as historian Daniel Martinez HoSang labels them, with an unprecedented burst of activism. In the late sixties and seventies, the United Farm Workers had inspired Mexican Americans, sparking a movement for political inclusion. A quarter century later, labor organizers targeting low-paid urban workers played a similar role, arousing the "sleeping giant" of Hispanic voters. In fact, many activists of the nineties had apprenticed with the UFW two decades before.

Consider two Los Angeles labor leaders, María Elena Durazo and Miguel Contreras. The children of farm worker parents in the San Joaquin Valley, both became organizers for the UFW, inspired by Cesar Chavez. Although they did not know each other, by the mid-eighties both were working for the Hotel Employees and Restaurant Employees Union, Contreras as an official at union headquarters in San Francisco, Durazo as a field organizer for Local 11 in Los Angeles. Durazo enjoyed great success among the city's Hispanic kitchen workers. But when the old-guard leaders of her local refused to conduct meetings in Spanish, she organized a dissident faction. In 1988 word of conflict in Local 11 reached union headquarters, and Contreras was sent to investigate.

Durazo and Contreras had very different styles. He was quiet but commanding, she was brash and rebellious. But soon they found common ground. Durazo's organizing owed much to her experience with the UFW, not only focusing on the workplace, but also reaching out to churches, schools, and other community organizations for support. Contreras knew that strategy well from his own UFW days, and he enthusiastically endorsed it.

The two shared the story of their relationship with a reporter from the *Los Angeles Times* a few years later. "We institutionalized the revolution," said Contreras. "Yes," Durazo interjected, "but on our terms, on our terms." Contreras laughed. "After that," he continued, "we started to work together on the same team." She nodded in agreement. "And from then on," he said, casting a sidelong smile at Durazo, "I couldn't keep her off me." Durazo vigorously shook her head. "This is where our stories differ," she said, laughing. In 1989, shortly before she won election as the new president of Local 11, the two married. Durazo went on to lead dramatic organizing campaigns among immigrant workers in Los Angeles. Contreras became president of the Los Angeles County Federation of Labor.

Meanwhile, UFW veterans in the Service Employees International Union (SEIU) were organizing L.A.'s janitors, most of them poorly paid immigrants. The SEIU's "Justice for Janitors" campaign featured boisterous street protests and confrontations with the LAPD. After much struggle, in 1990 the union won recognition from a slew of private contractors and negotiated a wage increase. It was the most significant labor victory for Californians of color since the UFW successes of the mid-seventies.

The passage of Prop 187 with its draconian attack on Latin American migrants convinced Contreras that the union movement had to play the long game, so he put members to work registering voters and persuading legal "green card" immigrants to apply for citizenship. The labor movement was certainly not alone in those efforts—many activists from across the state joined the campaign—but unions led the way, providing organizing prowess and people-power. By 1995, hundreds of California immigrants were applying for naturalization every day, more than in any other state. And once they completed the process, they voted at twice the rate of new citizens elsewhere. In the ten years following the passage of Prop 187, California gained more than a million new voters. The Hispanic share of the vote in statewide elections rose from 9 percent in 1990 to 14 percent in 2003.

During the conservative 1980s, California's traditionally Democratic Mexican American voters had begun to trend Republican. In 1990, 38 percent registered as Democrats, 34 percent as Republicans. But in the nineties they overwhelmingly rejected the Republican Party, and by 2003, 63 percent were Democrats, only 12 percent Republicans. Hispanic voters became the bedrock of the Democratic Party. Latinos and Latinas began winning more elections, filling seats in local and state government. The Latino Legislative Caucus in Sacramento rose from seven members in 1990 to twenty-two in 2002, all of them Democrats.

★

Among California's ethnic groups, none were more impoverished than Native Californians. They suffered the highest rate of unemployment, the lowest household income, the worst housing, the poorest schools. But inspired by the Red Power movement, during the 1970s residents of the state's nearly one hundred Native reservations began experimenting with ways to turn their limited sovereignty to advantage, establishing business enterprises that might create jobs and produce revenue. A few opened smoke shops, exploiting their exemption from state sales tax, but those were nickel-and-dime operations.

The Agua Caliente band of Palm Springs provided an example of bigger possibilities. Portions of the band's reservation lay in the heart of the city, and they negotiated an agreement with the municipal government to build a resort hotel adjacent to *Sec-he,* the ancient hot springs; they also agreed to lease a square mile of their land for an airport. But the city remained adamantly opposed to the band's more ambitious development plans—until 1977, when the U.S. Supreme Court ruled that federally recognized Native tribes had the right to use their reservation land as they saw fit. Soon thereafter, the Palm Springs municipal government agreed to a "joint use" agreement with the band. This didn't make the Agua Calientes rich, said Viola Ortner, chairwoman of the band's council, but it secured their future and promised increasing returns. "It allowed us to have things and do things that we wouldn't have otherwise had," she said.

The Agua Calientes had location in their favor. But soon

other Cahuilla bands of the Coachella Valley began opening small casino operations, offering high-stakes bingo and card games to the general public. When Riverside County authorities cracked down, closing a reservation casino near the town of Indio, the Cahuillas sued in federal court. In 1987, the Supreme Court ruled in their favor, and the following year Congress passed legislation establishing a procedure for states and tribes to negotiate gaming compacts.

By the early nineties, Natives on more than two dozen reservations—from the Kumeyaays in the south to the Yuroks in the north—had opened casinos generating nearly a billion dollars in annual revenue. Bands utilized the proceeds in various ways, but devoted much of it to community development, strengthening tribal courts and police, opening cultural centers, and running language preservation programs. "The real issue is not gaming," said Anthony Pico of the Viejas Band of Kumeyaays. "Gaming is hooked up to the right to self-government."

Governor Wilson, however, refused to negotiate with the bands, which led to intermittent conflict between casino operators and local law enforcement. Finally in 1998, during his last year in office, Wilson reached an agreement with the Pala Band of Luiseños that allowed for limited gambling. The governor then insisted that every band in the state had to accept the same terms. Considering that demand a violation of their sovereignty, reservation bands took their case directly to California voters, collecting a sufficient number of signatures to place a measure with far more generous terms on the November ballot.

For the first time in their history, Native Californians jumped into electoral politics, investing more than $60 million in an advertising campaign. Television commercials featured Native men and women speaking directly to voters, making the case that casino gaming offered their communities a historic opportunity for economic independence, as well as a chance to partially rebalance the scales of justice. Despite the strong opposition of Las Vegas casino operators, who waged an advertising campaign of their own, the proposition passed with 62 percent of the vote. Republicans opposed the measure, but Democrats and people of color voted overwhelmingly in favor. As one political observer noted, Native Californians were invisible to most of the state's residents "until they started writing checks."

★

In 1998, Democrat Gray Davis was elected to succeed Governor Wilson, winning by the largest margin of any Democrat since Pat Brown forty years before. He carried a number of populous, typically Republican areas, including San Diego County and "the Inland Empire" of Riverside and San Bernardino, all of which included growing numbers of Hispanic voters. Cruz Bustamante, a Fresno Democrat and speaker of the state assembly, was elected lieutenant governor, becoming the first Latino since the 1870s to hold statewide office. For the first time in sixteen years, Democrats enjoyed complete control of state government. Davis assumed office at the peak of the "dot-com boom," powered by the expansion of high-tech electronics, personal computers, and the beginnings of internet commerce. With substantial tax revenue, the Democrats increased spending for education, health services, and other programs that had suffered two decades of cuts.

But the good times were short-lived. In 2000, just two years into Davis's term, the state was hit with an unprecedented electricity crisis. The legislature had deregulated the state's electrical utilities, assuming that market competition would lower costs for consumers. Instead, wholesale energy prices soared, utilities were unable to meet demand, and the state suffered a series of rolling blackouts. The giant utility PG&E went bankrupt. As if that weren't enough, the speculative bubble in internet stocks burst and the dot-com boom went bust. California, the epicenter of the nation's high-tech industry, was hit hard. Tax revenue plunged and once again state government entered a period of political turmoil.

Davis and Bustamante succeeded in narrowly winning re-election in 2002. But shortly after his second inaugural, Davis was faced with the largest budget deficit in the state's history. Refusing to consider a tax increase to fill the gap, he reluctantly supported increases in state-levied fees, including drivers' licenses and auto registration. There was a public outcry. Conservatives gathered sufficient signatures to force a recall election in October 2003, only months into Davis's second term. Voters were required to make two decisions: whether or not Davis should be removed from office, and who should replace him if the recall was successful. Several dozen candidates were on the ballot, of whom the leading contenders were Republican mega–movie star Arnold Schwarzenegger and Lieutenant Governor Bustamante.

The ballot also included another proposition targeting people of color, the Racial Privacy Initiative, a constitutional amendment that would prohibit state and local government from collecting data on the ethnic identity of California's residents. Supporters argued that Proposition 54, as it was numbered, would advance the cause of a "colorblind" society. But opponents warned that the measure was a wolf in sheep's clothing. "We still live in a time when vigilance over discrimination is necessary," the *Sacramento Bee* editorialized. "Proposition 54 would only make us blind to it." Native California bands, flush with gambling revenue, funded a massive television campaign opposing the measure.

When the results of the election were tallied, Davis was

out and Schwarzenegger in. Exit polls indicated that White voters, turned off by Davis and intrigued with Schwarzenegger, supported both those outcomes by a significant margin. Voters of color went the opposite way, against the recall of Davis but for Bustamante. Exit polls indicated that many who cast their ballots against the recall neglected to vote for a replacement, giving Schwarzenegger a significant edge.

Prop 54, on the other hand, went down to a clear and unambiguous defeat. Republicans kept their distance from it, and Schwarzenegger opposed it. The campaign against the measure proved particularly effective and persuaded a critical segment of Whites, especially the young, to vote no. Native Californians had once again flexed their political muscle. In the first quarter of the twenty-first century, California voters would consider many more ballot initiatives, but this would be the last of the racial propositions.

MULTICULTURAL CALIFORNIANS

40

The First Step

California has long been a magnet for transplants. Over the course of the state's history they came in four great waves: during the gold rush, over the first third of the twentieth century, during and following World War II, and from the 1970s to the early 2000s. No region of similar size, anywhere on the planet, experienced such rapid growth over such a long period.

In the first two decades of the twenty-first century, however, California's growth slowed dramatically. Foreign immigration remained strong, although the number of migrants from Latin America dropped, and China overtook Mexico as the leading country of origin. The big change came in the pattern of domestic migration. From 2000 to 2020, people moving *from* California to metropolitan areas in Texas, Arizona, Washington, and other states, outnumbered those moving *to* California by more than two million. That was a dramatic development, and it had a large effect on the state's growth rate, which not only fell lower than that of states like Texas, but below the national average. In 2020, during the Covid-19 pandemic, the state's population actually dropped by more than 182,000, the first decline since the state began collecting statistics in the nineteenth century. California, the Census Bureau announced, would lose a congressional seat. Dowell Myers, professor of population studies at the University of Southern California (USC), put it succinctly: "Growth in California has stalled out—and that's pretty amazing."

California may have entered a new era. Historians rely on hindsight, and it's still too soon to know the various ways in which slower growth will transform the state. We can, however, consider whether the trends of the recent past are continuing along a familiar path or taking a new turn. Slow growth was something new, contradicting not only a long-standing pattern but California's very conception of itself, and it caught many observers by surprise.

By contrast, demographers had for some time pointed to a second major trend: the continuing reduction in the relative size of California's White population. Declining since the late 1960s, by the mid-1990s the proportion of Whites fell below 50 percent. People of color became a majority. In 2020, Hispanics (at 39 percent) surpassed Whites (at 37 percent) as the state's largest ethnic group. Another amazing fact, but certainly no surprise.

By the early twenty-first century, ethnic and racial diversity was evident everywhere in the state, not only in coastal cities but in rural counties, many with large resident communities of Mexican Americans and other Hispanics. Many suburbs also became more multicultural. The middle-class community of Walnut, on the eastern edge of southern California's San Gabriel Valley, went from nearly exclusively White to majority Hispanic, Black, and Asian in the span of a single generation. For kids growing up there in the early twenty-first century, multicultural was normal and interethnic relationships common. "My friends are a little bit of everything," sixteen-year-old Elisa Gutierrez told a reporter. Her BFF was White and her prom date Black. "I don't think I should be under pressure to 'act Mexican,'" she said. "We all breathe the same air."

Marriage statistics document the blurring of the color line. In 2020, a quarter of all California's registered marriages united individuals from different ethnic backgrounds, the highest proportion of any state but Hawai'i. Among unmarried couples living together, the interethnic proportion approached 50 percent. Children of "mixed race" made up the third-largest ethnic category among newborns, after Hispanics and Whites. Paul Richard and Michelle Hall, an interethnic couple residing with their two daughters in a suburb outside Sacramento, found their neighbors increasingly colorblind. "Before it was, 'Oh, are they your kids?'" Richard told a reporter. "Now, it's 'Your kids are pretty.'" Californians were increasingly comfortable with ethnic difference.

Nevertheless, in the second decade of the new century, hate crimes directed at people of color rose in California and throughout the nation. The state's ten largest cities recorded a 64 percent increase from 2014 to 2017. During the Covid pandemic, which originated in China, hate directed at Asian Americans surged. In Oakland, Carl Chan, president of the Oakland Chamber of Commerce, was attacked by a man shouting, "Fuck you, Chinaman." Across the bay in San Francisco, an elderly Thai man was body slammed and killed. Both attacks were perpetrated by young Black men. Fear and hatred of "the other" continued to haunt California.

★

Kamala Harris, elected 49th vice president of the United States in 2020, was the best-known "mixed race" Californian, the child of a mother from India and a father from Jamaica who met as graduate students at Berkeley in the early sixties. Harris's mother cooked Indian food at home and taught her daughters about Hinduism. The girls attended a Black Baptist church in Oakland and sang in the gospel choir. Harris graduated from Howard University, a historically Black institution, and received a law degree from the University of California. She pursued a notably successful career as a prosecutor, and was elected as San Francisco's district attorney, California's attorney general, and a U.S. senator before becoming vice president. "How do you describe yourself?" a reporter asked her during the presidential campaign. "As a proud American," Harris replied. Her Black and East Indian heritage were "of equal weight in terms of who I am," she said. "People exist through a prism and they are a sum of many factors."

Harris was one of many new faces reinvigorating California's democracy. Alex Padilla, whom Governor Gavin Newsom appointed to the Senate seat vacated by Harris, grew up in a Mexican immigrant household in Los Angeles. A talented student, he attended the Massachusetts Institute of Technology and graduated with a degree in mechanical engineering. He returned to California in 1994, during the turmoil over Proposition 187. "It hurt me," Padilla recalled. "I was coming home, proud of my degree, partly as a symbol of accomplishment of my parents' sacrifices and struggles. And here's this politician saying: 'California is going downhill, and it's the fault of people like your parents.' That shook me to my core." He ditched plans for an engineering career and went into politics, winning a seat on the Los Angeles City Council, then in the state senate. In 2015 Padilla was elected secretary of state, the second Latino in modern times to win statewide office (following Lieutenant Governor Cruz Bustamante in 1998).

The electoral success of men and women of color was unprecedented. During the 102nd Congress (1991–93), people of color held ten of the state's forty-five seats in the House of Representatives. Thirty years later, in the 117th Congress (2021–23), they held twenty-two of the state's fifty-three seats, a 91 percent increase. A sampling of their personal stories reflects the modern history of California.

Doris Matsui, representing the city of Sacramento, was born in a Japanese internment camp in 1944. Her parents, U.S. citizens who owned a fruit farm in the San Joaquin Valley, never spoke about their wartime experience at home. But upon learning something about the camps as an undergraduate at Berkeley, she began asking questions of her mom and dad. "And when the story was told," Matsui recalled, "the emotions came out. It was unbelievable." Her father remembered the cold wind that blew through the cracks of their plywood shack. "The best thing that came out of that experience," he told his daughter, "is that you were born!"

Karen Bass, representing a congressional district in Los Angeles, was the child of a mail carrier and a homemaker. She first became politically active at the age of fifteen, as a volunteer for Robert F. Kennedy during the 1968 Democratic primary. The first of her family to attend college, she earned a master's degree in social work from USC and spent three decades as a physician's assistant in South L.A. In the early nineties she helped organize and lead a Black-Hispanic neighborhood coalition that focused on grassroots rebuilding after the uprising of 1992. "Burning and destroying isn't healing," she told an interviewer. "Healing is putting it back together." Bass won a seat in the state assembly in 2004, and four years later became the first Black woman in American history to preside as the speaker of a statehouse.

Young Kim immigrated with her South Korean family to the American territory of Guam, then relocated to Hawai'i, where she attended high school. She came to California to attend USC, and after graduation became a naturalized citizen. For years she worked as a liaison to the Korean community for a southern California congressman, becoming well known for her TV show *L.A. Seoul with Young Kim.* In 2020 she won the congressional seat of her retired boss, representing a district that includes the multicultural community of Walnut. A third of her constituents are foreign-born. "My personal experience of being an immigrant, having gone through what this diverse immigrant community has gone through," Kim told a reporter, "really helps me understand the district."

The significance of the transformation of California's elected representatives was underlined by Peter Schrag, long-time editor of the *Sacramento Bee.* "California is a test case for something no nation had ever attempted before," Schrag writes: "to forge and maintain a modern, prosperous high-tech democracy out of the great ethnic and social diversity of people, many of them from the Third World."

★

In 2006, California's highly diversified economy seemed at the top of its game. The high-tech industry rebounded from the dot-com boom. The state produced more than $1.7 trillion in goods and services, making it one of the world's ten largest economies. Then, it all came crashing down.

To stimulate growth following the dot-com bust, federal financial authorities had lowered the prime interest rate. The cost of a thirty-year mortgage dropped to its lowest level since the 1950s, sparking a boom in housing sales—especially in California, where the median price of a home was 60 percent higher than the national average. With a majority of working families priced out of the coastal housing market, the demand for homes in the near interior soared. Home builders responded by constructing dozens of new single-family tracts. The Bay Area spilled over the coastal foothills into the Delta and the lower

San Joaquin Valley. Greater Los Angeles followed the freeways eastward, deep into the Inland Empire. Californians of all classes continued to embrace the suburban ideal, and lenders responded by offering borrowers with poor credit "subprime loans"—mortgages with variable interest rates and little or no money down. From 2005 to 2007, California accounted for 56 percent of all the subprime mortgages issued in the nation.

The result was a classic market bubble, which floats beautifully as long as demand remains strong and prices continue to rise. But the thing about bubbles is that they inevitably burst. When federal authorities raised the prime rate, fearing an outbreak of inflation, variable mortgages were adjusted upward and monthly payments increased dramatically. Many borrowers could no longer afford to pay, and defaults began rising. Meanwhile, with higher rates, demand for homes slackened and prices fell. Foreclosures put more properties on the market, and prices fell further. Mortgage holders were caught between declining home values and increasing monthly payments. Those who purchased at the peak of the market found themselves "underwater"—owing more than their homes were worth. The ripple of foreclosures became a torrent.

Mortgage lenders began going belly up. The tipping point came in 2008 when Washington Mutual Savings, California's biggest lending institution, closed its doors—the largest bank failure in American history. Wall Street financial firms, heavy investors in subprime mortgages, toppled toward bankruptcy, and in September 2008 the stock market crashed. It was the nation's worst financial meltdown since 1929. Unemployment rose to Great Depression levels, and a quarter million California families lost their homes. The state's interior regions were among the hardest hit in the nation. Entire housing tracts lay abandoned, modern-day ghost towns. As property tax revenue dried up, the cities of Vallejo in the Delta, Stockton in the San Joaquin Valley, and San Bernardino in the Inland Empire went bankrupt. The so-called Great Recession officially ended in 2009, but the suffering continued for years more. And for all intents and purposes, the whole mess began in California.

★

Overall tax revenue plummeted, and in 2009 the politically divided state government gridlocked once again over an astounding $42 billion deficit, the worst in the state's history. Partisan division intensified the crisis. Democratic legislators argued for a tax increase on upper-income earners to pay the state's debts. Republicans insisted on slashing taxes and shrinking government. Democrats championed positive government, while Republicans continued to argue that government itself was the problem. "The views of Republicans and Democrats," concluded the nonpartisan Public Policy Institute of California, "are the political equivalent of plate tectonics, moving in opposite and extreme directions."

Support for Republicans continued to shrink. From 1990 to 2010, Democratic registration in the state held steady at about 45 percent of all eligible voters, while registered Republicans fell to less than a third. Coastal counties, with the vast majority of the population, including large communities of color, were overwhelmingly Democratic. Only the state's less populous rural counties of the far north and the far east remained reliably Republican. Former conservative strongholds—the San Joaquin Valley, the Inland Empire, Orange and San Diego counties—became political battlegrounds.

Empowered by supermajority requirements, however, the Republican minority in the legislature continued to block a budget agreement. The state, forced to defer tax refunds, student financial aid, and funding for county governments, once again resorted to issuing IOUs. In the midst of the worst economic calamity in seventy-five years, Governor Schwarzenegger and Republican legislators forced Democrats to approve massive cuts in programs assisting the poor and unemployed.

This fiasco set the stage for the gubernatorial election of 2010, in which Democrats nominated former governor Jerry Brown. After leaving Sacramento in 1983, Brown had followed an unconventional political path, moving to the multicultural city of Oakland where he was elected mayor. Over two terms he built an enviable record by reducing crime, attracting investment, and building affordable housing. In 2006 he won election as California's attorney general. While Governor Schwarzenegger haggled with the legislature over cutting essential services, Brown sued a giant mortgage lender for "unfair and deceptive" practices and won an $8 billion settlement for California debtors.

Brown campaigned as the "can-do" candidate. "I want to summon Californians to a renewed, shared commitment to the state's real greatness," he declared. His political models, he said, would be California's great twentieth-century governors: Hiram Johnson, Earl Warren, and his father, Pat Brown. "These were the people who built the state, who were innovators and not ideologues." Brown won the election comfortably, joining Earl Warren as the only Californian elected to a third gubernatorial term. Also on the ballot was a Democratic-sponsored initiative abolishing the supermajority requirement for legislative approval of state budgets. It passed by an overwhelming margin. A century before, the election of 1910 had transformed California politics. The contest of 2010 was another historic "change election."

The supermajority requirement for any increase in state taxes, however, remained in force. Bypassing Republicans in the legislature, Governor Brown succeeded in placing an initiative on the 2012 ballot raising income tax rates for the wealthiest Californians. The new revenue would be dedicated to the state's public education system, once the best in the nation but by 2012 a crying shame, with per pupil spending 20 percent below the national average. This measure, too, passed overwhelmingly.

In the same election, Democrats won supermajorities in both houses of the legislature, culminating a long period of political realignment driven by voters of color, particularly Hispanics. In 2013, twenty years after Proposition 187, the new legislature passed a law authorizing driver's licenses for the state's estimated two million unregistered foreign immigrants. The legislation had both practical and symbolic importance. "No longer are undocumented people in the shadows," Governor Brown said at the signing ceremony, held on the steps of Los Angeles City Hall. "This is about the people who by their fervor, their faith, and their numbers have transformed California."

★

By the time Governor Brown completed an unprecedented fourth term in 2018, California had recovered from the Great Recession. The state's highly diversified economy had grown to become the fifth largest in the world. But California also suffered the nation's highest rate of poverty, and the wide gap between the incomes of rich and poor continued to grow. Home prices and rents remained extraordinarily high, with California ranked dead last among the states in the availability of affordable housing. Over several decades, environmental protection had been perverted into a bulwark of privilege, and as a result, young working families could no longer afford homes of their own. California suffered with the largest homeless population in the nation, with thousands of people living in tent cities or on the streets. Unaffordable housing was the principal reason people gave for leaving the state. The pandemic of 2020 exposed the depth of these problems. Los Angeles, with the highest rate of poverty and homelessness in the state and some of the most densely populated neighborhoods in the nation, became an epicenter, with one of the highest rates of infection. African American and Hispanic districts suffered disproportionately.

Structural problems persisted. In the condition of its roads and highways, bridges and tunnels, and other infrastructure, the state ranked forty-ninth. And despite improvements in education, California still ranked a scandalous forty-first among the states in per pupil spending. Enormous disparities existed between schools in affluent and poor districts. The state's students performed significantly lower than the national average in math, reading, and science.

Accelerating climate change intensified problems of drought, water supply, storage, and distribution. In 2020, the state's reservoirs were at record lows. Lake Mead, which holds Colorado River water, was at the lowest level since it was first filled in the 1930s. Antiquated electric transmission lines snaking across drought-ravaged forests resulted in huge wildfires. Sparks from a century-old PG&E line crossing the foothills of the Sierra Nevada were responsible for the 2018 Camp Fire, the deadliest in California history, which destroyed the town of Paradise and claimed the lives of eighty-five people. Eight of the ten largest wildfires in the state's history occurred between 2017 and 2020.

If unresolved, those problems will deliver a devastating blow to California's thriving multicultural democracy. The promise of equality is worth much less without economic opportunity and a livable environment. Simply growing the economy won't be enough. The solution requires a positive government committed to combating structural racism, miti-

gating inequality, rebuilding crumbling infrastructure, and re-
storing world-class public education.

★

In the twenty-first century, Californians began to confront the
dark side of their history. In April 2019, the city of San Diego
held an event commemorating the 250th anniversary of its
founding by Spanish soldiers and Franciscan missionaries.
Leaders of the Kumeyaay Nation were invited to participate.
Erica Pinto, chairwoman of Jamul Indian Village, a band with
a small reservation twenty miles east of the city, recounted the
Spanish arrival from a Native perspective. "When the ships
pulled in, our ancestors saw other humans who were suffering
from hunger and thirst," she said. "We welcomed them and
we fed them. After that, everything started to go downhill for
us." Angela Elliot-Santos, chairwoman of the Manzanita Band
of Kumeyaays, told the mostly White audience that although
they were not to blame for what had taken place in the past,
they had a historic responsibility. "You are the people who can
make sure this never happens again," she said. "You are the
people who can stop the dehumanization of the first peoples
of this land and all the peoples of this country."

San Diego County, with its glittering twenty-first-century
metropolis, has more Native reservations than any other county
in the United States. By 2019, the Kumeyaays were operating
eight casinos there, generating millions of dollars in revenue.
They used those funds to pay members and to improve housing, health care, and education. In lieu of taxes, they made direct
payments to the county in exchange for fire, police, and other
services. They supported a broad range of local charities.

The Kumeyaays assumed a respected place in local affairs. San Diego had celebrated the anniversary of its founding
many times before, but this was the first time Native Californians had been invited to participate. A reporter asked Chair-

woman Pinto about that after her talk. "So," he said, "the Kumeyaay have casinos, thus money, and thus clout. Or is that too cynical?" "No," Pinto answered candidly, "it's the absolute truth."

In 2019, California's population included an estimated two hundred thousand Native Californians from 171 bands and tribes, 109 of them officially recognized by the federal Bureau of Indian Affairs. That recognition vested them with limited but still significant sovereign authority. Sixty-two of those recognized bands and tribes operated casinos under agreements with state government, generating a total of $9.3 billion in revenue. They also paid hundreds of millions of dollars into a special trust fund administered by the state, which supported federally recognized bands and tribes without casinos.

But at least sixty thousand Native Californians belonged to bands without any official status, unrecognized by the federal government. They could not legally operate casinos, and had no access to the special trust fund. So while the living conditions of many Native Californians had improved considerably, others remained impoverished. Even in San Diego County, where all the Kumeyaay bands were federally recognized, a survey by the Census Bureau found that a quarter of Native households had incomes below the poverty line, which in 2021 was $26,500 for a family of four.

What Native Californians had in common was not reservation gaming, but shared historical experience. "Our people survived because we are resilient and courageous," said Erica Pinto. "That is our story, that is our history—and we're not going anywhere." Like Old Man Coyote, their most important spirit animal, Native Californians had survived, evading the grimmest of fates and exulting in the joy of being alive. Not only did Coyote remain an important character for Native people; he broke into mainstream popular culture as well. Maidu artist Harry Fonseca reimagined him exploring modern California like his Native brothers and sisters. In a series of striking paintings, he depicted the mangy Old Man dressed as a street-smart hipster in a black leather jacket, Levi's, and Converse high tops. "Some say that Coyote is on the streets and in the alleys," Fonseca wrote. "That Coyote lives in L.A. and San Francisco and eats out of garbage cans. . . . That Coyote doesn't like change. That Coyote is change."

★

There was indeed change. When PG&E went bankrupt in the early twenty-first century, the court created a Stewardship Council to administer the disposition of the utility's thousands of acres of watershed. In 2014 the council agreed to turn over the pristine Humbug Valley in the High Sierra to the conservation management of the Maidu Summit Consortium, an organization of several autonomous bands. Gary Snyder and Raymond Dasmann had imagined this possibility in the 1970s, but it took years of Maidu activism to achieve. For the first time in California history, ancestral homeland was returned to Native hands. "The Maidu people take solace in the knowledge that we will forever be connected to our homeland," said spokesman Kenneth Holbrook. "We have now reclaimed a future for our children that is uniquely Maidu."

The following year, the Pit River Tribe and the U.S. Forest Service announced a similar agreement, giving Native people a stewardship role over some 64,000 acres of their forest homeland. A lot had changed since 1971, when dozens of Pit River people were beaten and arrested for a symbolic occupation of that same land.

In 2018 the city council of Humboldt voted unanimously to return Indian Island, in Humboldt Bay, to the Wiyot people. The Wiyots had long hoped to regain possession of the island, which they considered a sacred place. In 1860 it had been the site of a horrible massacre by White vigilantes of 250 members of their small community, an atrocity reported by the young journalist Bret Harte. At the council meeting, former mayor Frank Jager presented a formal statement of apology. "Nothing we can say or do can make up for what occurred on that night of infamy," it read. "We can, however, work to remove the prejudice and bigotry that still exists in our society today." Afterward Cheryl Seidner, Wiyot tribal chairwoman, sang a song in the language of her people as members of the council stood with bowed heads. "We need to come together as a community," she said. "That rip in our society needs to be mended."

The following year, Governor Gavin Newsom issued an executive order, apologizing on behalf of California's citizens for the state's history of "violence, maltreatment, and neglect" of Native Californians. "Californians must reckon with our dark history," the governor said to a group of Native leaders from around the state. "We can never undo the wrongs, . . . but we can work together to build bridges, tell the truth about our past, and begin to heal deep wounds." Assemblyman James Ramos of San Bernardino, the first Native Californian elected to the state legislature, sang a song of thanksgiving while the group stood together. "It's healing to hear your words," Erica Pinto, representing the Kumeyaays, told Governor Newsom. "But the real results will live in actions. This is just the first step."

Acknowledgments

Christopher Rogers, my editor at Yale University Press, suggested this project to me at precisely the right moment. His advice and suggestions were enormously helpful, and this book would not have appeared without his assistance. The staff at Yale University's Sterling Memorial Library provided published materials and access to scholarly and archival databases online. Adina Popescu Berk took over editorial duties in midstream and didn't miss a stroke. Ash Lago handled administrative details. Weshoyot Alvitre drew the evocative illustrations. Bill Nelson created the maps. Anne Canright copyedited the manuscript, and Joyce Ippolito got it into print. I am indebted to them all.

Jeremy Garskof and Lalo Garskof, two of my grandchildren, read chapters and provided the perspective of young readers. Professors Michael Magliari and William Deverell furnished detailed scholarly criticism that strengthened my reading of the evidence and saved me from errors of fact. I am, of course, solely responsible for those that remain. As always, Michele Hoffnung listened as I read each chapter aloud, offering cogent criticism as well as needed encouragement. Thank you, Michele, for your love and support.

When I was a boy, my grandmother, Maude McFarlin Delaley, told me the kinds of stories that inspired this book. Stories about coming to California, about living and working in Los Angeles during the twenties and thirties, about the tragic loss of her son in World War II, shortly before my birth, and about her passionate support for organized labor, the Democratic Party, and Jimmy Roosevelt. Her tales of California history remain as vivid for me now as when I heard them, decades ago. They played an important role in making me a historian, so I dedicate this book to her.

Index

abortion, 391

Adamic, Louis, 304

aerospace industry, 371, 382, 412, 420

African Americans: case of Archy Lee, 213–14, 216–19; jobs for, 307–8; in Los Angeles, 306–9, 373–74, 414–16; migration to California, 350–51; in politics, 406–9, 411–13, 434; rights of, 216, 231, 252. *See also* civil rights movement

agribusiness, 401, 403–4. *See also* agriculture

Agricultural Workers Organization, 325

agriculture: and agribusiness, 403–4; in the Central Valley, 294–95; citrus growers, 252–54, 261, 301; cotton, 327; and early California peoples, 14, 16–17, 22, 88; at Fort Ross, 76–77; grapes, 379, 401; growth of, 341; hops farming, 323–24; and labor unions, 322–31; laborers

for, 320–31; in rural California, 403–4; in the San Joaquin Valley, 401; in Santa Clara Valley, 257–58; in Southern California, 251, 257; wheat, 257

aircraft industry, 304, 349

Alcatraz Island, 389–90

Aleutian Islands, 70–71

Aleuts, 70–74

Alexander, George, 286–87

Algondones Dunes, 55

Alien Land Law, 363, 364

Allayaud, Bill, 405

Alta California newspaper, 203, 204, 207, 208, 217, 229, 230

Alvarado, Don Mariano: arrest and imprisonment, 152, 155–58; and the Californios, 115–16, 117, 152; dismissal by Santa Anna, 132; as general of Mexican military, 118, 123, 127–28; and the issue of property rights, 193; vs. Micheltorena, 132, 134–36; as state senator, 188; wars of expansion, 203

Alvarado, Doña Francisca, 156
Alvarado, José Francisco, 92
Alvarado, Juan Bautista: after the Mexican American War, 170; arrest of, 134; avoiding politics, 183–84; as civil administrator, 109–10; education and family, 90–92, 94; as interim governor, 117, 126, 128–29, 131–32; as legislator, 114–16; in Monterey, 150; and the Native Californians, 118–19; negotiation with Larkin, 160–61; negotiations with southern faction, 117; plans for California independence, 105, 134–36, 151; in political service, 99; on Stockton's ultimatum to Castro, 163; and Sutter, 121, 123
Alvarado, María Josepha, 92
Alvarado, Salvador, 156
Álvarez, María Rufina, 92–93
American Communist Party, 327, 330, 331, 365
American Federation of Labor (AFL), 322, 374
American River, 121
Anaheim Colony, 251
Anderson, M. Kat, 16
anti-Semitism, 265, 274, 305
antiwar protests, 383–85, 388
Anza, Juan Bautista de, 55–56, 58, 83
Argentina, 78–79, 81
Argentina (frigate), 79
Argüello, José Dario, 84
Argüello, Luis Antonio, 85
Arroyo Seco Parkway, 340
Asisara, Lorenzo, 63–64
Assing, Norman (Sang Yuen), 230

Associated Chinese Teachers of San Francisco, 418
Associated Farmers of California, 328
Associates, The, 227, 228, 242, 245, 246, 247, 251, 259, 266, 281
Atchison, Topeka, and Santa Fe Railroad, 261
atomic bombs, 371–72
Austin, Mary, 298
Austin, Minnie, 258
automobiles, 302–3
Ávila, José María, 104
Aztec empire, 24–25

Baba, Kosaburo, 322
Baker, Edward, 217, 218–20
Banca d'Italia, 305
Bandini, Juan, 102, 117
Bank of America, 305, 328
Bank of California, 245, 266
Bardacke, Frank, 384
Bartleson, John, 127
basketmaking, 14–15
Bass, Karen, 434
Bay Area, 435–36
Bay Area Council of American Indians, 389
Bay Bridge, 340
Bay of Smokes, 28, 36
Bear Flag Rebellion, 157–58, 187, 205
beatnik generation, 369–71
Bell, Sally, 211, 212
Benton, Thomas Hart, 187
Bepp, Yoneo, 349
Berkeley. See University of California: at Berkeley
Bernard, Reuben, 241
Bethel, Rosalie, 17
Bidwell, John, 127, 154, 155

Bidwell-Bartleson Party, 142
Bigler, John, 229–30
Big Sur, 37
Bishop, Virgil, 17–18
Black Panther Party for Self-
    Defense, 385–87, 388
Bloody Island Massacre, 208
Board of Equalization, 247
Bodega Bay, 70
Bonanza Kings, 244–45, 266, 277
Booth, Newton, 242, 243
Boscana, Gerónimo, 65–66
Botts, Charles T., 185, 186
Bouchard, Hipólito, 78–82, 84,
    131
Boyarsky, Bill, 377
Bracero Program, 350, 374, 379
Bradley, Tom, 406–9, 412–13,
    415–16
Branciforte (Santa Cruz), 83
Brannan, Samuel, 173, 191–92
Bridger, Jim, 143–44, 145
Broderick, David C., 196–97,
    214–15, 219–20, 221
Brown, Edmund G. "Pat," 375–80,
    402, 438
Brown, Jerry, 402–3, 438–39
Brown, Kathleen, 421
Brown, Willie, 409, 411
Brown Berets, 386
Browne, J. Ross, 251
Brown v. Board of Education, 367
Buchanan, James, 215
Buffum, Edward, 180–81, 183
Bureau of Indian Affairs, 318, 319,
    442
Burkett, Frederick Marion Jr.,
    300, 355
Burnett, Peter H., 191–92, 209,
    217
Bustamante, Cruz, 427–29, 433

Cabrillo, Juan Rodriguez, 24–27
Caen, Herb, 369
Cahuenga Pass, 103, 167
Calac, Olegario, 256, 311, 317
Calhoun, John C., 187
California Agricultural Labor
    Relations Act, 403
California Association of Realtors,
    376
California Battalion, 161–62, 167,
    177
California Environmental Quality
    Act (CEQA), 395–96
California Federation of Civil
    Unity, 362–63
California Indian Association,
    313–14
California Indians. See Native
    Californians
California Institute of Technology
    (Caltech), 303
California Star, 204
California Tomorrow, 419
California Trail, 1
California Woman Suffrage
    Society, 279
Californian (San Francisco
    newspaper), 204, 226, 234
Californios: Castro and Alvarado's
    defense of, 99–100; condemn-
    ing the uprising, 117; and the
    constitutional convention,
    185; defeating Kearney, 166;
    deportation of "foreigners"
    by, 125–26; divisions among,
    136–37; and the goal of inde-
    pendence, 95–96, 105, 107–10,
    112, 115, 134–35, 151–52; land
    grants to, 192–93; Native Cali-
    fornian perspective on, 118–19;
    rebellion in Los Angeles, 165;

Californios (*continued*)
skirmished with "Bears," 159;
vs. Victoria
capitalism: crony, 277; industrial,
242, 282, 285; and the Progressives, 334; Sinclair's indictment
of, 332–33
Carrillo, José Antonio, 102, 184
Carrillo, María Antonia, 117
Castañeda de Valenciana, Emilia,
309
Castillo, Adam, 318–19
Castro, José Antonio: vs. the
Bears, 162–63; deportation of
"foreigners" by, 125, 126; deposing Gutiérrez, 115; education
and family, 90–93, 94; as governor of Baja California, 183–84;
in Monterey, 137; and the Native Californians, 107, 118–19;
negotiation with Sloat, 160–61;
negotiations with southern
faction, 117; plans for California
independence, 134–36, 150–52;
in political service, 99–100,
109–10; response to Stockton's
ultimatum, 163; returning to
California from Mexico, 170;
Stockton's denouncement of,
162
Castro, José Tiburcio, 92
Castro, María Modesta, 93
Catalina Island, 27, 36
Catholicism, 43. *See also individual missions by name*
Caucasian League, 245
Cavendish, Thomas, 34–35
Central Pacific Railroad, 227–28,
239–40, 242, 245, 247, 251
Central Valley, 3, 86, 88, 97, 123,
151, 239, 294–95, 342

Central Valley Project (CVP),
340–41, 401
Cermeño, Sebastian Rodriguez,
34–35
César, Julio, 64
Chambers, Pat, 330–31
Chandler, Harry, 333
Channel Islands, 27, 29, 82
Charles III (king of Spain), 43
Chavez, Cesar, 353, 379, 387, 403,
423
Chicanos, 386
Chico, Mariano, 112–14
Chinese Exclusion Act, 248–49,
268, 321, 323
Chinese immigrants: as farm
laborers, 245, 320–22; opposi-
tion to, 228–29, 236–37, 239,
243–47, 269, 294; rights of,
231; violence against, 244–45;
women, 229
Civilian Conservation Corps, 334
civil rights movement, 376,
385–87
Civil War, 221
Clappe, Louise Smith ("Dame
Shirley"), 178, 179–80, 182
Clay, Henry, 148
Clemens, Samuel (Mark Twain),
226, 235
Cleveland, Grover, 249, 267
Cliff House, 260
climate, 3–4
Coachella Valley, 315, 316, 426
Cold War, 360, 371, 381, 420
Cole, Cornelius, 179
Colorado River, 295
Colorado River Project, 340
Columbus, Christopher, 22
communism, 330–31, 365
Compromise of 1850, 190

Comstock Lode, 232, 244, 292
constitutional convention,
    183–84; creation of counties,
    188–89; formation of state
    government, 187–88; question
    of slavery, 185–86; question of
    statehood, 184–85; ratification
    of constitution, 186–87; second,
    247
contraception, 391–92
Contreras, Miguel, 423–24
Coolbrith, Ina Donna (Josephine
    Donna Smith), 233, 234–35,
    290–91
Coon, Nathan, 213
Corney, Peter, 80, 81, 82
Coronado, Francisco Vásquez de,
    22, 24
Costansó, Miguel, 40–41, 47, 49
Covid-19 pandemic, 431
Crespí, Juan, 44–45, 48, 49
Criminal Syndicalism Act, 325–26,
    328, 365
Crocker, Charles, 227, 228,
    242–43
Crocker, Edwin, 214
Cronise, Titus Fey, 16
Cuban Missile Crisis, 372
Cyane, USS (sloop-of-war), 130

Dana, Richard Henry, 86
Dasmann, Elizabeth, 397, 404
Dasmann, Raymond, 393–94, 396,
    397, 404–5, 443
Davidson, Sara, 378
Davis, Gray, 421, 427–29
Davis, Jacob, 265–67
Davis, Sylvester, 363
Death Valley, 2
Deaver, Michael, 381
Decker, Caroline, 330–31

Del Monte, 328
Democratic Party, 335–36,
    338–39, 375; Hispanic mem-
    bership, 424–25
Destruction of California, The
    (Dasmann), 393–94, 397, 405
Deukmejian, George, 412
Dewey, George, 267
Dewey, Thomas, 366
DeWitt, John, 348
Didion, Joan, 404
disease: among early Californians,
    18; diphtheria, 63; dysentery,
    40, 63, 324; malaria, 99, 222;
    measles, 63, 99; scurvy, 32, 40,
    45, 48, 80; smallpox, 99; spread
    by Spanish colonizers, 49, 51,
    60, 63, 99; syphilis, 63; tuber-
    culosis, 63
Donner, George, 144
Donner, Jacob, 144
Donner, Tamsen, 144
Donner Party, 144–46
Donner Pass, 1
"Double V" campaign, 351, 357
Drabelle, Dennis, 228
Drake, Francis, 32
Drakes Bay, 35
Durán, Narciso, 94, 97, 101
Durazo, María Elena, 423–24
Durst, Ralph, 323, 324
Dust Bowl, 341
Dymally, Mervyn, 409

earthquakes, 3, 41; San Fran-
    cisco 1906, 272–75
Echeandía, José María, 94,
    95–96, 98, 100, 102–3, 105–6,
    110
economic growth, 303–4, 349
Eden in Jeopardy (Lillard), 396

education: bilingual, 422; in colonial California, 89–90; funding for, 361, 427, 440; for Native Californians, 441; revamping history and social studies textbooks, 417–19; segregation in, 363, 364, 367

Eel River dam, 400

Eisenhower, Dwight D., 366–67

Elizabeth I (queen of England), 32

Elliot-Santos, Angela, 441

Elliott, James, 347

Emancipation Proclamation, 221

Employers' Association, 269, 273

End Poverty in California (EPIC), 333, 335

Endo, Mitsuye, 363, 364

environmental movement, 395–405

Espree, Edythe, 309

Estanislao (Yokut leader), 97–98, 105

Ex parte Archy, 214, 219

Ex parte Mitsuye Endo, 364

Executive Order 9066, 347–48

Fages, Pedro, 40–41, 53

Fair Employment Practices Commission (FEPC), 350, 362, 375, 377

Fallon, Michael, 380

Faragher, Alvin Robert, 341–42

Farías, Valentín Gómez, 107, 108

Farmers' Alliance, 278

Feather River dam, 400

Federal Housing Authority, 373

Feinstein, Dianne, 409, 411–12

feminism, 390–92

Ferlinghetti, Lawrence, 371

Fernandez, José, 92

Figueroa, José Secundino, 106, 107–10, 112

Fillmore, Millard, 209

fishing, 14, 28

Flores, Dan, 19

Flores, José María, 163, 165, 167

Foltz, Clara Shortridge, 279–80

Fonseca, Harry, 443

Font, Pedro, 52

Ford, Richard "Blackie," 324

Forrest, French, 126

Fort Ross, 74–77, 80, 106, 122, 128

Fortunate Eagle, Adam, 389–90

"forty-niners," 175. *See also* gold rush

Free Soil Democrats, 215–16, 219, 221

Free Speech Movement, 378

freeway system, 340, 361

Frémont, John Charles: arrest of Don Mariano, 154–57; as candidate for president, 215–16; in Monterey, 150–51, 161–62, 165–66; negotiation with Californios, 167–68; occupation of Los Angeles, 164; in San Diego, 162; as senator, 187; skirmishes with Californios, 159; as state senator, 190, 193

Fresno Bee, 328

Friedan, Betty, 391

Frumkin, Leo, 348

Frye, Marquette, 377–78

fur trade, 71–72, 84, 85, 122

Galaup, Jean-François de, 65

Gálvez, José de, 43

Garcés, Francisco, 58–59

Garcia, Jerry, 380

gasoline tax, 361

Gates, Daryl, 415

Gentleman's Agreement, 287, 323
geography, 1–3
George, Henry, 238, 243
Giannini, Amadeo Peter, 305
Gillespie, Archibald, 164–65
Ginsberg, Allen, 370–71, 397–98
Gitlin, Todd, 381
Gladstein, Richard, 331
Glendale, 304
Glenn, Hugh, 257
global warming, 405
gold rush: conflict between Whites and settlers, 182–83; prospectors, 172–76, 178; San Francisco, 6, 173; start of, 170–72; vigilante justice, 180–81; violence during, 199; waning of, 181–82; women and, 176–77
Golden Era (literary newspaper), 225, 233
Golden Gate Park, 380, 398
Gordon, Laura de Force, 279–80
Graham, Isaac, 115–16, 125, 126, 135, 136
Grant, Ulysses S., 256, 317
grape boycott, 379, 401
Grapes of Wrath, The (Steinbeck), 342
Great Depression, 6, 326, 332
Great Migration, 350
Great Recession, 437, 439
Greene, Marilyn, 344, 356
Grubbe, Jeff, 316
Guam, 37, 267
Guerra y Noriega, Angustias de la, 96
Guerra y Noriega, José de la, 117
Guerra y Noriega, Pablo de la, 113, 186
guest worker program, 350

Gutierrez, Elisa, 432
Gutiérrez, Nicolás, 114–15
Gwin, William M., 184, 187, 190, 193, 214, 221

Hackel, Steven, 51
Hall, Michelle, 432
"Ham 'n' Eggs" movement, 339
Hánc'ibyjim (Tom Young), 12
Hangtown, 191
Hanson, Victor Davis, 404
Hardy, James, 214, 216–17, 218
Harper's magazine, 291
Harriman, Job, 287
Harris, Kamala, 432–33
Harte, Bret, 224–25, 230, 233, 235–57, 256, 444
Hastings, Lansford W., 138–40, 143, 144–47, 150
hate crimes, 432
Hawaiian Islands, 71–72, 78, 80, 432; annexation of, 268; Pearl Harbor, 344–45
Hawkins, Augustus, 409
Hayes, Rutherford B., 245
Haynes, John Randolph, 278, 283
health insurance, 360
healthcare, 441
Hearst, George, 277
Hearst, William Randolph, 277
Hedgerow Vineyard, 258
Heizer, Robert, 209
Hetch Hetchy dam, 297–98
Hetch Hetchy Valley, 297
Himes, Chester, 351
hippies, 380
Hispanics: juvenile gangs, 354–55; in Los Angeles, 308–9, 414–16, 419; in politics, 427, 433–34; as voting bloc, 424–25. See also Mexican immigrants

historical empathy, 8–9
Holbrook, Kenneth, 443
Hollenbeck Junior High, 344–45, 348, 356
Holliday, J. S., 179
Hollywood, 304, 306
Hollywood Bowl, 335
Homestead Act, 258
homosexuality. *See* LGBTQ community
Honig, Bill, 417
Hoover, Herbert, 333, 335, 340
Hoover, J. Edgar, 347
Hoover Dam, 340
Hopkins, Mark, 227
HoSang, Daniel Martinez, 422
hospital system, 359
Hotel Employees and Restaurant Employees Union, 423
Howden, Edward, 377
"Human Be-In," 380, 398
human rights, 310–17
Humboldt State College, 393–94
Humboldt Times, 189
Humbug Valley, 443
Humphrey, Hubert, 388
Hundley, Norris, 341
hunting, 22
Huntington, Collis P., 227, 243, 281–82
Huntington, Henry E., 286, 299, 307
Hurtado, Albert, 122
Hutch, Ella Hill, 411
Hutchinson, C. Alan, 108
hydroelectric power, 301, 340, 400

Ide, William B., 154–56
If He Hollers Let Him Go (Himes), 351

Imperial Valley, 295, 326, 340
Inca empire, 24
Independence Rock, 143, 144
Indian Bar camp, 178
Indian Center of San Francisco, 389
Indian Citizenship Act, 317
Indian Island, 443–44
Indians of All Tribes, 389–90
individualism, 278
In Dubious Battle (Steinbeck), 328–30
Industrial Workers of the World (IWW), 282, 324–26, 330
Inland Empire, 427, 436, 437
International Longshoreman's Association, 337
internment camps, 348–49, 434
irrigation, 258, 294–96, 401
Irwin, William, 245, 263
Ishi (Yahi man), 314–15

Jackson, Andrew, 131
Jackson, Helen Hunt, 255–56
Jager, Frank, 444
Jamul Indian Village, 441
Japanese Americans: as farm laborers, 321–22, 323; as immigrants, 268, 269, 287–88, 306; in internment camps, 347–49, 363–64, 367–68, 434; Issei and Nisei, 346–47, 363; jobs for, 308; in Los Angeles, 308–9; opposition to, 287–88; in politics, 434; and World War II, 344–47
Japanese-Mexican Labor Association, 322–23
Jayme, Luis, 46, 47, 56–57
Jenkins, John, 197
Jesuits, 43

John Birch Society, 382
Johnson, Hiram, 283–86, 288, 324, 333, 334, 340, 347, 358, 375, 438
Johnson, J. Neely, 198
Johnson, Lyndon B., 377, 378–79, 382–83, 387
Jones, Mary, 142
Jones, Thomas ap Catesby, 130–31, 133–34, 140, 154
Jungle, The (Sinclair), 334
"Justice for Janitors" campaign, 424

Kearney, Denis, 246
Kearney, Stephen Watts, 166, 168, 248
Kelsey, Andrew, 205–7
Kelsey, Ben, 142
Kelsey, Nancy, 142
Kennedy, John F., 375
Kennedy, Robert F., 387–88, 434
Keseberg, Louis, 145–46
Kido, Koichi, 346
Kim, Young, 434–35
Kinajan, María Dolores, 54
King, Martin Luther, Jr., 387
King, Rodney, 415–16, 420
King, Thomas Starr, 220, 221–22, 225
Kintpuash (Modoc headman, "Captain Jack"), 241–42
Kittle, Robert, 58–59
Klamath River Jack, 17
Knifechief, Tom, 390
Kolonia Ross, 74
Konkow Trail of Tears, 223
Konnick (Nisenan sheepherder), 201
Korean Americans, 434–35
Korematsu, Fred, 363–64

Korematsu v. U.S., 363–64
Kuskov, Ivan, 72–74, 76

Labor Council of Los Angeles, 322
labor strikes, 266–67, 269–70, 287, 337–38, 358; in agriculture, 322–23, 324, 326–31
labor unions, 268–70, 278, 285–87, 304, 322–31, 324; Hotel Employees and Restaurant Employees Union, 423; Industrial Workers of the World (IWW), 282, 324–26, 330; International Longshoreman's Association, 337–38; Los Angeles County Federation of Labor, 424; Service Employees International Union (SEIU), 424; Teamsters Union, 402, 413; United Farm Workers (UFW), 379, 401–2, 403, 413, 422–24
Lake Tulare, 295
La Marr, Cindy, 400
land grants, 110, 119, 192–93
Land of Little Rain, The (Austin), 298
Lange, Dorothea, 342–43
Larkin, Thomas O., 133, 137, 138, 150–52, 157, 159–61, 184
Lassen National Park, 293
Lasuén, Fermin, 64
Lau, Gordon, 411
Lee, Archy, 213–14, 216–19, 220
Legaspi, José, 421
legislation: Act for the Government and Protection of Indians, 189; Alien Land Law, 363, 364; California Agricultural Labor Relations Act, 403; California

legislation (*continued*)
   Environmental Quality Act
   (CEQA), 395–96; California
   Land Act, 193; Chinese Exclusion Act, 248–49, 268, 321,
   323; Chinese tax, 230; Criminal
   Syndicalism Act, 325–26, 328,
   365; "direct democracy" amendment, 284–85, 288; electoral
   laws, 284; Foreign Miners' Tax,
   189–90; Fugitive Slave Act,
   190, 213–14; Indian Citizenship Act, 317; labor laws, 284;
   National Environmental Policy
   Act, 395; Pacific Railroad Act,
   227; Proposition 13, 397, 413,
   421; Proposition 54, 428–29;
   Proposition 187, 421, 424,
   433; Racial Privacy Initiative,
   428–29; Relocation Act, 388;
   support for state militias,
   208–9
Levi Strauss & Co., 264–67, 268,
   270, 274
LGBTQ community, 233, 410–11
liberalism, 84–85, 94
Librado, Fernando, 63
Lienhard, Heinrich, 201–2
Lillard, Richard, 396
Lincoln, Abraham, 221, 227
Lindsay, Lulu, 266–67
Lippitt, Francis J., 186
livestock: in Native communities,
   86–87; in Southern California,
   250, 254; at the Spanish missions, 50–51, 56–57, 62–63,
   85–86
Lizarras, J. M., 322
localism, 13, 15
London, Jack, 235, 274–75
lone star flag, 116, 125

Long Beach, 108, 304, 305, 307,
   335, 412
Long Beach Independent, 354
Loomis, Augustis, 230–31
Los Angeles: African American
   community in, 350–51; anti-
   Chinese violence in, 244–45;
   Boyle Heights, 305; under
   Bradley as mayor, 406–7, 409,
   412–13, 415–16; Californios rebellion, 133, 135, 165; Californios
   vs. Bears, 161; Dasmann's cri-
   tique of, 394; deepwater port
   at, 281, 303; ethnic divisions in,
   308–9; expansion of, 436; under
   Gillespie, 164–65; growth of,
   262–63, 281, 301, 303, 361–62,
   396, 412; Hispanic population
   of, 250, 306, 308–9, 337, 414–16,
   419; homosexual community in,
   410; labor unions in, 286–87,
   304; multicultural restaurants
   in, 419–20; Native Americans
   in, 388; occupied by Stockton
   and Frémont, 164–65; protests
   to overdevelopment of, 396; railroad in, 240; Rodney King riot,
   415–16, 420; segregation in,
   309; settlers in, 84; Stockton's
   capture of, 167; wartime economy in, 353; water for, 295–96,
   298; Watts neighborhood,
   377–78; during World War II,
   355–56
Los Angeles Aqueduct, 296, 298
Los Angeles Basin, 3
Los Angeles County Federation
   of Labor, 424
Los Angeles Herald, 296
Los Angeles Police Department
   (LAPD), 407, 414–15

Los Angeles Star, 210
Los Angeles State University, 396
Los Angeles Times, 286, 286–87, 299, 303, 317, 333, 337, 345, 347, 390, 391, 414, 420, 423
Loveless, Juanita, 355
Lubin, Simon J., 328
Lugo, Francisco Salvador, 91
Lugo, Leonicio, 310–12
Lugo, María Antonia, 91–92
Lynch, Judge, 280

Madley, Benjamin, 210
Mahoney, Margaret, 273
Maidu Summit Consortium, 443
Malcolm X, 385
Malibu Canyon, 28
"Man with the Hoe, The" (Markham), 321–22
Manojo, Cristóbal, 118
Manzanar, 348–49
Manzanar Free Press, 362
Manzanita Band of Kumeyaays, 441
maps: California, 5; of counties, 188; rivers and canals/aqueducts, 402
Markham, Edward, 321
Marshall, James, 170–71, 183
Mason, Richard, 170, 172, 174, 194
Matsui, Doris, 434
Maya civilization, 24
McBride, John, 138–39
McCarthy, Eugene, 387
McClatchy, James, 192
McDaniel, Hattie, 363
McDougal, John, 229
McFarlin, Dora, 300, 306
McFarlin, Marcellus, 300, 306
McFarlin, Maude, 300–301, 305–6

McKinley, William, 282
McLemore, Henry, 345–46
McMahon, Clarissa Shortall, 409
McNamara, James, 287
McNamara, John, 287
McWilliams, Carey, 342
Means, LaNada, 389
Melendres, Alejandrina Murillo, 61
Méndez, Felicitas, 363
Méndez, Gonzalo, 363
Méndez v. Westminster, 364
Merchants and Manufacturers Association, 286
Merriam, Frank, 337, 339, 358
Métini Protocol, 73
Metro-Goldwyn-Mayer, 338
Mexican immigrants: deportation of, 336–37; as farm laborers, 321–22, 326, 342, 349–50, 374, 379; jobs for, 307; in Los Angeles, 250, 306, 337; and the "racial propositions," 421–23; repatriation programs for, 336–37. *See also* Hispanics
Mexico: independence from Spain, 85, 93–94; Santa Anna's coup, 107; U.S. war with, 149–50, 153–54, 169
Michelson, Miriam, 274
Micheltorena, José Manuel, 132–36
Milk, Harvey, 410–12
Miller, Loren, 373, 378
Milliken, Randall, 62
missionaries, Spanish, 43, 44, 46
Mission Indian Federation (MIF), 317–19
Mission La Purísima, 87–88
Mission San Buenaventura, 63
Mission San Carlos Borromeo, 50–52, 62, 65, 67, 85, 110

Mission San Diego, 46–49, 51, 57, 60
Mission San Fernando, 103
Mission San Francisco, 62, 64
Mission San Francisco Solano, 76, 106, 110
Mission San Gabriel, 53–54, 56, 62, 65, 66, 104, 126
Mission San José, 62, 64, 97, 98, 122
Mission San Juan Bautista, 115, 135
Mission San Juan Capistrano, 65, 82
Mission San Luis Obispo, 92
Mission San Luis Rey, 62, 64, 66, 97, 109, 137, 251, 254
Mission San Rafael, 76
Mission Santa Barbara, 62, 87–88
Mission Santa Clara, 62
Mission Santa Cruz, 63–64, 67
Mission Santa Inés, 87
Modesto, 97, 297
monopolies, 242
Monterey, 130–31
Monterey Bay, 28, 37, 48, 83, 126, 157
Monterey presidio, 78, 79, 89–90, 98–99, 115–16, 125, 131
Morales, Beatrice, 352
Morro Bay, 33
Moscone, George, 411–12
motion picture industry, 304, 306, 338
Mountains of California, The (Muir), 291
Mt. Whitney, 2
Muir, John, 289–98
Mulholland, William, 295–96, 299
Murderer's Bar, 182
Murietta, Joaquin, 200

Murphy, Frank, 364
Mussel Slough shootout, 259–60, 277
Myers, Dowell, 431

Nash, Gary C., 418, 420
National Environmental Policy Act, 395
National Industrial Recovery Act, 337
National Organization of Women (NOW), 391
Nation magazine, 236
Native Americans: and Alcatraz Island, 389–90; Hopi, 59; Mojaves, 59; Tlingits, 72–73. See also Native Californian bands and tribes; Native Californians
Native Californian bands and tribes: Achuymawis, 19; Agua Calientes, 315–19, 425–26; Awahnechees, 222, 294, 316; Cahuillas, 16, 310–12, 315–19, 426; Chumash, 28, 29, 33–34, 87–88, 96, 97; Coastal Miwoks, 35, 70, 73, 75, 76; Cochimís, 44, 46–49, 54; Cupeños, 311–13, 317; Hupas, 174; Jamuls, 441; Konkows, 10–12; Kumeyaays, 21–22, 25–27, 36, 39–41, 44–47, 49, 56–57, 60–61, 426, 441–42, 444; Luiseños, 60, 66, 97, 109, 251, 254–57, 317, 426; Maidus, 10–12, 14, 123, 174, 222–23, 399, 400, 442–43; Miwoks, 121–24, 128, 135, 174; Modocs, 240–41; Monos, 17–18; Mono Lake Paiutes, 12–13; Nisenans, 171, 174, 182–83, 201–3; Ohlones, 37, 50–51, 62, 67–69; Paiutes,

16–17; Pimuvits, 27, 36; Pit
River Tribe, 399–400, 443;
Pomos, 16, 18, 28–29, 72–73, 75,
205–8, 400; Quechans, 15, 22,
55, 57–58, 84; Salinans, 62;
Shastas, 174; Sinkyowns, 211;
Tongvas, 27, 53–54, 62, 66;
Wintus, 18, 210–11; Wiyots,
224, 443–44; Yahis, 314–15;
Yanas, 19; Yokuts, 97, 99, 123,
315; Yukis, 400; Yuroks, 17, 174,
312, 426

Native Californians: and the 1836
rebellion, 118–19; as agricultural
workers, 251, 253; campaign to
exterminate, 203, 205, 208–11,
224, 238, 241, 314; casinos run
by, 426–27, 441–42; and the
civil rights movement, 388–90;
in colonial California, 82–84;
conflict with settlers, 182–83,
203–5; diversity of, 5–6; education for, 253; at Fort Ross,
74–77; loss of homelands,
398–400; meeting Europeans,
21–29; and Old Man Coyote,
18–20, 61–62, 118–19, 203, 398,
442–43; question of suffrage,
186–87, 189; and the railroads,
240–41; and the Red Power
movement, 425–26; removal to
reservations, 13, 209, 210, 222,
240, 241, 256, 310–19, 388, 398,
400–401, 425–26, 441–42; state
violence against, 204–12; Story-
tellers, 10–12; treaty negotiations with, 209–10, 254, 313–14,
401; working for ranchers, 174,
176

Navarro, Ramón Jil, 190
navel oranges, 252–54

Negro Victory Committee, 351
New Deal, 339, 340–41, 343, 358,
360, 401
Newsom, Gavin, 205, 433, 444
Newton, Huey P., 385
New York Times, 266
New York Tribune, 248
Nicolás José (Tongva man),
66–67
Nieto, Jacob, 274
Nieto, Manuel, 107
Nixon, Richard, 375, 390, 395
Nolasquez, Rosinda, 312
Norris, Frank, 276–77
North Beach district, 369–71, 397,
410
*Nuestra Señora de Buena Esper-
anza* (galleon), 33

Oakes, Richard, 389, 400
Oakland, 235, 267, 275, 282, 303,
321, 340, 358, 362, 363, 384–87,
418, 432–33, 438
Octopus, The (Norris), 276–77
Olsen, Laurie, 419
Olson, Culbert, 339, 346, 359, 365
Oregon Country, 149
organized labor. *See* labor unions
Ortega, José Francisco, 81, 84, 95
Ortner, Viola, 425
Otis, Harrison Gray, 286, 299, 333
Our National Parks (Muir), 293
Overland Monthly (literary jour-
nal), 226–27, 230, 233, 234–35,
237, 238, 255, 291
"Overland Trinity, The," 233
Owens, Florence, 343
Owens River, 298–99
Owens Valley, 296, 298
Oyama, Fred, 363
Oyama v. California, 364

Pacheco, Romualdo (father), 103–4
Pacheco, Romulado (son), 242–43
Pacific Gas and Electric (PG&E), 301–2, 328, 399, 428, 443
Pacific Ocean, 3, 30–31
Pacific steamship lines, 6
Padilla, Alex, 433
Palm Canyon, 316
Palm Springs, 316, 318–19, 425
pantheism, 290
Pardee, George, 282
Parrish, Essie, 29
Partridge, John, 271
Patencio, Francisco, 316, 319
Payeras, Mariano, 86–87
Pearl Harbor, 344–45
Pechanga Valley, 256
People's Party, 281
Pérez, Andrea, 363
Pérez, Juan, 39
Pérez v. Sharp, 364–65
Phelan, James D., 269, 270, 273, 274, 345
Philip II (king of Spain), 30, 34
Philippines, 30–31, 37, 42; war of independence, 267–68
Pico, Andrés, 166, 167
Pico, Anthony, 426
Pico, Pío de Jesús, 102, 105, 117, 136–37, 151; vs. the Bears, 162; and the Californios, 160–61; retreat to Mexico, 163–64; returning to California from Mexico, 170
Pimu island, 27
Pinto, Erica, 441–42, 444
Pit River Tribe, 443
Placerville, 191
plate tectonics, 2–3

Point Conception, 28
Polk, James K., 148–50, 153–54, 161, 165–66, 169, 174
population: decreasing White population, 431; diversity in, 419–20, 431–33; early migrants, 13–14, 16; ethnic minorities, 372–73; foreign immigrants, 113, 195–96, 305–6, 413–14; German immigrants, 251, 265, 268; growth in, 376; homeless, 439–40; immigrant labor, 6–7, 228–29; Japanese immigrants, 268, 269, 287–88, 306; Jewish community, 265, 305, 309; Kānakas, 72, 75, 80, 122, 124, 189; labor migration, 6–7; leaving California, 430–31, 439–40; *mestizos,* 83; *mulatos,* 83; overland emigrants, 126–27, 140–46, 260–61, 304–5; *pardos,* 83; Russian fur traders, 6, 42, 71; undocumented immigrants, 421–22; wartime migrants, 349; waves of migration, 430. *See also* African Americans; Chinese immigrants; Hispanics; Japanese Americans; Mexican immigrants; Native Californians; Spaniards
Portilla, Pablo de la, 102–3, 104, 105
Portnoy, Joe, 348
Portolá, Gaspar de, 43, 45, 48, 49, 50, 109
poverty, 439–40, 442
power supply: electricity crisis, 427–28; hydroelectric plants, 301, 340, 400; petroleum refining, 349; petroleum reserves, 302; power companies, 301–2

preemption claims, 259
Progressives, 283–86, 287–88, 333, 334, 338
property values, 396–97
Proposition 13, 397, 413, 421
Proposition 54, 428–29
Proposition 187, 421, 424, 433
Pullman Palace Car Company, 267
Punta de los Muertos (Dead Man's Point), 41, 45

Quechan people, 2, 15
Quintana, Andrés, 67–69

Racial Privacy Initiative, 428–29
racism: against African Americans, 307, 351, 355, 362–63, 373–78, 385–87; anti-Asian, 287–88; anti-Chinese, 294; anti-Japanese, 345–46, 362–63; anti-Mexican, 307, 354–55, 362–63, 373–75, 386; and hate crimes, 432; in hiring practices, 373; in the LAPD, 407; structural, 440
Railroad Commission, 247, 284
Ramona (Jackson), 255–57, 261
Ramos, James, 444
Rancho Los Alamitos, 107–8
Rancho Nuestra Señora del Refugio, 81, 84, 95
Rancho Petaluma, 119
Rarick, Ethan, 380
Reagan, Ronald, 379–82, 385–86, 401, 412, 413
real estate market, 435–36
Red Power movement, 425
redwood groves, 260
Reed, James Frazier, 144
religion: Christianity, 23–24, 43, 51–52, 63–64; Judaism, 265, 305, 309
Republic of Texas, 131, 148–49. *See also* Tejas (Texas)
Richard, Paul, 432
Riley, Bennet C., 183
Rivera, Fernando de, 44–45
Riverside, 251
Robinson, Robert, 216, 217
Roman, Anton, 226–27
Roosevelt, Franklin Delano, 333, 339, 346, 350, 364
Roosevelt, James, 366
Roosevelt, Theodore, 282, 285, 287, 293, 296, 297
Rose Bowl game, 3–4
Rosie the Riveter, 352
Round Valley Reservation, 400–401
Rowland, John, 126–27
Roybal, Edward, 407–8
Ruef, Abraham, 270–71, 274, 283
Russian American Company, 70, 72, 76, 127–28

Sacramento, 6, 191–93
Sacramento Bee, 268, 360, 428, 435
Sacramento Daily Union, 236
Sacramento River, 3, 121
Sacramento Settlers' League, 193
Sacramento Transcript, 204
Sacramento Valley, 240, 257
Saint Francis Dam, 299
Saint Louis, USS, 126
Salazar, Margarita, 309
Salem, Ole, 399
Salem, Rose, 399
Salinas Valley, 120
San Agustín (galleon), 35
San Andreas Fault, 2–3, 272

San Antonio (Spanish supply
  ship), 39, 45, 49–50
San Bernardino, 437
San Carlos (Spanish supply ship),
  40, 47, 49
San Diego, 441–42
San Diego Bay, 36, 39
San Diego presidio, 102, 105
San Fernando Valley, 103, 299,
  361–62, 415
San Fernando Valley State
  College, 391
San Francisco: anti-Chinese violence in, 245; Black community
  in, 219; Bret Harte's writings
  about, 225–27; Chinatown,
  260, 273; churches in, 220;
  Citizens' Committee, 273; Committee of Vigilance, 197–98,
  219, 245; earthquake of 1906,
  272–75; ethnic enclaves in,
  225–26; and the gold rush, 6,
  173; Golden Gate Park, 380,
  398; growth of, 263–64, 275;
  Haight-Ashbury district, 380;
  homosexual community in,
  410–11; immigrants in, 195;
  labor strikes in, 337–38; labor
  unions in, 270, 285, 304; literature in, 233; mercantile boom
  in, 195; Muir in, 290–91; Nob
  Hill, 245, 246, 260, 271, 273;
  North Beach, 369–71, 397, 410;
  police force in, 194; politics
  in, 196; "popular justice" in,
  196–200; vignettes from,
  271–72; water for, 296–98;
  waterfront property rights,
  194
San Francisco Bay, 28, 37, 48, 56,
  70–73, 83, 130–31

San Francisco Chronicle, 297, 369
San Francisco Examiner, 266, 269,
  322, 380, 420
San Francisco presidio, 67, 70, 97,
  348
San Francisco State College,
  388–89
San Francisquito Canyon, 299
San Gabriel Valley, 261
San Jacinto mountains, 310, 315
San Joaquin River, 3, 97, 121, 297
San Joaquin Valley, 88, 98, 259,
  295, 302, 327, 340, 358, 379, 401,
  423, 434, 436, 437
San José, 187
San Pedro, 28, 240
San Petro Bay, 36
Sandwich Islands, 71–72, 78, 80.
  See also Hawaiian Islands
Sang Yuen (Norman Assing), 230
Santa Anna, Antonio López de,
  107, 108, 112, 113, 118, 132
Santa Barbara oil spill, 395
Santa Barbara presidio, 81, 89
Santa Catalina. *See* Catalina Island
Santa Cruz, 83
Santa Fe Railroad, 300
Santa Rosa (French vessel), 80
Save Our State initiative, 421
Schlesinger, Alfred Jr., 418
Schmitz, Eugene, 270–71, 273, 274
Schrag, Peter, 435
Schwarzenegger, Arnold, 428–29,
  438
scurvy, 32, 40, 45, 48, 80
Seale, Bobby, 385
secularization, 96–97, 100, 101–2,
  107–8, 112, 122, 254
Segundo-Workman, Lois, 318
Seidner, Cheryl, 444
sequoia trees, 292

Serra, Junípero: death of, 62; as "father-president" of Baja missions, 43; on the Kumeyayys, 41; at Mission San Carlos Borromeo, 50, 51–52, 110; at Mission San Gabriel, 53, 54, 56, 57; in San Diego, 45, 46–47

Service Employees International Union (SEIU), 424

Sessions, Kate, 258

Seven Years' War, 42

Shasta Courier, 211

Shasta Dam, 340

Sherman, Moses, 298

Sherman, William Tecumseh, 198–99, 200

Sherman Indian Institute, 253

shipbuilding, 303, 349

Shuk (Pomo headman), 206

Shusterman, Carl M., 420

Sierra Club, 292–93, 297, 405

Sierra Nevada mountains, 1–3, 141, 290

silver mining, 232

Sinclair, Upton, 332–33, 335, 338–39, 409

Siskiyou Summit, 1

slavery, 148–49, 183, 190, 213–21

Sleepy Lagoon, 354

Slidell, John, 149, 153

Sloat, John Drake, 150, 154, 157, 159–62

Smith, Jack, 390

Smith, Josephine Donna (Ina Coolbrith), 233, 234–35

Smith, Leonard Herman, 356

Smith, Lucy, 18

smuggling, 84

Snyder, Gary, 20, 397–98, 443

social equality, 403

Social Security Act, 339

socialism, 278, 281, 332

Socialist Party, 282, 287, 334

Solá, Pablo Vicente de, 79, 80–81, 85, 87; on education, 89–91

Sonoma, 106

Sonoma presidio, 155, 156

Southern California Colony Association, 251

Southern California Edison, 302

Southern Pacific Railroad (SP), 259–60, 261, 266, 276–77, 281–84, 316, 328, 358

space program, 371

Spaniards: in Alta California, 32, 36–37, 39–44, 53–54, 56–57, 62–63, 74; in Baja California, 5–6, 21–22, 25–27, 33–38, 43; in the Caribbean, 22–23; in Mexico, 24–25, 42; at Mission San Diego, 46–49; as missionaries, 43, 44, 46; at Monterey Bay, 50–51; in the Philippines, 30–31; in *presidios,* 43

Spanish-American War, 267

Spence, David, 114, 115, 120

Spott, Robert, 312

Spreckels, Claus, 268

squatters, 259–60

Stanford, Leland, 221, 227, 240, 243, 277

Stanislaus River, 98

Stanley, William, 310–11

Starr, Kevin, 199, 340

state societies, 304–5

State Water Project (SWP), 375, 400

Steinbeck, John, 328–30, 342

Stephens, William, 325

Stockton, Robert F.: against the Californios rebels, 165–67, 168; issuing ultimatum to Castro,

Stockton, Robert F. (*continued*) 163; occupation of Los Angeles, 164; replacing Sloat, 161–62
Stockton (city), 186, 240, 437
Stockton Mail, 249
Stoddard, Charles Warren, 233–34, 253, 290
Stone, Charles, 205–6
Stovall, Charles, 213–14, 217–18
Strauss, Levi, 264–66, 269, 270
Street, Richard Steven, 323
Strong, Harriet, 280
Studer, Helen, 352
subprime mortgages, 436–37
suburbs, 361–62, 436
Sullivan, Dennis, 272
Sunkist brand, 254, 350
Sutter, Johann August, 6, 121, 127–28, 135, 138–39, 157, 171, 191–92, 201–3
Sutter's Fort, 124–25, 127–28, 138, 140, 146, 151, 173, 184
Sutter's Mill, 183

Tac, Pablo, 49, 60, 66
Tarabal, Sebastián, 54–56, 58–59
tax revolt, 397
Taylor, Bayard, 178–79
Taylor, Paul Schuster, 342–43
Taylor, Zachary, 149, 153
Teamsters Union, 402, 413
Tejas (Texas), 43, 113, 116, 118, 125, 127, 131, 153. *See also* Republic of Texas
Temecula, 254–56
Temkin, Vicki, 391
Terry, David, 217, 220, 221
Third World Liberation Front (TWLF), 389
Thompson, Lucy, 17
Tibbets, Eliza, 251–54

Tibbets, Luther, 252–53, 258
tourism, 260–61
Townsend, Francis E., 335
Townsend Clubs, 335
Toypurina (Tongva shaman), 66–67
Transcendentalism, 290
transcontinental railroad, 6, 227–28, 238–40
Treaty of Guadalupe Hidalgo, 169–70
Trevelyan, G. M., 8
Triezenberg, Bonnie, 420
Truman, Harry S., 366
Tulare Lake, 88
Tuolumne River, 296–97
Turtle Island (Snyder), 398
Twain, Mark (Samuel Clemens), 226, 235
Tyler, John, 131, 148–49

Unamuno, Pedro de, 33–34
Union Labor Party, 270
Union Oil Company, 395
Union Pacific Railroad, 227–28, 231
unions. *See* labor unions
United Farm Workers (UFW), 379, 401–2, 403, 413, 422–24
United States, USS (frigate), 130
University of California, 279, 302, 303, 365, 365, 433; at Berkeley, 177, 247, 258, 314, 342, 358, 361, 366, 367, 378, 381, 384–85, 389; at Davis, 361; at Los Angeles, 303, 361, 389, 407, 414, 418; at Riverside, 361; at Santa Barbara, 361; at Santa Cruz, 404
University of Southern California (USC), 431, 435

U.S. Constitution: Thirteenth amendment, 221; Fourteenth amendment, 231–32, 364, 427–28; Fifteenth amendment, 232

U.S. Department of Education, 418

Utopian Society of America, 335

Vallejo, Ignacio Vicente, 91–92

Vallejo, Mariano Guadalupe: and California independence, 105; as civil administrator, 109–10; at the constitutional convention, 183–84; dispossession of Native Californians by, 106; education and family, 90–91, 94; vs. Estanislao, 98–99; after the Mexican American War, 170; negotiations with southern faction, 117; plans for California independence, 151–52; taken hostage, 155–56

Vallejo, Salvador, 205

Vallejo (city), 437

Victoria, Manuel, 101–5, 112

Vietnam War, 372, 378–79, 382–83, 387; protests against, 383–85, 388

Vila, Vicente, 40

Visalia Times-Delta, 330

Vizcaíno, Sebastián, 36–37

von Wrangel, Ferdinand, 77, 106

Voorsanger, Jacob, 305

Warren, Earl: as attorney general, 346–47, 348, 358–59, 365; as governor, 357–58, 359–62, 364, 365–66, 375, 438; on Japanese internment, 367–68; on the Supreme Court, 366–67, 382; as vice presidential candidate, 366

Washington Mutual Savings, 436

Watsonville Pajaronian, 249

Watts Riot, 377–78

welfare system, 359, 382

Weller, John, 210

Whipple, Norman, 401

White, Stephen M., 281

White flight, 373

White supremacy, 189, 190, 210, 231, 245

Wiinu (Mono Lake Paiute woman), 12–13

wildfires, 440

Wilshire, H. Gaylord, 278, 334

Wilson, Luzena, 176

Wilson, Pete, 421–22, 426

Wilson, Woodrow, 285, 297

Wimmer, Elizabeth "Jennie," 170–71, 176, 177

Wimmer, Martin, 170–71

Wimmer, Peter, 170–71, 177

winemaking, 250–51, 257–58

Wise, Isaac Meyer, 265

Wobblies. See Industrial Workers of the World (IWW)

Woman's Congress, 280

women: abuse of, 52–53, 57; Chinese, 229; clubs and organizations, 280–81; in colonial California, 91–92; education for, 247; on the emigration trail, 142; empowerment of, 381, 390–92; as farm laborers, 323–24; as garment workers, 266–67, 274; and the gold rush, 176–77, 229; in horticulture, 258; in the labor force, 372, 351–52, 391–92; in labor unions, 330; in politics, 409,

women (*continued*)
411; prohibition of discrimination against, 247; and property ownership, 185; rights of, 252, 381, 390–92; suffrage for, 278, 279–81, 285; as writers, 234–35
Women's Christian Temperance Union (WCTU), 280–81
Wong Ching Foo, 248
Workingmen's Party of California, 246–47, 345
Workman, William, 126–27
World War II, 344
Wozencraft, Oliver M., 186
Wright, Guy, 420
Wyman, Rosalind Weiner, 409

Yellowstone National Park, 292–93
Yenari, Touru, 348
Yerba Buena Cove, 194
Yosemite National Park, 3, 297, 316
Yosemite Valley, 221–22, 260, 289–90
Young, Pauline, 309
Young, Sam, 18
Young, Tom (Hánc'ibyjim), 12
Yount, George, 206, 207

zoot suit hoodlums, 353–54, 362
Zúñiga, Gaspar de, 36

Also by John Mack Faragher

Women and Men on the Overland Trail

Sugar Creek: Life on the Illinois Prairie

Daniel Boone: The Life and Legend of an American Pioneer

The American West: A New Interpretive History
(with Robert V. Hine and Jon T. Coleman)

*A Great and Noble Scheme: The Tragic Story of the Expulsion of the
French Acadians from Their American Homeland*

Eternity Street: Violence and Justice in Frontier Los Angeles